CUTTING THE DRAGON'S TAIL

David and Lynda Chidell

MINERVA PRESS
ATLANTA LONDON SYDNEY

CUTTING THE DRAGON'S TAIL
Copyright © David and Lynda Chidell 1998

ISBN 0 75410 154 1

First Published 1998 by
MINERVA PRESS
195 Knightsbridge
London SW7 1RE

Printed in Great Britain for Minerva Press

CUTTING THE DRAGON'S TAIL

Dedication

We have written this for the sake of *Tin Hau* and all those who might dream about living on a boat and making voyages in distant waters. May *Tin Hau* be cherished for many generations to come, giving others the excitement, pleasure and sense of purpose she gave us.

Acknowledgements

During our building and sailing years, we were helped by many of our friends and respective families. Without their contributions there may never have been an adventure worth telling. The writing of this book has been a long-term project which hardly involved anyone else until we decided to have it published. We are grateful for the guidance received by our publishers, Minerva Press, and suggestions put forward by our editor to help us improve the story. We would like to thank Barry Lamprecht for generously allowing us to publish the various photographs which he took and which are attributed to him. Among the very few people who knew we were trying to put the story down on paper were Trevor and Sally Doran – sailing friends met in Corfu. We are enormously grateful for their encouragement in the early stages of writing and for being so willing to take on the horrendous task of checking our work for factual inconsistencies and mistakes. It is not their fault if the text still contains errors! We're also indebted to them for suggesting the title for the book.

21.3.98
David and Lynda

Preface

In 1982, the seeds of an idea were sown; an idea that was to change our lives – a dream that perhaps had always been there, but one that developed in our home overlooking Mbabane, the capital of Swaziland.

I had first visited Swaziland on 5th August, 1973, whilst on a student working holiday in Southern Africa, and had earmarked it even then as the ideal African country in which to live – a place with some of the most spectacular scenery on the continent. Unlike so many African countries, this one was united. There was only one tribe, the Swazis, and one much respected ruler, King Sobhuza II.

Like others before me, I was bitten by the 'Africa bug'; attracted by the wide open spaces, the warm climate, and the dignified but fun-loving people. In December 1975 I joined a couple, Peter Duby and Fiona Sawday, who had bought and prepared their own Land Rover for an Africa Overland journey and advertised in *The Times* for two people to share their adventure. Six months after leaving London, we reached Pretoria. Peter and Fiona then went to Swaziland. I chose to carry on to Cape Town where I obtained a job as a civil engineer at Simonstown harbour.

Two years later, on completion of the harbour extensions, I drove the 1300 or so miles to Swaziland to join Peter and Fiona in employment there. This lasted only eight months – although it felt like several years, such were the social and work activities with which I was involved. In the final fortnight, as I was preparing to leave, I met Lynda. I suppose we were destined to return to a country that had played such an important part in our lives (Lynda had been there since 1976); and return we did, in 1981. I was employed by the same firm of consulting engineers, but this time for a fixed contract period of two years.

We arrived towards the end of the winter dry season, a time of year when for months on end the skies are free from clouds. The land was brown from the lack of rain, especially in the hotter low veld areas and the roads were thick with dust. By November, however, the summer rains were well on their way and we started to experience incredibly violent thunderstorms. The heavens would open and rain would bucket down, turning the roads into mud baths.

We discovered that our house, being near to the top of a hill, was regularly struck by lightning.

We enjoyed hearing the beautiful Swazi language (siSwati) again – words like 'Sawubona' and 'Yebo', drawn out and slowly spoken, as though time did not matter too much. 'How far is it to Simunya?' I would ask a figure standing by the roadside clad in a western tweed jacket, open necked shirt, brightly coloured Swazi mahiya (skirt) and heavy building site boots with no socks. 'Ahh, little bit long way', would come the reply. 'How far to Mhlume?' I would ask. 'Ahhh, too far.'

We grew to know Swaziland very well, and explored its most remote corners. It will always be a kind of spiritual home to me, a very special place with some very special people. Not just the Swazis, but also the small and extremely varied international community – South Africans, British, Portuguese, Greeks, Dutch, Germans, French, Italians, Danish, Irish, Americans, Canadians, Australians, New Zealanders, Chinese and Japanese, to name but a few – all employed on various projects around the country.

Although much of our time in Swaziland was taken up with work, we were able to spend most evenings and weekends pursuing an amazingly diverse set of interests. I tried to set aside one evening a week to deal with a yachtmaster correspondence course I had started in England just before going to Swaziland, thereby gaining knowledge that proved to be extremely valuable. We found ourselves increasingly involved with local amateur dramatic performances, initially backstage and later – to my terror –on stage. I enjoyed more the obscurity of singing choral music with the Mbabane Singers – although the obscurity was somewhat shattered when the small choir was commanded by royal decree to sing the Hallelujah Chorus of the Messiah in front of tens of thousands of people at King Sobhuza's funeral. Other activities included sports such as golf and tennis, organised painstakingly by the Japanese. As if that wasn't enough, our New Zealand friends in the Usutu forest aroused our interest in orienteering (or how to get lost in the forest). We were the 'Mbabane link', placing advertisements in the local paper in an effort to swell numbers.

Our main relaxation, and something I really appreciated, was a visit once every fortnight to Sand River Dam, a low veld dam near the sugar estates of Tshaneni. There we would pitch a tent and spend an idyllic weekend dinghy racing in a Fireball built by and belonging to our good friend, Jeff Perring. In the evenings, we would light a fire and cook our meal in the open, as we contemplated the bright stars of the southern sky.

With so many things going on, it was perhaps surprising that we had time to think about what to do on completion of my contract – but think we did. An idea evolved, exciting possibilities were discussed, and a plan was formed that somehow tied together many of the threads of our lives up to that point. Might this be the time to make a move into something completely different? Could we consider selling our home and all our possessions, spending the rest of our lives at sea aboard a sailing boat? Could we make a living from a boat, by taking paying guests in an area such as the Greek islands and giving them the 'holiday of a lifetime'? Could this be our chance to create a more fulfilling lifestyle, in which we could get to know the oceans, live closer to nature, and explore as much of the world as possible?

The instinctive answers came straight from the heart. Why not sail off into the wide blue horizon and chase the sun? Why not set our sights on what we would really like to do with our lives? Why not do it now?

And so the project was conceived.

Contents

List of Figures

List of Maps

PART ONE
Construction

David Chidell

18

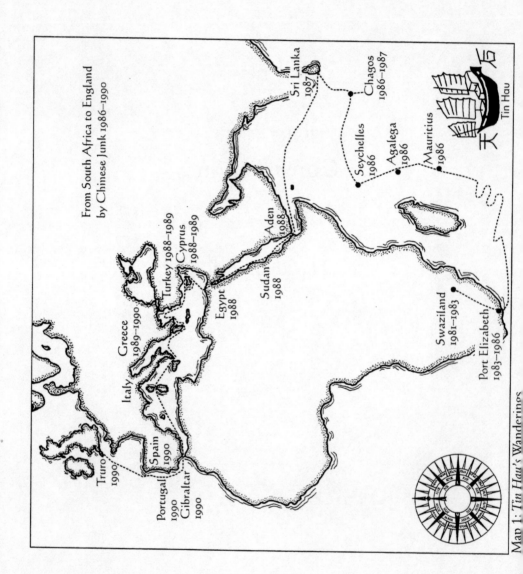

From South Africa to England
by Chinese Junk 1986–1990

Sri Lanka
1987

Chagos
1986–1987

Seychelles
1986

Agalega
1986

Mauritius
1986

Tin Hau

Aden
1988

Sudan
1988

Egypt
1988

Cyprus
1988–1989

Turkey 1988–1989

Greece
1989–1990

Italy

Spain 1990

Portugal
1990

Gibraltar
1990

Truro
1990

Swaziland
1981–1983

Port Elizabeth
1983–1986

Map 1: *Tin Hau's Wanderings*

1. The Case for Selling Up and Living on a Boat in Warm Climates

It took a number of months for our gut feelings to harden into a real decision. But the more we thought about it, the more sense it made.

Firstly, I looked at many of the people ten to twenty years older in my chosen career, and concluded that I was not desperate to follow in their footsteps. It looked like a future of suits and ties, rules, regulations and endless meetings; a life of worries about future prospects and employment, with either too much or too little work in the wrong place or at the wrong time. Every now and then my work had been fulfilling; there had been chances to be creative; I had enjoyed being part of a team, deriving satisfaction from a project that I had seen as being both necessary and attractive. But often the opposite seemed to be the case. Engineering schemes, top-heavy in management, would lead to ugly structures and buildings not wanted by many people. It was hard to see who could be blamed for this; it was as though everyone was powerless, caught up in a system that had gone wrong. I was aware that it would be a big step to give up a career I had pursued for more than ten years. I realised that by leaving the 'system' I ran the risk of being unable to join it again. I would be on my own. I knew that financially I could be making a major mistake; a regular salary is a sad thing to do without. Yet somehow...

Secondly, I was attracted by the concept of being involved in a project all the way from design, to construction, to final use. Most individuals in the building industry never have this chance, and do not see the overall results of their work. I imagined living inside our own creation, paying for it out of our own pockets, having full responsibility for any errors, and being able to change anything that needed changing without first having to appeal to a higher authority. That seemed like the real thing. There would be no one else to blame if it all went wrong. The buck would stop with us.

Thirdly, we were both equally inclined towards the idea and both in reasonably good health – although a bit touched by boat madness! It seemed better to do something really exciting and different at that time (we were both in our early thirties) than to wait for retirement and perhaps ill health. I wanted to make some sort of mark on the world, however small, while I could.

Finally, on totalling up the value of everything we owned and on researching what boats cost, we knew we had saved enough money to get what we wanted without having to borrow. Moreover, once living afloat in warm climates we would be free of many social and work oriented expenses associated with houses, cars, clothes, and stress-relieving hobbies and holidays. Our living costs would be much smaller, despite the cost of boat maintenance.

I am still of the opinion that it is not an extravagance to own a boat that serves as your only home – particularly if it can be used to provide an income.

2. Which Boat?

Our next decision was: which boat? All we knew at the time was that we wanted:

A boat that was satisfying to sail and could be taken around the world, using a rig that could be managed by one person, or two people at most.

A boat that was attractive to look at yet different from most contemporary yachts. I wanted some of the fishing boat – or small ship features – like high bulwarks, solid mooring bitts and a wheelhouse.

A roomy interior, comfortable enough to serve as our only home and large enough to accommodate charter guests in privacy with priority given to the size and quality of the berths, not their number. We wanted plenty of storage and good access to important items such as plumbing, electrical wiring, the bilge, and the main engine.

Good reliable equipment made by companies well-known throughout the world. Jimmy Cornell's ocean survey helped us here; for example, it led us to choose our Perkins 4.236 diesel engine.

A long keel and protected rudder; a boat that would take the bottom should we ever find ourselves in those colder, muddier and tidal waters found in places such as England.

A hull and deck built of steel. I understood steel and valued its strength; in the event of a collision, it dents rather than shatters. I had formed this opinion three years earlier on the final (forty-fifth) day of a 4,500 mile race from Cape Town to Uruguay. On drawing close to our destination – Punta del Este – we had hit a rock. Unbelievably, there was no damage.

A boat we could afford to build and afford to run. What the boat would be worth from the point of view of resale did not enter our reckoning at that time. We were sure we would *never* want to sell her.

3.   Second-Hand or New?

The other important question was: should we build a boat, or could we buy one second-hand? The second solution was tempting – so much work would be saved. A tried and tested boat could be chosen, and we would be able to see what we were getting. But how could we view boats from Swaziland without wasting vast sums on fruitless investigations?

We wanted to keep the idea on the boil and wrote numerous letters to boat-building companies and yacht designers in England and elsewhere. One reply, in particular, looked promising. Ronnie Nel of 'Nelco Marine', based in Port Elizabeth, South Africa, was prepared to build a steel hull of substantial size for a reasonable cost in an aircraft hangar used by a dozen or so amateur builders. He would construct the shell of our chosen boat. We would fit it out to our own interior and deck plans.

Building in South Africa would have certain advantages and I did not feel we would be supporting the apartheid system in any way. It is a beautiful country, as varied as the United States or Europe. The weather, although at times too hot for work, would definitely be better than England's cold and damp conditions. Availability of important materials like steel and hardwoods appeared good, and the cost of living low. Port Elizabeth in particular appealed, being the home of Lynda's father, mother, brother and sister and their families. It also seemed like a good place to seek employment should boat building plans go wrong or be delayed – which, in fact, is what happened. I already had a work permit for South Africa after my work there from 1976 to 1978.

The adrenalin was beginning to flow. We just needed to finalise our choice of boat and start moving.

4.   Our Choice

Our minds were made up completely when Ronnie introduced us to a book called *Cruising as a Way of Life* by the American designer and boat builder, Tom Colvin. We saw some plans of his boats. Lines drawings. Sail plans. Cross-sections.

We started to eat, drink and sleep boats. Our imaginations were racing as we thought about all the things we could achieve, and the places we could visit.

The excitement reached a head when it became clear that, unbelievably, we could afford to build the same boat Tom had owned and sailed for over a decade (sometimes without crew). What better recommendation could we have asked for?

Tom's home, *Kung Fu Tse*, was built of aluminium. Ours could be to the same design, but of steel. It would be fifty feet long, fourteen feet in beam, five feet in draft, and twenty-five tons in displacement. In other words, big! Much bigger than I had thought our budget would allow. We would get our long keel, our bulwarks, our ship-like mooring bitts, an enclosed wheelhouse, a separate engine room, watertight collision bulkheads fore and aft, a roomy interior, and a boat that looked good to sail and had been tested on many ocean voyages.

Only one aspect demanded a bit of a rethink: Tom Colvin's ideal floating home was a three-masted Chinese junk.

5. What Next?

After much deliberation we decided to go ahead with *Lilandza* (the first of a series of names we had for *Tin Hau*; this one being the Swazi word for a great white bird, discarded only when we came to realise it was simply a cattle egret). We paid for the drawings (about £850), increasingly happy with the idea of a junk. My being Hong Kong born was a bonus, a good omen.

Then came the formal appointment of Ronnie Nel. He was given a one year contract worth 33,000 rand (about £20,000 – the exact sterling amount being dependent on the exchange rate used). He signed an agreement to complete all the steelwork and a few additional items by April 1984.

Next we wound up our commitments in Swaziland. My work with EPD Consultants was over. We returned to England, sold our house in Midhurst, Sussex, and packed what we would need on the boat into seven bags (Lufthansa lost two). We flew back to Swaziland to collect our 'bakkie' (pick-up truck) and our various possessions, remaining there for a few days before setting off on the one thousand mile drive to Port Elizabeth. At first we stayed with Lynda's parents; then we moved to a caravan, which was to be our home for several months. This was followed by some house-sitting for Lynda's parents while they were away. Eventually we found rented accommodation of our own in Donkin Street, in the middle of Port Elizabeth. In all, we had eight homes in as many months!

Meanwhile, Ronnie was living up to his reputation: slow, but sure. At the time of our arrival in South Africa, nearly half way through his contract, he had assembled an impressive looking gantry, taken delivery of some steel, and partially made the keel.

I decided to look for employment, and was lucky to receive an offer almost immediately, as a structural engineer with one of Port Elizabeth's multi-disciplined consulting engineers, Hill Kaplan Scott (HKS). When not at work, I joined Lynda in a full scale hunt for boat materials; and when not involved with this, we were always busy designing and redesigning the interior, organising import permits and constructing various small items needed on the boat. In addition, Lynda spent three dusty and hot months at the caravan making a three foot long model, which we used to work out some of the peculiar junk details. We needed to learn about euphroes, friction blocks, snotters, parrels, sheetlets and lazy jacks. We wanted to become familiar with how the reefing worked, for example. We knew there would be no one to teach us once we launched.

On a depressing note, Ronnie's work, although very satisfying to watch, became slower and slower. We began to think we had made a big mistake and that the boat would never be finished. To make matters worse, the aircraft hangar, a truly excellent place for boat building, was declared unsafe by the municipality, and its demolition was ordered.

Even more upsetting, it was about this time I received news from England that my father, who had been ill with cancer for a year, had died. I had flown back to England the previous Autumn to see him, but it still came as a great shock to be without him – particularly as I would so much have liked to have shown him our completed boat and treated him to some sailing. He had sailed since a child and was responsible for my interest in the sport. For much of his adult life he had worked in Hong Kong, one of the homes of Chinese junks. As a younger man he had worked in South Africa, like his father. So I suppose my choosing to build a Chinese junk in South Africa must have come in some way from him.

We decided to keep extending the construction time allowed in Ronnie's contract, waiving the penalties we could have enforced. Lynda even became his welder for a week, not just to help, but also to make the point that we were serious about sailing this boat! Perhaps his male pride would be hurt...

One more target date was set, but this one was final. Ronnie had to hand over the forward interior of the boat (the 'forward area') to us by 8th February, 1985.

6. The Fitting-Out Starts

At long last Ronnie kept one of his promises. He finished his work in the forward area by the required date. We –mainly Lynda at this stage – had half a boat to tackle.

Where should we start? Would our lack of skills be a problem? We knew that over the next year or so we would have to carry out all sorts of tricky work involving carpentry, plumbing, electrics, painting, diesel mechanics, refrigeration, and the fitting of specialist yacht equipment. To make matters worse, at the time of our arrival in South Africa our only tool was an old food mixer converted twenty years earlier to a drill and disc-sander by my great-uncle Charlie in Northern Ireland!

However, we could read. We could learn from others. And we were determined to build a boat as perfect in detail as we could possibly manage. With hindsight, I would say that our work was as good as many professionals could have done, and often more robust; the main difference being that our work probably took twice as long to carry out, as we groped with unfamiliar territory.

Our first task in the gleaming white interior was to add insulation (necessary in a steel boat to reduce noise, to eliminate condensation and to help with interior temperatures). We decided to use three millimetre cork sheeting, sealed by fibreglass tissue at all frames and stringers. This was firmly glued to the hull with contact adhesive everywhere above the waterline. Combined (as was usual) with an inner wall or ceiling panel, this proved tough, effective and durable.

Then came the flooring, followed by the installation of the main electrical wiring – heavy twin and earth cabling, running through sleeved twenty millimetre diameter holes in each overhead steel deck frame. Uncle Charlie's drill was not man enough for this! So our first Black and Decker electric drill had to be bought. The sizes of the cables were worked out during lunch breaks at work, when the electrical engineers turned their attention to more interesting 'junk' items. The aim was to minimise the voltage drop in each of the fifteen twelve-volt circuits.

In the meantime, Lynda set herself up as master carpenter and plumber, and worked methodically aft from the forward collision bulkhead. Figure 1 shows the interior and deck plans we were using at that time (1985–1986), being our seventh – and, we thought final – attempt at the perfect layout. However, as the years went by and we gained experience of life afloat in extremely varied climates and conditions, we changed even this! The revised layout is shown in Figure 2. I have also shown some cross-sections (see Figures 3 and 4).

Lynda's first job was the forward heads (this was one of the areas we changed later in Cyprus, by which time we had other priorities and felt that two heads – even in a charter boat – were enough!) Then came the master cabin with its large double berth and single sea-berth, and aft of this the two two-berth 'charter cabins', each with their own heads. Aft of the charter cabins Ronnie was still occupied, cutting, grinding and welding away in areas destined to become the engine room, the galley, the saloon, the lazaret and the wheelhouse (also called the pilothouse). Forward of where Lynda was working was the large forepeak locker, in which we planned to stow our two anchor chains and keep all our spare paints and ropes.

Our stock of power tools had increased by this time to two drills, two jigsaws, an angle grinder, a belt sander, an orbital sander and a vacuum cleaner. We were also lucky to have the use of another boat builder's circular bench saw and his planer/thicknesser. Later we bought our own portable circular saw and also a portable router. Besides our open-backed vehicle, our most useful piece of equipment was probably the Black and Decker workbench. Also, to prevent ourselves becoming totally dehydrated, we had – on loan – two portable electric fans.

7.   March 1985: The Turning Point

Although we were having the satisfaction of at last seeing some progress on *Tin Hau*, it was worrying to see Ronnie's work slowing almost to a standstill. Additionally, the hangar demolition contract had just been let by the council to Ronnie, of all people! We would shortly have to move. We needed new premises. We needed to work out how to shift a half-built steel hull. And we needed a replacement for Ronnie. Although he had taken on an assistant, a welder by the name of Mr Fredericks, Ronnie himself had definitely run out of steam and was going no further. This was a very disturbing situation for us with no easy answer.

The solution, we hoped, lay with the press. We approached the local newspaper, the *Eastern Province Herald*. Before we knew what was happening, a reporter visited us, together with a photographer, Barry Lamprecht, who later became a crew member on our epic maiden voyage. The visit led to a long article. Then we were the subject of a radio programme. Finally, South

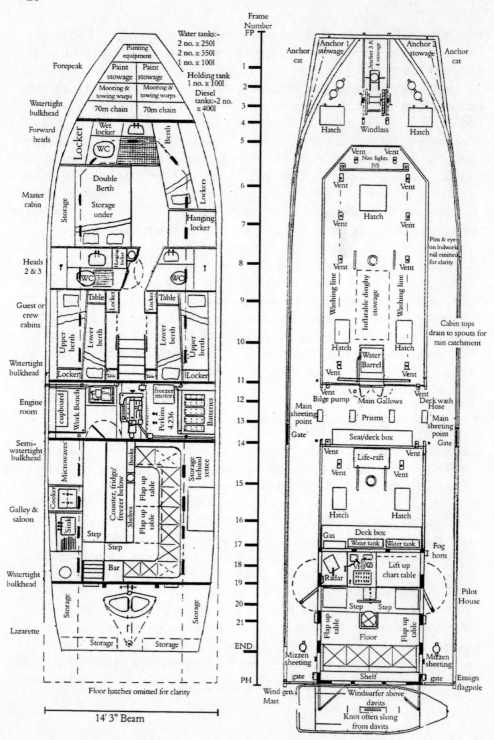

Figure 1: *Tin Hau's* Original Deck and Interior Plans (1986)

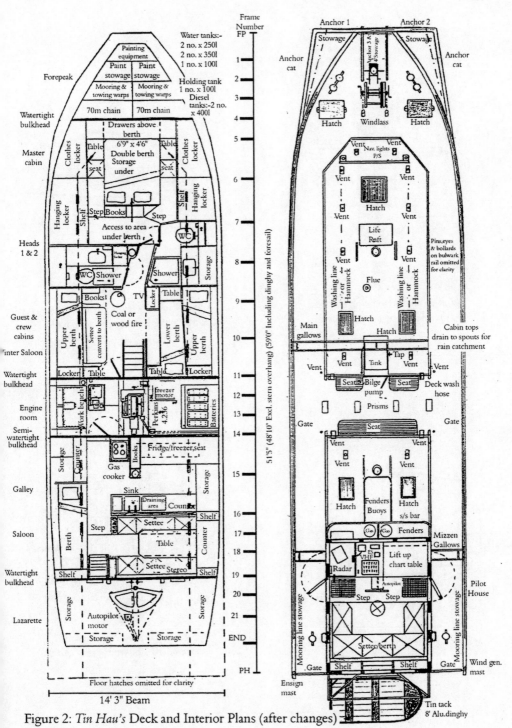

Figure 2: *Tin Hau's* Deck and Interior Plans (after changes)

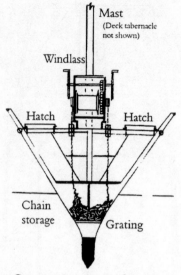

Cross-section viewing forward
at frame 4 (showing forepeak)

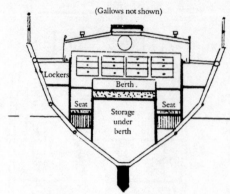

Cross-section viewing forward
at frame 6 (showing master cabin)

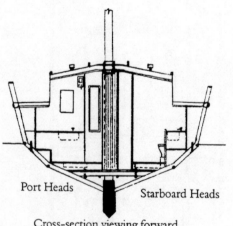

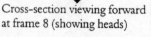

Cross-section viewing forward
at frame 8 (showing heads)

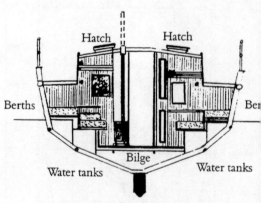

Cross-section viewing forward
at frame 10 (showing guest cabins)

Figure 3: Forward Area Cross-Sections (after changes)

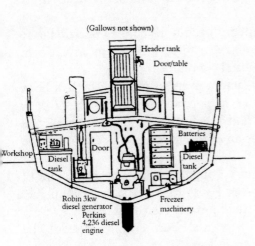

Cross-section viewing forward at frame 13
(showing engine room; midships deck area)

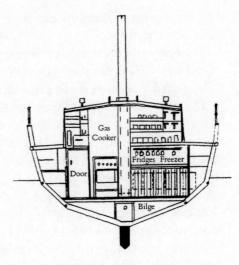

Cross-section viewing forward at frame 15
(showing galley)

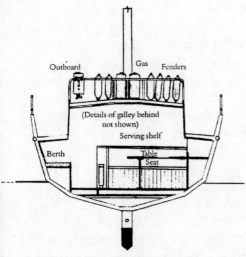

Cross-section viewing forward at frame 17
(showing saloon)

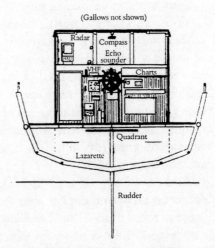

Cross-section viewing forward at frame 20
(showing pilot house)

Figure 4: Aft Area Cross-Sections (after changes)

African television found us and started paying regular visits in preparation for a documentary film.

No offers of new premises were forthcoming, but the council declared they would allow all unfinished boats in our hangar to be finished in an adjacent hangar (in my opinion in the same structural condition).

Ronnie's most recent excuse for his lack of progress was that he had been having difficulties finding large-diameter steel piping for our through-deck mast supports. 'Why not try Algoa Oil and Pipeline?' suggested Hashim, one of my friends at work. That proved to be an excellent idea. In fact, it led to the end of all our problems.

On phoning the company, I was put through to a man by the name of Graham Moolman, commonly called – as I was to learn later – 'Munchie' Moolman. 'No problem,' he said – his stock phrase. He could supply just the pipes we required, cut to the lengths we wanted. Furthermore, it would be done that day. What a refreshing change from Ronnie!

Having helped us with our mast collars, Munchie listened carefully to our story and applied his mind to how *Tin Hau* should be moved.

'Why not jack her up and roll her round to the other hangar?' he suggested.

'Roll her on what?'

'A dozen four inch diameter steel oil pipes,' he replied. 'We can lend you some.'

'And how can we pull or push the boat?'

'With a mechanical horse,' he said, 'I can arrange one for you, if you want.'

Munchie proved as good as his word. We organised the strengthening of the cradle and managed to jack it up and get the pipe rollers into place. A day was set for the four hundred metre move – 28th February. Early that lovely, clear, sunny morning, our gang of friendly 'volunteers' arrived at the hangar, closely followed by Munchie and his baby (Munchie spent much of the day changing nappies) and the mechanical horse (a lorry without its trailer). The move went smoothly, although it took some time. The cost was measured in cans of beer, not rand.

'And now for your next problem', said Munchie, when we had finished. 'You need a replacement for your Ronnie Nel. I have an idea.'

He proceeded to tell us how Algoa Oil and Pipeline employed some of the best welders in the country, qualified to the highest levels and able to meet the exacting standards of the offshore oil industry. Perhaps one or some of these men might be persuaded to take up the challenge of completing *Tin Hau's* steelwork, working weekends and evenings. 'Leave it to me', said Munchie.

Sure enough, about a week later, a vehicle turned up at the boat and two men clambered out. They strolled up to the hull of *Tin Hau* and proceeded to examine her critically, without saying a word. Perhaps these were Munchie's welders? They told us they were, and we learnt their names – Tony Bryant and Paul Miller, originally from Yorkshire and Glasgow, respectively. However they were *not* impressed, and we were made to feel more and more glum. They disappeared as abruptly as they had arrived, muttering something like 'perhaps we will be in touch'.

We carried on with our joinery, depressed by the thought that not only was Ronnie's speed of work a problem, but his standard of welding was deficient too. However, we were comforted by the knowledge that his earlier work, in constructing the framework of *Tin Hau*, was well done. At least we were past the stage of having to refer to the lines drawings, which made the remaining welding work much easier to explain. I gave Tony and Paul a long list of what still needed doing, in the hope that they might be tempted.

And tempted they were – or perhaps what they really felt was pity for two crazy idealistic dreamers in need of help. Their offer came through very quickly. They were prepared, they said, to complete all the steelwork on *Tin Hau* in a period of little more than thirty weekends, and they named a figure for their work which was acceptable to us. We breathed a sigh of relief, paid Ronnie what was due to him and gave Tony and Paul the go-ahead. At last, everything started moving quickly, and the work was of a very high standard.

8. Twelve Busy Months

During the twelve months prior to the launch, Lynda and I worked harder than ever before, conscious at all times of the importance of getting things right. One nut insufficiently tightened, or one shackle sized wrongly, could have been enough to lose the boat and not just our lives, but those of our crew as well. I was under no illusions about the seas off the South African coast, and the vast distances we would have to cover in an untested boat.

We applied all our time and effort towards the construction of *Tin Hau*, with no breaks at all except those required for sleeping, eating and a few enforced hours taken on Christmas Day. I did, however, have a significant distraction from boat building during the first three and a half months of this period, in that I had still had a normal office job. Lynda, on the other hand, just had the boat. On viewing our efforts, one visitor to the hangar – a retired sea captain – declared over and over again in amazement, 'You people are not playing, you're not playing games...' As though people could consider building a boat a game!

Having said all this, perhaps it is worth making the point that although we were usually filthy, bruised, cut, tired and hot for weeks on end, we were happy – in a perverse sort of way!

9. Away from Port Elizabeth

Not all the work going on during this period was taking place in Port Elizabeth. For example, the three sails were being made in Hong Kong by the sail maker, Cheong Lee. They were done extremely well, but too quickly – in that we received them before the shipping papers. This caused a degree of panic, as we took measures to avoid paying expensive demurrage charges at the harbour.

In Swaziland, Jeff Perring was building a twelve-foot plywood sailing dinghy to Tom Colvin's design. I wanted the very best of dinghies, and needed to know its shape and form in good time so we could plan where it could be stowed and how it could be launched.

In the Transvaal, our anchor chains were being prepared; the first step in the seemingly unsolvable riddle: Which comes first, the chain or the gypsy?

In Natal, the aluminium masts were being extruded by Huletts Aluminium. I will return to the subject of our chosen boat masts and their associated rigging. Ronnie had just said: 'Go out into the Knysna forest and cut down a tree.' Tom Colvin had given little in the way of a detailed specification.

Even further afield, in England, Perkins Diesel Engines of Peterborough were preparing three large wooden crates containing the engine and all the stern gear. Years later, I could still phone David Read (who was then area manager – Africa) with any query concerning our engine – an engine which never let us down.

In Southampton, Fast and Freeze handled the freezer; again, a subject on which I could write at great length. I remained happy with our decision to use the twelve-volt ship's batteries as the power source, although three years later I constructed a transformer so that the freezer motor could also run off mains alternating current.

Kelvin Hughes of Southampton supplied various Admiralty Sailing Directions (Pilots), charts and our VHF radio, but they made the mistake of writing an illegible invoice – illegible, that is, to the South African customs officers who immediately charged the maximum duty. On the subject of customs, all the duties we paid were reimbursed when we left South Africa, but only after some protracted wrangling with the South African bureaucracy in Pretoria. This concession applied only to import duty, not to Sales Tax (the South African equivalent of VAT at that time).

Mars Electronics supplied our most expensive piece of electronic equipment, the radar. In spite of their most helpful suggestions, it never worked properly and we were thankful to see it replaced in Cyprus with an updated model, the Vigil RM. This device was invaluable. I always felt I was cheating when I turned it on, as navigation became so easy. With such features as the 'variable range marker', the 'variable bearing marker' and 'track', it became much simpler to monitor shipping; moreover, in poor visibility this was our only set of eyes.

Aladdin's Cave in Bursledon, Hampshire, who specialised in second-hand or surplus chandlery, sold us various items, including our three Lavac toilets (a good, sound make) and – on hearing it over the telephone – a hand-held foghorn.

London Yacht Centre proved to be our final choice of a large UK chandler geared towards export, and they proved quite satisfactory. We placed a huge discounted order with them, having spent weeks scrutinising their Simpson Lawrence catalogue. Amongst the items we chose which were successful were the Barton cruising blocks, Scanmarin fenders, Marlow rope, Henderson Mark V pumps and Duff anodes; however some items (such as a plunger operated foghorn) were very poor, and had to be thrown away after a few weeks (or months) exposure to marine conditions.

Later we were more experienced in the choice of yacht equipment, and could see well beyond the plastic veneer, the brass plating or the exaggerated description in the catalogue. Our original principles, however, never changed:

Do without it altogether, if possible.

Go for well known manufacturers and proven makes of equipment.

Buy quality items – the sea will punish anything second-rate.

Before buying, always work out every detail of how and where the article will fit on the boat.

Remember the KISS principle ('Keep It Simple, Stupid'); remember that everything must look right as well as perform efficiently. These principles are ably summarised by the formula:

$$\text{Satisfaction} = (\text{Beauty} + \text{Performance}) \div (\text{Complication})$$

Don't waste too much time and money dilly-dallying. 'Deeds not croaks' was a phrase I learnt as a child from a picture book about a contented frog.

Try to get two or more uses out of each article, if possible.

A good example of the final principle was provided by our four plastic buckets, which we considered to be amongst our most valuable pieces of equipment. They were given the prime stowage position on deck under the open slat midships seat, held in place by shock chord – not even a deck box lid had to be opened to get to them. They were used regularly for many purposes such as deck washing, laundry, 'bucket baths' at sea, storing scrubbing brushes and other cleaning aids, and providing a temporary home for any fish caught or shells collected.

We eventually received all this equipment on time in Port Elizabeth, but just about every shipment had its dramas. One of the more amusing ones (if we could still find room for a sense of humour) was the time when a British clerk in the Home Office decided to apply his own personal sanctions and ban exports to South Africa of goods of a sensitive nature. This included our radio and radar. It took a lot to persuade him that such actions would only harm us – British citizens – and would have no effect on South Africa's political system.

Before returning to the main story, perhaps this is an appropriate moment to consider the important subject of money. Barclays bank had already proved their cunning and skill to me fifteen years earlier, when they had taken to bribing students at universities with free hand-outs of pens and other goodies. This time they were impressive once again, and what they told us removed much of the financial risk in building *Tin Hau* overseas. I learnt that by using the 'forward rate of exchange' system, I could order all the rands I needed well in advance, at fixed rates of exchange, and on certain agreed dates. The really good news, however, was that the exchange rate was expected to vary in our favour during the boat building period, to such an extent that at the projected end of it (1985), we would be receiving twice as many rands for each pound as at the beginning. This meant that we could budget a higher figure in rand terms than had previously seemed possible.

Having cleared with the South African banks that foreign currency brought into the country would be permitted to leave in the form of a boat, I signed several forms with Barclays agreeing currency transfers at four specified dates in the future. What impressed me so much was that, when each of these dates came up, I saw that the rates estimated by Barclays were never more than one per cent in error, and the error was always in their favour. How did they know so far in advance how the exchange rates would vary?

On this occasion the international banking system did us no harm. There were many times later, when we were having to work with four or five different currencies simultaneously, that we longed for an easier means of handling money. Ideally there would be one world currency, one basic system of taxation, and one broad set of customs rules. In such a world there would be no currency speculation, legal or illegal. No black markets. A huge reduction in regulations and bureaucracy. Substantially less smuggling – and the crime that goes with it. And we – and other travelling folk like ourselves – would be spared so much of the unjustified suspicion of zealous officials that at times made life afloat rather difficult.

But how could such a utopia ever come into being? Too many international bankers, lawyers, financiers, politicians, officials, agents and criminals would lose their livelihoods. That would never be allowed to happen!

10. Some Technical Matters

This story would be incomplete without mention of some of the more important technical details involved in *Tin Hau's* construction. The non-technically minded, keen to draw nearer to the launch and our subsequent adventures on the high seas, can pass over the next few sections, in which I propose to describe briefly the following:

> The sails, yards, battens and running rigging
> The masts and standing rigging
> The steering
> The windlass, chain and anchors
> Plumbing
> Power generation
> Paints

The reader should therefore skip to section 11 (page 75) unless he or she is particularly interested in some of the details of how to construct a large steel junk.

On finishing the book, if fired with the thought 'I would like to sell up, build a boat and take to the life afloat', the reader should return to these pages – which hopefully will have become more significant.

10.1 THE SAILS

Changing headsails on a wet heaving foredeck may be the racing man's idea of fun, and a pleasure he would not want to be without, but not everyone who goes to sea feels the same way. Cruising folk generally like to keep as dry as possible on deck. They like work to be easy rather than difficult. And they like it to be cosy and warm down below. Sharing a berth with a wet sail bag is *not* considered desirable. Bagging and unbagging of sails is something to be avoided.

One solution to the problem of how best to stow and reef sails, commonly adopted on cruising yachts nowadays, is the 'furling' headsail – a foresail that can be wrapped round and round itself to various positions of reef, and eventually to the fully stowed position. The same system is sometimes used on the mainsail. There are, however, two main drawbacks: firstly, the very considerable costs involved; secondly, the fact that the complex furling equipment *can* go wrong. Anyone who believes Murphy's laws, as I do, knows that anything that can go wrong will go wrong, and this will happen at the worst possible moment. A sail that will not come down spells total disaster. In the course of our travels, we came across numerous yachtsmen with problems over their aging furling gear – sometimes waiting months in port for a spare part.

I had originally thought we would choose furling headsails; then we started to learn about Tom Colvin and the junk rig. I considered carefully all the advantages and disadvantages of this rig, and concluded that what had been right for centuries of Chinese families living aboard their junks would also be right for us. We would have one sail on each mast, ready at all times for use; a simple means of reefing with no complex gadgetry; no worries about sails splitting from top to bottom (as has happened to me on other yachts); no expensive winches; and no stowage of sails below decks.

Later we had experience in the junk rig, but at the outset of our venture in 1983 we could only have trust and blind faith in the oracle, Tom Colvin. As he seemed to have an answer to every problem I raised, I decided not to become too involved in a study of all the different junk sail variations, which are as numerous as western sail variations. Tom's latest arrangement for *Kung Fu Tse* would be good enough for us. I sent a copy of his drawing to Cheong Lee in Hong Kong, together with instructions on the material to be used.

Figure 5 shows the details of *Tin Hau's* three sails.

It will always be a matter of regret to me that I was unable to experiment with the basic sail shapes, batten arrangements, and mast positions – even

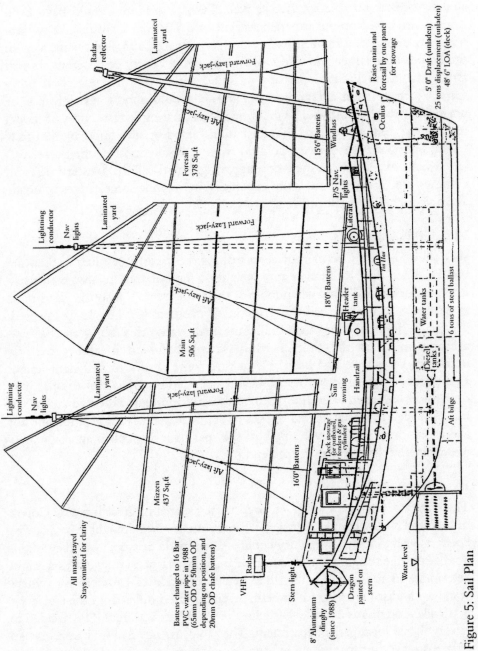

Figure 5: Sail Plan

though we may have had a near optimum arrangement. Obviously, changes in these areas would have been major and expensive, affecting not just the sail and deck plans but the interior as well. Perhaps nothing would have been gained. Yet, based on our experiences on board *Tin Hau*, I would like to have tried, for example, a mizzen twenty per cent smaller and slightly aft, a main fifteen per cent larger and also slightly aft, and a variety of different foresail arrangements, including – perhaps – a small self-tacking jib on a short bow-sprit. To make such alterations on *Tin Hau* would almost certainly not be practical or worthwhile, but I would find it fascinating to test a fleet of model junks on a pond, and to see the information gained used to build another full-sized junk rigged vessel (we would not want to build another one ourselves!) Large sums of money are spent on improving what I call the 'western rig', and volumes are written about it by experts. Why cannot some funds be made available for refining the junk rig?

10.2   THE YARDS

We followed Tom Colvin's advice in making the yards much heftier than the battens, since they carry the entire weight of the sail and are always in use – even in storm conditions when most of the sail is reefed. Also the yards need to be heavy, so that the sail will drop quickly and easily when being lowered. We made them of laminated Philippine mahogany, this being all that was available to us at the time. Having experienced yard breakages on two occasions, I wish we had been able to find some spruce of sufficient length and thickness, so that we could have done without the laminations. The dimensions we used were fine, each yard being approximately two and a half inches thick and five and a half inches in depth at the halyard position and for about one third of the total length of the spar, tapering off to approximately two inches by three inches at each end.

10.3   THE BATTENS

The battens – six on each sail – proved to be an area of great interest. Colvin had indicated they could be made of aluminium, but we thought this might be noisy, as well as expensive. They could also be made of wood, but they might not be strong enough. Or they could be made of plastic piping, but this might deteriorate in the sun. Finally, they could be made of bamboo, but where could we find some in Port Elizabeth, seven hundred miles from the tropics?

Lynda took this as a challenge and set off on a bamboo hunt. She decided to start with the local parks department. They told us they had no bamboos of a large diameter, but that we should try the museum.

Taking their advice Lynda went to the museum, where she was more successful. She learnt that a citrus farm about twenty kilometres out of town, Amanzi Estates, used bamboo for windbreaks. She phoned the owner of the estate, Mr Niven, and met with a most favourable response.

'Take as much as you want,' he said, 'as long as you look after the cutting and the transportation.'

So we enjoyed a welcome break away from the hangars and drove to Amanzi Estates. There, to our amazement, we found that the bamboos were huge. They had been planted at least fifty years before and were obviously of sufficient size for our purposes.

What size did we want? What exactly are the wind pressures on a junk sail? How 'bendy' should a junk batten be? What sail camber should it allow? How strong should it be? How heavy? Do bamboos need any special treatment before they can be used? How can they be straightened if they are cut crooked? When will they turn from green to brown? How long will they last? Are there different species of bamboo, some good for our use and some bad? What do the Chinese do?

These questions went round my head for weeks as I searched for the answers.

The lengths we required were shown on Tom Colvin's drawings: eighteen feet for the main, sixteen feet for the mizzen and fifteen and a half feet for the foresail. I am using feet and inches because Tom, being American, gave all his dimensions in this way. We actually had great problems in South Africa finding an imperial tape measure. Luckily, having been brought up to understand both systems, I was able to switch easily from one to the other. I like to use millimetres when taking and writing down a measurement, but I think in feet and inches when visualising a feature such as the length of a berth, or my own height.

The required diameters and wall thicknesses of the bamboos were much harder to assess. I spent some time researching bamboo in general and also carrying out various theoretical calculations.

Luckily for us, it was at about this time that Port Elizabeth was visited by two junks on their way westwards. One was *Rajah Laut*, a beautiful Malaysian junk, skippered by a quietly-spoken and obviously highly competent German called Wolfgang. The other, *Elf Chine*, had come all the way from Canton under a mixed nationality crew (mostly French) in their twenties. She was twenty-five metres long and built only five years earlier in the traditional manner of a South China Seas trading junk. Whilst admiring the beautiful woodwork and many features, such as the long tiller operated by block and tackle and the huge capstan for raising the mainsail (operated by two or more people), we were horrified to hear the tales of breaking masts (one more was to break in the Atlantic before they got back to France) and the sheer man-power (or womanpower) needed to operate her. I was happy with our philosophy of being prepared to combine the best of the east with the best of the west. Our masts would be made of aluminium if I thought that was best. On a more positive note, South African bamboos – or at least those found near Durban – were highly praised. 'The best we have found anywhere,' said the crew. I wondered slightly why they had had such experience in looking for bamboos in so many countries. Did they break often? However, on balance I was encouraged. The Amanzi Estate bamboos were becoming more and more desirable.

We also learnt from the crew of *Elf Chine* that the maintenance of bamboos was nil, that we must cut them at the right time in the lunar cycle (this we ignored!) and that we must cure them by floating them for some weeks in the sea to leach out the sugars in the sap.

Armed with a bit more knowledge, we set off again for the Amanzi Estates, this time with two cars in the company of Jan and Jeff, visiting from Swazi-land. We passed a most enjoyable few hours sawing, hacking and tugging at selected bamboo poles. I had decided at this stage to go for diameters of between two inches and three and a half inches. Generally, the best bamboos were in the middle of the thicket, where they were hardest to reach. However, by the end of the day, with the aid of ropes, chains and the vehicles, we had thirty-one fine poles laid out on the ground. This would be a large enough number from which to choose the eighteen we actually needed.

Back in Port Elizabeth, I examined these poles more carefully, cut them roughly to length, weighed them and placed them in the swimming pool belonging to Lynda's sister and brother-in-law (Sally and Wally Wessels). A swimming pool was considered more practical than the sea; and, being winter, no one was wanting to swim. The main inconvenience to Sally and Wally was that the pool's automatic 'Kreepy Krawly' cleaner had to be removed.

Some months later, the poles came out again, looking much the same – green and crooked. We took them on the back of the bakkie to the hangar, making several trips. Then we lashed them tightly to the hangar's vertical girders in an effort to straighten them.

A further two to three months passed whilst the bamboos turned from green to golden brown. The moment of truth came when we unlashed them from their supports. Would they spring back to their original shapes?

The answer, thankfully, was no. They emerged straight. On weighing them, I discovered that their weights, which had worried me earlier, had more than halved to a respectable four to nine kilograms per pole, which worked out to be between 0.8 and 1.6 kilograms per metre length.

At this stage I needed to determine which poles should be used in each batten position. It was clear that the uppermost two battens on each sail needed to be the largest. The lower battens could be smaller, as they would probably not be loaded at all in strong winds, lying within the stowed bundle of the reefed sail; and, when unreefed in lighter winds, the wind forces would obviously be less.

I decided upon a simple load test for sizing the largest battens: Lynda's brother, Andy, weighing eighty kilograms, would have to stand on the middle of a bamboo resting on supports sixteen feet apart. The bamboo should not deflect more than twenty-four inches or less than nine inches and, on bouncing, it should not break.

This crude but effective rule of thumb resulted in us choosing three to three and a half inch diameter bamboos for the upper pair of battens on each sail and two to three inch diameter bamboos for the lower ones. For the lowermost batten (or 'boom'), I made the size slightly larger than that strictly needed for wind loading. We felt that some weight was needed at the bottom of the sail.

Luckily, we had more than enough poles available for the eighteen 'working' battens. We decided to carry three poles on deck as spares; and we rejected the six worst poles as being surplus to our needs.

Having worked out the loading in this way, I was able to use the knowledge later when it came to designing the masts. Also, I could check that the entire running and standing rigging was designed to the same loading – in other words, the sails were as strong as the battens; the battens matched the masts; the masts matched the deck and keel steps and also the stays; the stays matched the dead-eyes; and the dead-eyes matched the bulwark eyes and shackles. All very well in theory, but gale number three on our maiden voyage produced two zones of weakness, as will be seen.

One important aspect of the traditional Chinese batten escaped me at the time, which we were to regret afterwards. We would have done better to have used two smaller bamboos per batten position, rather than one large one, and these should have been staggered with respect to each other. For example, the uppermost mainsail batten should have consisted of two 2½" diameter bamboo poles each sixteen feet long and overlapped to make up the required length of eighteen feet. This would have been better than one three and a half inch diameter pole just greater than eighteen feet in length. The problem was that due to the nodules in bamboo it was impossible to cut a pole exactly to the required length. As a result of this initial misjudgement (eventually put right in Cyprus), we had innumerable headaches with our sheetlets catching the short protruding lengths of batten on the leach of each sail. This meant scaling up the sail to free the snarl-ups, often in the middle of the night and in bad weather.

Apart from this one mistake, we were very happy with our bamboo battens. In spite of all the misuse we gave them, only one ever broke.

10.4   THE RUNNING RIGGING

Moving on from the battens to the running rigging, I started with the most familiar ground to me from past sailing experience – the main halyards, the ropes needed to haul up the sails. Again, working on the old principle of keeping it simple (and thus long lasting), I did not want halyard winches. I preferred to use block and tackle.

I envisaged the weights involved in hoisting the largest sail, the main (refer to the sail plan). First we would just have to lift the twenty-five kilogram yard clear of the stowed bundle. Then the yard, the top panel of the sail and one batten (say forty kilograms in total). Then two panels of sail. Then three. Then four, five and finally the full six panels of sail (say one hundred kilograms at this stage – getting heavy!) I decided to allow a further one hundred kilograms for the fact that the sail might be partially filled with wind. Thus I calculated that in extreme conditions, a weight of two hundred kilograms would have to be lifted, ideally by one person weighing only sixty-five kilograms. This would require a mechanical advantage of three-to-one, assuming that all the person's weight is on the halyard; but, allowing for block friction, I felt I needed a purchase of four-to-one. This meant a double block on the yard (we used Barton cruising blocks, costing about seven pounds each in 1985) and a double block with becket at the masthead.

We quickly discovered, however, the problem with the block and tackle system: when the sail was fully up, we were left with a mile of rope at deck level – or to be exact, in the case of our main, thirty-five metres. This had to be stowed quickly and conveniently. Over the period of our trials on *Tin Hau* we evolved a system that still remains. For each sail we made a pin rail which we lashed to the standing rigging at about chest level just above the halyard cleating-off points on the bulwarks. The procedure with loose halyard rope was then to coil it directly on to a selected pin (holding the increasingly heavy coil was thus avoided). When finished, the entire coil would be turned upside down on the pin, ready for lowering. In the case of a one panel reef, the top three turns would quickly be uncoiled and laid out on the deck, prior to uncleating the halyard. For a two panel reef, six turns would be laid out. This way we avoided nasty rope tangles. Time was often very short when reefing or lowering sails.

After the halyards used for hoisting the three sails, the next set of ropes to mention are the three spare halyards (also twelve millimetre three strand polyester). Each of these was positioned on the opposite side of the mast to the principal halyard, and on the same side as the sail. They proved to be invaluable for bosun's chair work at the masthead.

Then there were the ten millimetre lazy jacks – yet more rope running to and from the mastheads, making the Chinese junk rig seem still more complicated to the uninitiated eye. We used to watch people an quay walls gazing for hours at *Tin Hau's* spaghetti as they tried to work out the function of each line.

The purpose of lazy jacks is to support in a bundle well clear of the deck some of the sail, when reefed, or all of it when fully lowered – another junk speciality. The slope of the bundle and the height it rests above deck is controllable. We found this extremely handy, as by 'reefing up' (raising the bundle) we could obtain very good visibility forward and, in harbour, enjoy full standing room under the stowed sails.

Tin Hau had two lazy jacks per sail, an aft one cleating to the bulwark rail on both sides (port and starboard), and a forward one cleating to one side only. Figure 6 shows how they work.

Now comes one of the most debated parts of a Chinese junk's running rigging, the sheeting system – the ropes needed to adjust and control the sails when sailing.

A large part of the skill of sailing is the way in which these ropes (or sheets) are set. In western yachts, the sheets are normally attached to one point on the sail (to the boom in the case of the mainsail). In junks, however, there is a significant difference. Generally, *each* sail batten is attached to a sheet, directly or indirectly via sheetlets and bridles. Unfortunately this means considerably more rope, but the strain on the sail cloth is much reduced, with obvious advantages.

Not knowing any better, initially we used the system recommended by Tom Colvin, with separate sheets and sheetlets and traditional euphroes and friction blocks (see Figure 7). These were made of Oregon pine, salvaged from the demolished floor of Port Elizabeth's opera house. We decided also to adopt the double sheeting method – two sets of sheets and sheetlets per sail.

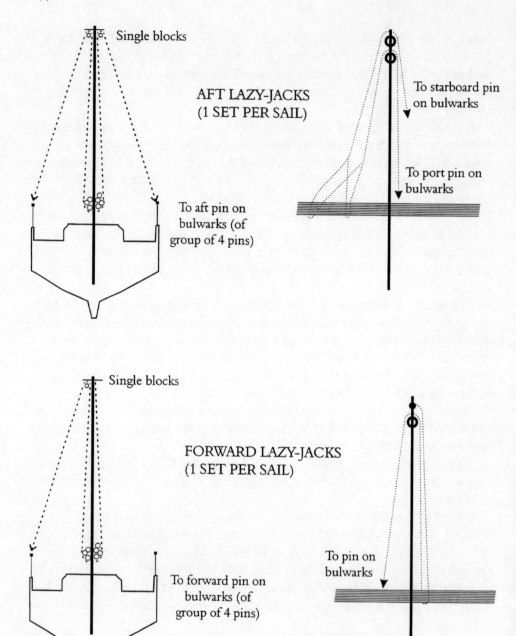

Single blocks

AFT LAZY-JACKS
(1 SET PER SAIL)

To aft pin on
bulwarks (of
group of 4 pins)

To starboard pin
on bulwarks

To port pin on
bulwarks

Single blocks

FORWARD LAZY-JACKS
(1 SET PER SAIL)

To forward pin on
bulwarks (of
group of 4 pins)

To pin on
bulwarks

Figure 6: The Lazy-Jacks

While we never had any regrets about the latter (there are many advantages; particularly the ability to hold the sail steady, sheeted amidships or near midships, when motor-sailing or simply stopping in mid-ocean for a rest), we had reason to change the former. We decided during our maiden voyage that euphroes and friction blocks were not for us. Balancing on the cabin top, or worse still on the pilothouse roof, to reduce sheetlet lengths was no fun, and positively dangerous at times. (If this was not done the euphroes touched deck level, catching every obstruction they could find.) The procedure had to be carried out all too often on our maiden voyage, whenever reefing or unreefing was required (typically, four times a day). Reefing from full sail (six panels) to five panels required no adjustment. But from five panels to four each sheetlet had to be shortened and the excess tied up on the euphroe (two per sail, and perhaps all three sails). From four panels to three there was no further adjustment, but from three to two (winds in excess of gale force by now), once again we had to shorten the sheetlets, and this time in extremely difficult conditions. Reefing a junk was meant to be easy!

We planned various changes during the maiden voyage, and experimented with them in Mauritius and later throughout the Indian Ocean. However, it was not until we reached Cyprus that the bulk of the alterations were done, and even after our arrival in England there was still one last adjustment. Much as we loved the traditional aspect of euphroes, and much as we were proud of our first efforts at woodwork on *Tin Hau*, they had to go. With the euphroes went the sheetlets and friction blocks. We were left with just the sheets and western blocks.

Figure 8 shows the final arrangement we adopted. Note the totally new gallows frame – like a football goal post. This raised the sheeting blocks as high and as far outboard as possible, with good provision for coiling the excess rope. There were no further problems of sheets catching on doors, cabin top drain spouts, deck seats, and all the other places that used to be a problem when the sheet blocks were at bulwark level. Note also that we decided in the end to sheet the upper part and the lower part of the sail separately. This was useful in controlling the sail's twist and thus its performance, but the main reason we chose this system was to ease the hoisting load. One continuous sheet through numerous blocks on the gallows frame had resulted in too much friction. Hoisting was difficult.

In conclusion, the final sheeting system – with which we were very happy – had four stainless steel pins per sail for cleating-off purposes. Each sail had a port top, port bottom, starboard top and starboard bottom sheet. With three

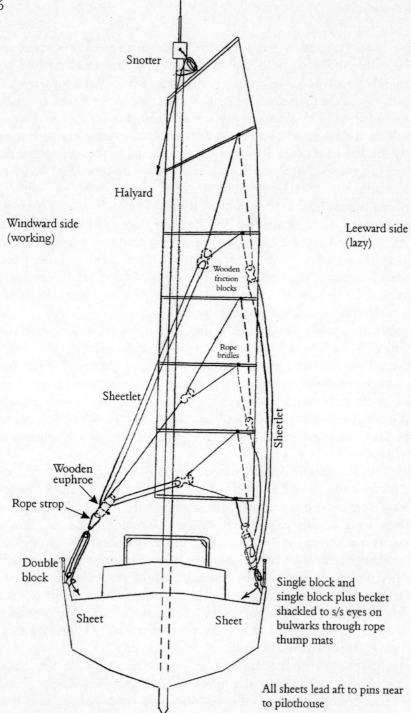

Snotter

Halyard

Windward side
(working)

Leeward side
(lazy)

Wooden
friction
blocks

Rope
bridles

Sheetlet

Sheetlet

Wooden
euphroe

Rope strop

Double
block

Single block and
single block plus becket
shackled to s/s eyes on
bulwarks through rope
thump mats

Sheet

Sheet

All sheets lead aft to pins near
to pilothouse

Figure 7: The Original Sheeting System (1986)

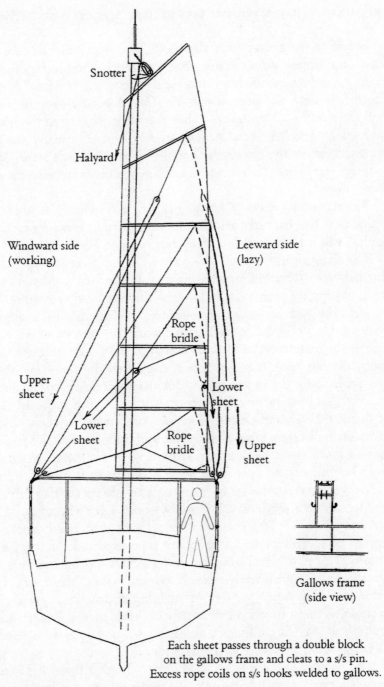

Snotter

Halyard

Windward side
(working)

Leeward side
(lazy)

Rope
bridle

Upper
sheet

Lower
sheet

Lower
sheet

Rope
bridle

Upper
sheet

Gallows frame
(side view)

Each sheet passes through a double block
on the gallows frame and cleats to a s/s pin.
Excess rope coils on s/s hooks welded to gallows.

Figure 8: The Final Sheeting System (1992)

sails, there were twelve sheet pins in total, together with twelve excess rope hooks.

Before moving away from the sheets, it is worth mentioning that the new main and mizzen gallow frames had a number of secondary functions. They gave us improved washing line and hammock slinging positions. (The hammocks were all important on *Tin Hau*. A good all-round watch could be kept from them – in comfort – while the autopilot steered the boat.) Also they gave us an excellent sun awning arrangement. It usually took less than a minute to set up the awning; and in the places *Tin Hau's* crew liked to be, sun awnings were vital. They made the difference between utter contentment and sheer misery.

The remaining items of running rigging and other lines not yet mentioned include the flag halyards, sail ties, snotters, parrels, bowsing tackle and down-hauls, I will explain these briefly as they relate to *Tin Hau*:

The flag halyards: we chose – very wisely as it turned out – to have three flag halyards (three millimetre, eight plait standard polyester), one on each mast, passing through a single block at the masthead cross-tree. Additionally, we flew the Red Ensign on its own flag pole aft. We used the mizzen mast (starboard side) for the courtesy flag of whatever country we might be visiting. The main mast (port side) was used for any house flag we wanted to fly (normally our Junk Rig Association flag). And the foremast (starboard side) was available for the yellow quarantine flag ('Q') flown on our first arrival in a country (not necessary everywhere, nowadays). Lynda made all our flags, most of them in Swaziland before *Tin Hau's* keel had even been laid, including a complete set of signal flags. The other useful function of the flag halyards was as a means of passing equipment from deck to masthead. Whenever I was up there I would often forget items such as screwdrivers, pliers and shackle pins. Lynda would send these up to me in a plastic bag via the flag halyard.

The sail ties: Jacqui (much more of whom will be heard later) was given as her first job on *Tin Hau* the task of end-splicing three hundred and fifty short lengths of six millimetre three strand rope needed for tying the sails to the battens. This may have turned her into the best splicing hand in the Southern Ocean, but, unfortunately, except on the yards, these ties later became redundant. They had a habit of undoing themselves, given enough time. Eventually, the solution we found for a cheap, easy sail tie that would never undo itself was six millimetre shock cord. Rope such as is used for dinghy sheeting would also have been satisfactory.

The snotters: I imagine many readers will not know what is meant by the term 'snotter' on a Colvin junk. We certainly did not know when we first became involved. The Chambers English Dictionary gives three meanings for 'snotter': first, as a verb: 'to breathe through an obstruction in the nostrils: to sob, snuffle, blubber'. This was not the one. Secondly as a noun: 'the wattles of a turkey-cock'. Also not the one. And finally 'the lower support of the sprit'. This is nautical and nearer the mark. English junkies call the snotter the yard hauling parrel. But we became used to Colvin terminology. It is actually the rope used to hold the yard close to the mast (one per sail, ten millimetre polyester in our case). It is redundant when the sail is fully hoisted or in its stowed position, but is vitally important in each of the four reef positions. Without it the yard would bounce all over the place. One end of the snotter is shackled to the yard halyard block. The other end is taken once round the mast, back through a ring or shackle on the yard and thence down to one of the bulwark pins at deck level.

The parrels: These were required to hold each batten close to the mast. *Tin Hau* had six per sail. We read a number of articles about parrel chafe being a problem, and we found this to be true – our original rope parrels were showing signs of wear after the first few sails. So when a roll of industrial webbing was offered to us, we jumped at the opportunity. A wide flat area rubbing backwards and forwards against the mast was obviously more desirable than a rope. We cut eighteen pieces to the correct lengths (each about a metre long) and Lynda sewed the ends back on to themselves to form two loops into which ten millimetre rope was spliced. The webbing was then led around the mast and the two rope ends tied to the batten, one at the sail luff and the other at a point about two metres back. The actual position and the tension of the parrel is critical. If it is too tight, difficulties result over hoisting and lowering the sail. If too loose, the sail hangs too far away from the mast. The latter occurs, of course, only when the wind is blowing from the side on which the parrels are located. When the wind blows from the opposite side the battens are pushed up against the mast and the sail takes on an altogether different shape. Since *Tin Hau* had three masts, we alternated the side of the mast on which the sail was placed. On the mizzen and foremast the sail was to port. On the main it was to starboard. By doing this we reduced the possibility of one tack being more favourable than the other. I actually much preferred the look of the sail when it was 'hanging from its parrels' – in other words, when the wind was blowing from the parrel side. I have always been mystified when reading the view stated in various junk articles that the opposite tack (when the battens are pushing against the mast) produces the better performance.

The hauling parrel, bowsing tackle and downhauls: These are three more of the controlling ropes that may occur on a junk sail. We experimented with them on *Tin Hau* and Figure 9 shows the arrangement we finally used.

The hauling parrel and bowsing tackle were rigged only on the foresail. They are very important for reefing. Without them the sail took on a horrifically distorted shape.

On the mizzen and main we rigged two simple downhauls which we used occasionally, whilst close hauled, to remove some of the creasing in the sails. Whether or not this helped our windward performance is hard to say.

10.5 THE MASTS

I am glad we chose aluminium masts. They proved to be one of the few fixtures on the boat that required no maintenance, in spite of constant exposure to wind, rain, sun and salt, and heavy abrasion from the battens and the yard. They were not even anodised.

It took nearly as long to organise the masts as it took to build the boat. Right up to the last minute there were problems. But Huletts Aluminium were successful in the end, even though the mizzen and main masts – promised initially in one length – came eventually in two halves, expertly sleeved and joined at Port Elizabeth's university.

The sizes that were supplied, after much to-ing and fro-ing between myself (as designer) and David Whitby (the local Huletts representative) were as follows. Main and mizzen masts: 12.3 m long, 168 mm outside diameter and 7.9 mm wall thickness. Foremast: 9.5 m long, 140 mm outside diameter and 9.5 mm wall thickness.

The alloy had a greater yield stress – and thus strength – than mild steel, but would not corrode. It was a special marine grade (reference D65S).

Lynda's model had demonstrated to us that a small cross-tree was required at each masthead to stop the battens fouling the stays, and Tom Colvin subsequently confirmed this. We used a solid aluminium bar two inches in diameter and welded it through the mast, notching the ends to receive the stays. It was also useful for supporting the ancillary masthead blocks, such as those required for the lazy jacks and flag halyards.

I chose to have the mast cap made in wood (Philippine mahogany) in order to provide a convenient attachment point for the various steel fittings and to keep them electrically isolated from the mast, thus avoiding galvanic corrosion problems. The foremast carried our Firdell Blipper radar reflector. And the mizzen and main masts carried lightning conductors, together with various navigation lights (the port/starboard light, the steaming light, an all round

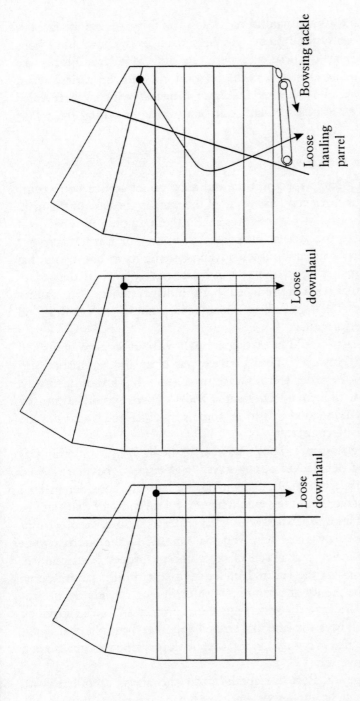

Because of the angle of the mast, the bowsing tackle on the foresail is important when the sail is reefed. The fixed block is shackled to the tabernacle. The movable forward block is clipped to the lowermost batten using a carbine hook. The rope is secured on to a cleat welded to the tabernacle.

Figure 9: The Hauling Parrel, Bowsing Tackle and Downhauls.

white anchor light, and two all round reds). On the forward and aft faces of each mast cap were galvanised steel eyes held together by four long bolts passing through base plates. These eyes were used for the halyard blocks, the spare halyard block being shackled to the forward eye and the main halyard shackled to the aft one. Here, however, I made a mistake which was revealed in a dramatic manner on 'that Sunday', our first overnight outing from Port Elizabeth.

10.6   THE STANDING RIGGING

We followed Tom Colvin's specification and subsequent advice concerning the stays. He called for three stays each side of the mast in the case of the main and the mizzen; and just two on the foresail. But before going into details, I should mention one of the eternal junk debates: to stay or not to stay your masts? Unstayed masts have undoubted advantages, the main one being that the sails are totally unobstructed and so can be let out as far as is desired. A further advantage is that costs are reduced, both initially and later (in maintenance). Also, windage aloft – and noise – is reduced, resulting in less drag and thus slightly better performance.

I knew that our masts would be strong enough without stays to withstand just about any wind. However, Tom's advice was clear and emphatic: Stay your masts – loosely – in order to minimise masthead whipping in a seaway. He felt that continual movement backwards and forwards would eventually cause mast failure. I understood this to be some sort of fatigue fracture, such as has been known to affect aircraft.

Not wanting to go against Tom's advice, particularly in something as important as this, we decided to adopt stays – a decision I never regretted despite the extra work involved. Perhaps in future I would consider making the shorter masts unstayed, but they would have to be exceptionally strong.

The next question about the stays was: what material should we use? After some thought, I chose galvanised wire rope as opposed to the alternative of stainless steel. The former was much cheaper and, if properly maintained, promised to last as long as the latter. I understood that should failure occur there would usually be plenty of warning; worn or fraying strands are noticeable well in advance. We gave the stays their initial protection, once rigged, by applying a mixture of beeswax and linseed oil (another bosun's chair job). Subsequently, about once every two years, I went aloft with a toothbrush and a small tub of rust converter.

Haggie Wire Rope of Port Elizabeth made the stays, complete with thimbles at each end; eight altogether – not sixteen, as might be thought. We specified that each stay should be double length, that is it should take one complete turn round the mast just above the cross-tree and return to the bulwarks on both port and starboard sides.

Each thimble was shackled to a dead-eye made of lignum vitæ to Tom Colvin's specification, and tied to its partner by a rope lanyard (six turns). The lower dead-eyes were shackled directly to welded eyes on the bulwarks; and here I made another annoying mistake. Those eyes should have been of stainless steel, not mild steel. I never found a way of painting them effectively to stop rust – unsightly, but in this case not dangerous.

The real problem with the dead-eyes, however, was their metal straps. Originally these were of stainless steel, but they contained a ninety degree bend – too sharp. We had failure after failure on the maiden voyage from the third gale onwards. By the time we reached Mauritius we had made numerous temporary lashings. Eventually, they all were replaced by galvanised straps (another story involving dozens of people of many nationalities!)

The final area of note concerning the masts is the way they were supported at deck level. Again we had a decision to make: to take them right through the deck to the level of the keel, or to step them on the deck in a tabernacle, with just a small compression post between deck and keel?

The latter interfered considerably less with the interior arrangement, but, in the case of the mizzen and main masts, I chose the former. We were prepared to put up with a seven inch aluminium pole coming through the middle of the accommodation. We would disguise it somehow, yet keep all-round access to the securing wedges. In the case of the mizzen, we would build a supporting bridge in the bilges across the propeller shaft. There were many disadvantages, yet it seemed to me I was choosing the stronger alternative, and I did not fancy having too many protrusions on deck that might rust and cause maintenance headaches.

With hindsight I was right, but the mistake we made was not to keel-step our third mast – the foremast. Instead, a tabernacle was constructed, as interpreted from the designer's drawing – and what a mistake that proved to be. It nearly led to a major disaster during the maiden voyage, which took a year to sort out afterwards.

Before leaving the subject of the masts, perhaps I should answer one of our three most common quayside questions (the other questions being 'Why has your rudder got holes in it?' and 'When are you leaving?') 'Why does your mast lean forward?', someone would ask, pointing at the foremast.

This could be answered glibly: 'Because it was shown that way on the drawings', or 'Because the Chinese often do it that way'. But the real answer is clear enough. The mast rakes forward so that the foresail, which hangs from the top of the mast, is positioned well forward of the bow. It can thus be of a reasonably large area (378 square feet in our case). If the mast had been vertical, there would only have been room for about 150 square feet of sail, a reduction of 228 square feet. Moreover, in order to maintain balance, the mizzen would also have had to have been reduced by about the same amount. A sail reduction of 456 square feet out of our total of 1,321 square feet. A thirty-five per cent loss – quite significant!

The counterpart to the raking Chinese mast on a western yacht is the bow-sprit. Beautiful as these are, they are frequently a liability when it comes to berthing or anchoring, and we were glad to have been without one.

10.7   THE STEERING

We were presented with a bewildering number of alternatives when it came to working out the best steering system for *Tin Hau*. The rudder itself, the rudder post and the rudder port (the fixed tube through which the rudder post passed) were all detailed by Tom Colvin. But the rest was more or less left for us to work out. Not having had much prior experience of this sort of thing, I had to tackle it from first principles. I considered worm steering, hydraulic steering and the push-pull system, but concluded they all had their drawbacks, either in cost, complexity or inadequacy. The simplest solution – a tiller was out of the question with a wheelhouse. There was no room for it. I calculated that had we had a tiller, its length would have had to have been more than ten metres, two-thirds of the length of the boat! Even by adopting the Chinese system of block and tackle, attached to the end of the tiller, the length required would still have been excessive, given that we wanted to have a pilothouse.

Having said this, our 'emergency' system was a two metre long tiller made of steel pipe, machined square at one end to drop over the top of the rudder post. I was careful to have an eye welded on the other end of it, the plan being to obtain additional purchase by shackling a pair of double blocks to this eye. In the event of a failure of the main steering system (assuming the rudder and its post were still intact!) the plan was to unbolt and remove the helmsman's seat, drop the emergency tiller into position (facing aft, not the normal direction), and use the tiller immediately for steering. Should the emergency become 'long term', we would then rig up blocks and tackle, and sit on the settee right at the aft end of the wheelhouse, squinting at the compass.

The whole subject of emergency steering was close to my heart, as I had had considerable personal experience of it. In my Cape to Uruguay race of 1979, our main steering broke irretrievably on the third night out of Cape

Town. For the following forty-two days we relied on an increasingly worn 'emergency' wooden tiller. Having been through this, I was not prepared to take any chances on *Tin Hau*!

Returning to *Tin Hau's* primary system of steering, I realised there were two main design factors: firstly, the helmsman would have to be able to manage the wheel in any foreseeable weather in which we might be sailing; secondly, the rudder, its bearings, shackles and all linkages would have to be designed for the occasions when all attempts at steering the boat had been abandoned and the wheel lashed. Perhaps one day we would be in this situation, lying ahull in a gale. I let my imagination run wild. I visualised mountainous waves breaking hard against an unyielding four foot square unbalanced rudder. What a pounding it might have to take. And what a disaster if we lost it! With this in mind, I resolved to take the utmost care while it was still easy to do so on dry land.

After much thought and on becoming acquainted with the size of the lazaret (Tom Colvin's terminology for the stern locker, at that time another new word to me) and the arrangement of the wheelhouse, I decided to adopt a system based on a large steel quadrant welded to the rudder post and connected to the wheel via a series of wire ropes, tensioners, chains and sprockets (or gear wheels such as one sees on a motorcycle). Most of the components would be situated inside the lazaret and so would not only be sheltered and free from corrosion problems, but also very accessible for inspection and, if necessary, maintenance or repair. Figure 10 shows the arrangement as finally constructed. Although this should be largely self-explanatory, I will comment on some of the details:

The gearing: I learnt early on from reading magazine clippings and nautical books that there would be no advantage in having the rudder turn more than thirty-five degrees in either direction. Beyond this, the advantages gained from extra turning ability would be offset by the disadvantages of braking and stalling effects. Likewise I learnt that the wheel should not be allowed to turn more than three revolutions to starboard or three to port. 1080° of wheel (three 360° turns) to thirty-five degrees of rudder represented a mechanical advantage of just over thirty, which I decided was sufficient, even with a small two foot diameter wheel (which could always be increased in size at a later date, if desirable).

In order to achieve this mechanical advantage, I realised I would need as big a quadrant as was physically possible (item 6 in Figure 10) and also an intermediate shaft with a pair of gear wheels on it, one large and one small (item 7 in Figure 10). At that time I had never heard of the term 'slaveshaft',

Key to Figure 10: The Steering System

1. *Rudder* ex 10 mm plate, stiffened horizontally. Three rows of diamond shaped holes. 50mm x 50mm angle on trailing edge.

2. *Lower bearing.* Simply a steel 'cup' welded to the keel, machined exactly to fit the rudder post. Well greased steel disc in cup base to reduce friction. Greasing points fitted.

3. *Upper pillar bearing* bolted to steel framework.

4. *Rudder post* ex 65mm diameter solid bar, weighing 80kg. Welded (after installation) to the rudder plate. Square head for emergency tiller.

5. *Rudder port* ex 90mm OD 8mm thick pipe welded to hull and bulkhead tie.

6. *Quadrant* ex 10mm steel plate with weight-reducing cut-outs; 0.6m radius. Welded to rudder post. For plan view see Figures 1 or 2.

7. *Vertical slave shaft* ex 45mm diameter solid bar. Two pillar bearings, three gear wheels (eleven teeth to the quadrant, twenty-two teeth to the wheel slave shaft and twenty eight-teeth to autopilot slave shaft).

8. *Wheel slave shaft* ex 25mm diameter solid bar. Two bearings, two gear wheels (eleven teeth to the vertical slave shaft. Fifty teeth to the wheel shaft).

9. *Wheel shaft* ex 25mm diameter solid bar. Two bearings, one gear wheel (fifty teeth to the wheel slave shaft). Key-way at end for wheel. Forward end can be extended for external steering.

10. *Wooden wheel* with spokes. 0.6m outside diameter.

11. *Helmsman's seat* reduced over two years from a second-hand draughtsman's chair with arms and tilting back to just the seat portion.

12. *Compass* (Sestral Moore) mounted high and upside-down, well clear of all steelwork (to minimise magnetic problems).

13. *Rudder stops* (2 No.) to prevent the quadrant (and thus the rudder) from rotating more than thirty-five degrees in either direction.

14. *Emergency tiller* lashed and stored in the lazarette.

15. *Autopilot slave shaft* ex 20mm diameter solid bar. Two bearings, two gear wheels (twenty teeth to the vertical slave shaft, forty-four teeth to the autohelm motor).

16. *Autohelm 6000 motor* installed eighteen months after launching.

17. *Number seven:* the name we gave to the two ropes that lash the wheel and thus – in some conditions – steer the boat.

18. *Rudder indicator* (perspex). Mounted on the rudder post.

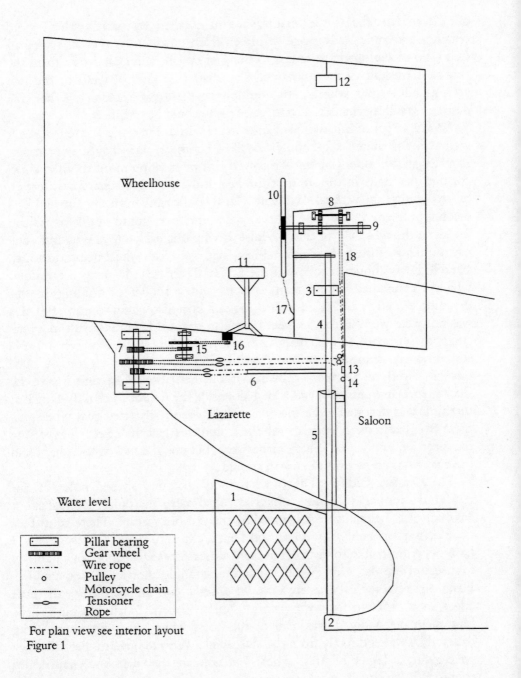

Figure 10: The Steering System

but I learnt later that this is what it is normally called. By inserting this I could obtain a mechanical advantage of fifteen from quadrant to vertical slaveshaft (the ratio of the quadrant radius to the gear wheel radius) and two from the vertical slaveshaft to the horizontal slaveshaft (the ratio of teeth in the two corresponding gear wheels). By multiplying these two factors together, the desired overall mechanical advantage of thirty could be obtained.

So far, so good; but two problems materialised. First, the lazaret, big as it was, was not quite long enough to allow room for the chains, wire ropes, shackles and wire tensioners. We solved this by creating more room; a small cut-out was made in the stern of the hull and a two-foot square box section made to house the vertical slaveshaft. Hardly noticeable from the outside! The second problem could easily have gone unnoticed until we were afloat. Luckily I thought of it in time. Whilst driving our bakkie to the hangars one day, thinking of the boat as usual, I imagined *Tin Hau's* wheel being turned to starboard. My thoughts followed the action all the way down to the rudder, which I concluded would turn to port; and a rudder protruding in this direction would result in a forward moving boat also going to port. But this was not what we wanted! A wheel turned to starboard should result in a boat going to starboard. I had made a big mistake, and cursed myself for my stupidity. My immediate reaction was to find Tony. In his customary calm way he solved yet another problem without hesitation. A second horizontal shaft (item 9 in Figure 10) was added alongside the first one (item 8), which at that time was destined to be the wheel shaft. Identically sized gear wheels on these two shafts were made to interlock, and this had the effect of reversing the direction of rotation. Shaft 9, therefore, became the new wheel shaft; and the boat would now turn the way it should.

The Chinese rudder: The three rows of diamond shaped holes in our rudder, traditional in Chinese junks, provoked more questions than just about anything else. People were fascinated by this curious feature. There must be a good reason for them, they think, and I am inclined to agree. Unfortunately, I have never been able to give a genuinely satisfactory explanation and I am yet to meet anyone else with good first-hand junk sailing knowledge who could.
From our personal experience, I would observe two things. Firstly, the hole edges are a problem from the painting point of view. Small, grasping shells love them. Secondly, I was glad of the holes when our rudder was being battered by waves directly from the side, while we were hove to. Perhaps they were giving a degree of stress relief? But why are they diamond shaped, not round? Why so small?

Many suggestions have been made to me. Manoeuvring in harbour is meant to be easier (on *Tin Hau* it *was* reasonably easy). Turning of the rudder meets with less resistance. Turbulence and stall zones are created with beneficial eddy currents. However, not having experienced *Tin Hau* without her 'holey' rudder, I can make no comment on the views offered by the experts, whether they be naval architects or aeronautical engineers. One day, I hope, the puzzle will be solved.

The other mystery is the two inch by two inch angle welded to the four foot high trailing edge of the rudder. As we gazed at our wake and watched the bubbly, disturbed water leaving this last bit of *Tin Hau's* structure, we often wondered how this might help. The angle was not just detailed on the drawings, but it was also emphasised to me as 'extremely important' by Tony Richardson of Southampton, the owner/builder of *T'ai Shan*, sister ship to *Tin Hau* (we were lucky to 'discover' Tony early on during our boat building days, and we have kept in touch with him ever since).

Rudder position indicator: At first we had no rudder position indicator and, in spite of the groove on one of the wheel spokes, it was sometimes hard to know in which direction the rudder was pointing. It was easy to think it was lying dead central, whereas really it was ten degrees off dead centre with the wheel one whole revolution to – say – starboard. Lynda solved this problem neatly by cutting a small circle of perspex with a central void that fitted over the square head of the rudder post. One segment of the perspex, made visible through a slot in the woodwork, was marked 30°, 20°, 10°, 0, 10°, 20°, 30°. As the rudder post turned, the marking on the perspex would line up with a single line drawn on the woodwork. This was all that was needed to tell us the rudder position. No electronics, no delicate needles – and hardly any expense.

10.8   THE WINDLASS AND CHAIN

Tin Hau's windlass has such a history to it that it is worthy of some detailed description. We do not even know where it spent its early days, probably at the top of some slipway in South Africa where it would have given years of service launching and hauling out boats. We came across it – following a tip-off from Ronnie – in one of Port Elizabeth's more intriguing junk shops, which goes by the name of EP Buyers and Sellers. This is a place where I could easily have spent a whole day if I had ever had the time, containing rooms full of every conceivable domestic and industrial item, usually at bargain prices.

Sitting in one corner, buried under piles of cloth, was a three foot high winch, dusty and neglected but otherwise looking in good shape. I was pleased to find it described as a 'crab winch' in my Simpson Lawrence catalogue, and was able to read a technical specification. The new price, I noted, was about fifty times the junk shop price. So, with some trepidation about how we would make it suitable for *Tin Hau's* foredeck, we bought it.

The first job was to strip it down, send the mild steel cheek plates for sandblasting and priming, and then reassemble it with a longer main shaft on which we would fit two chain gypsies. Also the drive shaft would need modifying and two handles welded on to each end. The aim – which we achieved – was to construct a hand operated windlass, capable of being used by one person when hauling up anchors, or by two people simultaneously. I also wanted to have an easy system for setting two anchors at the bow, each being attached at all times to about seventy metres of chain, which, when not in use, would lie unobstructed in the forepeak.

As mentioned earlier, the problem was: what comes first, the chain or the gypsy? The local chain manufacturers did not make gypsies. And the gypsy manufacturers, who could supply chain, were abroad. There seemed little point in importing nearly half a ton of eleven millimetre chain when it could be bought for a reasonable price and to a high quality in South Africa. So we decided in the end to place an order with McKinnon Chain of Benoni.

The problems started with the two gypsies. Simpson Lawrence in Glasgow agreed to make them to match a small sample of our chosen chain. But when it came to delivery we thought we would take advantage of the fact that Lynda's parents were about to have a holiday in Britain and would be staying in a certain London hotel. We gave the address of the hotel to Simpson Lawrence and the estimated date of arrival of Lynda's parents. All was going smoothly at this point; the gypsies were made on time and delivered to the hotel. However, the hotel staff took fright and thought that such a small, heavy package might be a bomb. They refused to keep it and redirected it back to Scotland.

Thus began a long and involved correspondence concerning the where-abouts of the gypsies – but we got them in the end. They fitted the chain (more than many gypsies do!) and it all ended happily.

10.9 THE ANCHORS

The most commonly seen anchors on cruising yachts are the CQR, Danforth and Fisherman. These were all available – in different sizes – at yacht chandlers. But the price of the larger ones was exorbitant. Also, I was not happy with some of the well-known weaknesses (for example, the Danforth's shank is often known to bend on being pulled excessively from the side); and I was having great difficulty in working out convenient stowage positions.

Bearing all this in mind, I decided to design our own anchors, and have them made locally.

Danforth and Northill anchors (the latter being used by Tom Colvin on *Kung Fu Tse*, and unfamiliar to me then) are both convenient for welded construction, and so these appeared to be the most viable choices. I liked the idea of having two different anchor types, both ready to drop at a moment's notice.

Taking advantage of having a drawing board at work and structural steel design books at hand, I spent many a lunch hour designing and detailing the anchors. The main factor to remember on the Danforth is that the angle between the flukes and the shank is critical. It must be about thirty-two degrees. After that, it was a matter of minimising weight where not needed and keeping the fabrication as simple as possible. Ronnie's brother actually made our anchors, very proficiently and at a reasonable cost, a complete 'family' of Danforth types – fifty-six kilograms, twenty-eight kilograms and fourteen kilograms – and one single thirty kilogram Northill type. The two smaller Danforths were kept on deck as spare anchors and for stern use, the smallest one also being used at times as a very generous dinghy anchor. The largest Danforth and the Northill were stowed on the two 'anchor cats'. Such was the efficiency of the windlass that I ended up using the heavy fifty-six kilogram Danforth as our 'working' anchor. Originally I had thought it would only be used in storm conditions.

The anchor cat idea of the Chinese is, I think, a very good one (refer to the deck layout plan in Figures 1 and 2). The anchors are securely stowed clear of the hull and overhanging the water, yet they can be dropped in seconds. On weighing anchor, once the anchor itself was clear of the water and hanging from the bow roller, I used the boat hook to reach the eye of a short length of rope permanently spliced on to a point two-thirds of the way along the anchor shank. I then led the rope over a small roller on the anchor cat, clipping the eye to a carbine hook which was kept permanently shackled to a double block through which, along with a similar block shackled to the boat a metre aft, a rope was reeved. At this stage I would turn round and pull on the end of the rope. Once the anchor crown had swung outboard tight up against the anchor cat, I would cleat off the rope on to one of the bulwark pins. The whole operation usually took thirty seconds on a good day, when no anchor washing was required.

We had been well trained in anchoring techniques years earlier when flotilla sailing in Greece with the first flotilla company operating there, YCA (Yacht Cruising Association). They taught us how to select the best spot to drop anchor, how to drop it at the right time when moving ever so slightly astern under power, and finally, to dig it in securely with the engine for a few seconds under high revs. With *Tin Hau* we added a few extra rules which became standard procedure.

First we made quite sure that both chains were well marked at ten metre intervals so we knew how much we had let out. The best marking system we found in the end – after a bad experience in Aden – was to tie brightly coloured ribbons to the chain – one ribbon denoting ten metres, two marking twenty metres, three marking thirty and so on. Every so often we would replace a tatty ribbon; mainly the ten, twenty, thirty and forty metre markers on the port chain, being the most commonly used.

When about to anchor, I would normally take the wheelhouse position and Lynda would be at the bow (opposite way round when hauling in the anchor). I would then use my fingers to indicate how much chain I wanted let out. Three fingers would be fairly normal, meaning 'please let out thirty metres of chain'. I would have noted the reading on the echo sounder as being four and a half metres, added three metres to this (the vertical distance between the echo sounder transducer and the bow roller), and multiplied the result by four (sometimes as little as two and a half, sometimes as much as six, depending on the circumstances). This may sound a complicated calculation, but making it came to be second nature after a while. The sums became more complex when tides were involved. I would then have to allow for varying depths of water. The biggest problem was in allowing for other boats already at anchor or yet to arrive.

Our final anchoring rule was always to add an 'anti-snub' rope. We kept two ten metre long sixteen millimetre nylon warps handy at the bow for this purpose. Once the anchor was down and secured, we would shackle one of these ropes to the chain, tying the other end to a mooring bitt on the bow and selecting the length of anti-snub required (say, five metres). We would then let the chain out until the 'anti-snub' just took the boat's weight in a strong gust. Then the windlass brake would be reapplied. By doing this we found we could eliminate all those noisy and alarming jerks we would otherwise have got. These were now being absorbed by the stretchy nylon warp. But if the rope broke, the chain was there to act as a 'back-up'.

10.10 PLUMBING

Amazingly enough, it was the plumbing that turned out to be the hardest, the most uncomfortable and the most soul-destroying task in *Tin Hau's* construction. However much we tried to make it otherwise, pipes usually had to be connected in the most inaccessible of places. What made the work so unnecessarily difficult was the annoying clashes between the metric and the imperial systems of measurement. Our imported British toilets and pumps were mostly imperial (I thought Britain went metric years ago!), whilst the South African plumbing fittings were generally metric. Time and again we would find ourselves attempting with all our strength to push one and a half inch (thirty-eight millimetre) hoses on to forty millimetre spigots. It became clear early on that this could only be done by first dipping the hose in boiling water for twenty seconds or so to soften and expand it. Invariably this took place under the cabin sole in the bilge, an area that took half a minute to squeeze into and several minutes to wriggle out of! I suffered bruises, grazes and razor blade cuts; also burns from the boiling water. Then there was the frustration when I found I needed another hose clip or spanner, which necessitated the long crawl out of the bilge before starting on the water boiling routine all over again.

Since we had to bring all water to the hangar in our vehicle (we had no mains water there), it would usually be some days before we could carry out any tests. Anxiously we would search for any leaks. But, sadly, we would just about always be disappointed. There would be a slow leak somewhere.

Subsequently we decided that one of the main causes of these problems was the specially ordered imperial hose we had managed to obtain in South Africa. Good and flexible as it was, we found that the spiral groove on the inside encouraged leaks. In the end we learnt to deal with this by melting the groove closed using the flame of a lighter.

What do you do when you have to go back perhaps for the third time to a place you utterly detest? I grew to hate some of the more inaccessible areas of *Tin Hau*. But there was little choice. The work had to be completed. More discomfort. More bruises. More cuts – 'I'm only happy when I'm bleeding,' I would mutter to myself. 'Keep calm. We *are* making good progress. Boat building is fun. Many people would give anything to do what we are doing. We are the lucky ones.' But finally I would not be able to take any more, and would let fly with every swear word I had ever learnt. Poor Lynda felt the same way. Once she got so stuck in the bilge that her only escape was to be pulled out by the legs, just like Pooh down Rabbit's hole.

It was at about this time Tony and Paul found a name for me to show their respect (at least Lynda told me it could be interpreted as respect) – 'Captain Bilgeman'. It took only a few weeks, however, for this to be shortened to 'Captain Bilge'. Then 'The Bilgeman'. Then 'The Bilge'. I was being accepted! Finally it was 'Hey, you, Bilgie!' All this was fine. We had fun working together. But one day, when I was in my usual position (in the bilge), wearing my usual clothes (just a pair of shorts and some heavy building site boots), I thought the welders went too far. All that could be seen of me through the floor hatch opening was my bare stomach. I was happily 'doing my own thing' down there. Paul or Tony or someone (I never saw who) decided that this was the time to weld a few fixing lugs to the underside of the deck at a point directly above me. Every time the red hot slag fell on me I would yell, try to sit upright, bang my head on the underside of the floor, fall back and then receive the next smattering of slag. We had a good working relationship!

Thanks to having had such a long period of 'waiting for Ronnie', we had been able to educate ourselves on the subject of boat plumbing. Since we were planning to be a charter boat, we obviously needed something a bit more complex than the basic – and effective – 'bucket and chuck it' system. On the other hand I did not want an array of electric pressure pumps that might go wrong or use too much power.

After much thought, we decided to install a freshwater system that made maximum use of gravity. All that was required was a small header tank. By placing it high enough, we ensured there would be enough water pressure for our wash basins, showers and the galley sink. Individual pumps on the fittings would not be needed, nor any form of electric 'master pump'. Once a day I would operate a hand pump (a Henderson Mark V) to lift water from the four main tanks; these would be interconnected through a number of valves living in the depths of the bilge (designed and assembled by Lynda and known as 'the monster').

Figure 11 shows the main freshwater and salt water plumbing features we adopted, including modifications made in Cyprus, where – amongst other things – the sea-cocks were much improved. It had been wrong – even dangerous – to install bronze yacht fittings on a steel hull.

One good feature of our freshwater system was that I always had total control over the amount of water being used on board (often a problem on cruising yachts). I learnt early on to make the pumping a daily chore, during which I would count the number of strokes made with the pump handle. Then I would place a dot representing this number on to a graph. Figure 12 shows a sample month (when we were in Mauritius with Jacqui and my mother, and later on passage to the Seychelles). All that was required to make the point to a newly joined crew member or guest that they were using too much water was to show them the graph and hopefully alert them to the way its shape had changed since their arrival. I didn't have to say a word. The graph did the job. Immediately, the water consumption rate would decline. The

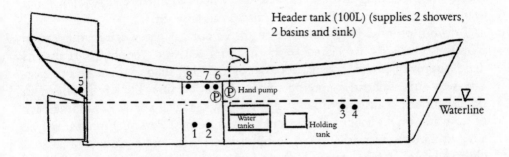

INLETS
(with strainers)
1 For engine cooling only
2 For freezer, galley tap, deckwash hose and the two heads

Header tank (100L) (supplies 2 showers, 2 basins and sink)

Hand pump

Water tanks

Holding tank

Waterline

OUTLETS   3 & 4 Port & starboard heads
5 Galley sink
6 Holding tank waste water or bilge water
7 Freezer cooling water
8 Engine cooling water

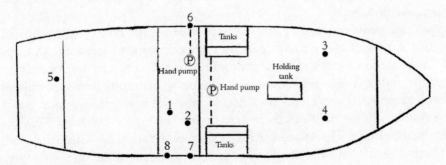

Tanks

Hand pump

Holding tank

Hand pump

Tanks

All main seacocks (at positions 1, 2, 3, 4) are heavy-duty plastic ball valves threaded onto steel pipes welded to the hull.

Figure 11: Fresh Water and Salt Water Plumbing (after changes)

concept of having to be frugal with water or questioning its quality is unfamiliar to a surprising number of people. After all, they think, water just comes out of the tap. Lynda and I would normally use about twenty-five litres of water between us each day on *Tin Hau* (this would vary from ten litres to fifty litres, depending on where we were and what we felt we could spare for laundry and washing dishes). In a house, where admittedly sea water is not available, I estimate we use nearly ten times this amount.

I do not propose to go into the details of our gas pipework or the engine plumbing, with its associated freshwater and sea water cooling circuits, its diesel supply lines and its exhaust outlet pipes, other than to mention one near omission – the salt water cooling circuit siphon breaker. Luckily I realised in time that our exhaust manifold was just below sea level and so siphoning back of sea water might happen. I contacted David Read of Perkins Engines, and he advised us by return of post to install a water trap and a siphon breaker. I observed later, whilst cruising, that there were many boats on which these precautions had not been taken. In one case it was only the tight-fitting rubber blades of the water pump which for many years prevented flooding of the engine. When eventually a blade broke, the engine was severely damaged.

I am no expert on diesel engines, the opposite, in fact. However, I have noticed that most of the problems that occur are not due to a fault in the engine itself, but from some fault in its installation, and generally in what could be termed its 'plumbing'. This seems to be a 'grey' area for which no one takes full responsibility – neither the engine manufacturer, nor the boat builder, nor the owner.

One final point concerning *Tin Hau's* plumbing: our rainwater catchment area. In the tropics many yachtsmen rig up some form of tarpaulin when it rains, and ingenious methods exist for piping trapped rainwater into the tanks. From the outset I was extremely keen on being self-sufficient in drinking water in these rainy areas, and I wanted to have the best possible rain catchment system. This turned out to be yet another reason for choosing *Tin Hau* as the boat to build. The raised central cabin tops are ideal for rain collection, and Tom Colvin, with full knowledge of this, had detailed a rim all the way around them, eventually leading to drainage spouts (two on the aft cabin and two on the forward one). The plan was to collect the initial run-off in buckets and use this for laundry and deck baths. Once the water running off was clean, we intended to connect short lengths of hose pipe to the spouts and lead the other ends directly into the main water tanks.

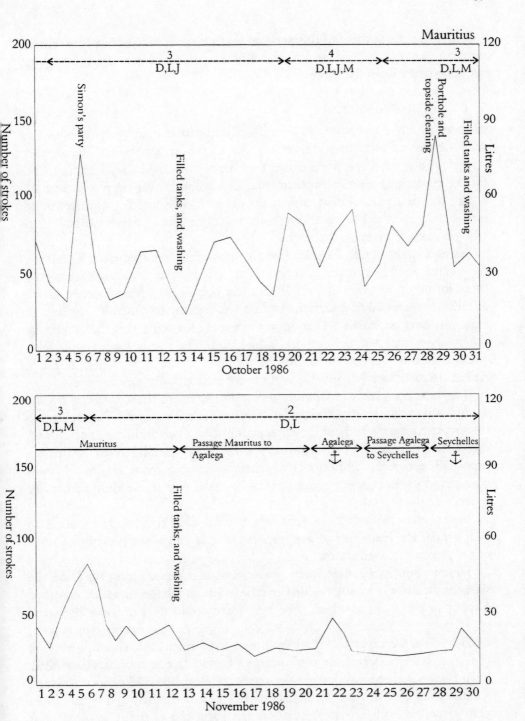

Figure 12: Water Consumption Records.

Such was the success of this scheme that we went for sixteen consecutive months, between Mauritius and the Red Sea, without ever having to seek drinking water from the shore.

10.11 POWER GENERATION

We wanted a home that would be self-sufficient in as many ways as possible, and one area of great importance was that of power generation. We needed power for domestic use, for lighting, for starting the engine, refrigeration, and for the running of nautical instruments. One solution was simply to have no engine (or, on a smaller boat, one that could be hand-started), no gadgetry, no refrigeration, and oil lights throughout. I admire those people we have met who do manage to cruise this way.

Being a larger vessel, *Tin Hau* had an engine that required electric starting. Given that we had to have batteries for this, I thought it made sense to use them for other purposes as well. With some help from a friend named Garth at HKS, I proceeded to design the twelve-volt lighting circuits. We resolved to make the best possible installation at the outset, knowing that this would be much easier than adding lights and cables later. The result was a good, clean, trouble-free network of light fittings throughout the boat. I also installed circuits to cater for any nautical instrumentation we might care to have.

The next question was: should we supply power to these batteries by any means other than the main engine's alternator; and if so, how? This led me to undertake a lengthy study of the choices available: a petrol driven generator? A diesel driven generator? A wind generator? Solar panels? A free-wheeling propshaft generator? Additional alternators on the main engine? I even considered a generator we could operate by pedal power, building up our leg muscles in the process.

In the end, I decided we definitely needed additional power sources to supplement the main engine, and proceeded to install a combination of most of the aforementioned alternatives.

First we bought a Rutland wind generator and mounted it on a pole on the starboard quarter, running the power cable through a large ammeter mounted directly in front of the wheel. The helmsman could thus measure the wind speed in amps. We knew exactly what four amps of wind was (a typical trade wind, such as we experienced all the time in Mauritius), or ten amps of wind (a Port Elizabeth storm), or half an amp of wind (a common dawn or dusk lull). However there was one problem with the Rutland wind generator which we never resolved despite our best efforts. This was the half to one and a half amp growl or hum, a nasty vibration felt particularly in the pilothouse at certain wind speeds. At times I would quite happily have thrown the wind generator into the sea because of this, but reason would prevail. Its free power generation was just too useful. In the trade wind areas it looked after all our power requirements, which included the fridge/freezer (then being run just as a fridge).

The next acquisition was a Lucas propshaft generator. I felt that the potential cost-free power offered by the propshaft, free-wheeling while sailing, was just too good to miss – even though it would only be available on passage and not at anchor. It was much easier to install this at the outset than at a later date. We bought a large bronze pulley which we slid over the propshaft before it was fitted in position, and connected it via a rubber drive belt to the generator mounted on a bracket below the cabin sole. Along with the drive belt in use we fitted three spares, tied out of the way, to prepare ourselves in case of future problems associated with a broken belt (of course, we never had such problems!) As with all our generators, we fitted an in-line ammeter so we could see what current the batteries were receiving. Generally this was an additional fifteen amps when motoring, a useful four to six and a half amps when sailing at four to six and a half knots and nothing when sailing any slower (the propshaft did not turn).

Our fourth means of power generation was, in our case, a waste of time and money: a solar panel. We bought one at the same time as the autopilot in 1987 and fitted it on the pilothouse roof, an ideal location. I had thought I was buying thirty-six watts of power giving three amps of current at twelve volts. But I found to my disappointment that the maximum amount of current the solar panel was able to feed into the batteries was one and three-quarter amps, only lasting for a couple of hours. For another two hours the current might be one and a half amps; and for a further two hours only one amp; a total of eight and a half amp-hours over a sunny twenty-four hour period. I know this could have been improved slightly if we had set up a system whereby the panel could have been manually tilted every few hours to face the sun, but I did not want that complication. As our solar panel had cost about the same (about £300) as the wind generator, which would produce eight and a half amp-hours on a terrible day (virtually no wind) or up to two hundred amp-hours on a good day (storms!), I felt that its 'value per amp' was very poor.

In addition to all the twelve volt DC chargers, I decided to install a three and a half kilowatt air cooled, diesel powered, two hundred and thirty volt AC generator, made by Robin (costing 1,900 rand, or £1,100, in 1984). This enabled us to have two hundred and thirty volt 'mains' power on board when it was required. Those occasions were rare, but, when they did occur, our

Robin generator was most helpful. It rendered 'usable at sea' all our electrical power tools, and this was invaluable in the odd emergency as well as for certain maintenance tasks. It also gave Lynda full use of the various kitchen appliances acquired during her 'shore life'. It made our small one hundred watt plastic mini washing machine operational, when we needed to wash more clothes than could be handled by a bucket or two. It also powered the microwave ovens. During the building stage, our two small microwaves had been the sole means of cooking in our flat. These had later been fitted on the boat to supplement the gas cooker and they were most useful in, for example, the Chagos Islands, where our two fourteen kilogram gas cylinders were made to last much longer than their normal four months.

Our final means of charging the batteries was what is commonly called 'shore power', an AC power supply from the shore taken to the boat through an electrical cable, and then distributed throughout the boat (in our case, to an array of two hundred and thirty volt power sockets). We used a simple £10 car battery charger, left connected all winter long, to trickle charge the batteries – taking care that they were electrically isolated from the hull. Without this precaution considerable galvanic corrosion could have occurred to the hull underwater.

We first came across the luxury of shore power in Larnaca Marina (except for a brief spell in Port Elizabeth), where a new and ugly power requirement revealed itself – heating. Twice later, we were to have shore power – in Corfu and in Cornwall, both being places where we spent winters afloat. Our solution to the heating problem gradually improved from thicker sweaters, to thermal underwear, to a one or two kilowatt electric fan blower, to a 1.2 kilowatt oil filled thermostatically controlled electric radiator, to a Camping Gaz catalytic heater (not used in England where we found Camping Gaz refills cost ten times as much as in Greece in the same year!), and finally in Truro to a wood and coal burning stove, bought in Spain and installed amidships. Additionally, we double glazed our portholes to eliminate problems of condensation on the inside of the glass.

The best way to deal with the heating problem is quite obvious. Avoid climates where heating is required! This reduces clothing costs as well!

There are two areas where I would like to see *Tin Hau's* power generating capabilities improved. Firstly, I would like to see a different type of regulator on the engine's alternator – one that allows the maximum rated current (seventy amps in our case) to flow during most of the charge cycle. These regulators are available, but I never bought one as I was wary of the possibility of damaging the – otherwise good – existing alternator. It was always frustrating, however, to motor with only – say – twenty amps showing on the ammeter when I knew the batteries could accept the full seventy amps.

Secondly, I would like to have had a large – say forty amp – battery charger (with isolated primary and secondary coils) for use in conjunction with shore power or the Robin generator. This would have been a wonderful safety feature, as it would have provided a rapid means of recharging the batteries at sea, should they ever have mistakenly been allowed to run flat. The Robin generator, unlike the main Perkins diesel, could be hand-started.

Before leaving the subject of power generation, I feel I should comment further on the most important component of the power circuitry – the batteries. We had had early trouble with these in Port Elizabeth, where I had made the mistake of buying some second-hand batteries at a 'bargain price'. On becoming more acquainted with these, I realised I was not prepared to trust our lives to them. So we advertised them for sale, successfully in the end, but only after several false attempts, including one where I learnt over the telephone all about South African pigs. We were being offered one pig, or 'vark' in Afrikaans, for each battery. I had to ask for the word to be repeated several times before I realised what was going on. At first I couldn't understand why I was being so needlessly insulted. The South African 'v' sounds like an 'f'.

Later, I knew exactly what I was looking for; the number of batteries I wanted (five), the type (lead acid), the capacity (about one hundred amp-hours each), and the general shape and size that would fit inside the engine room. I then contacted the Willard factory, glad to have another useful facility right on our doorstep – Port Elizabeth being a motor car manufacturing city well geared towards industry of all types. Willard supplied exactly what we needed at a reasonable price. Six years later, after much care and attention, those batteries were still going strong.

10.12 PAINTS

Steel is one of the best materials for boat building, but it has one severe drawback. When exposed to air and water, particularly salt water, it will rust. I knew right at the beginning that the way in which our steel was painted would be of paramount importance.

Before becoming too involved in paint research, however, I had some earlier decisions to make. What sort of steel should we use? There are some types that corrode less than others – for example, Corten steel or stainless steel of the correct grade. Then there was the possibility of not using steel at all in some areas, instead employing wood, aluminium or other materials.

Looking back, I feel I was right to dismiss Corten. It would have been available in straight sheet form, but then the large flat areas of *Tin Hau*, where paint was easy to apply, were never a problem. The troubles with Corten would have started on seeking the various specific steel sections like flat bars, angles and hollow tube – about twenty shapes and sizes in all. Some of these might have been impossible to acquire, or at least would have caused us unnecessary delays and expense. I did not want to end up with a mixture of Corten steel and the steel we eventually chose, ordinary mild steel.

I was prepared, however, to mix mild steel with other materials, or avoid the use of it altogether in certain areas. The pilothouse, for example, was constructed of wood over a steel frame; the cabin hatches were made in wood (and later remade of superior wood); the porthole frames were made in the same mistakenly chosen wood (and later reconstructed in bronze); and the eyes to which the moving sheet blocks were attached were made of stainless steel. There were some places where originally we used mild steel and afterwards changed to other materials; for example, the forepeak hatches (changed to aluminium); the davit framework (changed to stainless steel); the gate hinges (changed to stainless steel); the wind generator mast (changed to aluminium, perhaps mistakenly, as aluminium whips about much more than steel) and the deck boxes (removed altogether and changed to a most useful open structure made of stainless steel pipe). I was aware before we started building that steel boats often corrode from within, and so we were extremely conscientious about all our work on insulation above floor level, bilge painting, ballast epoxying, and drainage below the sole. As a result we had no problems in these areas.

However, I underestimated the extent of the potential corrosion problem on deck. We discovered that nasty brown streaks would appear in two circumstances: firstly, wherever localised rubbing occurred; and secondly, wherever steelwork was kept permanently damp by contact with wood or other materials. After five years afloat, *Tin Hau* had the correct assortment of materials on deck (nearly), but we certainly learnt the hard way! One regret I will always have is that, when Munchie Moolman offered to obtain for us at a reasonable cost some stainless steel pipe for use as handrailing, I turned him down, thinking: what's special about the exposure of the handrailing? Now I know better. Unthinking yachtsmen and officials just love to grab it with their boat-hooks, chipping off the paintwork and causing me days of work to put right.

In case it may seem that we had all the ideas, perhaps I should emphasise that often only the final decisions came from us. Ronnie, Paul and Tony were always suggesting better ways of doing things. For example, in order to minimise painting problems, Ronnie had recommended flat bars for the bulwark and hull frames, keeping angle bars only for the overhead deck frames.

Most of the detailing, however, had originated from Tom Colvin and was shown on the drawings – or at least on a separate sheet of steel scantlings, as the drawings were for an aluminium boat. One detail, which we particularly appreciated from the point of view of painting, was the one he made of the bottom of the keel. He specified for this an eleven metre length of 200 mm by 200 mm by 25 mm thick (eight inches by eight inches by one inch) steel angle weighing eight hundred kilograms, placed on its corner to form a V-shape. Vertical plates were welded to the top of each of the arms of the V to form the upper section of the keel. But what we liked so much was the generous thickness of steel in the area of the boat most likely to hit the seabed, together with the way the sides of the V could be painted easily whenever *Tin Hau* was hauled out for antifouling. Only a few isolated points on the bottom of the V could not be reached with a paint brush. This sort of detailing was just as important as the type of paint used.

The next question to be answered was: how should the steelwork be prepared in readiness for painting? We decided to take some items, such as the mooring bitts and the air vents, for hot dip galvanising prior to being welded into place. However the bulk of the steelwork was not treated in this way. Instead it was sandblasted and primed before use, this being a much easier job in warm, rain-free Port Elizabeth than in, say, England. We could have left all of the sandblasting until after assembly, but it was more encouraging to watch the growth of a tidy matt-red skeleton than to watch a growing 'rust-bucket'; and thanks to Ronnie's tardiness we were at the watching stage for a long time! The importance of good sandblasting has since been well demonstrated to me; paintwork lifted or blistered in the one or two areas I know, or think, were not sandblasted.

At last, we reach the painting itself. I am glad to be writing about it and not doing it. Clean fingers are such wonderful things to have! It was a massive job on *Tin Hau*, taking about one thousand five hundred hours altogether. We were most fortunate to have received help from many sources, such as from Mark and Tandy Helliwell (Lynda's son and daughter), out in South Africa from England for their summer school holidays (winter in South Africa); Ronnie and his gang on the initial interior steel painting; Kim Ockenden, who came all the way from Cape Town to give a total of six hard weeks doing considerably more than just painting; Clive Battell, who passed his two week 'holiday' with us beavering away from dawn to dusk; likewise, Jan and Jeff, visiting again from Swaziland; and another useful young volunteer, Nigel. Then there was Ike, whom we employed for a total of one hundred hours (the lazaret became known as the 'Ike house'); Lynda's father, Ernie (Royle), who came regularly every Thursday afternoon for nine months, complete with 'sustenance' baked by Lynda's mother, Marjorie; my mother, Margaret (Chidell), our faithful supporter, out from England for another so-called 'holiday'; Lynda's brother-in-law, Wally, who tackled some of the tightest spots in the bilge, adopting his usual perfectionist principle ('if you do a job, do it properly'); Lynda's brother, Andy, equivalent in muscle power to two normal mortals, who helped us with many tasks; Hugh Jagoe and Chantal Kraus, a couple we grew to know and like, who were at that time considering the construction of their own boat; Bill from the yacht club; and last, but by no means least, Jacqui and her mother, Wendy.

The paints we used over the shop-primed steelwork were numerous: two-part coal tar epoxy on the hull below the waterline, mixed in the easy ratio of 1:1, four thick coats in all, alternating in colour between brown and black. The final coat was a special one in preparation for the two coats of copper based scrubbable antifoul paint. Above the waterline on the hull we applied (mainly by roller) two coats of two-part aluminium-coloured epoxy primer, followed by two coats of epoxy black paint – a type that could be overcoated with a different colour, if required, although we both admired Henry Ford's famous dictum 'Any colour as long as it's black.' The deck area, including the cabin top, was given the same treatment, except the top two coats were white instead of black. The final job was to mask off all the areas where we might tread, and then apply two further coats of non-slip white epoxy paint, mixing the normal white epoxy with what we termed 'wood flour', fine wood powder obtained from sanding machines. Sand is often used for this purpose, but we decided that the surface thus obtained would be too hard on kneecaps.

On subsequent maintenance painting, we kept to the same specification below the waterline, but above it and on deck we switched to two-part and subsequently one-part polyurethane paints. We discovered to our cost that the epoxy paint powdered in the sun and it was a lengthy business to clean and sand it in preparation for an overcoat.

There were various special areas of exterior paintwork, including the two 'oculi', Tin Hau's eyes, which were welded and painted on the bow – and aligned to scan the horizon – thus depicting a trading junk as opposed to a fishing junk. On the stern we had a beautiful Chinese dragon, painted in red and yellow (later changed to black, red and yellow) by our friend Ivor Sing

Key. First he drew the dragon on his drawing board, then he set himself up on a scaffold to paint the real thing. This took four days, during which time he was bitten to pieces by mosquitoes. Ivor may have suffered, but the dragon was a work of art.

Inside the boat there was plenty of painting to be done: three coats of coal tar epoxy in the bilges, and two coats of two-part white above the waterline, subsequently covered by the cork insulation and more paint. Most of the interior woodwork was varnished, and we found that by doing it properly in the first place, with much sanding between coats and extensive use of thinners in the first coats, it rarely needed any further treatment. Some woodwork, such as that forming the ceiling panels, was painted with an excellent non-drip jelly-like satin gloss paint made by Plascon Evans; this was called Velvaglow.

Plascon Evans, who in South Africa are licensed to produce International yacht paints, deserve a special mention, although much of our excellent treatment from them was due to our contact there, a long-standing friend of Lynda's parents, Don Durham. He helped us in the early days when I was struggling over the types of paint we needed (which weighed – wet – a quarter of a ton in total). He proceeded to make it his personal responsibility that we never had any delays or problems. We were very lucky to have had such a friend, and years later we were to see more of him on board *Tin Hau*.

11. The Build-up Towards the Launch

May 1985, found me scouring our newly acquired British Admiralty routeing charts of the Atlantic and Indian Oceans (one for each month), gleaning all the information I could from these wonderful sources. Even though there was still an enormous amount of work to be done – in fact most of the boat to be built – it really did seem that the biggest difficulties of the construction had been overcome and that *Tin Hau* would be in the water within a year. I had to give some advance thought as to what would happen after that.

Assuming we stuck to our original aims of becoming a charter boat in Greece or Turkey, the first question of navigation was: Do we leave Africa to the left or the right? Do we sail up the Indian Ocean, Red Sea and through the Suez Canal? Or do we sail up the Atlantic Ocean, entering the Mediterranean Sea at Gibraltar?

I knew there were two types of weather conditions we would prefer to avoid, the first being hurricanes (or cyclones) and the second being prevailing headwinds. A Chinese junk would get nowhere in either. I knew the type of weather we would like most: winds dead abeam or just aft of abeam, force three to six and plenty of sunshine, with temperatures over twenty-five degrees centigrade.

With this in mind, I worked out that in order to reach Cape Town, four hundred miles to the west (and thus setting off to leave Africa to the right), we should be ready to sail from Port Elizabeth by February or March before the onset of the adverse westerlies. There would be little point in leaving any earlier than February, as the summer south-easterlies in Cape Town, although favourable in direction, are extremely strong – often blowing at gale or storm force for days on end. By March or April they are much less violent and Cape Town is generally basking in its best weather of the year. If we departed from there without too much delay, it would be feasible to reach the steady South Atlantic south-east trade winds within a week. Perhaps we would stop for a break in St Helena before setting off on the long haul northwards during which we would encounter first the south-east trades, then the doldrum equatorial belt, then the northern hemisphere's north-east trades (before the hurricane season), then – assuming we could bear to pass by the West Indies – the Horse Latitudes, and finally the North Atlantic's prevailing westerly winds bringing us to the Azores, Portugal and Gibraltar. After Gibraltar there would still be enough of the summer left to sail the length of the Mediterranean to Greece, making many stops on route and arriving, say, in October, after an eight month passage from Port Elizabeth.

If we were not ready to leave by April, then none of the above would be possible and we would have to wait in Port Elizabeth until the following February, perhaps losing our customs drawback sums valid only on items re-exported within two years.

Alternatively we could set off for the Indian Ocean. If we did this (leaving Africa to the left), we would have to start our voyaging with a midwinter passage to Mauritius, in which gales, although generally favourable in direction, could be expected on one day in five. Then we would have to proceed northwards, before the November cyclones, in good trade wind beam reach conditions towards the Seychelles and the entrance to the Red Sea. I concluded that the best time to sail up the lower half of the Red Sea was from January until March. However, the northern six hundred miles appeared to present a near-insurmountable problem. In this area, on-the-nose headwinds seemed to be a permanent feature, not of gale force strength, but strong enough to stop all progress in the right direction. Perhaps we would be able to 'coastal hop', anchoring along the coasts of Sudan, Egypt and Saudi Arabia, but politically this did not look easy. Assuming a successful outcome, our next obstacle would be the Suez Canal. Fine, as long as it remained open to shipping; but hadn't there been one or two problems in the past in this area? On reaching Port Said, the remaining four hundred miles or so to Greece in early spring would be a pleasure, and we would arrive at the nearest Greek island in May – after twelve months of 'snakes and ladders' adventuring from Port Elizabeth.

Having done this much preliminary passage planning, I resolved to complete the construction of *Tin Hau* as quickly as possible, so we could take the easier option of the Atlantic route. I set my sights on launching her in January 1986, and being ready to set off by March; perhaps a somewhat ambitious target, but with Tony and Paul on the job (and the third man in their team, Lenny, keeping things moving in the background), and with Lynda and myself now able to work unimpeded, it seemed that we could at long last move quickly and effectively.

However, one further change would still have to be made. Much as I appreciated my work at HKS, and the company of those who worked there, I would shortly have to give it up and start working on the boat full time. From HKS's point of view the timing seemed good, in that my work on various long standing projects such as Livingstone Hospital (the African hospital in Port Elizabeth), was just coming to an end. Perhaps Port Elizabeth was finally heading for the recession that had hit Johannesburg two years earlier?

Regrettably, before I could submit my notice, an unexpected event happened. On 26th April I was called into the office of Mike Williams, HKS's manager. Initially he told me that my department head was leaving at the end of the year. Then he went on to say that another engineer from a branch office with no work was being transferred to Port Elizabeth on 1st July to become the new department head. Finally he came to the point – there was no room for three senior structural engineers, even for a month or two, and so my services were no longer required after 30th June. I was being made redundant! This may seem unimportant, in that I was about to leave anyway, but it was a sharp blow to my morale and confidence. Even a slap-up party at which I was given a generous leaving present did not remove totally the sour taste at the way in which I was departing. I was aware that this was more than just the completion of a job. This was the final break from 'normal life'. For fifteen years I had kept my eye on safeguarding the future, particularly from the point of view of employment. Now I had cut all the ties – or at least they had been cut for me.

On 26th July, 1985, Mark and Tandy flew in to Port Elizabeth airport from England for their school holidays. They were arriving in a South Africa torn apart by all sorts of suffering and atrocities in the townships, but of course they saw very little of this. The system kept visitors out of the problem areas – in fact, most white South African citizens never saw the inside of an African home. I had had a glimpse of the disturbances during my work for HKS, which took me to some of the local trouble spots. During one site visit, while fifteen feet below ground level in a test pit where I was sampling the subsoil, I remember looking up to see the pit perimeter lined with black faces peering down. Knowing what they were going through in their homes, the thought crossed my mind that it must have been tempting for them to do a bit of 'back-filling'. One less white man! But I smiled at them, got on with the job and later, on chatting with them, realised how unfair my thoughts had been. These were just light-hearted, friendly school children, full of fun and life. How could I have thought otherwise, particularly with all my happy memories of racially harmonious Swaziland? Was I being naïve, or were other people showing undue prejudice and unnecessary fear?

Lynda had seen much more of the violence in the townships than I. She had worked as a trainee paramedic for the Red Cross in the casualty department of Livingstone Hospital on Friday and Saturday nights. She had seen stab wounds, burns and disfigurations such as most people never encountered. She wanted medical qualifications and capabilities beyond the basic first aid she might need to be able to perform on the boat. Over an eighteen month period she emerged top of her class with a useful EMA (Emergency Medical Assistant) Paramedics qualification. Unfortunately, she was unable to attend her graduation ceremony in December 1984, as she was taken into hospital that day for an operation. Luckily she recovered sufficiently from this to start the heavy boat work two months later.

Our other training exercises for the boat included some practical follow-up to my yachtmasters courses. From our upstairs veranda in Donkin Street I would use my sextant to 'shoot the sun', and subsequently calculate a position line and draw it on the chart. I was somewhat dismayed to find our position to be anything from fifteen miles offshore to fifteen miles inland! This was with an £80 Davis Mark 25 plastic sextant, which I had thought would be our number one sextant to be backed up by a spare – and cheaper – plastic 'Ebco'. However, my mother kindly gave me a quality metal sextant at this point, so the Davis became my spare. Immediately I achieved much better results.

Our final piece of training was spending every Thursday evening for about a year going to ham radio classes. I passed the Amateur Radio Operator's exam in the end, but Lynda could not sit it, as the dates conflicted with her paramedics exam. I valued the theoretical knowledge gained, which was pretty complex at times, but unfortunately we never bought an 'amateur radio' (a long range short wave transceiver with amateur frequency bands). It was just too expensive and could not be classified as a boat necessity. We went one day to the National Amateur Radio meeting held in a hotel close to our flat. Sitting at the back I noted one fact: seventy-five per cent of the men at the meeting – there were hardly any women – were bald! I decided that when I qualified on this count, I would perhaps indulge in this interesting hobby! For the moment life should revolve around boats and one boat in particular.

Mark and Tandy's arrival at the airport neatly coincided with Lynda's birthday. Tony and Paul knew this, and they did something about it, typical of their sense of humour and creativity. We arrived a short time before the plane was due and went to the airport waiting lounge. We moved immediately to the window to look across the runway to where *Tin Hau* was being built a quarter of a mile away. Imagine our surprise when we saw a huge banner proclaiming: 'Happy Birthday, Lynda'.

At last, most of the work we still had to do was at the boat itself. Lynda thumped away at her Yankee screwdriver all day long; and, in total, we used 20,000 brass screws on the interior woodwork. We also did well on forty millimetre by seven millimetre stainless steel bolts (about 2,000), which became our standard size after we discovered a treasure trove of these at one of the local scrapyards. How they got there, we never knew. Bakkie load after bakkie load of plywood, timber battening and tongue and groove panelling was transported to the boat. The panelling we used in the forward area was South African pine, which never gave us any problems, but in the aft section of the boat and in the pilothouse we moved on to a superior timber called black-wood, which, besides being extremely hard, has a beautiful and varied grain.

One of Tony and Paul's first actions was to condemn many of Ronnie's long seam welds on the plating. Luckily for us, one weld on the hull had already revealed itself as defective when rainwater from the leaking roof of our new hangar had found its way through Ronnie's so called watertight cement screeding over the ballast and then worked its way out again through an appallingly bad keel weld. I fixed the roof and then spent days in the cramped conditions under the cabin sole epoxying over the ballast. Johnny, employed by Tony and Paul for much of the lengthy welding operations, fixed the defective weld. He then went on to spend two solid weeks grinding out and re-welding to a very high standard any length of weld that looked suspect, using power from a large diesel generator our gang had organised. Fortunately, Ronnie had not gone too far on the seam welding. His work had mostly been on setting up the framework and tacking in place the plating. If he had been allowed to continue in the same way we could have ended up with a leaking boat that would have required much time, expense and effort to put right. Perhaps that would have been the end of our efforts to build *Tin Hau*. Once again: thank you, Tony, Paul and Johnny for your expertise, generosity and sheer hard work!

The months raced by; the weekly highlight being Sunday lunchtime, when we gathered together our scrap timber in preparation for a South African braai. Tony and Paul would join us once the sizzling meat was ready. Sitting outside in the glorious sunshine, enjoying our Castle lagers and the latest of Lynda's salads, followed by a delicious sweet, we made the most of our twenty minutes of shared bliss.

By November, the welding work was just about complete. I had been organising the supply and the sandblasting of the remaining quantity of steel needed, and in this had been helped considerably by a local steel fabricating company called Project Services. The manager, Brian Burns, had shown such sympathy towards us, and understanding of what we were up against, that he supplied the final order not just at discount price, but free of charge!

With the steelwork over, Paul and Lenny left us to continue life as before, a job well done. Tony remained a constant visitor, supporter and helper. Something about the whole *Tin Hau* project had hooked and besotted him. Or was it something else? He saw the generator installed. He arranged for his friend, Eddie, a man of considerable success in his own field – refrigeration – to help with the freezer installation. And, on 2nd February, Tony assisted on the big day for the Perkins engine. It had been installed over the preceding weeks, and a 'mock sea' had been made, using a drum of water outside the boat from which the cooling water was drawn and into which the exhaust returned. All that was required was to turn the key. Would she start after nearly two years in her timber crate?

At eleven o'clock exactly I turned the key one notch to the right and the red light came on. So far so good. Another notch to the right and hold for a few seconds, with bated breath. Third turn and chug, chug, chug – the engine was running. What a moment. I cannot describe the feeling of life that seemed to enter the boat and the pleasure that first throb gave us. We had made a silent vow to Perkins that we would put up their 'Powered by Perkins Engines' plaque if the engine started at the first turn of the key. Well, it did, and the plaque was fastened to the console just below the instrument panel. We had the engine on and off several times that day, at first idling, then running the propeller in forward and in reverse. After all the excitement, we sat down with our supportive friends and had a few glasses of bubbly.

Work in anticipation of the launch now reached a frenzy. I finished off the installation of the twenty-seven round portholes and the fourteen pilothouse windows (six millimetre and ten millimetre armour plate safety glass, respectively), having devised my own test for the glass panes. On their collection at the suppliers, I had climbed a four metre ladder and dropped a few of them on to the floor, somewhat to the surprise of the other customers! There was a loud crash, but nothing broke and I was satisfied.

We started gathering together and loading on board all sorts of equipment: the Abavi rubber inflatable dinghy, the second dinghy to *Knot Often*; my windsurfer, a present from Lynda in Swaziland; crockery, cutlery, pots, pans, linen, bedding and cushions; engine spares and other spares; tools; the Walker log; the lead line and the echo sounder; the radar, VHF, radio direction-finder and compasses; the liferaft, lifejackets, harnesses, wet weather gear, flares, EPIRB, fire extinguishers and an extensive medical kit; a carefully filled 'panic bag', ready for that day should we ever find ourselves cast adrift in mid-ocean; our tape recorder and lifelong collection of cassettes; mooring lines, towing warps, anchors and chain; catalogues, manuals, licences and other papers; sewing machine, typewriter, camera, binoculars, accordion and guitar. The list goes on...

Inside, everything was taking shape. Lynda was completing all the curtaining, blinds and upholstery. Spare wall space started sprouting some of her weavings. Cupboards and lockers were filled. Endless drawings were made showing stowage positions. It really was extremely fulfilling seeing everything coming together so beautifully. Regrettably, however, we had no time to sit back and savour what was being achieved – to quote Lynda's newsletter: 'Poor David, at this stage, was hopping about the boat like a rabbit in a warren from one tunnel to the next, his presence required by anyone and everyone, usually at the same time...' We just had time to be aware that we were probably in the middle of the most exciting and productive phase of our lives so far, with promise of more to come.

On 15th February I decided that the launch might be only three weeks away; and since it would probably take three weeks to organise, we should start considering the subject as a matter of urgency. Another Munchie Moolman job, I thought, knowing his capabilities and contacts. So I went on hands and knees to him once again and asked him how we should set about transporting twenty-five tons of steel junk twenty kilometres to the harbour, keeping costs to a minimum. 'No Problem,' he replied; and when the day of the launch arrived he proved his attitude to the world at large by standing prominently at the head of the convoy through town wearing a tee shirt with the words 'NO PROBLEM', clearly displayed.

Munchie organised the cranes and the low-bed, and we liaised with the police and contacted the traffic, electricity and telephone authorities (lines had to be temporarily lifted along the route). We met the harbour master, Captain Ted Page, and found out where we could berth. A launch date was set – 10th March, and we arranged that as the first phase in the procedure *Tin Hau* would be jacked up on her cradle once again and rolled out of the hangar to a point where the cranes could reach her. This was set for 22nd February.

All went as planned on the day, and we moved out of our flat and on board *Tin Hau* for the first time. I remarked to Lynda that this would probably be one of the calmest and most trouble free 'anchorages' ever. Although *Tin Hau* was now extremely visible from the airport buildings across the runway, we were not disturbed by sightseers. The route to the hangars was too rambling and remote for most people. Neither was the plane traffic beside us a nuisance. In fact we never stopped taking childlike pleasure at each of the landings and take-offs. By evening most of the manmade noises ceased and we only had the crickets from the nearby scrub to contend with. The stars were really bright and the nights warm.

The space left behind in the hangar was immediately put to good use. After a thorough spring-clean, I laid out the three masts on trestles and set about the job of rigging them and fixing the lights. In the meantime, Lynda started a small factory, printing tee shirts. Her father had organised one hundred and fifty blue tee shirts through his contacts in the clothing business, and Lynda had made a silk screen stencil showing a picture of our boat with the words '*TIN HAU*' in English and Chinese. She printed all the tee shirts at an incredible speed and hung them up to dry on the masts, the visual impact being like that of a Chinese laundry.

On the boat we applied the final coat of antifoul paint and bolted on the zinc anodes, eight four kilogram anodes on the hull, two 2 kg anodes on the rudder and a single anode on the propshaft. These were our protection against galvanic corrosion, recommended and supplied by Duff Anodes of my home town, Chichester. The cradle was bound to the boat by webbing, as the plan was to use the cranes to lift the boat itself, not the cradle – which would simply hang below. I had put my head well and truly 'on the block' by deciding to cut four holes in the bulwark frames, two on each side, to which the crane strops would be shackled. Normally, long broad slings are placed under a boat when it is lifted by a crane or cranes, but I saw no reason for this in our case. The slings would have had to have been specially made, and so they would have been very expensive. Also I did not relish the idea of the hull's paintwork being rubbed. I calculated that the four 'strong points' on the bulwarks could take a load in excess of ten tons each, and assured everyone that if they failed to do so it was entirely my responsibility.

The last task was to lift the three masts on to *Tin Hau's* side deck. With this done, we were ready! We settled down to sleep on 9th March, keenly anticipating the following day.

12. The Launch: 10th March, 1986

The day started cool and cloudy, We were up bright and early and had barely breakfasted when we heard the drone of a heavy engine approaching. Loadstar, as usual, arriving before the scheduled time. Following close on their heels came the press, the telephone and electricity authorities, officials from the airport across the way, and one of the two thirty ton cranes. The second crane arrived a bit later.

Loading took almost two hours. The somewhat treacherous route we were planning covered a number of nasty hills and bends. As an additional precaution, therefore, to stop *Tin Hau* sliding free, Tony tack-welded the steel cradle to the low-bed platform. Our traffic escort checked the permits and the routes once again. Many stories were told of previous boats hitting bridges, high voltage electricity cables and overhanging buildings or trees. But the go-ahead was given. The convoy started moving towards the harbour. Two police officers led on their motorcycles, followed by the low-loader carrying the boat, myself in our faithful Isuzu bakkie, Tony in his Beetle, a police patrol car, and then a long line of vans and cars that grew in length as the journey proceeded.

We moved slowly through town past the residential area of Southdene, left on to Walmer Road, down the steep Upper Valley Road, sharp left into Lower Valley Road at Plate Glass Building – where my old employers, HKS, were situated (on seeing *Tin Hau* going past, nearly everyone at HKS stopped working to take the afternoon off and follow the excitement). We then proceeded up the steep hill to St George's Park (where cricket test matches were played in earlier years) and right into Rink Street then left into the busy Cape Road at the Horse Memorial, right into Mount Road and down towards North End, one of Port Elizabeth's oldest light manufacturing and commercial districts, into Main Street and thus to the docks, crossing the railway lines on one of the many hideous flyover bridges constructed in the name of progress when the docks were separated from the city by a modern elevated 'freeway'.

Lynda was waiting for us at the dock gates with the news that plans had been changed on where we should launch and berth. For reasons unknown, we had been redirected to a different part of the harbour. This presented no problem other than that someone (Lynda) had to wait at the original berth to inform friends and family of the new location.

At two o'clock the fun started. The cranes were ready to act, and the low-bed was in position right on the edge of the quay wall. I climbed on board along with Tony. Jacqui and Lynda stood by with pots of paint and brushes waiting to touch up any areas where antifoul had been rubbed off during the move. The operation began with the slow taking up of slack in the lifting cables. Boat and cradle were then gently hoisted clear of the low-bed which drove off, its work complete. The cradle was lowered to the ground and all the webbing ties holding it to the boat were undone. *Tin Hau* was lifted in the air again, this time with all her underwater profile visible to the crowd. Lynda and Jacqui rushed in to do their bit and I came down to bolt on the two remaining zinc anodes. The motors whirred as the two crane drivers commenced the delicate business of edging *Tin Hau* outwards over the water. Unexpectedly, with just two metres to go, they stopped. The load was too much. *Tin Hau* went back into her cradle, which had been manoeuvred sideways, until it was overhanging the quay wall by almost half of its width. With *Tin Hau* supported in her cradle the cranes were able to reposition themselves as close to the water as possible. Again *Tin Hau* was lifted. This time the cradle was dragged along the quay well clear of the launch site. *Tin Hau* was edged outwards and seawards once more, and lowered towards the sea. But still there were problems. The out-riggers of one of the cranes threatened to lift. All we needed was one dropped boat and two overturned cranes! Some rapid rethinking was necessary. Munchie and the boys rose to the occasion. A third, lighter crane was ordered, and the crowd resigned itself to yet more waiting in this real-life drama, their spirits not dampened in the least by the drizzle which had just turned to rain.

The third crane arrived and was set up to lean its weight on the offending out-riggers. Up went *Tin Hau* for the fourth time, and out towards the water. With only half a metre to go all three crane drivers became jittery, but this time Tony and I on board could do something. We removed all the fenders. Moreover, the crowd could help; they pushed on the side of *Tin Hau* to gain those few inches so she was clear of the quay wall. This was just enough for the crane drivers, who gratefully lowered their load slowly towards the water. I anxiously waited to discover two things. At what level would she float in the water? And would she leak?

As the water touched the keel and then the broader expanse of the hull for the first time, I marvelled at the way in which an inanimate land object could suddenly be transformed into a fabulous creature of the sea. I raced backwards and forwards below decks, checking all the sea-cocks and pipes for leaks, but everything was fine. The bilges were dry.

Back on deck, I watched the sea surface draw closer to the top level of the antifoul paint, which I had purposefully painted high, five inches above the theoretical design waterline. I was relieved to see the bow come afloat with four inches of antifoul paint showing. But the water at the stern covered the line by an inch, which made us, on average, three and a half inches deeper in the water than we should have been, equivalent to three and a half tons in weight. Allowing for two and a half tons of diesel, water, spares and possessions, this made us one ton, or four per cent, overweight. Not too bad, but I was not at all happy about being down in the stern and I prayed that later we would be able to do something about it.

Meanwhile, everyone else was oblivious to my thoughts, and I quickly forgot them myself. We were afloat, and the launch, in spite of the delays, had been a success.

Lynda's mother did the honours with the champagne. She uncorked it and showered us on the foredeck several metres below her (it was low tide), with the words 'I name this ship *Tin Hau*. God bless her and all who sail in her.' The TV camera recorded the magic moment – this was probably the first three-masted steel junk to be launched on the African continent – and scores of other cameras clicked. Hand shakes and relief all round. The first stage of our dream had been achieved.

We were not given long to rest. The third and smallest crane remained behind to drop the three masts into position. Andy joined Tony and myself on the boat, whilst Munchie took up his position – prominent as usual – astride the cross-trees of each mast as they dangled in the air. The crane operator could not see the deck of the boat, so Munchie fulfilled the role of go-between. The main and mizzen masts dropped into place easily enough. The foremast took slightly longer, as it had to be guided between the cheeks of the tabernacle, raked at the correct angle, and then drilled to receive the two securing bolts. In accordance with tradition (to bring good luck), coins were placed under each of the masts – a British fifty pence coin under the main mast, a Swazi fifty cents under the mizzen mast, and a South African fifty cents coin under the foremast. We finished just before darkness fell, and were more than ready to relax and celebrate. A crate of good South African beer was waiting.

There was still no peace for the wicked. We received an urgent request from the harbour officials that we move immediately. The quay was needed. I replied that we had not yet tested our engine, steering, anchors and a hundred other items. Could we wait at least until the morning? Or could we man-handle *Tin Hau* along to the end of the quay using warps? The answer was a firm no. Regulations. When I asked where we were to move to, I was told that it was to the original spot where the launch was meant to have taken place. 'Don't worry,' they said, 'we will call a tug.'

One was, in fact, already hovering, so I relented. We would move. The tug came alongside. Mooring lines were passed across, and off we went across the harbour on our first outing. We were cast off near to our designated berth and thankfully tied up without any problems. This time we really did feel drained. Kind friends drove our cars round for us, and thoughtful ones arrived with flasks of soup and sandwiches for the weary crew. We felt shattered and bruised, but at the same time contented and excited about the future. My last thoughts before dropping off to sleep were of mooring lines and fenders carving themselves against the quay wall with the rising and falling tide. Nautical thoughts – at long last. The days of sleeping on land were over.

13. Afloat at Last

We woke up on Tuesday, 11th March, to the sounds of seagulls, harbour cranes and the gentle lapping of water against the hull. Other sounds were less readily identifiable, such as the mysterious cracking and hissing of creatures on the seabed ten feet below. In time everything would become familiar, and anything unexpected – such as a sharp change in the wind strength and direction, or the arrival of a new boat – would result in instant wakefulness. For the moment, we still thought in terms of sleeping at night, being awake during the day, and treating weekends as different.

All this was to change as we grew into our new roles as 'boat people'. In fact it reached a stage where we coined a phrase 'land people' to describe those people we observed from *Tin Hau* – who obviously lived on land, probably in a town or city, and whom we assumed were not in touch with so many of the things which became of overriding importance to us – such as the phase of the moon, the direction and strength of the wind, and the type of cloud cover. They would have no understanding of the relief we felt when dawn came at sea after a cold, black night. Nor would they understand our endless efforts to conserve water and our concern about the disposal of waste. A true land person is more preoccupied with his or her motor car, telephone or video player, and is concerned about insurance, pensions, social security, holidays and personal safety. An extreme land person loves photographing boats but will not set foot in one, loves the seaside but will only look at the sea from the shelter of a car, and shows no appreciation of some of the wonders of the modern world, such as drinking water that comes out of taps, electricity brought right to the home, and the humble water closet. It is amazing how often the subject of toilets ('heads' at sea) comes up between two boat people meeting each other for the first time.

Returning to the smaller world of *Tin Hau's* saloon on 11th March, Lynda and I were enjoying our first breakfast afloat as we contemplated the long list of 'jobs to do'. We were galvanised into action when we heard the familiar sound of a Volkswagen Beetle engine on the quay wall above. Tony had arrived. This meant work and no more hanging around talking about it.

The first job was to crawl into the bilges and wedge into place the mizzen and main masts, securing them where they passed through the deck. The foremast would need some further attention.

'Coffee, Tony?' I asked hopefully.

'No, don't be so idle,' came the reply. 'There's an engine waiting.'

I went down below to open sea-cocks and check stowage. There were no apparent problems. We were in a position to turn the key in the pilothouse. This we did, and the engine roared into life, enjoying its first taste of huge quantities of genuine sea water. We engaged gear, forwards and in reverse. All seemed in order as we strained against our mooring lines.

Over the next few days, we commissioned the three heads (they worked), our waste water bag in the bilges, the deck wash hose, the radar, the VHF, the freezer, the navigation lights and the wind generator. The latter proved to live up to the manufacturer's claims by generating four amps of current in twenty knots of wind, and cutting out at eight to ten amps during our first quayside gale. The only electronic instrument that totally failed right from the beginning was the Seafarer 700 echo sounder. Once again, we were lucky to receive some generous free assistance from a local electronics genius, Dave Johnson, who actually worked out and drew the circuit diagram before we received it from Seafarer in England. Despite his best efforts, he did not succeed in fixing the instrument until his third attempt four weeks later, by which time we had bought a replacement which was posted from England. From 1986, therefore, *Tin Hau* had two echo sounders, one in commission and in working order and the other in its box as a spare – not a bad precaution given the importance of this device.

On Friday, 14th March, Hugh and Chantal arrived from East London and became our first overnight guests on board. They proved to be much more than guests, as they beavered with us for four days on various painting and rigging jobs. Our eight mast stays had all been measured in position, taken to Haggie Wire Ropes for end swaging and returned the same day. They were ready for fixing in place along with the dead-eyes and lanyards. Before this could be done, we had to make our first trip under our own power around the harbour, as the harbour survey team required our space to be vacated for a few hours so they could take some soundings. Using springs, we managed to get away from the quay wall. The re-berthing also went without mishap, my first somewhat nerve-racking experience of handling what was more like a small ship than a yacht. I knew I had much to learn.

The next day we brought all three sails over from the hangar to the quay wall and started the job of lashing the bamboo battens and the laminated timber yards into place. Our hangar space was looking more and more empty and I spent some time clearing it out completely.

By now the quay wall sported a steady crowd of onlookers and well-wishers. Rumour had it that special coach trips were being run from town to see the strange junk! We carried on regardless, trying hard always to be polite and receptive to the comments and questions – the most common one being, 'When are you leaving?'

Perhaps the moment has arrived to introduce someone briefly referred to earlier, but not mentioned at any great length – Jacqui Wilmot. She was to play an important part in *Tin Hau's* early days, and came into our lives in a most unusual way. Back in December 1984, when the first article on *Tin Hau* had been written in the *Eastern Province Herald*, Jacqui (then a schoolgirl aged 16) had been living with her parents, brother and sister, in Mill Park; at that time we were house-sitting for Lynda's parents in the area. Jacqui's grandparents, Bob and Sheila Palmer, were visiting their daughter, son-in-law and grand-children for Christmas, and Sheila, on idling through the local paper, came across the *Tin Hau* article and our name, *Chidell*. Since Chidell had been her maiden name, and as there are not many Chidells around, she decided to track us down. Sure enough, we were quite closely related, although until the *Herald* article we had not even known of each other's existence. It turned out that Jacqui's mother, Wendy, and I had shared the same great-grandfather.

Right from the outset, Jacqui set her mind on joining us on *Tin Hau* wherever we might be going; and, despite opposition – mainly on account of her age – from her grandparents, parents and ourselves, she achieved all she set out to do. To see such determination, enthusiasm and courage from someone so young was really uplifting for us all, and many a time we were helped by Jax. The first proof of her dedication came in all the work she did with us while still on shore; and on Tuesday 18th March, she moved on board *Tin Hau*, leaving us eight months later after many happily shared experiences.

Lynda had a huge number of important jobs to do below decks, mostly concerned with stowage. Ship's stores, equipment and furnishings all needed to be sorted out and given their places, secure against a possible ninety degree knock-down or even a three hundred and sixty degree roll.

This left Jacqui to help me on deck with the mass of running rigging, the three sail bundles having just been moved on board. Lazy jacks and parrels were cut and rigged, as were the halyards, snotters, sheets and sheetlets. Jax, and Lynda when she had time, back-spliced all the cut rope ends, whilst I moved on to the next piece of 'spaghetti', usually at the top of the mast. I could never stop appreciating the view from there, and was always reluctant to leave.

On Saturday, 22nd March, we took *Tin Hau* around the harbour for the second time, for the purpose of swinging the compass under the direction of a friend of Lynda's parents by the name of John Walker. A deviation card was produced, but the error, twenty-eight degrees, was still far too much. John said he would repeat the operation once he had acquired some better magnets from Cape Town. However, the outing and the general progress since the launch was so encouraging that I decided we could phone Jeff in Swaziland to invite him to come down. He and another Swaziland friend, Jan Borrell, were to be two further crew members on the maiden voyage, and had long since planned a three to four month absence from their work. Jeff managed a respected construction company in Swaziland called Construction Associates; and Jan was one of those increasingly rare multi-skilled white farmers still farming in black Africa. We were indeed lucky to have these two along with us, especially with such little pressure on us from them as to the departure date.

Our sixth and final crew member (including ourselves in the count) has also been mentioned earlier – Barry Lamprecht, a photographer from the *Eastern Province Herald*. Never having had any experience of nautical matters, I think it was with some trepidation that he finally 'signed on'; and he certainly proved to be another valuable addition to the *Tin Hau* clan. I, for one, really appreciated seeing the whole venture through one more set of eyes and from a different perspective. Barry saw the sea as something almost magical or mystical, and a phrase he often used during the maiden voyage was 'this really is the last frontier, the last frontier for man to explore!' He would at times almost jump up and down with exhilaration and at other times wear an expression of terror all over his face.

Barry's press influence was utilised on two nagging problems almost immediately. Firstly, we had already approached the fire station in the hope of acquiring some redundant canvas fire hose which we wanted to cut into two foot lengths for use as anti-chafe on our mooring lines. We had received a polite 'no' by way of a reply. Barry, however, asked the same question and came back with large quantities of just what we needed.

His second action was even more useful. We had been shocked to receive an astronomical bill from the tug, the *Blue Jay*, for fifteen minutes of work on the day of the launch. The amount was almost equal to the total cost of the launch. Naturally, I went immediately to see Ted Page, the Port Captain, who had always been helpful and courteous in his dealings with us. He said he would see what he could do. Some days later I was summoned to his office and told he could not help. The matter was already beyond his control. On occasions like this a friend in the press – in this case, Barry – can be extremely useful. He went to see the port press office, threatened to spill the whole story to the *Herald*, and the result was all I could have wanted, a letter of apology in which all charges from the *Blue Jay* were waived.

This represented just one of the numerous paperwork jobs and worries I could have done without. Another concerned our customs drawback. Some of our imported items had been in the country for nearly two years, the cut-off limit for any refunds coming our way. I had to come up with some good reasons as to why we had been delayed and why I did not want to set off to sea quite yet. It was difficult to convey the sense of urgency and plead our cause when visiting the various customs officials secure in their box-like offices lost amongst numerous corridors and never ending fire doors.

I was helped by Rod May of our friendly shipping agents, Rholig, and eventually we saw the 'big boss', Mr Theron, Controller of Port Elizabeth customs. He had to refer the whole matter to Pretoria, but the final verdict was not too long coming and at least partially favourable. We were granted an extension to 1st June, by which time we had to leave South Africa if we wanted total reimbursement of the customs duties we had paid.

Another official department we had dealings with was the South African Department of Transport. We asked them to check that *Tin Hau* was being constructed in accordance with their normal standards, thinking that the resulting certificate might prove useful in the future. A Mr Ter Stege from the DOT visited the boat at the hangar and made some constructive comments which we were able to implement during the building stages. Later he called on us at the harbour on a few occasions to carry out some more thorough inspections.

The most important item of boat documentation we had to arrange was the small ships British Registration Document which, luckily for us and thanks to the RYA (Royal Yachting Association), was extremely easy and inexpensive to acquire. This new and considerably simplified system of registering a small British-owned pleasure vessel had only just come in – for once bureaucracy had moved in the right direction. The end result was a most impressive looking pale blue wallet something like a British passport. In all the places we visited it was always accepted, although often with some puzzled looks. The item most foreign officials needed that could not be found on the Registration Document was the Port of Registry. At first I tried to explain what RYA meant and where Woking – the RYA's offices at that time – was, but later I answered the question in a simpler manner by just saying 'London'. Most officials had heard of London and were happy with the answer.

Besides the British Registration Document and the South African DOT certificate there were of course numerous other papers, books and documents we had to carry. On the personal side there were our passports, our crew's passports, any visas required for foreign countries (although we always obtained these on arrival), driving licences (in case we got near a motor car), VHF radio operator's licences, Lynda's paramedic certificates, my yachtmaster and ham radio course certificates, and our South African tax clearance papers. For the boat we had a radio licence and call sign ('MEUD 4'), various test certificates on some of the materials used, such as the aluminium masts and the galvanised chain, manuals on every item of equipment we had bought and, finally, a most useful ship's stamp and ink pad which I would bring to bear on every official paper that came my way. On leaving South Africa we received an impressive looking clearance certificate never looked at by anyone since.

One area of paperwork we ended up having nothing to do with was insurance. We never had any personal insurance, nor any comprehensive boat insurance. Both were far too difficult and expensive to obtain. On meeting those rare long distance cruising boats carrying insurance we were glad not to have been in their position. We met one cruising couple who had to carry a third crew member at all times or else their insurance would have been null and void. Finding suitable crew had often been a problem for them and had caused them much inconvenience. We could not believe that they had never been allowed – by a remote insurance company – to sail their beautiful boat, *Leisurely Leo*, across a sea or ocean on their own.

On another occasion, we were planning a passage from Larnaca in Cyprus to the Turkish mainland and had worked out the safest and most direct route, given the winds that looked most likely over the following forty-eight hours. We found to our amazement that certain other boats were unable to go with us round the eastern 'pan-handle' of Cyprus because their insurance did not allow it, and any variation was too complex to arrange in the time available. So they took the more difficult and dangerous way round to the west of the island.

Time and again we observed that it was yachtsmen with insurance who treated their yachts with the least care and were the most prepared to take foolish risks. Yacht owners without insurance were much more cautious. I feel that insurance companies, through no real fault of their own, have not helped improve safety standards at sea. And when claims do occur, often the long drawn out wranglings end unsatisfactorily for the boat owner.

Having said all this, we did make a few half-hearted efforts to obtain comprehensive boat insurance while in South Africa, but abandoned these when we realised that the annual premiums were probably going to amount to more than all our other annual living costs put together. Furthermore, one of our boat-building friends, also an insurance broker, advised strongly against it. When we asked him whether he insured his boat, he said, 'Yes, but on a post-dated basis.' He never had to pay any premiums in advance, but if an accident occurred he could still make a full claim as long as he paid some of the premium in arrears. We wondered how often this sort of thing happened in the world of insurance.

Three years later in the Mediterranean we learnt of a German company, Pantaenius, who for only £60 per annum would cover us against the risk that had always worried me the most – that of colliding with or damaging someone else's boat or causing personal injury to a third party. Apparently there were no unacceptable conditions attached. So in the end we did acquire some – limited – form of insurance.

14. The Trials

It would take too long to describe in detail all that was going on during this crucial period of our trials. I suspect the reader would rather not hear about the problems of our leaking water tank lids, or our efforts to sort out the dinghy davits, or my further escapades in the bilges or at the top of the masts. Painting jobs never seemed to end. Nor did the stowage and provisioning activities.

Yet by Monday, 31st March, we were in a position to go outside the harbour for the first time and try out the sails. Lynda, Jax and I cast off early in the morning in very little wind. We motored clear of the harbour entrance and hoisted all three sails, waiting to see what would happen. Everything went quiet as the engine was turned off and we revelled in the peace and tranquillity of the open sea. For the moment, Port Elizabeth was behind us. What would happen with the sails? I secured the sheets and waited hopefully. Slowly *Tin Hau* picked up momentum, but in the wrong direction – Backwards! This was wonderful. I had no idea that we had built a boat that would sail in reverse. We decided to leave things as they were for the moment, lash the wheel and have some breakfast. As we enjoyed our cereal, Cape seed loaf and coffee, *Tin Hau* continued her sternwards drift, also quite happy.

Once the washing up was done, however, I thought it was time to try some more conventional sailing. I asked Jax and Lynda to 'back' the foresail by pushing on the lower battens and the boom until they were well outboard. I sheeted in the mizzen fairly tight, and, sure enough, *Tin Hau* started on a slow turn away from the wind. Once we had turned about forty-five degrees, I instructed Jax and Lynda to let go the foresail and re-set it correctly. I adjusted the main and mizzen, and forwards we went. Gracefully, serenely, majestically.

For a couple of hours we enjoyed ourselves, tacking or gybing on the turn. Finally the moment came to return to the hustle and bustle of the harbour. What a pity! Still, we knew there was more to come; and *Tin Hau's* first sail – if it could be called that, in such little wind – was a success.

Later that day Jan and Jeff arrived from Swaziland to move aboard. With them, and staying for just one night, were Jan's wife, Kim, and daughter, Marika. They all looked remarkably fresh after their thousand-mile drive. We caught up on the latest news and gossip from Swaziland before immersing ourselves once again in engine exhaust valves, bilge pumps (there was a slight leak around one pump), and radio aerials.

Over the next two days we had two further gentle sails and I decided it was time for the next major landmark in equipment testing. We would try out our anchors. With this in mind we set out during the afternoon of Thursday, 3rd April, despite hearing that some of the worst storms and highest seas on record were occurring two hundred to four hundred miles to the west of us. However, there was still little wind in Port Elizabeth, and the time available for our trials was becoming increasingly short. We headed out towards the harbour entrance, where, admittedly, the swells did look big. I knew we were in for some fun, but I felt we could continue. It would be better clear of the entrance.

That proved to be a slight error in judgement. I think it took only the third incredibly steep climb up onto a crest followed by an even sharper fall into a trough for me to decide to head back. I warned the others that I would be turning to port. Lynda checked the stowage below. We had no sails up to steady us and so I anticipated a heavy roll. I picked my moment, and rotated the wheel, hoping we could make it through one hundred and eighty degrees on one crest. However, it was not to be, as something totally unexpected happened. One third of the way into the turn the wheel came off in my hands!

My heart nearly stopped, but luckily my reactions were reasonably quick. I managed to push the wheel back on to the shaft, matching the square key to its keyway, just before the shaft had a chance to spin; by continuing to apply forward pressure on the wheel, I still had control. I turned rapidly to starboard back to our original course and the crisis was averted as we descended sharply into the next trough. I maintained my pressure on the wheel, judged the following crest, and completed a safe about-turn to port, heeling to a maximum of only thirty degrees. Back in the harbour I breathed a sigh of relief. The loss of our steering at a narrow harbour entrance between two breakwaters in such big swells could have led to the loss of the boat!

Accidents never happen singly. We should have remembered that – not that such a thought would have prevented our next problem. I had decided that in view of our close shave, the day's 'trials' were over. We would return to our berth, especially as the wind had just changed sharply to the south west and increased in strength. However, once more my plans were thwarted. This time, during a mock approach to the berth (it was not an easy berth to come alongside), the engine controls failed abruptly and I could not engage reverse gear. There was only one way to stop. I ran forwards to the anchors, unlashed one and dropped it, all in the space of fifteen seconds. It held and, luckily for us, brought *Tin Hau* to a standstill just before the approaching mudbank. Our planned day of 'anchor practice' had turned into the real thing. The anchor had proved satisfactory.

We spent a few minutes looking at the gear cable in the engine room, carried out what we thought was a temporary repair, and pulled up the anchor, setting off towards the quay wall once more. However, yet again everything went wrong (a passing thought went through my head – one of the alternative names suggested for *Tin Hau* had been *Wot Went Wong*). I could not engage reverse. This time our heading and position was slightly different. I had no choice but to drift towards the quay, berthing in a spot fifty metres from our normal one. Thanks to the crew's good use of fenders, tyres and their arms, this operation went without any trouble, and we warped our way along the quay wall back 'home'.

The following day we found that the cause of the steering failure was one tiny grub screw, supplied with the wheel, which had come undone in spite of my having drilled a matching hole for it in the shaft and having personally tightened it up hard with an Allen key. My mistake had been not to allow for vibration. I should have applied Loctite or a similar compound to the screw's thread to stop it working loose. The weakest steering link that I had wondered about at the time of installation had been discovered!

The reason for the engine control failure was similar. In this instance it was a screw on the gear cable at the engine that had vibrated free. Loctite was again applied in liberal quantities; a new bracket was made and the problem solved. I went all over the boat applying Loctite, having just discovered its existence and what it was for. I consoled myself with the thought that this was what 'trials' were all about, and at least we had been lucky so far in avoiding any serious harm.

Work carried on over the next few weeks as we sorted out *Tin Hau's* teething problems and learnt how to handle and sail her. Unfortunately all the batteries (weighing about twenty-five kilograms each) had to be taken out and returned to Willards, since unexplained signs of acid were appearing in the battery tray. Willards discovered that the casing of one battery was cracked and they gave us a replacement free of charge. Other electrical problems were sorted out by another of those wonderful helpers that seemed to materialise out of thin air, Dickie Henderson. Yet more volunteers checked over the freezer and the engine. A scuba diver, Gert, examined the hull underwater and reported that everything looked fine, except for some sharks that were paying an unexpected visit to our length of quay wall. Meanwhile, Munchie Moolman continued with his generosity by bringing us a ten kilogram yellowtail he had caught the previous night.

The *Herald* kept *Tin Hau* in the news with a huge front page photograph of her under full sail off Port Elizabeth. Sue and Debbie Ryan came round one breakfast to interview Jacqui for a special feature article.

I had decided by now that we were too late to head for Cape Town and the Atlantic. Our destination would be Mauritius, and specifically a particular bay in Mauritius that sounded idyllic, Grande Baie. We learnt more of the waters we would be crossing when we met a Canadian yachtsman by the name of Brock who had just arrived from Mauritius, sailing on his own. He had taken an incredible 107 days, having been blown all over the place by headwind gales. At one point he was in polar regions among icebergs. His boat, *Asylum*, was in tatters, but his spirit was undaunted.

On Sunday, 13th April, the time had come for our first overnight sail, and since I wanted to be free to try out some astral navigation and not be too burdened down by other duties, I was glad to take on John Walker as acting skipper for the trip. The plan was to sail due south from Port Elizabeth, see what the waves were like in the Agulhas current and turn round after twelve hours or so. We left at midday in a force four to six easterly and encountered almost immediately a nasty short chop of a sea with waves about six feet in height. Thus began what we remember now with sheer horror as 'That Sunday', our most miserable experience on *Tin Hau*. My stomach turns just thinking about it.

The wind freshened considerably and wave heights increased as we continued southwards out of sight of land. With all sails fully set (with hindsight we were absolute fools not to have reefed), we raced along at seven knots. The lee deck was regularly awash and to me it seemed we were totally out of control, but John Walker, the skipper, was unworried. I experienced for the first (and almost the last) time the sensation of seasickness, and felt indescribably ill and light-headed. Jan, Jeff and Jacqui were in a huddle on the dry port quarter, throwing up a week's worth of good food into the sea below. John stood at the wheel, legs securely braced for each wave, looking calm and confident as every ship's master should be. Lynda proved her toughness by remaining in full control of her senses and not showing any inclination towards seasickness.

Just before dark, Jeff and I managed to communicate to each other that perhaps it would be wise to turn back now, not at midnight as originally planned. We spoke to John and he agreed with the idea. 'We will gybe,' he said. Jeff and I muttered something about 'wouldn't tacking be safer?' as we remembered all those capsizes we had suffered during gybes on his Fireball dinghy. But we were in no state to argue.

The wheel was turned to starboard. The foresail came across and then crash! – the main swung over, followed by the mizzen. But what was happening? The mainsail had fallen down and was lying in a most precarious position. Total chaos ensued as we rolled heavily and lost steerage way. No one had time to pull in the log line which we were towing, and on turning on the engine to regain control, the line caught the propeller.

'Cut the log line,' I ordered. 'Drop the foresail. Reef the mizzen. Secure the main – what has broken? Close the pilothouse door,' I couldn't get the words out fast enough.

We all forgot our seasickness and sprang into action. Thankfully, after a few minutes *Tin Hau* was under control again and we were heading back home. Would the engine and a reefed mizzen give us enough power to clear Cape Recife, the headland that protected Port Elizabeth? How far had we been set to the west by the mighty Agulhas current and the easterly wind?

Darkness fell and we could look for the lighthouse at Cape Recife. At last it was spotted just to starboard. We had to win all the ground we could to the east. The engine was revved as it had never been revved before, and slowly we managed a few extra degrees to starboard. As long as we kept the lighthouse just on the port bow we would be all right and able to get home on one tack. By now the crew were wet and cold and being sick once more. John and Lynda remained steady and strong. I really felt for the poor engine, wondering exactly how much line was still round the propshaft, and I tried to work out why, apparently, the main halyard had broken.

By midnight it was clear we would reach Port Elizabeth and, in fact, at one o'clock in the morning we tied up alongside the quay. The safety and lack of motion in the harbour was absolutely wonderful. I found a berth, collapsed, mumbled something about 'never going to sea again' and promptly slept for sixteen hours until five in the afternoon, returning to bed at nine!

It is amazing how one can bounce back! Forty-eight hours after 'That Sunday', I was thinking what a good day's trial it had been. We had found some weaknesses. We had learnt our lesson about the log line. Never again did we allow it to become tangled with the propshaft. As for the failure of the main halyard after the most violent and unnecessary gybe we were ever to undergo, I found that the steel eye at the masthead to which the halyard's double block had been shackled had been torn open. It took several days to work out how to improve on the system, but finally the solution was found, thanks to Rob Wicks and Stuart Young of a company called Rimtex. We unbolted each of the masthead plates with their single welded eyes, and replaced them with some new plates on to which short lengths of chain had been welded, everything being galvanised after fabrication. We then reconnected the double blocks, shackling each one to the lowermost of three dangling chain links. The plan worked, and a week later we were comforted by the knowledge that another potential problem had been averted by action taken while still in Port Elizabeth, which to me, at least, was more than living up to its reputation as the 'Friendly City'.

On Saturday, 19th April, Jan left us to go to Swaziland, very much on the understanding that he would return a few days before the date of our departure, whenever that might be. It was a pity that he missed the events of the following day, which proved most entertaining. This was the day arranged for *Tin Hau's* Chinese commissioning, starting at half past three, organised entirely by the Chinese community but set up in the first place by our friend, Ivor Sing Key, the painter of *Tin Hau's* dragon.

We spent the morning preparing for the party and dressing the ship overall, taking care to place the flags in the correct order (an order that did not spell out some signal). Everyone arrived as planned and we were presented with a brass dragon plaque, a Chinese flag, and some good luck, health and happiness cards before we all moved on board; some thirty-five people in all. In the wheelhouse we enjoyed some delicious Chinese food, and passed a happy afternoon feeling properly blessed and encouraged. However, conversation rapidly faded come early evening, and after some polite goodbyes everyone had suddenly gone. Afterwards we found out the reason. Half the party had been feeling seasick! We had become so acclimatised to the boat's motion that we had not even noticed that we were moving. We had been given a truly wonderful afternoon, and felt bad that we had unwittingly caused discomfort to our generous friends. Hopefully no one was put off boats!

One subject talked about a lot at the Chinese blessing was the name we had chosen for our boat '*Tin Hau*' (pronounced 'tin how'), a name well known to any Chinese person from the coastal regions of southern China and Hong Kong, but less known elsewhere.

Initially we had wanted a Swazi word, as our boat was effectively conceived in Swaziland. We had considered a number of names, the favourite becoming '*Lilandza*'. However, after a while, Lynda got the feeling that a boat with the hull form and sails of a Chinese junk should have a Chinese name. We started to think of all the alternatives, trying to pick a word that would not just have a significant meaning, but also one that would not be too hard to spell, pronounce or be remembered by others.

As early as 1983 we had been given a small figurine of the Chinese goddess of the sea, patroness of fisher folk and queen of the heavens, Tin Hau (or T'ien Hou), by my cousin, Pat Loseby, who had lived (and sailed) in Hong Kong for most of her life. She told us the whole story of Tin Hau and we learnt of the importance of the goddess to the junk people of Hong Kong, even today. Every year a festival is held in Joss House Bay on Tin Hau's birthday (the twenty-third day of the third moon). Pat told us how it was normal for a junk to carry a figurine of Tin Hau on board and that, for this reason, she was giving one to us, together with the promise that each year our boat would be remembered at the festival. As far as calling our boat '*Tin Hau*' was concerned, back in 1983 we had never considered it, assuming it would be sacrilegious.

Two years later when we sent to Pat for approval the first of our proposed Chinese names, 'P'an-T'ao', she consulted her Chinese friends and came back to us with the definite advice, 'No. P'an-T'ao is bad joss.' We learnt that it was associated with death and not immortality as we had originally thought. 'Why don't you consider calling her Tin Hau?' she asked. She herself had owned a boat called 'Tin Hau' many years before.

So, 'Tin Hau' it became.

Tin/Heaven   Hau/Goddess

We were at last reaching the point where the departure from South Africa on *Tin Hau's* maiden voyage looked imminent and real. Each day, many important loose ends were being tied up, such as the rope handholds in the pilothouse, the cills over the doors, the pin rails on the shrouds, a cork notice-board under the chart table lid, spare fuses and bulbs, photocopies of log sheets and sextant calculation sheets, a satisfactory stowage system for the windsurfer and for the liferaft, wooden stopper plugs for the through-hull fittings for use in emergencies, tool boxes, a very comprehensive medical and dental kit (I think Lynda was looking forward to a chance of some amateur surgery on her husband!), mug and tea towel holders... and a host of other items. We continued to go out each day for test sails, initially only tacking through one hundred and seventy degrees, but eventually bringing it down in slight seas to one hundred and thirty degrees, very much aware that this was the area in which further junk research, as well as future *Tin Hau* experimentation, would almost certainly bring great improvements.

Jeff left us for two and a half weeks to attend to business in Swaziland, but he was back on 16th May, as loyal, supportive and humorous as ever. By this time we had completed our twenty-first trip out of the harbour, and had given many people the unusual experience of sailing a junk off Port Elizabeth. We had been trying all sorts of sail combinations and learning when each was applicable (see Figure 13). For example, we used full sail (six panels of the foresail, six panels of the main and six panels of the mizzen) in winds of force four or less. In winds of force five we would reef to five-five-four (one panel less on the mizzen than on the other two sails). At force six we would reef to four-four-three, and at force seven or eight to three-three-two. In order to reduce pressure at the wheel when sailing downwind, particularly if the sea was in any way rough, we would drop the mizzen sail an extra two panels, sailing at five-five-two in a force five. We discovered how well *Tin Hau* would sail dead downwind, goose-winged, with the main out to starboard, the mizzen to port and the foresail sheeted amidships. Later we would find many more combinations and their uses, sometimes quite extraordinary, like sailing with the mizzen alone.

This may all sound rather complicated to the non-sailor, or over-simplified to the expert. Yet for us at the trial stage, learning how to sail a junk was one of our main objectives. Before we had launched, our knowledge of junks had been limited to what we had read. We remembered one story in which a junk had been shipped from the Far East to Sydney, Australia, where she was sailed for the first time. The owner found to his dismay that the performance was terrible, and he paid a Chinese junk master (or 'laudah') to come to Sydney to sort out his problems. The laudah was immediately successful. I am not sure whether or not this story is true, but it made us aware that there could be more to sailing junks than met the eye. As it turned out, our fears were unjustified. Learning how to sail *Tin Hau* proved to be relatively easy, and we were – and still are – impressed with the junk sail's advantages and simplicity.

One manoeuvre we practised again and again was our man overboard drill, not so much because I was expecting to lose anyone overboard with our good, high, fixed handrails, but more so that each and every one of us would become familiar with handling *Tin Hau* under sail. 'David overboard,' I would yell suddenly, throwing a sealed plastic bottle into the sea. Then I would press the stopwatch button on my wristwatch and wait for some action – hopefully! Another time it would be Lynda. Or Barry. Or Jeff. Or Jax. Our rescue times varied from three minutes to fifteen minutes. At least we always retrieved the bottle.

On Sunday, 18th May, after our twenty-third time out of the harbour, I phoned Jan in Swaziland to say we were ready. All being well, and depending on the forecast, we would leave on the following Saturday (24th May). Lynda and Jax cooked forty or so meals for six persons at Andy and Carol's house, bringing them back to *Tin Hau's* freezer once they had been fully frozen

Full sail (6-6-6)
Wind Force 1-4
Smooth to moderate sea

Motor-Sailing and reefed (0-2-2)
Wind forward of abeam Force 7-8
Very rough sea

Reefed (4-4-2)
Wind aft of abeam Force 5-6
Moderate to Rough sea

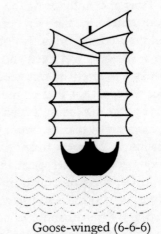

Goose-winged (6-6-6)
Wind dead aft Force 1-4
Smooth to slight sea
Foresail (sheeted amidships) not shown

Figure 13: Typical Sail Settings

ashore. We were going to eat well! I spent an afternoon preparing a star and planet chart for May and June in the approximate area of our voyage. I wanted to know in advance which navigational planets and stars would be useful, and roughly where they would be in the sky. We also worked out watch-keeping lists. Jeff would be in charge of one watch with Jan and Jax; I would have the other watch with Lynda and Barry. Subsequently, especially when we had an autopilot, Lynda and I were happy to take the boat on our own, but on the maiden voyage with an untested boat, no autopilot and a potentially dangerous section of the ocean in midwinter, I definitely wanted crew.

On Tuesday, 20th May, we took a TV crew out for a quick sail, but found out later that the entire interview was drowned by wind noise! On returning to the harbour we received an upsetting phone call. Jan could not join us after all. He was having major problems on the farm. This was a great disappointment to us – Jan was the ideal sort of person to have along; he had proved most capable on all the jobs he did for us, particularly those involving mechanical work. He was exceptionally strong, the original gentle giant. His sense of humour was always evident. He had already shown much generosity and encouragement towards us.

Without Jan I urgently needed to find another crew member, and we only had three days before our planned departure! A number of people came to mind, Tony and Andy being the obvious choices, but I knew already that they had too much in the way of work and family commitments. Another possibility, a young lad of twenty-one called Jean-Marc Gabriel (commonly known as 'Angel') had been showing some interest in *Tin Hau* over the past few weeks. We knew he was keen to reach Mauritius and, after that, Réunion, in order to report for French military training. He was obviously physically fit and used to the sea, being a keen participant in what to me always seemed one of the toughest of marine sports – surfing. He belonged to that exclusive band of lunatics to be seen miles out to sea on their own in the roughest of conditions in midwinter, permanently seeking the ideal wave. I had seen such people in Cape Town, and again in large numbers in the Eastern Cape. Only one group of nautical enthusiasts have surpassed the surfers in terms of guts and insanity – the offshore windsurfers, for whom I have nothing but the most profound respect and admiration.

It didn't take much to persuade Jean-Marc to join us. He was happy with the daily charge of five rand we asked from each crew member to cover his or her food expenses; and he accepted responsibility for his own travel costs from Port Louis onwards. In no time he found a place on the deck to stow his surfboard, and he agreed to be at the quayside at six o'clock in the morning on the day of our planned departure.

This left us two days to complete our provisioning, fill our diesel and water tanks and the gas cylinders, make arrangements for our faithful car (it was left for Andy to sell), complete the paperwork with the customs, harbour and immigration officials, pay a final visit to the dentist, and say our farewells to so many wonderful friends and well-wishers. My feelings about South Africa were as mixed as ever. I knew I would miss the wide open spaces, the smell of Africa, the sunshine, the beautiful scenery, the wine and the food, and above all the African people of all colours, races and creeds. But it would be good to be free of all that bureaucracy and away from a sort of shadow that hung over the whole country, and of which we had been most aware whenever we had made the occasional visit to South Africa from Swaziland. 'What guns do you have in your car?' we would be asked by the South African immigration officials on entering South Africa at Oshoek. 'What fruit do you have?' the Swazi officials would ask on our return (importation of fruit to Swaziland was not allowed). It was like returning from a huge, somewhat frightening metropolis into a gentle, friendly village.

I paid one last visit to the helpful meteorological office at Port Elizabeth's airport on Friday 23rd May, receiving print-outs of forecasted weather maps for seven days ahead (which, except for the first day, proved totally wrong!) I came to a decision: we would leave at seven o'clock the following morning. I anticipated that the passage to Mauritius, a distance of about 2,700 miles along the dog-legged route we would have to follow given the prevailing winds, would take between four and six weeks, although nothing could be certain in the Southern Ocean.

PART TWO

The Maiden Voyage

Lynda Chidell

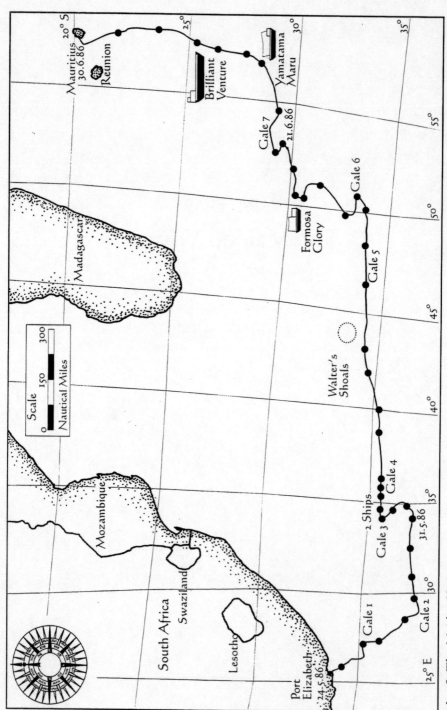

Map 2: The Maiden Voyage

Dots (●) represent noon positions

As soon as David had received the weather reports for which he had been waiting, Barry and Jean-Marc were notified that they should report on board no later than six o'clock the following morning. The rest of us had made lists of last-minute shore activities we wished to carry out before departure. Now it was to these that we all turned our attention. Haircuts. Luxury treats to buy. Hot baths. (The latter featured on all four lists!)

I never asked my family what their feelings were when the news finally came that we were about to set off. I know that my own were a mixture of nervousness and excitement, and I'm sure the rest of the crew felt the same way. Those family members staying behind handled it so calmly that it made parting very easy for us.

Tony spent our last evening in port aboard *Tin Hau*. We had always said that the seventh (unoccupied) berth would be reserved for him. We strongly urged him to join us on the adventure which lay ahead, even though we realised and appreciated that his work and family commitments at the time were too great for him to be able to do so. Tony had given so much of himself to *Tin Hau* – it had been more than just another job to him. We knew that a part of Tony would feel let down and unfulfilled unless and until he had experienced cruising aboard *Tin Hau*. It was with very heavy hearts that we said farewell to him that night. He would not be at the quayside the following morning to see *Tin Hau* sail away; he had told us he didn't think he could stand it.

Departure day dawned and, after a quick cup of coffee, Jeff, Jax, David and I commenced work on departure details. Barry and Jean-Marc arrived promptly at six and very quickly stowed their personal belongings. Family, friends and a large number of unknown persons gathered at the quay. Andy was handed the keys of our trusty van, along with all the gear we were leaving behind. It was his task to dispose of it for us.

Tensions were mounting minute by minute as small jobs were completed and final checks made. Barry's boss came aboard to take pictures for the newspaper and Barry found himself at the other side of the lens for once. At last we were ready. There were tearful hugs and kisses for all those who had given us so much support during the preceding months. As the crew stepped off dry land for the last time, a bottle of champagne was thrust into my arms by an unknown well-wisher. A much appreciated gesture of friendliness from the Friendly City we were about to leave.

Precisely two minutes after the appointed hour, our umbilical cord was severed. All lines were cast off and all hands turned to the stowing of fenders and coiling of mooring warps. Sails were raised in the harbour for the benefit of all those who had turned out of bed so early to give us the rousing send-off they did. A foghorn salute was given by a neighbouring trawler as we left the quay and glided towards the control tower at the entrance to the harbour. Permission to proceed was granted on the VHF at half past seven by the Port Controller as, for the last time, we made our way between the breakwaters. The first change of watch was scheduled for eight o'clock.

As soon as we were clear of the harbour we carried out a 'cleansing' of the boat. Chinese mythology would have us believe that junks attract demons and evil spirits while connected to the land. These spirits inhabit a dragon which dangles its tail in the wake of the boat. By performing a figure-of-eight manoeuvre, one cuts the dragon's tail thus releasing the spirits into the deep. Most seafarers, ourselves included, are too superstitious to ignore such folklore. Cutting the dragon's tail became a feature which marked the beginning of every voyage.

David had set the watch system at straight four hourly intervals with two dog-watches from 4 p.m. to 6 p.m. and from 6 p.m. to 8 p.m. The three Js made up the one watch – Jeff, Jean-Marc and Jax – and the other consisted of David, Barry and myself. It was a logical division of experience, strength and other skills. The system ensured that we all had the opportunity to experience dawn and dusk watches, as the rota meant one watch did not get the same spell on successive days. The initial course was set to take us well clear of land and across the Agulhas current to a point on latitude 35°S, south-east of Port Elizabeth, where we expected to meet the prevailing westerlies. These, we hoped, would carry us a long way towards our goal of Mauritius.

Our first day brought favourable winds which helped us achieve our initial aims. By dawn of the second day we had lost the wind altogether and found ourselves wallowing uncomfortably on a lumpy sea. Though we had crossed the current, skipper felt it was sensible to put as much distance between it and ourselves as possible. Reluctant though we were to use fuel unnecessarily, the engine was turned on to motor or motor-sail for as long as we felt we were at risk of being blown back towards the current and the coast of South Africa.

Dawn on our third day presented a more definite change in the weather. A force four easterly which gradually increased to force five and backed to east-north-east. By breakfast time the sea had risen a bit, and the motion of the boat had become uncomfortable enough to put four of the crew off their food. Those of us who had happily sailed in force five winds along the coast or in sheltered inland waters were now learning that the same strength wind can be a very different kettle of fish out in the open sea. We were experiencing the effects of a long fetch for the first time. In spite of being, by noon, 192 miles from land, there were a surprising number of small birds around. A lot of them looked, to my untrained eye, like land birds. By this time we were experiencing mini-gale conditions for the first time.

Our fourth day at sea was something of a milestone, in that it was the day we discovered we had a stowaway on board – a seventh crew member. David had been playing about with various settings of the wheel and sails in an attempt to see if it was possible to reduce the amount of human effort needed to guide the boat. After what seemed to me like a very short time indeed, he had worked it all out and with the help of a couple of newly-spliced heavy gauge lines (my only contribution to the exercise), we had our seventh 'crew member'. Officially given the name 'Number Seven', he was warmly welcomed by all aboard. This discovery was made during our night watch and it was with great enthusiasm that David, Barry and I planned an amusing introduction for the off-watch when they eventually came on duty. The chess board was brought out of its locker and set up on the wheelhouse settee. I stationed myself out of sight in the galley, but ready to make a quick entrance and not miss the fun. Jax was the first to enter; she came in and said a few dopey words, looked around, then her eyes widened as she stared first at the wheel, then at the compass. The penny finally dropped as she saw that the wheel was lashed, and she let out a squeal of delight. Being first in, she was able to get into hiding for the arrival of Jeff and Angel. Number Seven was an absolute blessing. The discovery came none too soon, either, as by the end of that day, the sea had roughened and the wind had increased to force seven to eight.

Shortly after that, we had a spell of northerly winds, which, despite the moderately rough sea, made easier sailing. Several of the crew were still experiencing the misery of seasickness. It was time, in my opinion, that we had some decent wind and weather to get them over it and then we could, perhaps, enjoy the voyage. The first few days are always a problem on any passage. For a first voyage, good weather conditions at the start are desirable to acclimatise the crew quickly. Unfortunately, we were not so blessed. It took a little while for everyone to settle down. The shifts, which alternated very short spells of sleep with relatively long periods of physical and mental strain, were harder going than any of us expected, though they eventually became routine. We all had difficulty getting off to sleep during our first day or two. When we did sleep we didn't always feel rested afterwards. The first reason was that our muscles did not relax, but continued to work, stabilising our bodies. Secondly, we knew that the wake-up call would come all too soon. Thirdly, one becomes attuned to the feel or rhythm of the boat in relation to the weather/sea conditions and slight changes can trigger in-built alarm systems into action. The last two factors kept our minds from switching off, and consequently we could not sleep as deeply as we might have wished.

It was almost a week before any of us had enough energy to bathe (albeit a sea-shower), or do the laundry. With six people on board and no idea how long the journey to Mauritius might take, we had to be very careful with our water consumption. Sweet water was for drinking, brushing teeth, cooking and washing faces only. Everything else had to be done in sea water. We had bought a large number of salt-water soap tablets at great expense. What a flop. They would not lather at all. We resorted to using shampoo for bathing as well as for hair. It lathered very well – but made the decks slippery.

By this stage we had almost finished the commercially baked bread we had taken aboard in Port Elizabeth. Jax and I worked out a system for the baking of bread and muffins. Bread would be made by the midnight to 4 a.m. watch, and set in the oven to bake. A mixture for muffins would be made and set aside for baking in the next watch ready for breakfast. We got this arrangement down to a fine art and were turning out more than passable bread and rolls within days. By the end of the voyage we had progressed to croissants.

At the end of the first week, with 488 miles completed (much less than the skipper's target, to his disappointment), everything on board was beginning to return to some semblance of normality. Jean-Marc set the first fishing-troll and, in spite of the skipper's scepticism, managed to land a one and a half kilogram tunny within an hour. A smoother sea and gentler breezes were partly responsible for the uplift in spirits. Also, we had the unique experience of seeing – at close quarters – an awesome albatross which we christened 'Trossy'. There is nowhere on earth quite like the middle of an empty ocean. So much we take for granted on land becomes a matter of vital interest and importance. Every natural phenomenon, every living creature, is of consuming interest to the long distance sailor. Those creatures which keep small boats company at sea become 'friends' (which probably explains why all our longer term visitors or companions were given names). Trossy, 'our' albatross, was the largest bird we ever saw at sea. It flew figures-of-eight across our wake for hours at a time, day and night.

Week two, which started out reasonably well with fair weather, quickly turned into a nightmare, rapid switches in wind direction, with even more rapid rises in wind strength and barometric pressure. Even though we kept hourly records of the barometer readings and wind strengths, soon it was not possible to predict switches except by observing the approach of squally conditions. This was all very well during daylight hours, but impossible at night – especially when there was no moon. The wheelhouse contributed to the sense of unreality in that it took away the physical contact with the weather which many yachtsmen develop into a kind of sixth sense barometer. It also heightened the sensation of being out of control on a 'downhill run' when sailing on a dark night. If there was no moon, the sensation changed to that of feeling that one was steering the boat in an ever-tightening circle. These sensations disappeared as soon as one went out on deck, feeling the wind constantly blowing from one direction. Odd, to say the least.

2nd June was a depressing day for all of us. Jeff discovered that one of the stainless steel dead-eye straps had snapped, and, worse still, that the foremast tabernacle doubler plate was lifting off the deck! It was unfortunate that we were in the teeth of a very nasty gale (winds of up to sixty knots), and unable to do much of any practical value. We desperately needed a calmer stretch to do anything worthwhile to repair the damage. Jeff and I sorted out the dead-eye by fixing a rope strop to it and re-reeving the lanyards. That job was the least of the worries though, as the masts were supposedly capable of surviving without stays. Every time one of us ventured to the foredeck for an inspection it seemed that the gap was widening and the rip in the weld was getting longer.

That gale produced the most frightening conditions I had ever seen. The waves were huge. When I was able to bring myself to look out of the pilot-house windows, the spray was flying horizontally off the wave crests. The sea was an ominous shade of grey with foam swirling about on the surface which added to its evil appearance. Occasionally the very crests of the waves would tumble over themselves, but just before they did it was possible to catch a flash of green water. I'm not sure why, but those particular flashes filled me with fear. Our sails, by then, were as reefed as they could be without actually bare-poling and the wheel was lashed. *Tin Hau* was effectively somewhere between lying ahull and being hove-to. The pounding she took during that storm was terrific, and apart from the dead-eye problems and the tabernacle failure she stood up to it well. Most of the crew had gone off their food again. Just as well as it would have been very difficult indeed to have produced a 'proper' meal in conditions where food took off from cooking pots like Harrier jump jets and crockery flew off horizontal surfaces like flying saucers. I did try cooking in these conditions one night. The meal ended up all over the place. Four servings were lost accidentally – the final one was hurled by myself in a fit of temper at being unable to cope. David kindly cleaned up the mess while I sobbed my heart out. Since then we followed a policy of having nourishing do-it-yourself food available for that kind of weather. Far more sensible that the crew should be able to eat little and often and, more importantly, when they felt like it.

During the worst of the weather we spotted a trawler some miles to the north of us. Twelve hours later we spotted another ship some distance away. Keeping track of them while ducking and diving in wave peaks and troughs, however, was impossible. We were very frustrated at not being able to make contact with these vessels on the VHF.

Eventually the gale abated sufficiently for us to be able to get out on deck and consider how to tackle the foremast problem. The doubler plate had ripped right across the aft end like a flimsy piece of toilet tissue. Jeff had woken us with the news that, in his opinion, we could well lose the foremast and the sail unless urgent action was taken. The obvious thing to do first was to get the sail right down, use the engine to hold the boat head-to-wind as far as possible, and do our best to jury rig the mast. The waves were still enormous. It remained too rough to operate the generator – given the exhaust outlet position we had at that time – or risk taking power tools out on deck. The wind was dying down though. So, with luck, we could at least do something with ropes, and work out a way to carry out a more permanent repair. Driving rain squalls continued to blast down on us for the first hour or two. Jeff and I got the forepeak hatch open between squalls to sort through mooring lines. Eventually we chose two long twenty-four millimetre diameter polyester lines with bights already spliced on the ends, and a third line of the same diameter, but a little shorter, for an interim stay. Our plan was to lash the foremast, from a point about one third of the way up, to the boom gallows aft. This would, we hoped, make it secure enough to send someone aloft to drop the bights of the other two lines over the masthead. The worry was that the added weight of a person suspended from the masthead, which already leaned forward, might just tip the balance and send it toppling. This was a job for a lightweight crew member, not just any volunteer. Even though this was logical, Jeff was not happy about our choice, as the lightest crew member (other than Jax) was also the most important – the skipper. Without giving us too much time to brood on that aspect of it, David got himself into the bosun's chair, clipped on to the spare foremast halyard and had himself hauled aloft. The job went quickly and easily and it was with some relief that we sent him back to the wheelhouse as soon as he was down again. Angel had had the unenviable task of trying to keep the boat head-to-wind during all this. Barry, Jeff and I continued the jury rigging work on deck, tensioning and securing the new 'stays' well aft to the very solid handrails. We wore harnesses all the time we were out there and were very glad we did as we were constantly being buffeted around by the high seas and several times were slammed over by breaking waves. There was one which knocked all three of us over and we were flung to the extent of our harness lines. I doubt we were in serious danger of being washed overboard, but it was comforting to know that we had the extra security of the harnesses. We had several trips to the warmth of the wheelhouse for a change of wet-gear and a hot cuppa. Jax competently took control of the galley and ensured that all had a good, hot and nourishing meal as soon as we were able. She also prepared a number of rope strops ready for replacing the broken straps of the dead-eyes which, by that time, were many. Night fell before the desired level of calm had been reached. So work was left until the next day.

5th June was much calmer in every way. The sea had gone down and the wind had virtually died out. The previous night David had pinched two heavy aluminium angles from the depths of the anchor locker. (Supports for the draining grid beneath the anchor chain.) These we intended to use to strengthen the deck. Bolted across the weld-rip in a fore and aft direction, they would help to reduce the tendency of the mast to tip forward. Once the generator was operable, David and Jeff drilled holes through one face of the angle ready for positioning on deck the following day. Our main worry then was that the third and final drill bit of the right size would not last long enough to drill the holes through the deck and doubler plates. Two had already been blunted going through the aluminium. All the men concentrated on the work to be done on the deck, and Jax and I attended to the business of keeping the boat moving. For once we were going in the right direction, even if under motor rather than sail. Our distance out of Port Elizabeth at that point was 616 miles. The work on the foredeck took all day and was finally completed at five thirty. A hearty cheer went up when the sails were hoisted again. A tired crew drifted lazily but contentedly through the most deserved happy hour on record.

Shortly after we had enjoyed our evening meal, the westerly breeze started to intensify and all hands were called to the task of shortening sail. No sooner had each reef been taken in than the wind picked up further, requiring yet another two panels of reefing. When there was virtually no sail left up, (the sails were at two-zero-two), the crew all piled into the wheelhouse and shut the doors. Clearly we were in for another night of miserable weather.

The crew had just had time to sort themselves out, and Jeff taken the helm from me, when a rogue wave hit *Tin Hau* on the starboard side. There was an alarming clap as a wall of water hit the wheelhouse. The aft deck spotlight was still on after the reefing, so I had a clear view of this wave as it washed over the cabin top ahead, also of the port handrails as they dipped into the clear green sea. Bodies tumbled on to the port side, a tangled mass of arms and legs. The wheel spun cruelly out of Jeff's hands, smashing one of them with violent force. By the time *Tin Hau* had righted herself and we had collected our wits, Jeff's injured hand had already swollen to the size of a small melon. He was very dazed and obviously in a great deal of pain. Jax and I got him down to the saloon and made him comfortable on the floor wedged in by some cushions where we knew he would be safe if he passed out. Jax dug into the freezer for all the ice she could find, which we packed in plastic and bound lightly round the injured hand. Jeff was still conscious, so we were able to administer some trauma tablets to reduce the swelling and relieve the pain. The swelling was far too severe for us to tell whether or not any bones were broken. Only time would tell.

Once the panic was over, we tried to work out exactly how far we had actually gone over. Usually *Tin Hau* sails at around twenty degrees off the vertical. The maximum angle of heel experienced previous to the rogue wave had been about forty degrees. David was prevailed upon to work it all out mathematically, and concluded we had heeled to about sixty degrees.

The wind direction which accompanied this onslaught was, for a while, reasonably favourable and we were being chased by the waves – a situation never before encountered. This led to the discovery of yet another problem. We had suddenly got a gushing fountain in the galley sink. It appeared we had placed it too low for these conditions. Jax gallantly mopped up the flood until I had worked out how to solve the problem. For immediate remedies, the simplest solutions are usually the best. We took off the drain hose at the sink end, stuffed a wooden bung in it, and clamped it to a point well above sea level. With the sink outlet blocked off we used a chuck-it method of disposal till a more permanent change could be made.

That night everyone was either too frightened or dispirited to want to go to their berths. We all preferred to find a space on the settee or floor in the galley or saloon, and spent the night together. There was a lot of lifting and dumping of the boat by the confused waves. At one point all the cassette tapes leapt over their fiddle bars and landed on the sleepers on the saloon side of the cabin. The rail height was almost half that of the cassettes standing on end, so the reader can work out how heavily the boat was dropping into the troughs. Furthermore, it was the coldest night we had yet had.

The following day, the sea was still very rough and the waves continued to break over *Tin Hau*. The sea was running too high for David to gain accurate sun sights. What he did get appeared to put us back sixty or seventy miles. In view of the continued bad weather that night, the fact that we were miles from any shipping lanes, and the exhausted state of the crew, David decided to put the not-under-command lights on, ordered a hearty meal for everyone, and then suggested we all had a night off and attempt to get twelve hours sleep.

That was the only time in all the years we sailed *Tin Hau* that we ever abandoned watch. In the circumstances, it was a very wise decision as the crew had had it rough for days. The respite refreshed everyone and greatly improved morale. By the time we emerged from our short hibernation period, the wind was still blowing hard (from the wrong direction of course) and the sea was lumpy and high. However, there were indications that a moderation could be expected, and we were all feeling better able to cope again. By then we had completed our second week at sea, covered 734 miles, and – though we had been mentally and physically battered – were prepared for more.

The third week started much better, with blue sky, rainbows, soft fluffy clouds and, later, plenty of sunshine. Ideal wind, too. We still had not reached the first week's target point and ahead of us was a place we were dreading: Walter's Shoals. This was a patch of relatively shallow water miles from anywhere, which was pin-pointed on the routeing chart as being the worst spot for a likely gale. For the first time on the voyage it was warm enough for everyone to divest themselves of their sea boots, and even to remove sweaters. All the exposed feet, looking like albino prunes, caused some amusement. The skipper had his first bucket bath of the trip. We all thought it was about time he did, but didn't like to say so. Trossy had remained with us, but we had been too absorbed in other things to notice. The best news was that Jeff's hand was going to be fine. I'd had a chance to give it a thorough examination once the swelling was reduced, and was very relieved to find nothing broken.

On 9th June we had a double celebration, passing the week one waypoint and our first time zone. The celebration took the form of a treat – Jax and I made chocolates. We catered for everyone's favourite which included cherries, almonds, peppermint cream, coffee cream and brandy praline. The following day was also worth noting in that we reached the thousand mile mark. The weather was sufficiently mild, and the wind gentle enough, for us to carry out some routine chores. A number of sail ties had come loose or fallen out, several parrels needed tying up again, and the snotters had become so chafed they needed turning end-for-end.

We passed the dreaded Walter's Shoals without incident. The gale never materialised. We did, however, nearly run over a dozing albatross. He paddled away at the last possible moment, panicked into a most ungainly takeoff. Albatrosses are so large they need to take off from the crest of a wave in order to get airborne.

12th June was notable because we made our best day's run. 147 miles from noon to noon, bringing our total to 1,305. The last couple of hours we were pushing it, though, sailing over-canvassed in order to make as big a 'score' as possible. Once the figure had been verified, we reefed to make the helm lighter. Even then we were making six and a half knots, at times feeling a bit out of control. By 4 p.m. on that day, it was evident we were set to go through another gale. We were recording gusts of up to sixty knots. We spent the night hove-to, and awoke to find the wind had died. We were able to raise all sail as soon as the crew had risen from their bunks.

We were by now far enough into our voyage for Jacqui and myself to do a stocktake of food supplies. Everything we had taken on in Port Elizabeth had been recorded, so it was possible to work out how much we had consumed. Perishables, like bread, were not expected to last the voyage and substitutes had been planned. All our quantities proved to be good except for sugar. I had obviously misjudged the amount of sugar six people would consume, and hadn't realised that Jean-Marc had an inordinately sweet tooth. He ladled sugar on to everything that didn't require tomato sauce (his other passion). Rationing had to be started at once, and the shortfall made good with the other sweeteners we carried.

By the time the domestic sorting had been completed, the wind was up once again. We were recording gusts of fifty-five knots. Everyone was getting heartily sick of the heavy weather conditions we had encountered. Barry was totally mesmerised by the waves. He spent a lot of time clinging to the handholds in the wheelhouse scaring himself (and others) witless. As often as not, he would provide the galley with a running commentary on the state of the waves. He had Jax and myself grabbing for handholds many a time while cooking – false alarms in reality, because *Tin Hau* would merely rise up the extra large waves in the same way she took all the others. Sometimes the professional side of Barry overcame his morbid fascination, and he would be strapped on to something on deck trying to capture, on his innumerable cameras, the sheer size of the waves. His most dramatic picture of the waves was taken from inside, as he cleverly framed them with the wheelhouse windows. I wondered what we would have been able to record with a video camera, and suspected that may have given us a more dramatic keepsake.

All our windspeeds were measured using a hand held anemometer at deck level. As I understand it, yachts with wind monitoring equipment at the masthead get a far more accurate picture of the true strength. Had we had such equipment fitted, our readings would probably have been twenty per cent higher. As far as measuring wave height is concerned, it is really a matter of judgement on the part of the crew. There was no equipment for measuring it on our boat. Our yardstick was the pilothouse roof, knowing its height was twelve feet above sea level. Figures and estimates varied. David was the only person who had had previous ocean sailing experience and therefore was possibly better able to give an accurate assessment. I do know the rest of us felt his figures were always on the low side, perhaps because he insisted on measuring what he called the 'significant wave height', an engineer's term meaning the average height of the highest one third of all waves. The highest he noted was five metres (sixteen feet). It is easy to see how such figures can be distorted and how the term 'tall stories' originated.

The fourth week started with a bump – quite literally. It was another of the many days we spent hove-to. We were following the established watch routine for this state; that is, just one person on watch while all the others tried to sleep, or at least to conserve strength. David and I were cabinised, he asleep and I about to get up. *Tin Hau* was being tossed about like a cat's toy. As I sat up on my berth, a wave hit the boat quite hard. The lurch was sufficient to throw me against the lee cloth, which tore free of its anchor point (later we changed to lee boards). Everything on the bed, including me, was unceremoniously dumped on the hatch in the cabin sole, with such force that the hatch broke and dropped on to the suspended flexible holding tank below. The ties slinging the tank snapped too, and the whole lot ended up in the bilge. David slept through it all and awoke to my indignant cries for help. The bedding which had gone down with me had got so tangled that I couldn't lift myself out of the bilge, and I was lying there like a turtle that had been turned on its back. No serious injury to life or limb, but more than a little damage to be repaired. Meanwhile, David and I had the 'hole-in-the-floor' to negotiate for a few days, until the weather had calmed sufficiently to make a new hatch.

During the heaviest of the weather, David did all the sextant work from inside the wheelhouse. Clipping harness lines from one handhold to the next gave him a sling into which he could lean while bracing his feet at the base of the bulkhead. It was an infinitely better method than struggling out on to the deck with that precious sextant, fastening himself securely, taking the sight and getting the sextant (and himself) covered in spray. All his navigation proved to be just as good from inside as out.

That gale in the middle of June was probably the most demoralising. We crossed longitude fifty several times, and apparently lost a lot of hard-won ground as well. More dead-eyes needed replacing and the sugar ration had to be decreased to three teaspoons per person per day! The crew were becoming almost mutinous in their belief that it was wrong to attempt to make our 'easting' so far south. We felt that the gales were more prevalent down there and that if we made some northward progress first we might find it easier to work our way east. David's original plan had been to go south to latitude thirty-five, there to pick up the prevailing westerlies, use them to take us east, then head north to catch the south east trades which would take us to Mauritius. The headwinds which bedevilled us at the outset had forced us into going further south than planned – almost to the Roaring Forties. We reasoned that it would do no harm to try and get back up towards latitude thirty, then try and make the three hundred miles of easting we still required. The arguments went round and round. David was adamant he was not going to head north till we had made those vital three hundred miles to the east. The crew felt frustrated because we thought it would take longer his way. Added to this, everyone was feeling cheated of the warmer climes they had been expecting. It was still very cold, being almost midwinter down there.

On the bright side, we had the birds providing endless hours of entertainment. Even better, the unusual experience of seeing a rainbow at night. It formed an almost complete circle around the moon and was as vivid as its daytime counterpart.

By 19th June we had covered 1,711 miles, but still needed three hundred more to the east. David took the decision to head more towards the north. Though not entirely sure it was the right thing to do, he was at least content to have made a decision on which we could act. Moreover he had to some extent mollified the crew.

Morale improved immediately, and was further strengthened by the appearance of a ship heading straight for us. We warmed the radar up, tuned in the VHF and took bearings on her. She appeared to be on a collision course with us. Later we concluded that ships altered course to investigate, after picking us up on their radar sets. David ordered the engine to be turned on and ticking over, in case we had to take avoiding action. At a distance of 3.3 miles she veered a little and the bearings confirmed she would pass on our port side. We were unable to raise her on the VHF until she was close enough for us to get her name. Communication was difficult but we hoped we had got off a message to family and friends who would be glad to know that we were safe. This was the first encounter we had ever had at sea. The *Formosa Glory* had created great excitement, and provided a talking point for hours thereafter. I had been baking caraway rolls for breakfast when the ship was sighted. They came to no harm in spite of being abandoned halfway – in fact they made a delicious addition to the lively breakfast which followed. In all the excitement, the engine exhaust valve was not shut properly, and this caused a problem when we later wanted to start the engine. Fortunately, there was no damage done and it was only a matter of emptying the water trap on the exhaust system. The wind died that night and we motored right through till dawn.

Sometime during the dark hours we were joined by a pilotfish. He was spotted the next morning swimming along about six inches ahead of the stem, making use of the forward thrust of the small bow wave we were creating. By then we were coasting along under sail in a very gentle breeze. It was fascinating sitting on the anchor cat just watching him surf along. His progress looked so effortless. Looking down over the aft bulwarks we could see right down to the keel. The water was the prettiest inky blue in the sunlight. The barnacles on the section of the stern not covered by antifoul paint – mere babes when we had set off – had grown considerably.

The light breeze faded into nothing, and David decided to get the engine on in the calm and attempt to reduce the one hundred and seventy miles of easting still needed. We saw more night-time rainbows – although not as distinctly coloured as the first. The clouds were becoming more and more like the ones David was expecting to see in the trades. In the early dawn they were tinted pink by the rising sun. Daybreak is an awe-inspiring time in the middle of the ocean. Colours are magnificent. The pilotfish had been joined by another and we christened them Cain and Abel. After some hours of motoring we stopped the engine to carry out some routine checks. While doing so, the boat drifted gently backwards, which confused Cain and Abel dreadfully. Next thing we knew, they had swum round to the stern and were guiding us, rudder first, back the way we had come. It took them a good half hour to catch up once we started motoring forward again.

The excess battery charging needed to be diverted, so we chose that day to make ice-cream. Altogether we made six litres. The power surge was absorbed by the extra hours of freezer time. Our ice-cream maker was the old-fashioned hand-churned sort. Each crew member had to churn for a minimum of ten minutes on each flavour, qualifying him or her for a share of that ice cream. The system worked well and it was a great treat.

The lull did not last long and we were soon back to the more familiar force sevens and eights. The seas grew rough again, though not as high as they had previously been. Initially this bout of heavy weather was adverse, but eventually it backed to the right direction for us. It had to be used to our advantage in spite of the fact that helming was heavier work than some of us could comfortably handle. On the plus side, David was pleased to see *Tin Hau* performing so well downwind in biggish seas. What a pity we were unable to log a full day of running – we might have bettered our 147 miles. As it was we made 111 miles, bringing our total to 1,921. Barry spotted the first flying fish (thereafter referred to as 'flish'), which had all except the helmsman out on deck scanning the sea for more. Though the wind moderated in the evening, it was still taking us where we wanted to go. Morale was improving as we began to sense victory. Skipper appeared for dinner dressed in a three-piece pinstripe suit, complete with yellow wellies, amusing us all till he entered the wheel-house. What an assault – he had dosed himself liberally with three different brands of aftershave!

My home-baking book was proving to be an absolute godsend. I had never had much success with yeast cookery before. Every recipe we tried from that book was good and we had no flops at all. The variety of bread rolls, loaves and yeast cakes we turned out was amazing.

Barry sighted the next ship during the forenoon watch. She was the *Yamatama Maru* bound for Texas with a cargo of oil from Borneo. Our first contact with the outside world for six days. This time we had a sighting of human beings as well. (The Taiwanese aboard the *Formosa Glory* had not shown themselves.) We were greeted with waves from the flying bridge and bon voyages over the VHF as well as a 'toot' salute.

More 'flish' were in evidence after the ship had disappeared from our sights. They are incredibly tiny, fly with rapid 'wing' movements, and travel relatively long distances skimming over the waves and swell before plopping back into the water and disappearing from sight. The noon sight confirmed that we had passed the 2,000 mile mark. Altogether a heady day. It was calculated that we should have entered the trade wind area, though there was still no sign of them. The wind was constantly shifting and gusting in nasty little squalls of rain. The swell gradually lengthened, but without significant wind. We had at last completed our easting and were set on a northerly course with only four hundred miles to go. Cain and Abel had deserted us and there was no sign of life on the miles and miles of empty sea; only *Tin Hau* and her motley crew.

Our first contact with our destination came when we picked up Plaisance aero beacon. Theoretically having a range of three hundred and sixty miles, I was chuffed to have heard it even though the signal was very weak. Though the conditions were far from ideal in sailing terms, they had improved in that we were marginally more comfortable. The seas were less frightening, the temperatures warmer, and our goal getting appreciably nearer.

David turned in early one evening, leaving Barry and myself to complete what, till then, had been an uneventful watch. All continued well – light wind and the odd rain squall – until our final hour. Suddenly we were hit by a severe squall driven by a strong wind. Barry, on the wheel at the time, lost control of his steering and somehow ended up one hundred and eighty degrees off course. We had far too much sail up for the strength of the gusts which had tried to flatten us. It had literally gone from force two to force six or seven in a matter of seconds – a phenomenon we encountered a number of times in the Indian Ocean. It was less problematic during the daytime, but there was no way of detecting the onslaught in the dark. We all got very wet trying to sort out the tangles caused by the blast and it took a while getting *Tin Hau* back on course. Barry was very dazed – he didn't really know what had happened at all.

After several such incidents we followed a policy of automatically shortening sail at nightfall, especially when we were short-handed. We did not lose a great deal in terms of distance covered and were better able to deal with the unexpected.

The wind turned adverse again and produced a choppy little sea. The freezer was shut down – partly because we had a bubble showing in the sight glass which oughtn't to have been there, partly because we had just about reached the end of our pre-cooked meals. Number Seven handled the steering for us and we were able to get on with various chores which had presented themselves.

We were gradually drawing closer to Mauritius. A glorious sunrise preceded the next favourable wind. We sighted yet another ship at noon. This time we had no problems making contact and I was delighted to speak to the captain of the *Brilliant Venture*. I put a request for Captain Anderson to send a radio message for us. He offered to go one better and send a ship's telegram giving our position and ETA at Port Louis, as well as a report that we were all well. This constituted a great kindness on his part and was greatly appreciated by ourselves. I learned later that this was the only communication which reached our family. The telegram was 'phoned through' to them and they were very relieved to hear that all was well, especially since they had reached the point of expecting a phone call from us from Mauritius.

We adopted a new policy then, and stuck to it throughout our cruising! Never give definite dates of arrival, and be as non-committal as possible. This not only avoided panic on the part of the family when we didn't show up, but also saved us worrying about their worrying. We did set ourselves targets for every voyage after the maiden one, and almost always made them within a day or two; but they were only targets to aim for. David always maintained that the most dangerous and undesirable condition at sea was having an appointment to be kept no matter what. We were at sea to be free.

Cain and Abel reappeared and were joined by a third, bigger, pilotfish. Barry dubbed the new arrival FBI. I never did find out why. We were also aware of more birds of the land variety; small birds with a piercing, almost shrieking, call, still unidentified years later.

The sugar was holding out – just – as were all our other provisions. My cigarette supply was running short though. Each crew member who smoked (there were four of us out of six) had been asked to take care of their own tobacco requirements; estimate their needs for five weeks and add two weeks for good measure. Jean-Marc had grossly underestimated his requirements and had run out of cigarettes at the end of the second week. Jeff and Barry both smoked pipes, though Barry occasionally had a cigarette or two as well and had allowed for this. Each crew member had a small stowage box in the wheelhouse, a place to keep small personal bits and pieces. Feeling sorry for Angel, Jeff had loaned him one of his spare pipes and Barry and he had clubbed together to give him a bit of tobacco. I had passed on two of my precious packets of ciggies. Jean-Marc kept his smoking paraphernalia in his stowage box – as did the rest of us, in ours. The only difference being that Jean-Marc also kept his sea soap there. When he finally ran out of the collected gifts of tobacco and we were unable to give him any more, he was collecting the tobacco left in the butts of our cigarettes, putting them in his box, and hoarding till he had enough to fill his pipe. The resultant smoking mixture was heavily tainted by the soap. We were all treated to the heavy mixture of pipe smoke laced with carbolic (or whatever sea soap contains). Ugh.

I was trying to get another fix on Plaisance aero beacon when I spotted our seventh ship – a decidedly odd-looking motor vessel. We thought it might be an inter-island coaster plying between La Réunion and Mauritius.

David estimated our position to be one hundred and twenty miles from Port Louis. We had had good winds for the previous eighteen hours, though still not ideal, direction-wise. Everyone was becoming quite hyped up; Barry running around doing 'personality pictures', Jean-Marc doing some fibreglass touch up work on his surfboard, Jacqui and myself getting our laundry up-to-date and washing hair and bodies and so on – all in preparation for arrival which we hoped was imminent.

There was a very exciting moment when David sighted the most enormous school of dolphins about to cross our bow. We estimated there were between one hundred and one hundred and fifty of them, travelling at about fifteen knots in a very determined way.

Barry and I spent endless hours climbing on and off the wheelhouse roof hoping to be the first to spot land and have the pleasure of calling 'Land ahoy'. A Mars bar had been promised to the lucky lookout. David had drawn two intersecting circles on the chart, one around Mauritius and one around Réunion (the latter having a larger ring because it was a higher island). The idea was that we should have been able to see each of the islands from within their respective circles, and if within the intersection zone ought to see both. It goes without saying that this only works in ideal conditions. We were unable to see either – not even at sunset, when we had calculated our best chance would be. Sod and Murphy, our constant invisible companions of the previous thirty-six days, decided the time had come to give us one more dose of their medicine before the voyage ended – one last night of nasty weather. Like Jeff earlier, Jax had the wheel snatched out of her hands when *Tin Hau* was struck by another of those sudden squalls, with almost the same result for her hand. After treating her and sending her off watch, I stepped in for her helming tricks but dozed while the others did theirs. I stayed on to do my own watch but was dismissed by David before we had completed the full four hours. We still had not seen land and I went to bed feeling thoroughly disgruntled.

On 30th June, David crept into our cabin at six thirty and said that land was visible. Hardly pausing to drag on my clothes, I raced up the companionway and stared at... nothing. The land was totally obscured by misty drizzle and low cloud.

By eight o'clock, at the change of watch, a clearer picture was emerging. Dramatic mountain peaks were offering their profiles to our view. David and Jeff were having quite a job deciding which peak was which in relation to the Pilot information we had. This was an essential fact they had to establish in order to know exactly how far up or down the coast we were in relation to Port Louis. We had got all that way with no navigation problems at all and suddenly it was a problem knowing where we were. As we closed with the shore, however, more and more details became available to help, and eventually David was able to pinpoint our position exactly.

The crew were completely entranced. Seeing land again was the best prize anyone could have dreamed up for us after our thirty-seven day battle with the elements. The vision before us of a lighthouse and lower buildings centred on large tracts of cultivated land. A strong smell of molasses emanated from burning sugar cane in fields surrounding factories. The beautiful mauve mountain peaks provided a stark contrast to the gentler sloping green hills. It was almost too much to absorb.

We were still one and a half hours away from the end of our voyage, but we were determined to have everything ready for that great moment of arrival and at the same time were determined to miss nothing of the approach. We hoisted our 'Q' flag, and the very colourful Mauritius courtesy flag, as well as breaking out the Red Ensign. For good measure we added the burgee of the Junk Rig Association and our own 'house' flag.

We discovered, to our surprise, that a VHF facility had been introduced at Port Louis since our Pilot Book had been written. This was useful as we were able to receive courteous directions on where to berth and how to go about clearing in. Picking our way through the maze of buoyed and anchored trawlers was no problem. Neither was finding the customs quay and the berth we had been instructed to go for. In among the fishing boats we found what we were looking for, and tied up alongside a Swiss boat called *Bubblehull*.

Within two hours we had gone through all the clearance procedures and were free to go ashore. *Tin Hau* had completed her maiden voyage. Not without problems, it's true, but we had all made it more or less intact, with a third of our water and food and half of our diesel unused.

There is absolutely no way one can adequately describe the minute details or the see-sawing of emotions one feels when taking part in an enterprise of this kind. David had been through similar sailing experiences before. For the rest of us it was all totally new. We each coped with what came our way in our own manner. Each had his or her private fears and joys and benefited from the experience in one way or another. We were relatively free of the personality clashes so often associated with this type of journey – partly because we elected to take people we already knew well and trusted. There were a few small resentments and a few disagreements. But looking back they seem so small and insignificant in the greater scheme of things.

We owe a debt of gratitude to Jean-Marc Gabriel for being willing to slot into the sixth berth at the last minute. His practical skills were valuable so many times. His physical strength and stamina took a lot of beating.

Our intrepid 'pioneer of the last frontier', Barry, had never set foot on a sailing boat before but cast his lot in with ours for the duration – whatever it might yield. His unflagging enthusiasm for getting the most out of each new experience was very moving. He gave us so much in the way of entertainment as well as a magnificent treasure trove of pictures which span the life of *Tin Hau* from birth to the loss of her maidenhood.

Jax, that little girl who joined us for the adventure of a lifetime and who returned to her parents a much matured young woman, proved her worth beyond anyone's expectations. She was always cheerful, even though she must have been dreadfully homesick at times and terrified at others. Jacqui is that rarity – a natural at the helm of the boat. She was willing to take on any job to ensure the smooth running of her watch, and the same for the efficient running of the ship. When the rest of the crew had to leave us to return to their 'other' lives, Jax remained with us for another few months. I'm glad she could and did stay on to enjoy *Tin Hau* in pleasanter circumstances; it was a just reward for her determination and sheer hard work during the trying times.

No words can express what it meant to have Jeff, our far too modest watch leader and Skipper's right hand, with us. He offered patient support in all things, right from the earliest planning stages. *Knot Often* was the most admired dinghy wherever she went, and we had loads of fun in her. We could never have done as good a job of building her as he did. Jeff's dry sense of humour and wonderful enjoyment of ridiculous things gave us endless pleasure and helped to keep things in proportion when so often they may have grown too much to bear. We still owe you an 'easy' sail on *Tin Hau*, Jeff.

A skipper's job is never an easy one. David's was no simpler for having a raw crew and untried ship to command. He was surely the most patient skipper in the Indian Ocean, and kept us all together without a cross word. We were all full of admiration for his navigation skills (rare in these days of Satnav), which were spot on.

As for myself? Well, I survived to tell this tale and more...

The authors with the completed model-posing for
the local press in the hangar
Photographer Barry Lamprecht

Moving from hangar to hangar (February 28th, 1985)

The final stages of fitting out

Moving out of the hangar in readiness for the launch (22nd February, 1986)
Photographer Barry Lamprecht

Transportation across town
Photographer Barry Lamprecht

Crossing the railway lines
Photographer Barry Lamprecht

The launch (10th March, 1986)
Photographer Barry Lamprecht

First time out of Port Elizabeth harbour (31st March, 1986)
Photographer Barry Lamprecht

Trials
Photographer Barry Lamprecht

David at the top of the main mast
Photographer Barry Lamprecht

Tin Hau under full sail-South Africa

Photographer Barry Lamprecht

The maiden voyage crew (except Jean Marc)
Clockwise from left: Jax, Jeff, Barry, Lynda & David
Photographer Lynne Wilmot

Maiden voyage-reefed for strong winds
Photographer Barry Lamprecht

At anchor in Mauritius-Jeff sailing *Knot Often*

Anchored off Agelega-islanders beaching the fishing boat

Agalega children on the jetty

Royal Marines visiting Salomon Atoll

Paradise

Sri Lankan fisherman

PART THREE
Indian Ocean Islands

Lynda Chidell

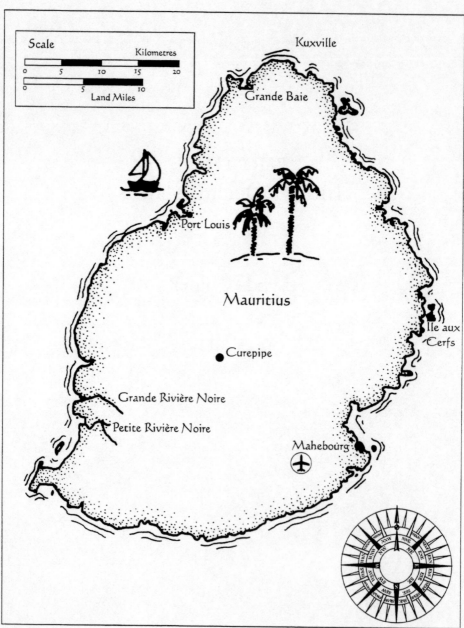

Map 3: Mauritius

1. Land of the Dodo

We had a total of four and a half months in Mauritius – just long enough to get a feel for the island and its very varied people. It was a colourful country in every sense of the word. The tropical vegetation was not just the gold and green associated with swaying palm trees, but a whole rainbow of bougain-villaea hues from the palest lemon to vivid reds and purples. So many of the plants growing wild and in gardens were of varieties seen by the rest of the world only in hot houses and botanical gardens. The pride of all flowers in Mauritius was the wonderful anthurium, the beautiful waxy lily-like flower grown in shades of pink, orange and red.

The population of the island was no less colourful, drawing, as it did, from four ethnic groups – French/English Europeans (generally ex-colonists), Indians (mostly ex-slaves or indentured labourers from the sugar plantations), Africans (mostly ex-slaves) and Chinese (immigrants over the last century). The year before our arrival the population had passed the one million mark. So many people occupying such a small area of land (thirty-five miles by twenty miles) should be applauded for their example on how easy it is for diverse groups to co-exist in relative harmony. Each follow their own cultural traditions and religions, giving rise to a number of festivals and holidays, many of them celebrated publicly in the streets of the villages and towns. We witnessed the Festival of Lights (Divalee), but regret we missed the Chinese dragon festival, where homage is paid to Tin Hau. Jax was invited to an Indian wedding – a great honour for her, as it was a traditional wedding to which tourists would not usually be invited.

During our stay we managed to get to most parts of the island. We went to many places aboard the boat, but started inland explorations with a hired Mini-Moke. That did not last long as driving around was a nightmarish experience. Driver behaviour was definitely French in flavour, although people drove on the left side of the road. Roads were narrow, often dirt tracks. Cyclists and pedestrians abounded, not to mention household pets and next week's bacon. Animals were a continual hazard, and if we were not wide awake we were likely to get a thorough soaking from the overhead irrigation systems adorning the cane fields. The fields occupied every available inch of arable land on the island. Sugar was the main export, with textiles close behind.

We visited various places with *Tin Hau*. Cap Malhereux/Kuxville was the northernmost place where we anchored. We dropped our hook just off the private beach belonging to the small holiday complex owned and run by a charming German couple, Fritz and Elke Kux. They invited us to take *Tin Hau* into their anchorage; it was probably the largest boat ever to have done so. We measured 0.9 metres on the echo sounder and knew that we touched at 0.8 metres (add 0.8 metres for the true depth). We must have scraped over the reef at high tide. It was a fairly unsheltered anchorage and the only protection was provided by the surrounding reef. It was there that Mark and Tandy had their first taste of coral reef diving and tropical fish viewing.

Grande Baie, the north-western end of Mauritius, was our base for the duration of our stay. It is a large enclosed bay, well protected from the wind and sea, and our choice of 'cyclone hole' should we have needed one. Moreover there were no mooring charges or regulations. Grande Baie was built up on all sides, though not so one felt it had in any way been spoilt by development. The entire village of Grande Baie consisted of a main road which wound round the bay, with a few small branch roads and little else. Buildings were more or less all on the landward side of the road, leaving the beach with palms and casuarinas clear down to the water. The village was well endowed with restaurants, including three Chinese, 'La Jonque' (how apt), 'La Pagode' and 'La Charette'. All kinds of 'noddles' were listed on the menu including 'shrink fried' ones, presumably meant to be shrimp fried noodles. A steakhouse owned by Nobby someone-or-other, 'Phil's Pub' offering European-style pub grub, and two excellent French restaurants, 'Le Grillon' and 'La Perle Noire'. At one time or other we tried them all (they were not expensive), and found each to be good.

Grande Baie had a notorious roll. Boats at anchor were constantly moving to the rhythm of the sea. Even when the ocean beyond the reef appeared calm, there would be a gentle rocking to and fro.

Sound is greatly amplified when it passes across the water and this was something we experienced in no small way in Mauritius. During one of our spells in Grande Baie the local elections were being held. The candidates drove around from midday until mid-evening, exhorting the local populace to vote for them, daily for two weeks. We felt very uncomfortable having to listen to this electronically amplified racket, doubled in volume, passing across the water. We were also bombarded by what we took to be an eisteddfod taking place in the nearby Hindu temple. Next door to this was the Moslem mosque (complete with minaret and muezzin calling the faithful to prayer at the prescribed hours every day). The somewhat quieter Catholic church was also nearby.

There were a few tourist hotels including probably the best on the island. Grande Baie was definitely the place for visiting yachts to head once formalities had been completed at Port Louis. It was a must for all those boats on the 'coconut run' (circumnavigators doing the Australia-South Africa-Panama-Pacific route). Réunion islanders with sailboats tripped across for weekends and holidays. And there were South Africans doing a three to six month stint of island hopping. The lovely yacht club in Grande Baie opened its doors to all who wished to join as temporary members. On Bastille Day the French contingent arrived from Réunion, rafted up their boats and proceeded to throw the most magnificent party for yachtsmen and yachtswomen from all over the world. We met and made friends with so many people during our stay – a number of them transients like ourselves, but others who lived and worked on that lovely island.

Port Louis, the capital of Mauritius, was probably the scruffiest and smelliest town I ever had the doubtful pleasure of visiting. If one could just hold one's nose long enough to get from the harbour to the up-town area, then it was a fascinating and rewarding place to explore. Like most capital cities, it was sectioned into distinct areas with differing functions. Where we found one 'quincaillerie', we would find a whole host. In Port Louis, they occupied a whole street a stone's throw from Chinatown. The latter consisted of numerous little stores – all with the same jumble of brightly coloured plastic whatnots vying for one's attention with pyramids of equally interesting looking jars, tins, packets and boxes filled with curious cure-alls of the traditional Chinese medicinal kind. All the buildings housing these were once so beautiful – chalet style, with steep pitched roofs of timber shingle and pretty shutters at the windows. When we saw them, the shutters hung from rusty, broken hinges and little paint remained on the woodwork. All had seen better days. Of the two or three floors, the upper ones were used as homes or gambling dens. At night the click and clack of Mah Jongh tiles and poker chips formed part of the background buzz of the city.

All government buildings and offices were painted a cool grey. Government House was no exception. Standing in the square beneath this once imposing building, flanked by two magnificent 'flamboyante' trees, was a statue of Queen Victoria. What amused (or should I say bemused) us was the attached plaque, which described the late lamented as 'Our much regretted Queen'. We still have not found out if it was her association with Mauritius or her death which was much regretted...

You may get a negative impression of Port Louis if I continue in this vein. There was a great deal to be enjoyed and admired about the place; for example, the natural history section of the museum, and the Merchant Navy Club, which offered hospitality to visiting yachtsfolk – a relaxing, cool refuge in a steamy town.

Rivière Noire is a small village at the south-western end of the island. It is shown on the map as two distinct sections, Petite and Grande – we tried the former, but chickened out as the depth sounder showed less and less water under our keel. We mainly visited the Grande section when we went down south. It is a large indentation in the land mass, with high hills giving good protection from all directions except to seaward. There is no reef protection. In the unlikely event of the wind coming off the sea, it was advisable to get out. It was utterly peaceful – especially after the bustle of Port Louis – and was the only place in Mauritius where we were aware of land birds. Unrestricted views of the sun setting over the sea were marvellous. From there, too, many of the tourist 'musts' were much more accessible. We made forays inland to Cassela Bird Park – magical – and La Vanille Crocodile and Monkey Farm. We travelled up the Black River Gorge to the falls (written about by Gerald Durrell in *Golden Bats and Pink Pigeons*), and tried to get to Chamarel to see the coloured sands. Black River was the centre of the big game fishing industry. Marlin of gigantic proportions were regularly caught from boats operating out of the area, then taken back for processing in the smoking factory. Smoked marlin was a delicacy on the island.

Some of our readers will be wondering how we kept ourselves occupied. Our days became less routine than for years, and no attention was paid to clocks or calendars. We kept an ongoing list of jobs which needed doing on board and each of us had daily chores to get through. Other than working on these, we spent most of our time getting to know the land and its people, and trying out new and unusual local foodstuffs.

We also spent time reading about the history of Mauritius and generally absorbing the atmosphere, in preparation for what might be the start of some charter work.

Even though the area we had originally planned to do charter work was Greece, we wondered if perhaps we had already reached the ideal spot. Calmish seas (on the west coast, at least). Good sailing winds. Sunshine. Coral reefs and interesting bays, all close to a perfect base, Grande Baie. Moreover there were hundreds of holiday-makers keen to spend some of their time afloat, especially on an unusual looking boat. We thought we should try day-chartering instead of our initial plan of having guests on board for periods of a week or more. With *Tin Hau's* large amount of deck space, day chartering would work well. So why should we go any further?

We started making discreet enquiries about the regulations. David did all the ground and leg work on this, and spent hours to-ing and fro-ing between the boat and the official departments twelve miles away in Port Louis. He was assured, at the highest government level, that chartering was 'no problem' (the stock phrase for everything in Mauritius – even printed on souvenir tee shirts). He was guided by the Minister of Tourism into the maze of officialdom he had to negotiate in order to legalise our intentions. We duly set out to comply with all the requirements, which seemed quite reasonable. The first step was a survey by the Mauritius marine authority – quickly accomplished, and *Tin Hau* was certified as having passed muster at the scrutiny. The other two requirements were a work permit and a residence permit.

At this stage in the proceedings we were approached by the owner/skipper of one of the charter boats operating in Grande Baie. He asked if we would be prepared to consider a link-up with his operation. We had been very impressed by his methods – or what we could see of them – and of the three extant charter companies operating out of Grande Baie, his was by far the best. We agreed, after a great deal of discussion, to go into an association with him and his wife. Desmond and Terry Cohen had started their business with *Hummingbird*, a sleek modern yacht. They had reached a point where they had more guests than they could handle and needed a second string to their bow. As they had many repeat guests they were happy at the idea of being able to offer a different kind of sail as part of their package. They had cornered the upmarket end of the trade and Desmond's marketing strategy had secured their future for some time.

Their idea was to retain us for a given number of day charters per month at a fixed rate, and any extra days were to be paid on a fee-per-charter basis. Des and Terry would see to all the catering for both boats at their shore base as well as looking after all the administration work. All that and heaven too... Yes, well, it did seem too good to be true. All we needed to set the whole thing in motion were two bits of paper. David made numerous visits, wrote endless letters and made lots of phone calls to try to speed things up so we could start work in November. Nothing seemed to help. We had endless visits from officials from this and that department (complete with uncles and aunts); a veritable stream of visits from magistrates and police officers, leading to impromptu tea parties aboard *Tin Hau*.

During this time we had Margaret over for a visit from the UK, and between the official visits we were able to do some sightseeing with her. We also introduced her to the wonders of snorkelling on coral reefs.

Just before she left us at the end of October, we received a bombshell of a letter, a reply to our months of hard endeavour:

> IP 111/86-1 Passport and Immigration Office,
> Police Headquarters,
> Port Louis,
> Mauritius.
> 29th October, 1986
>
> Sir,
>
> I am directed to inform you that your application for a residence permit has <u>not</u> been approved.
>
> You and Mrs Lynda Elizabeth Chidell should leave Mauritius forthwith.
>
> I am,
>
> Sir,
> Your Obedient Servant
>
> Passport and Immigration Officer
>
> Mr. David Wallace Michael Chidell,
> c/o Yacht Tin Hau,
> Grand Baie Yacht Club,
> GRAND BAY

The signature was illegible, but the letterhead looked official enough. We had had our answer. Not the one we had wanted or were expecting – in fact it was all totally unfathomable – but at least someone somewhere had given a firm instruction.

With the onset of the cyclone season imminent we had to make a vitally important decision. Should we stay and fight the decision? If so, what would we then do if our appeal failed? We didn't want to set off to sea knowing that we might have to contend with a cyclone. Or should we leave within the next few days before there was any possibility of a cyclone, just the two of us, towards a very uncertain but, perhaps, exciting future?

Our immediate decision was to enjoy the three remaining days of Margaret's stay and then sort out our problems in ('no problem') Mauritius.

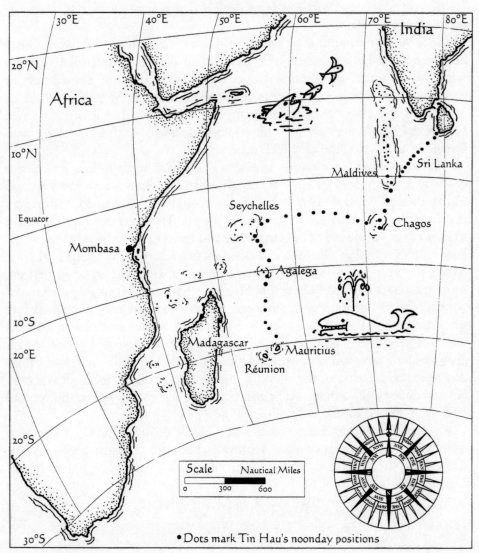

Map 4: Mauritius to Sri Lanka

By this time, too, we had lost Jacqui, who had returned home to start her university education.

Once we were on our own again, we made up our minds. We would head northwards to the Seychelles. The prospect of one thousand miles of trade wind sailing across an ocean was appealing. David had had enough of his endless trips to Port Louis and ceaseless interrogations at the police station (at one stage he saw a piece of paper stating that 'D.W.M. Chidell is not wanted by Interpol'). Although we were bitterly disappointed not to be working with Desmond and Terry, the time had come to leave.

Our most urgent task was to provision the boat. This would have to be for one year, as we had no idea of what lay ahead and no time to find out. Des and Terry, though devastated by our ill-fortune (and theirs), helped us through that hectic run-around in every way they could. They accompanied us down to Port Louis on the eve of our departure and spent the evening with us at the Merchant Navy Club. We all had a fairly shrewd idea of why things had gone wrong but no proof to back those suspicions. We strongly suspected that the Immigration Office had been given false information about us by persons not wanting the competition of another charter boat in Grande Baie. Perhaps the signature on the letter was not even that of a bona fide government official? Desmond and Terry worked at finding out the true reasons for our abrupt dismissal long after our departure, and though they had even stronger feelings that our ideas were right, they never did gain any conclusive proof. It was very sad saying farewell to them – they had become such good friends, and we had built such dreams together...

Another dream we had to shatter as a result of our summary expulsion from Mauritius was that of Tony visiting us there for Christmas. However it was not too late for him to reschedule his flight and change it for one to Mahé, in the Seychelles.

2. Mauritius to Seychelles

The day set for our departure dawned clear and calm, with hardly a breath of wind. We cleared Port Louis at 10 a.m. and ghosted out of the port to make our way northwards. Our plan was to wave a final farewell to *Hummingbird* as she entered Balaclava Bay on a lunchtime charter. We made it to the rendez-vous and cut the dragon's tail in front of the assembled guests aboard *Hummingbird*. Having performed this ritual, we set sail for the distant

LOG BOOK OF THE TIN HAU   BOUND FROM MAURITIUS TO AGALEGA   ON TUESDAY NOV. 18 - 1986 - DAY 7

TIME	LOG	ON WATCH (HELM / LOOK-OUT)	COMP. COURSE REQ (TO STEER (LOG) / MADE GOOD)	COURSE STEERED (TRUE / MAG)	ALLOWANCES (COMP VARN / DEV / LEE-WAY)	ESTIMATED TIDAL STREAM (SET / RATE)	WIND (DIR / FORCE)	SEA	BAROMETER (mB) (READING-MAG / TEND-ENCY)	TEMP (AIR °C / SEA °C)	CLOUD COVER	HUM & VIS-IBIL-ITY	REMARKS
0000	452	N°7 / D	025	025 / 025	12°W 2°W / 5°		ESE 3-4	3/4 Mod	1013 ↑	23	⊕	82 G	Mrs Birthday. No postman.
0300	406	N°7 / L	025	020			ESE 3-4	3/4 Mod	1011 ↑	24	⊕	82 G	Happy Birthday Skip !!
0500	477	N°7 / D	025	025 / 045			ESE 3-4						0500 Set No.7 closehauled so as to calculate moon + star sights. Speed reduced 5.5
0600	481	N°7 / D	025	040			ESE 3	3/4 Mod	1012 ↑	24	⊕	81 G	3.5 Knots. 025 C → 045 C
													Position at 0500 11°54'S 56°14'E. Course to steer for south point of Agalega = 017T or 031C (without leeway) or 045C (with leeway and allowing for possible current). presently doing 3.8 knots closehauled 045C OK. Est. Log reading Agalega 567
0900	491	N°7 / L	045	040			E 2/3 M		1015 →	25	⊕	73 VG	
1200	501	N°7 / L	045	041			E 2/3 M		1015 →	25	⊕	72 VG	1300 - sighted whales (3 at least) ½m off stbd bow
1500	510	N°7 / L	045	040			E 3 M		1011 ↑	24	⊕	84 VG	
1800	520	N°7 / D	055	050	12°W 2°W 10°W	2 Kn?	ESE 3	3/4 mod	1011 ↑	24	⊕	84 G	Afternoon sunsight shows strong westerly current. Land/all Agalega tomorrow possible. not feasible?
2000	526	N°7 / L	055	050			ESE 3/4 M		1012 ↑	23	⊕	88 G	
2200	534	N°7 / D	055	060			ESE 4 Mod		1012 ↑	23			SIGNATURE OF SKIPPER ....

POSITION : NOON POS. LAT. 11°40'S LONG. 56°23'E LONG LOG 106 M. DAYS DISTANCE LOG 106 M. DAYS DISTANCE ACTUAL 109 M. DAY'S AV. SPEED (ACTUAL) 4-5 Kn.

DIESEL : TANK READING - PORT 350 L (END OF DAY) STANDARD 360 L .... DIESEL CONSUMED DURING DAY ... NIL ..... ENGINE RUNNING HOURS DURING DAY ... NIL ..... DAILY RATE OF CONSUMPTION L/H ... NIL

WATER : TANKS FULL V/S L/P V/S ..... TANKS EMPTY ... NIL ..... TANKS IN USE ... V/P ..... TOTAL ENGINE RUNNING HOURS 225.07

Figure 14: Ship's Log (sample page)

Seychelles with the sounds of hand clapping, cheers and *Hummingbird's* foghorn fading astern. We kept radio contact with them till the last possible moment by which time it was dusk and we were only just out of sight of land.

We had very light winds for the first few days but all the wind was from a direction which made it possible for Number Seven to do the steering for us. The days were warm and sunny and we were able to get an all-over tan. At midday the sun was almost directly overhead, and it was during this passage that David excitedly announced that the midday sun was now in the southern sky – the familiar position for anyone used to living in the northern hemisphere. The evenings generally brought squally showers but rarely anything too heavy to handle. We had a few small islands and shoals to avoid on our way, but also one group where we hoped to stop. We never did see either of those we had to miss – good navigation on the skipper's part. David celebrated his thirty-fourth birthday at sea. I had had no opportunity to find a gift for him before our departure, and what money there was in my purse was spent on last minute extras for the voyage. However, I did manage to concoct a present and a party of sorts, and he loyally said it was the best birthday ever. The following day, a week out from Port Louis, we were due to sight and put into the Agalega islands.

I was hit, during the course of the midnight watch, by a severe squall for which I required David's help, as the helm was too heavy for me to hold in those conditions. We had too much sail up. Visibility had dropped to a minimum and the squall gave every sign of turning into a mini-gale. We shortened sail, which helped a bit with the steering, but it was obvious that we could be in for a spell of very rough weather and navigation was going to be difficult with the reduced visibility. The proximity of the islands of Agalega was now becoming a matter of some concern. We had little way of telling how close they were and could not risk running up on them unawares. David did manage to get a dawn sextant sight of the bright southern star, Canopus, together with the moon, at 4.45 a.m. This made our position fifteen miles south-south-west of the southern island of Agalega. Since the wind was from the east, now at a strength of force seven to eight, David decided we should harden up as much as possible. He did not want to end up directly downwind of the Agalega islands and therefore unable to reach them. Our new course was north-north-east and our speed was reduced to two and a half to three knots. He insisted we had to keep going, keep a good lookout, and hopefully we should soon see land. Failing this he would try to take a sight of the sun to determine our position more accurately.

By half past eight we had still seen nothing. David was virtually dead on his feet and I was exhausted. The wind had built up quite a steep sea and both of us were far too tired to cope. The decision was made to heave-to. We got everything battened down, re-lashed the anchor (which had slipped slightly in its cradle of rope), put the storm covers over the vents to stop the deluge of spray finding its way down below and snuggled ourselves in to sit out the weather. David went below to sleep and I set the timer in the wheelhouse and dozed under a duvet on the settee there. At half past eleven the sun threatened to show its shape through the clouds for half a minute. I shook David out of his sleep and he stumbled out on to the deck with his sextant to take a reading. Twenty minutes later he had drawn a position line on the chart which put us beyond the islands, to the north of them. What a disappointment! It seemed we were not destined to stop at Agalega after all.

I continued with my pilothouse watch. Every time the timer rang I roused myself to do a radar and visual sweep of the horizon. I kept watch like this till half past two when I went down below to get something to eat. The last of the Mauritian pineapples went down well. David surfaced around then and we both went back up to the wheelhouse.

At around half past three I spotted a smudge on the horizon off the port bow. At least I thought I did – I guess I thought I was seeing things as there should have been nothing visible in that direction at all. David climbed up on to the wheelhouse roof with the binoculars to get a better view. He confirmed that I had indeed spotted land. It could only be Agalega which we had thought was behind us! (David re-worked his sun-sight some days later and found that because of his tiredness he had made an arithmetical error that had resulted in our position line being drawn wrongly.) A radar check still gave no indication of land though, in spite of the fact that it was only five miles to the north of us – as we were about to verify. Our first radar from Mars really was useless, although the repairs we carried out in Sri Lanka did improve it slightly.

Had we time to make landfall before darkness fell? Never has a boat so quickly started sailing again. We didn't waste time getting up more sail, just re-set them to get moving. We rushed past the southern tip of South Island and gratefully entered the calmer waters in the lee of the land. The only likely looking anchorage was at the north-western tip of North Island, twelve miles away. Could we get that far in less than two hours? The palm trees raced by two hundred metres to starboard of us, giving us a wonderful sensation of speed, as we did our best to beat the approaching dusk. Later, we both agreed it was one of the most exciting sails we ever had on *Tin Hau*.

We made it to the point where we were able to see the anchorage by the crumbling jetty in the fast fading light. We continued to sail as hard as we could, but by the time we had lined our compass and *Tin Hau* up for the entry, the jetty was no longer visible. A vehicle had been brought to the water's edge and a torch was being waved about in the dark. Supposedly this was to assist us, but it gave no indication of how close to the shore we really were. David had got the anchor ready to drop. All sail was down and temporarily stowed and we moved forward slowly under motor alone. We had just enough way on to control her against the heavy rolling swell. The radar proved to be of some value here as we were able to pick out various details on shore and work out just how far off we were.

The positioning of the anchor at this spot was crucial. Too far in we could have gone aground, yet only one hundred metres offshore the water was hundreds of metres deep. The chart showed a narrow platform of seabed suitable for dropping the hook. Our echo sounder was not being very helpful. It was hard to read accurately in the dark, so David was casting a lead line to determine the depths. It took several tries to get the anchor to hold. After each failed attempt David had to wind in the full seventy metre length of anchor chain, dangling vertically below, by hand, as we drifted out into rougher waters. Eventually we were satisfied that we had got it down reasonably securely. Once settled we had a quick drink and snack supper before hitting the berth for a really good sleep. At least I went to bed. David stayed in the wheelhouse, the echo sounder shallow depth alarm sounding every time a fish swam beneath the transducer. He was worried about the strong currents which ran parallel to the shore. He told me afterwards that these changed in direction half way through the night. At one point, he said, he could almost have stepped out on to the beach, by then visible in the moonlight.

When making ocean passages, we always had the dinghies well stowed and covered (at least until Cyprus, where we made many changes to the stowage arrangements). In this mode, though the main dinghy was on davits, it took quite some time to get it all unpacked for launching. We had, therefore, to decide if a visit to the islands was going to be worth the effort. Our main reason for the stop was to get a bit of rest. We watched the activities on the shore for a while – there was a good sized cluster of people assembling on the beach. Eventually we realised they were preparing to launch a boat. Logs were rolled into position on the steeply shelving sands and a boat was run out over these. Several people got into the boat and it was launched by the rest of the men on the land. The boat drew alongside *Tin Hau* and permission was requested for two of the men to board. We were asked who we were and what we wanted. We explained that we merely wanted to have a break from sailing, but if an opportunity presented itself for us to visit the island(s) then we would like to do that too.

Agalega is a dependency of Mauritius, and it is forbidden to land on any of the outlying islands without a permit obtained from the Government. The senior official on Agalega was the head of the police unit stationed there. It was he who had come out to the boat to meet us. Sergeant Bhurton suggested that as 'the lady is not well', he could obtain permission – by radio – for us to land. I started to contradict him – then bit my tongue as I realised he was looking for a reason for us to be allowed to stay. The boat then left us so that the officer could go and make his request.

Permission was obtained and we were granted a period of forty-eight hours on the island. Sergeant Bhurton came out again to stamp our passports and officially welcome us to the islands. When the fishermen who had brought him out to the boat returned to collect him, they collected us too. They had, all the while he was aboard *Tin Hau*, been fishing off the surrounding reef. As soon as we had stepped ashore and they had landed their catch, we were handed the largest croissant (a large red fish with lilac spots and a crescent tail) for our supper that night. We were introduced to two young islanders from the village of St James who were instructed to take us to visit the shrine of Sacré Coeur, and then for a long beach walk.

On our return we cut inland through the coconut groves, where one of the lads shinned up a palm and brought down a couple of king coconuts. These were quickly and skilfully opened and we were handed one each to drink. The nut was then split and we were given pieces of the outer shell to use as spoons to scoop out the jelly-like flesh of the fruit. Many people do not know that the coconut they see on supermarket shelves is nothing like the nut fresh off the palm tree. A 'drinking' coconut is a very young form of the fruit, with a much more succulent flesh and considerably richer milk than the harder, drier version of the matured fruit. The nut on the tree is a larger item altogether, still bearing its green or golden green outer skin, which is very smooth. The pointed end of this nut is shaved off with a machete to reveal the fibrous interior – at this stage white – surrounding the inner nut which we usually call the coconut. When the kernel is visible, the machete is again used to lop off a tiny bit of the inner shell. The coconut is then ready for drinking.

By the time we got back to St James, the manager of North Island was waiting with a jeep to take us on a guided tour. His main aim was to take us to view the newly constructed airstrip. It had been built some time before but had never been used. The airstrip existed for emergency and strategic purposes. There was no tourism and certainly no plans for any in the future.

The total population on the two islands was three hundred and fifty in 1986; sixty per cent of these being juveniles. There were around one hundred labourers and the rest of the adult population were either wives or administration personnel. The main occupation was centred around copra and coconut oil extraction. Their only contact with the outside world was the ship which called on average once a year, and a radio link with the Seychelles and Mauritius. All their provisions would arrive on that ship and be off-loaded by small boats on to the jetty in our anchorage. There was no money on the island. All the provisions went to the government store, from where they would be drawn by the islanders on a book system. Earnings by the Illois would be credited to the store in each islander's name, then purchases would be offset against these. If, at the end of a contract, an islander was to choose to return to Mauritius, he would be paid any money owing to him then. Electricity was provided on each island, between nightfall and 10 p.m. only, by two large generators. Water from wells was used for washing, and drinking water was obtained from rain catchment. Accommodation was in the form of shanty type houses constructed of corrugated iron sheeting. These would blow down every time a cyclone hit the islands, and the sheeting would be collected after the storms to rebuild the homes. The islanders were natives in the sense that many of them had lived on the islands for several generations – descendants of old slave stock, mainly African. The administrators were mostly Mauritian. Some of the Illois were repatriates from Chagos, unable to settle in Mauritius when the Chagos archipelago was ceded to Britain at the time of Mauritian independence.

It poured with rain in the morning of our second day. Robin Bhurton paced the shore for ages before coming out to fetch us. He brought the island's Meteorological Officer with him to meet David. When the fishermen came back to take us ashore, they brought us yet another whopping great fish (this time a rock cod) for our dinner that night. Once ashore, Robin took us to the island's 'capital', Vingt-cinq, so called in memory of the twenty-five strokes which used to be administered, in that spot, as punishment to slaves for their misdemeanours.

We were shown over the remains of the police headquarters – they had been devastated by a cyclone the previous year. Being brick built, they were not so readily replaced as the shack dwellings. We met the duty officers who were playing a game of dominoes in the canteen. In the whole history of the islands, no one had ever spent a night in the cells – in fact no one had ever been locked up at all. The authorities were justifiably proud of this record of crimelessness. The police cells were put to good use as stores for salted fish and octopus, as well as providing a room for stretching and drying the shark-skins for sega drums.

From the police station we were driven to La Pointe at the southern end of the island so we could look across towards South Island. This is accessible by jeep across the sand bar at very low tides. After a wander around that end of the island we were returned to St James and the care of the Aglae family: Jean-Claude, Linda and their three children. Jean-Claude was a very talented craftsman (a welder by trade), working as a contract labourer on Agalega as there was no work for him on Mauritius. In his spare time he fashioned all sorts of wonderful things from coconut shells and found objects washed up on the shore. A modern display case in a corner of their home was full of models made by him. Each had been done without the benefit of plans and was accurate to the most minute detail. There were planes, racing cars and sailing ships, to name but a few. The most intriguing item of all, however, was the full set of drums, such as those a pop band might use. The drums were hand made from diesel barrels and sharkskins by Jean-Claude, who played them as well.

I could go on for ever about our two day stay on those islands. The people were so hospitable. They had nothing (by most westerner's standards), yet they were willing to share what little they had. We really were very grateful to them for enabling us to share for a while the peace and tranquillity of their simple lives. All we could do in return was to satisfy their curiosity by showing them round *Tin Hau*. We must have had about forty of them on board at the same time, mostly children. Without doubt we have never come across people more worthy of our trust or children quite so well behaved.

Robin came out on the day of our departure to officially stamp us out, and he also gave David a birthday gift from the people of Agalega – a large cowrie shell. Jean-Claude accompanied him and brought four fresh eggs from their only chicken, together with a few shells for my collection and a carved coconut-shell basket for David as a birthday present from the Aglae family. They had already given us one of the half dozen cassettes they owned, a tape of sega music. Jean-Claude was horrified when he learnt that we did not carry on board a single cassette of sega music. With the Aglae's gifts came the following letter:

Good morning   for 22.11.86
    Mr David and Mrs Lynda
I do not sure if you can come today because the little boat is no
good. My wife, my children and I wish you and Lynda a Happy
Christmas day and a new good year.
My wife, my children and I kiss David and Lynda a Christmas day
    your best friend in Agalega.
      Jean-Claude
      Linda
        Jerry
          Jenny   AGLAE
           and
             Jonny.
      Bye Bye.

By a quarter past two in the afternoon we had all our lines in and the anchor
up, and we were on our way once again.

On 24th November we collected a passenger. A common noddy with an
injured wing landed aboard *Tin Hau* in a very drunken manner. He stayed
with us for a couple of days, resisting all attempts on our part to feed him.
Eventually he had mended enough to fly off.

Temperatures gradually increased as we moved further north, but the
winds dropped. By the 27th we had the most unbelievably calm sea. It literally
looked like a sheet of glass. We sat all night in that eerie atmosphere. Towards
midnight a whale sounded right alongside, it spouted several times before I
thought of getting out the Aldis lamp in order to have a good look at it. The
light frightened it off, and by the time it disappeared beneath the surface I
realised that I was shaking with fear.

If possible, it was even calmer on the following day – even the slight swell
had disappeared. David has a picture he took from the anchor cat which shows
his toes reflected on the water. Land was spotted at 8.23 a.m. – a faint blob
beneath a bank of cloud. We were seeing Mahé from about sixty-five miles
offshore. We motored throughout the day and switched the engine off at dusk.
We had no intention of entering a strange harbour in the dark if we could help
it. We decided to drift in international waters just outside the twelve mile
limit. At sunset we were buzzed by what appeared to be a small military
aircraft. I had to do a quick scramble for cover as I had been sitting on the
pilothouse roof in the Emperor's new suit.

Soon after the departure of the aeroplane we were further investigated by the most ugly creature I have ever seen. David spotted it first and called for me to get his camera. All I could see at first was a boiling, seething mass of movement off the starboard quarter. The churning was caused by two pilot-fish – each about three feet in length. They were piloting a large brownish fish with creamy coloured spots along its back. This creature was – we estimated – between twenty-five and thirty feet long, and turned out to be a whale shark. They are, apparently, very curious creatures as we found out for ourselves when it proceeded to nose its way alongside, gently bumping us along the starboard side of the hull. Eventually it swam slowly away from our stern. We thought it was feeding on the millions of tiny copper coloured things swimming on the surface of the calm sea. We raised some of these in a bucket for closer inspection but were unable to tell just what they were. My guess was that they were some kind of plankton, but I had always understood that plankton was microscopically small – so I was probably mistaken.

3. One Thousand Miles from Anywhere

We set off early on Friday, 28th November, once again under motor, for Victoria Harbour. On arrival at the harbour light we were immediately boarded by a host of very officious gun-toting individuals. The customs, health and immigration people were not too bad. It was the naval officer and his machine-gun-wielding lackeys who gave us a hard time. We were inter-rogated about the supposed third crew member whom the Lieutenant Commander claimed to know we had aboard. What had we done with him? Where were his papers? Why was he no longer on board? Who were we trying to fool saying we had made the passage with just two people on such a big boat? His band of yobbos searched the boat from stem to stern, even going through our photo albums page by page. They clumped about in hobnailed boots; I don't think they knew the 'shoes off' rule commonly followed on small boats. We had to re-stow all our goods in order to have the booze sealed into the settee lockers in the saloon. Eventually, they left us and indicated we could proceed to the designated yacht anchorage within the harbour. This yacht basin was crammed with boats of every description, both local and visiting. Given the poor holding ground, we were somewhat surprised at how close to one another they were anchored. Once we had set our anchor, we had a quick lunch, launched the dinghies and set off into town to try to make a couple of phone calls.

By the time we had got ourselves sorted out, the banks had closed and we had no means of getting any money. We had two important calls to make, one to Margaret and one to Tony. We knew we could call Margaret collect, but we could hardly do the same to Tony who was at work. We ended up asking Margaret to contact him for us. The calls could not be delayed as everything was about to close down for three days – Victoria was preparing for a papal visit. (David later joined the crowds at the National Stadium to see the Pope's arrival and hear the mass.) We were told everything would stay closed till Tuesday.

Message sent, we set off into the town for our first taste of the Seychelles. What a culture shock. After Mauritius this was really quite something. Broad, clean streets with proper pavements and neat grass verges bordered with tropical plants. Very westernised shops with their wares artistically and neatly displayed, unlike the jumble in the retail establishments of Port Louis. We did, eventually, manage to change some cash and went in search of the fresh produce market, hoping to find something left on the stalls. There was very little choice and even the local vegetables and fruit were very expensive. Most produce was imported from East Africa. One thing we found to be good value was the packs of spices. These were available as either curry or sweet spice selections in either ground or whole form.

The Seychelles archipelago is situated about one thousand miles from any other large population centre (the population at that time was about sixty-four thousand). It comprises almost one hundred islands covering an area of approximately 160,000 square miles of ocean, nearly twice Great Britain's land area. Seychelles' land area, though, only totals about one hundred and sixty square miles. The islands are unusual in that there are two distinctly different types. Low lying coral atolls, covered with sand and a few palm trees, and granite islands that have higher profiles and are typified by small cliffs and enormous boulders on the beach. The people, known as Seychellois, are descended from Africans, Indians and Asiatics, with – for good measure – a tiny dose of European too. Dark skinned, with essentially Eurasian features, we sensed they were much slower to smile than the islanders we had met elsewhere – almost as though they were looking over their shoulders, conscious of being constantly watched.

Victoria harbour was tucked under a high and quite steep outcrop covered in deep green vegetation. Cloud drifted over the summit of this hill almost the whole time we were there. The heat in the shelter of the basin was phenomenal, and we had no awnings rigged to shelter us from the merciless onslaught of the sun.

On our arrival we were granted the two week visa generally issued to visiting yachts. We had to submit an application for an extended visa if we wanted to stay any longer. There were additional special permits needed if we wished to go to any of the designated anchorages on the outlying islands or elsewhere on Mahé. We planned to get the application in and processed before Tony's arrival, then go to either La Digue or Praslin for Christmas. We also needed time to carry out permanent repairs on *Tin Hau's* foremast tabernacle. We had not done these in Mauritius, having decided instead to await Tony's arrival – no one in Mauritius could touch his expertise. Our temporary repair had certainly been good enough for the coastal cruising there, and David had gambled that it would also be good enough for the relatively easy passage to the Seychelles (we did not have a lot of choice). However, it was not a good idea to go any further without carrying out these repairs, as we had less confidence in the weather and sea conditions beyond the Seychelles.

In view of all the uncertainties, David and I decided we would do little or no sightseeing until after Tony had joined us. We used our time to get things done on *Tin Hau*. We made sail covers, looked for a boatyard, and started making arrangements to buy and import an autopilot. We'd reached the point of feeling it was a necessity – we didn't want any more manual steering on short-handed passages. Delivery of parts and equipment for boats was said to be relatively easy in the Seychelles. David wrote letters of enquiry to various autopilot manufacturers around the world, and we took advantage of the postal service to send out about one hundred Christmas cards, using postcards as these were easier to find.

Something we always do when we arrive for a lengthy stay in a new country is to register with the British High Commission. We did this in Victoria. As a result we were invited to attend a cocktail party aboard some visiting Royal Navy ships, HMS *Andromeda* and HMS *Nottingham*, accompanied by the RFA *Orange Leaf*. We were the only guests to arrive by water and had a fairly undignified scramble up the quay wall near the gang-plank where all the ratings were lined up, resplendent in their whites. Other guests were being dropped off in chauffeur-driven vehicles. Our somewhat dishevelled appearance did not preclude us from being greeted with smart salutes and being piped aboard like everyone else.

Officers told us the Royal Navy had not had an easy time on arrival either. First of all they had had to re-anchor three good sized ships because the authorities were not happy with the places they had selected. Then they were moved a second time. They were not allowed alongside till virtually the last minute, which had made their arrangements much more difficult. The final straw came when they were told they would have to leave before five o'clock in the morning. I got the impression they were no more charmed with their reception than we were with ours.

In spite of the heat and humidity, David found the energy to take several longish early morning walks to various parts of the island with Dusty, Tasmanian owner of a very attractive wooden boat called *Sagan*. On one occasion (on a public road) they found themselves being grilled by armed men. What are you doing? Where are you going? Where have you been? Apparently they were within close range of the State President's house. Like many leaders of similar countries France Albert René, the head of state, was paranoid about his personal security. Anyone and everyone who was in any way out of the ordinary, either in looks or in behaviour, was immediately and automatically deemed a suspicious character. This was evident from David's walking incident, from our interrogation on arrival, and particularly from our subsequent treatment.

Our two week period was drawing to a close. We had quietly completed a number of outstanding jobs and managed to get to know some of the other cruising folk. We'd spent several hours in the delightful, friendly, yacht club and had received daily parcels of mail from different collection points. Some letters, well out of date, had travelled backwards and forwards several times before finally reaching us.

On our 13th day in Victoria, David went to the immigration office to find out how our application to remain was progressing. He was shattered to be told that we were not being granted an extension and that we should prepare to leave the following day! David patiently explained to them that it was practically impossible for us to leave at such short notice as we were unseaworthy owing to damage and being short-handed. At this information, they agreed to defer a decision until we had been visited by an inspector from the harbour office who would assess the damage. This inspector came and inspected and told us he would recommend that we be granted an extension of at least three weeks in order to carry out essential repair work.

The following day, Friday, we received a summons from the immigration office. This summons did not reach us till half past four in the afternoon. David shot up there and was astounded to be handed our passports, already stamped out of the country with that day's date – Friday, 12th December, 1986. He was given the following letter:

Mr. David Chidell   Our Ref: IMM/7/4/2
Skipper Yacht 'Tin Hau'
c/o Seychelles Yacht Club   12th December, 1986
Victoria.

Dear Mr. Chidell,

RE: YOUR APPLICATION FOR EXTENSION OF YOURS AND
YOUR WIFE'S VISITORS PERMITS

Reference is hereby made to your above application, but I am to inform
you that your request has not been approved.

You are henceforth informed to make the necessary arrangements to
leave Seychelles this very day (i.e. 12/12/86).

Yours sincerely,

S. POMPEY
FOR: DIRECTOR OF IMMIGRATION AND CIVIL STATUS

David left that office, shaking with emotion. Can you imagine the responsibility of trying to mobilise a sailing vessel at such short notice? How could
the authorities in a country so involved with the sea show such a total lack of
understanding of nautical matters? First, it takes time to plan a route and a
sailing boat cannot just leave in any weather. Second, one requires time to
replenish stocks of food, fuel and water. Third, the crew needs to be in a
rested state, both physically and mentally. Finally, what on earth were we
going to do about Tony's arrival on Sunday? We had no way of getting in
touch with him to apprise him of the situation.

At this point we decided it would be wise to contact the British representatives on the island in the hope that they could find out why we were being
refused the time needed to get *Tin Hau* into order. We went ashore to make a
phone call to the British High Commission, the first time we had ever made
an appeal for help to any British government department, at home or abroad.
David was told that unless he was arrested and jailed there was little they could
do before Monday. We would have to sort out our own problems in the
meantime.

As though there were not enough reasons already, we hadn't a hope of
complying with the demand to leave that day because we could not get to the

harbour office – it was closed – and they had our ship's papers. We could not leave without these. So we decided to lie low throughout the weekend till it was time to go to the airport for Tony. That we did, by bus – half fearful of being picked up and arrested as illegal immigrants. There we met up with an expatriate friend who had kindly offered transport back.

Once we had Tony safely installed on the boat with us we explained the situation to him, pointing out our options as we saw them. First, we could appeal to the authorities for time just to get the work done, then leave the Seychelles, with Tony finishing his holiday on board another boat (Dusty and Mary – and others – had offered to have him). Second, we could appeal for time to get the main work done, then put out to sea for the remainder of his stay, returning to Victoria just before the day of his return flight. Third, we could leave as the authorities wanted – with Tony if he so wished – but with the risks of an unseaworthy boat and of being short-handed... to sail where? Our choices of destination were severely limited at that time of the year. Back where we came from was out of the question because of cyclones. West to Mombasa was possible, but how were we to know if the authorities there would allow us to stay? North to the Red Sea? David did not want to tackle that difficult area without first having the chance to improve *Tin Hau's* seaworthiness. The only real choice was east to the Chagos archipelago, British Indian Ocean Territory, directly downwind and as far away from anywhere as the Seychelles. It was uninhabited, except for one atoll, Diego Garcia, leased to the United States as a military base. As far as we knew, we would be allowed to stay there until the winds were favourable for the onward passage to Sri Lanka. This would mean at least five months anchored within a deserted atoll. There was something extremely attractive about that proposition after all our troubles with governments and authorities.

We discussed all these possibilities with Tony and decided to see what would happen ashore the following day. Assuming the worst, Tony adamantly declared that he would go with us; we needn't worry about being short-handed. Also, he would help solve the problem of the foremast tabernacle, somehow. He was not one to desert his friends in a time of need, he insisted, whatever the cost to himself.

Once again, it looked as though Tony was going to be our lifeline, and he had only come to us for a brief holiday! We scanned the two charts we had of the Chagos archipelago and concluded that the target to aim for – mentioned by other yotties as being good – was Salomon Atoll.

On the Monday morning we armed ourselves with a long letter of appeal to the immigration authority explaining our position and how we could now because of Tony – get our repair work done quite quickly. We took a copy of this letter to the High Commissioner and asked him to get us an interview with a senior officer at Immigration – as high up as possible. This he did – first having thanked them for not having arrested us over the weekend! He then asked for some indication as to why we were being treated in this manner. The answer to that was that it was a matter of internal security. The High Commissioner was no wiser than we were as to what exactly that signified. We took our letter of appeal over to Immigration and were instructed to come back at three o'clock in the afternoon for their decision. Meanwhile, we had a few hours to get emergency provisioning and refuelling started.

David reported to Immigration at the appointed time and was immediately called in to the presence of the lady minister responsible for the department. He was told in no uncertain terms that we had to leave. He spent half an hour trying to have the decision reversed, but without success. Finally, he asked if we could have at least until the following day to get all our preparations done properly. This request was granted grudgingly. In view of their unreasonable attitude towards our unseaworthy state, he told them it was the least they could do. We felt their attitude was unreasonable because it is accepted virtually anywhere in the world that boats or ships in distress have the right to be able to enter a port for the purposes of repair or to seek shelter during serious heavy weather conditions or when medical problems warrant such action. Furthermore, according to David's notes on maritime law, the decision as to whether a ship or boat is seaworthy or not rests entirely with the master of the vessel. In addition, insufficient crew is, in itself, enough to make a boat unseaworthy for certain voyages. We had been able to make considerable use of Number Seven between Mauritius and the Seychelles, as the winds had been mainly from the beam. But the downwind passage to the Chagos islands would be altogether different – skilful and physically tiring manual steering would be necessary all the way, with the possibility of accidental gybes ever-present. Add to that the dubious tabernacle, still unrepaired. We were convinced that the Seychelles government was contravening international maritime law, but they obviously did not see it that way. The impoundment of *Tin Hau* was beginning to look like a distinct possibility. We really did have to go.

Our final day was a crazy rush of jobs. In addition to all those started on the Monday, we had to notify family that we were being moved on again. Tony had to get in touch with his wife to let her know that he would not be returning in three weeks but in five months at the earliest! She, in turn, had to notify his bosses. We also contacted the High Commission again to let them know what had happened and what we were now doing – under protest. They were still unable to shed any light on why we were being evicted. The selection process for permits appeared to be fairly random. An American boat was also being summarily kicked out, we learned. Yet there was a German yacht in harbour that had been allowed to stay for six months. The latter had a horrifying story to tell of a recent misfortune which made us happier about leaving in spite of all our efforts to be allowed to stay. Someone from the shore had swum out to the yacht and brutally raped the lady on board, who, at the time, had been on her own.

By six thirty we had completed all our tasks, but we were far too exhausted to set off that night. We decided to chance it and leave quietly in the morning.

First light on Wednesday, 17th December saw all of us on deck. We had fenders in and the anchor up and everything ready to go by half past five. We slipped out of the basin and past the Victoria light. All sail was raised and I went below to get the kettle on for a cup of coffee. Next thing I knew, a Navy patrol vessel cut across our bows and ordered us back into port. After working so hard to get rid of us, they now wanted us back? Unbelievable! I went below to turn off the boiling kettle. I was in such a state that I managed to tip the kettle full of boiling water all over my right hand – scalding it very badly indeed. Back we went, using full engine power – and valuable supplies of diesel – to go at the speed required by the gun-boat. We tied up alongside another boat which had also been turned back.

We were boarded by the same Lieutenant Commander who had given us such aggro on our arrival. He proceeded to rant and rave at David, yelling that we had no right to leave port without stopping for a security check. David let him get it all off his chest and then calmly told him that we had followed (to the letter) the printed directions we had been given by the Lieutenant Commander himself on our arrival. The officer continued to bluster for a while, but finally conceded that we had done all that was required of us according to the instructions on his sheet of paper. He went off muttering about the left hand not knowing what the right hand was doing, and we were left wondering when, if ever, we would be free to leave. All our papers had once more been removed for scrutiny at some office in town and we, along with the crew of the other yacht, had to prepare ourselves for what might be a long wait. A while later the passports and ship's documents were returned. We were told once again to get out of the Seychelles immediately. No explanations. Certainly no apologies. We cast off our mooring lines without delay. But it was not until we had passed Frigate island and worked our way twelve miles beyond it that we felt we were able to breathe freely.

Almost as far back as I can remember, I have had a longing to visit those enchanting islands. My father was stationed there for part of the Second World War. I had built fantasies round the pictures in his album. All I can now say is that I have been there, seen nothing, and the Seychellois are welcome to it. Even had we not had the reception we did, there were so many rules and regulations limiting the movements of visitors and particularly the movement of sailing boats that we would not have been able to have done much exploring anyway.

In the flurry of activity which surrounded our exit, no thought was given to our departure ceremony. The dragon's tail was cut unintentionally on that occasion when we almost lost a vital navigation chart overboard. Wielding a boat-hook each, Tony and I fished for the sheet of paper as David skilfully brought *Tin Hau* round onto the reciprocal course. Miraculously we were able to fish the page out of the water, and David continued the figure eight to put us back on course. The small chart turned out to have been inessential, it was merely a convenient copy of a bound-in page of the almanac! Did our goddess have a hand in pointing out our omission?

4.   Towards the Chagos Archipelago

Our first few days out of Mahé were gloriously sunny with gentle breezes – a good chance to give Tony a crash course on the art of sailing. It wasn't long before we could leave him with a two hour night watch on his own. We saw Russian trawlers almost daily. We did wonder whether they were spying on us and reporting back to Victoria, that being the port from which they operated. We also passed a French fishing boat, the *Drennec* of Concarneau, which resulted in David and the French skipper screaming at each other in fits of delight on the VHF: 'Nous sommes voisins, nous sommes voisins' ('we are neighbours'). Somehow, in the depths of the Indian Ocean, France to us (and obviously England to the Breton) seemed like home.

Our progress on the one thousand mile passage to Salomon Atoll was consistent and steady. We were aided considerably by the half to two knot current. Lots of flying fish landed on the decks – enough each night for a light breakfast for the three of us.

It blew slightly harder on Christmas Eve – just as I had organised a fancy dress cocktail hour for us all. Steering was rather heavy especially with my severely burn-blistered hand – so Tony and David did mine for me. We put the clocks forward as we entered a new time zone. We had hoped for a unique twenty-three hour Christmas Day.

25th December got off to a good start with winds suitable for Number Seven to steer the boat. *Tin Hau* ghosted along under his control in the beautiful starlit night. Our wake was bright with phosphorescence as Jupiter and Mars slowly set together behind us.

At half past eight, Santa arrived with a sailor's tog-bag full of gifts. After opening all of these, we had a leisurely breakfast and then decided to send up a hoist of flags spelling out 'Merry Christmas', just in case we should see a vessel at sea. Within minutes of running them up the mast, a ship appeared on the starboard beam! As the wind continued to drop and the sea became calmer, we drew in all the sheets and set the sails amidships. We wanted to enjoy Christmas properly and in a relaxed manner. What better way than stationary, in mid-ocean, hundreds of miles from the nearest land?

In the evening we had our Christmas dinner out on deck as we watched the sun set. The feast consisted of a canned ham, glazed in beer with pineapple rings, cherries and cloves; roast potatoes and roast pumpkin for the fresh vegetables. This was followed by home-made plum pudding with tinned cream and lashings of brandy. I had managed in our last frantic shopping expedition to lay my hands on some crackers, so we also had two each of these, and beer or wine to drink with the meal. We had coffee with chocolates and liqueurs to finish. Simple fare really, but it made one of the most memorable celebrations ever.

The calm spell lasted right through Boxing Day and for half of the following day, which was probably a good thing as the log readings for this period contained items such as: 'Recovering from Christmas dinner. Where's T? and come to that, where's D?'

On the 29th we encountered our first heavy weather of the voyage; torrential rain and a sudden increase of wind strength to forty knots. David's log entry shows that he was helming. He found it impossible to hold *Tin Hau*. First he tacked accidentally, then gybed unintentionally several times. Tony and I were trying desperately to reef the sails. Eventually we got two panels down on the foresail and three off the main. Another note in the log reads: 'Now we know the main mast can take an accidental gybe with full sail up and thirty-five knots of wind'. Luckily the sails, battens and masts withstood this punishment. However the foremast tabernacle did not! The shackle on the starboard temporary stay broke and the doubler plate started to lift about three-quarters of an inch off the deck with every wave. One of the foremast dead-eyes went, so we had to set up a strop for that. The rain lashed down and we were hardly able to see what we were doing, but we managed to set up further temporary stays in time to save the mast. This weird weather lasted for

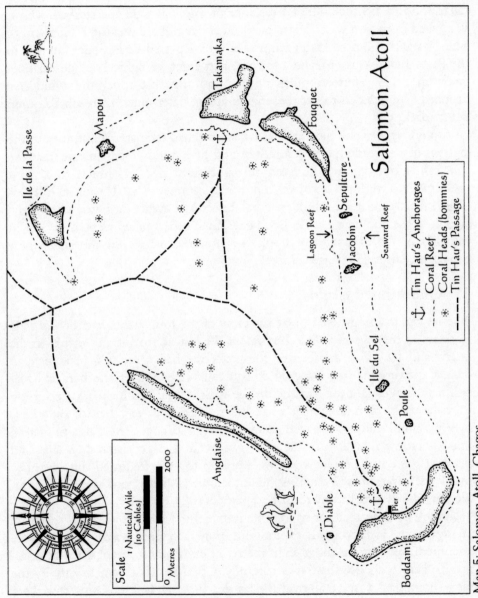

Map 5: Salomon Atoll, Chagos

a full five hours with winds anywhere between force two and seven.

Peros Banhos atoll (the first of the Chagos islands) was picked up on the radar at 3 a.m. on the 30th at a distance of four miles off the starboard bow. We gybed from port to starboard tack and at dawn there was the excitement of land on the port beam. At ten minutes to six we passed Ile Fouquet (an islet in the Peros Banhos group), and at quarter past eight we sighted our destination, Salomon Atoll, fourteen miles dead ahead. By that time, the wind had dropped. We decided to get the engine going, determined to reach Salomon before dark.

At midday we took the log in as we approached the narrow entrance to the lagoon. It was reading seven hundred and fifty miles, which meant that the free ride given to us by the equatorial current had amounted to a most welcome two hundred and fifty miles over fourteen days. It took us till two o'clock to negotiate the hidden coral heads and weave our way across the lagoon to the anchorage at Ile Boddam. Three other yachts were at anchor in the lagoon. We dropped our hook two hundred metres off the beach near *Shahla*, an Australian flagged sloop.

5. Uninhabited Islands

The new year was ushered in by the crew of the four yachts anchored off Ile Boddam in the lagoon at Salomon Atoll. We built a roaring camp fire on the beach and let off a number of fireworks we had saved for just such an occasion. Everyone had a supply of bottles of one kind or another, and reef fish had been caught for cooking on the coals. David had his piano accordion to make music at midnight. We had not realised how very British *Auld Lang Syne* was until midnight arrived. Only the single-hander, Peter, aboard *Shahla*, knew what it was all about. The other two boats, Swiss registered *Okeanos* and *Sarah la Noire* had no idea what we were up to, nor, it turned out, did they usually celebrate New Year. In spite of that, we all had a good time and it was nice to have their company to make a party of it.

It took no time at all for us to settle into the new routine. Our first priority, as always, was to thoroughly explore our immediate neighbourhood. We were anchored over coral in about eight metres of crystal clear water. Each boat, on arrival, had to choose their spot carefully. Coral heads known mostly by the term 'bommies', rose up all over the lagoon. We each had to ensure that there were none in the vicinity of our anchor chain or, indeed, within the area through which our boat could possibly swing.

Boddam was the 'main' island of the atoll. Some twenty years previously it had been inhabited. There were three distinct beaches on the lagoon side of the island. Between two of these there were the remains of an old stone built jetty, overgrown with mangrove. Our usual landing place was just to the north of this jetty, where there was ready access to an inland path. Our first exploration covered the seaward side, which was very rough and rocky – good for catching crabs and eels, but of little additional value in terms of survival. The lagoon beaches, aside from the beautiful coral sands, gave access to densely packed palm trees up to eighty feet in height. On our first wander along these beaches, Tony and I were convinced we had located chickens on the island. The yottie's grapevine had hinted that bantams had been seen at times. We distinctly heard clucking every time we passed along a certain stretch of shoreline. On closer investigation we discovered – somewhat to our disappointment – that the clucking was a warning signal being passed along the shore from burrow to burrow by a type of fiddler crab! So much for our hopes of finding a source of free-range eggs.

Back on the boat, it was obvious that we would have to make some changes to ensure our comfort during our stay on the atoll. The heat was intense and we needed to find a way of covering the decks in order to maintain a cooler temperature down below, as well as provide shade for outdoor activities. We had very little in the way of awning material. We had purchased some gardener's shade cloth in South Africa which, as it turned out, proved unbeatable for giving protection from the sun without cutting off the cooling breezes. This was now rigged in strategic places to give some relief. We also had the sail bags in which the sails had been shipped. Junk sails do not need bags as they are permanently bent on the mast. Once the bags were opened they gave quite a sizeable spread. Not terribly elegant, but we were not too concerned about looks. Comfort was the overriding concern.

Afternoon siestas became a necessity in that climate. Each of us went off by ourselves to enjoy the siesta in a different way. Tony's delight was to smear himself with oil and lie out in the full sun on the wheelhouse roof. He usually took up a poolside beanbag to lie on. David's favourite spot was the settee in the wheelhouse – dozing and reading – but always with the doors open to catch whatever cooling breeze there was. I also liked to read, preferably lying down. My own choice of location, however, was out on the deck where there were only hard surfaces on offer. It was not long, therefore, before we had collected two stout wooden poles from the shore and I had cobbled together a hammock to sling between the forward and main boom-gallows. The body of the hammock was made of long strips of webbing interwoven to form a mat.

This proved so popular that later we had two canvas hammocks made, which were slung to port and starboard of the main mast when needed.

Siesta time was also the time when we had lines overboard in the hope of catching fish. None of us had ever really done any serious fishing before and it was absolutely vital that we learnt how, or else we would get heartily sick of corned beef. Peter was a willing instructor in the arts of 'handline-over-the-side' and 'trolling-a-line-from-the-dinghy' as well as underwater harpooning. We were well supplied with hooks and lines, and had a number of lures for trolling in the ocean. We had given little thought, though, to the more static forms of the art. We hadn't a clue what to use for bait. Left to myself I would probably have gone in search of winkle-type shells – the sort of thing I had used to feed tiddlers when I was a child. Peter showed us what we needed and how to prepare the bait on the hook. He had found that live hermit crabs were the most successful and easiest form of bait to use. He brought us our first batch one evening and tipped them into one of our plastic deck buckets. That night we all lay awake getting used to the sound of these little creatures parading round and round the base of the bucket. I really hated the idea of using these dear little crabs as bait as they held an endless fascination for me. Their behaviour was so weird...

The hermit crab, for those who are not familiar with it, does not have a hard shell of its own. In order to protect its vulnerable soft body parts, it borrows or steals a shell from another creature. As the soft body grows, the hermit discards his small home for a bigger one. We saw hermits occupying snail shells, top shells, augers, mitres and harp shells – but never did they occupy cowries. Occasionally they grew big enough to use coconut shells, and once we observed a hermit who had taken a fancy to a bright green shampoo bottle top. He really was a comical sight, scuttling along the sand with his salmon pink legs splayed out beneath his lime green house.

In order to use the hermit for bait, it had to be removed from its shell. If the crab was in a new shell, it was possible to remove him from the shell without breaking it. In most cases, though, it was necessary to crack the shell and remove it from the crab. For this purpose we kept a chopping board and hammer handy on the deck. We all tried our hand at fishing during our stay at Salomon, but eventually it became one of my jobs. Even if the others caught anything, it was always my lot to do the gutting and cleaning. From a raw beginner who sent loads of good flesh over the side with the bones and guts, I worked my way towards being a fairly competent fish filleter who could send completely flesh-free skeletons back to the deep.

Line fishing from the boat was moderately successful at first – we caught quite a few worthy fish from the port and starboard quarters in the early days. It did not last long; a five foot barracuda soon learned to lie in wait for our baited hooks to be dropped. He always knew when we were about to sink a line – he must have felt the vibrations of our hermit crab shelling exercise. After hauling up a number of tailless half-fish we gave up fishing from *Tin Hau*. From then on we had to rely on trolling from the dinghy or line fishing over one of the bommies some distance from the boat.

Barry the barracuda was a well known personality in the cruising world. He was – we assumed – an elderly barracuda who had grown too old to hunt in the normal way. Or perhaps he was just too lazy. Whatever, he had certainly developed a skill for wresting catches away from other fishermen. He was an infernal nuisance when we were fishing, and was very intimidating to have around when you wanted to swim or had to get into the water for mainte-nance work. However we really came to feel that he meant us no harm, and we got used to having him around. Indeed, if none of us had seen him for a while we would feel concerned for his welfare. When we did manage to land fish without his noticing, it was possible to call him to the boat with a few taps of the hammer on the board, then to feed him the scraps. We have some delightful memories of him virtually standing on his tail waiting to be fed. It was not unknown for him to follow us if we went off in the dinghy, though he seemed to prefer his station in the cool shade of *Tin Hau*. We have a picture of him swimming alongside Peter. It was an unwritten yottie rule that Barry was not to be taken if he should ever be so foolish as to be caught. In fact this happened during our stay. Peter landed him one morning, took a quick snap of him, cut the line just short of his inch-long teeth, and deposited him back in the water. Within two days he had rid himself of the dangling steel tracer Peter had had to leave in his mouth.

We made a number of visits to the interior of Ile Boddam. We never took any great pleasure in these excursions as they were very uncomfortable. Nowhere in the world have I come across such an active mosquito population. The odd thing was they were very territorial – never straying beyond the vegetation line. The beach was perfectly clear of them and we never had a hint of them on the boats. Once we set foot into the long grass or the jungle, however, we would be eaten alive. There was no good time of the day to visit – they carried out twenty-four hour dive-bombing patrols. The only way we could keep our bodies reasonably itch-free was to smear them all over with foul smelling insect repellent or to wear plenty of protective clothing. As the reader can imagine, it wasn't exactly pleasant in the equatorial climate to have to dress for the Arctic.

The need for variety in our diet made such visits necessary from time to time. The legacy of the Illois who had lived on Boddam was a small number of surviving fruit trees, among them a number of high yielding lemons, an orange, a grapefruit and some limes. Also, there were a couple of huge breadfruit trees. Earlier cruising visitors had left maps showing the position of papaya, bananas and guavas. We tried several times to locate these, but either the land was too overgrown to reach them or they had long since died off. We did discover a curious fruit for ourselves in our need for something new. We had never seen its like before but were daring enough to try it anyway. The fruits were waxy ovoid blobs which grew in clusters on the trunk of a small tree. They were pale lemon green in colour with a very astringent juice. Boiled or stewed with sugar they were very similar to stewed apple. We later learned that it was a common fruit in the tropics and went by the name of billing. Apparently it has a very high vitamin C content.

There were still a number of buildings standing on the isle, although they were in a very dilapidated state when we were there. It could hardly be described as a ghost town, as one never got the impression of any number of buildings together. Each was isolated from its neighbour by the overgrown vegetation. It was saddening to see these lovely old stone and timber buildings tumbling down. The roof of the church had long gone, but all the walls still stood and there were even a few old pews left. Weeds grew up through the flagstone floor and all the doors had gone, but there were still a few panes of the stained glass windows intact.

One of the houses had been officially designated the yacht club by the British representatives down on Diego Garcia. They kept a log book there for the use of the yotties to record their presence on the atoll and to record any events or discoveries. There were, too, pots of paint and drawing materials for our use. The idea was to decorate the walls of the clubhouse with a patchwork mural. Each visiting boat was expected to add something to commemorate their stay. Several previous visitors had restored bits of old furniture they had found on the isle and installed them in the clubhouse. There were still several serviceable rainwater tanks and the gutters leading to these worked well. In addition there were a couple of wells, but the water from these tended to be a bit brackish. We never needed to avail ourselves of either as we had sufficient tankage to manage between tropical downpours when we were able to replenish our supply.

The ruins were mainly domestic dwellings, but there were one or two copra sheds still standing. One of these had a roof and quite a lot of heavy lifting tackle suspended from the girders. There was a rail track from this building to the jetty and the chassis of a small rail cart on the lines. Altogether it was a place for the imagination to run riot, wondering how the inhabitants had done this and that, who had lived where, and so on.

Exploration of all the other islands was also done over the weeks we were there. Sometimes we sailed in *Knot Often*, sometimes we rowed or motored in *Bizzy* (my 'rubber duck'). Each of the isles had something new to offer; either unusual shells, different birds, food not available elsewhere, or simply a change of scenery.

We also enjoyed snorkelling over the coral heads – sometimes purely for the pleasure of seeing the brightly coloured corals and fish, but more often because we hadn't caught any fish for days and fancied something fresh to eat. On these occasions we could take giant clams from the coral – delicious eating, but only after they had been left in clear water for twenty-four hours to cleanse their innards!

We had heard along the grapevine about the delicious meal one could have if one could locate and catch a coconut crab. On one expedition Tony and Peter managed to do so, and they also found some turtle eggs. We always tried to weigh the effects on the environment of our using such things for food against our own needs of survival – it was obviously important that we should have a fresh, balanced diet. We were aware of the desperate struggle for survival faced by some species of turtle. Although hundreds of eggs are usually laid just beneath the sand on a beach, very few of the eggs or baby turtles survive the attacks of rats, other rodents, sea-birds and man. Those that do have to contend with yet more dangers once they reach the sea. We had not had any eggs for so long that we thought that just once we would try some. We also succumbed to the temptation of the coconut crab on two occasions but desisted when we learned that they are, in fact, a protected species known as 'the Queen's crabs'. The only other meat we had on one occasion – was an adult turtle. Peter had caught and killed one, but he had no means of preserving the flesh. In order that it should not be wasted, we all joined in the eating of it. We made it clear, though, that we did not wish to see any more caught.

For the record, coconut crabs are large land crabs which somewhat resemble lobsters. They live in burrows dug out of the boles of palm trees. The crab's pincers are huge and capable of cracking open a mature coconut –

its staple food. One average sized crab provides sufficient meat for a meal for three people, it is so large.

Turtle eggs look just like ping-pong balls. They are almost identical in size, and dent in a similar way because the shell is leathery rather than brittle. Though I am told they scramble well, we did not cook ours that way. I chose to hard boil them, which was a mistake as the white never set! What we ended up with was a yolk just like that of a chicken's when hard-boiled, but with a runny white.

Turtle meat is very like veal and, surprisingly, does not have anything of a sea taste. No further turtles were caught during our stay on the atoll. I hope it was as a result of our dislike of killing such beautiful creatures and our concern for their numbers. It was very hard to reconcile our needs with our ethical feelings when, on such a remote isle, turtles appeared to be so abundant. Nor was it easy to retain our principles when we knew that others elsewhere, with less needs than our own for fresh food, were heedlessly harvesting whatever they could catch. It was good to discover during our travels that the majority of cruising folk are reasonably sensitive in this respect. Most would take only what was needed for personal consumption and even then they would be selective. To give an example, one young couple we met were expert crabbers. But they always examined the crabs they caught – never taking females with eggs.

Earlier I mentioned some details of the coconut. The reader may be interested to know just how many ways we were able to use this very versatile fruit. When we first started our cruising I had little idea how to get a coconut open, let alone how many parts of it I could use. The young coconut was best for quenching the thirst. It also had edible flesh, but as I explained earlier, this was very jelly-like in consistency. A truly ripe coconut is one that has just fallen from the tree. It has a small quantity of very clear 'milk' and crisp nutty flesh. Once the coconut has been on the ground for some time – long enough to start 'sprouting' – it has developed a spongy substance in the void. This 'sponge' made very good eating indeed. Coconut cream can be obtained from the ripe nut, by draining the milk and grating the flesh into it. Once strained, this yields a creamy liquid which is delicious in cocktails, with chocolate powder, on cereals, or in curry sauces. Finally, the trunk of the very young palm tree can be stripped of its outer leaves to reveal a pale green succulent leaf which can be used in the preparation of 'millionaire's salad' also known as heart-of-palm, or palmiste. Where palms are under cultivation, usually at a spacing of about ten metres, heart-of-palm salads are not really practicable. It would be foolish to destroy a whole tree for such a small end result. But on

Boddam we were more fortunate. The palms had gone so wild that they were much too close together, almost choking each other. It was easy for us to find a young tree for this delicacy.

Breadfruit, too, is a versatile foodstuff. We used it generally to make chips, fritters and mash. But it can also be used raw as a salad ingredient, and when over-ripe its flesh can be scooped out and served with sugar as a sort of fruit fool. Unfortunately it had a flavour we soon grew tired of, and the sticky latex which covered everything during its preparation was also a bit off-putting. The fruits grew on relatively tall trees, which we had to scale in order to pick them (we also tried harvesting them from the ground with long poles). Getting them tended to be a two-person job – one to climb the tree, and one to try to catch the fruit when it was dropped. It was not easy for the 'monkey' to return to earth with the fruit.

Initially we were very sparing in our use of lemons as the trees from which we picked them were not particularly productive. It was only after we saw Peter with a bucketful that we thought of asking him where he had found his. To our surprise and delight, he led us to a small grove (four trees, I recall), where there were enough sound lemons lying on the ground to fill a number of buckets, and leave plenty more ripening on the trees. This really was treasure. We made jars and jars of lemon curd and bottles of lemon squash. The fruit juice made lovely salad dressings and was put to many other uses. Young lemon leaves were often used in the wrapping of whole fish inside aluminium foil prior to baking on a beach fire. The zingy lemon flavour was better than that obtained from the fruit.

Quite frequently during our stay on Salomon, ships would pass close to the atoll. We habitually turned our VHF radio on at such times in case any of them tried to establish contact. We had heard, via the grapevine again, that the British authorities based an Diego Garcia made periodic visits to all the atolls in the archipelago. On or about 14th January we were delighted to hear a very British voice calling sailing boats on Salomon Atoll, and announcing that they were Brit customs. I grabbed the mike and responded to their call. It transpired that they had planned to call in at Salomon that day, but due to a very high running swell were unable to enter on the landing craft. They then proceeded to enquire what boats were in the anchorage (just us and *Shahla*) and whether we were in need of any assistance. Here was my opportunity to ask for help with the repairs. I handed the mike over to David, who had a far better idea than I of what was needed. A long conversation followed, with David giving details of what we required to carry out better – but probably still temporary – repairs to the foremast tabernacle. He requested they arrange to have made a steel plate of a certain shape with various cut-outs and notches (it was 'drawn' over the VHF) and that they bring this and a small portable welding plant to Salomon on their next visit, if possible. The customs and naval officers to whom we had been speaking agreed to see what could be organised but warned us that we would not know what could be done for at least four to six weeks.

I'd like to make the point, here, that Diego Garcia is a port closed to civilians. Shipping, other than that having legitimate Naval business, is not allowed to visit the base for any reason. Attempts to do so are actively discouraged by both the US personnel and the British administrators, with good reason. It has been known for vessels to use the excuse of (faked) emergencies to gain entry in order to have a good snoop. (By his own admission, a well-known journalist, Simon Winchester, had done just this – thereby making it far harder for the genuine cases following in his wake.) Knowing all this in advance, we had deliberately not approached the authorities for assistance and at no time did we ask for any help other than the supply of materials and loan of equipment to carry out the repair work ourselves.

Approximately six weeks after initial contact, we were visited by a small landing craft serving the supply vessel, the *Alex Bonnyman*, working out of Diego. The officer manning the high speed rigid hull inflatable boat brought a message that the 'powers' at Diego Garcia had decided we should be granted restricted entry for the purposes of carrying out essential repair work in the dockyard. We had to decide on a date and were then given instructions on entry procedure. We chose Tuesday, 3rd March– and proceeded to pack up at Salomon.

Diego Garcia was some one hundred and thirty miles to the south, across the Great Chagos Bank. We had a terrific sail aboard *Tin Hau* on our way there. The excitement started from the moment we were leaving the lagoon, when there was an almighty tug on my fishing line. It took two of us to heave in whatever was on the other end. Tony and I hauled away and eventually had a five-foot shark dangling from the port quarter. At that moment, David needed help with the sailing of the boat – the coral reef was only yards away. The steel tracer was rapidly cut with a pair of pliers and we lost our catch and my best lure. We concluded that the Great Chagos Bank had been an enormous atoll with a series of islands around its perimeter. As we approached this rim at high speed at quarter to three in the afternoon, we prayed the chart was correct and that we would not hit the coral. It was thrilling to watch as the inky nothingness of the ocean changed to azure blue. Suddenly we could see

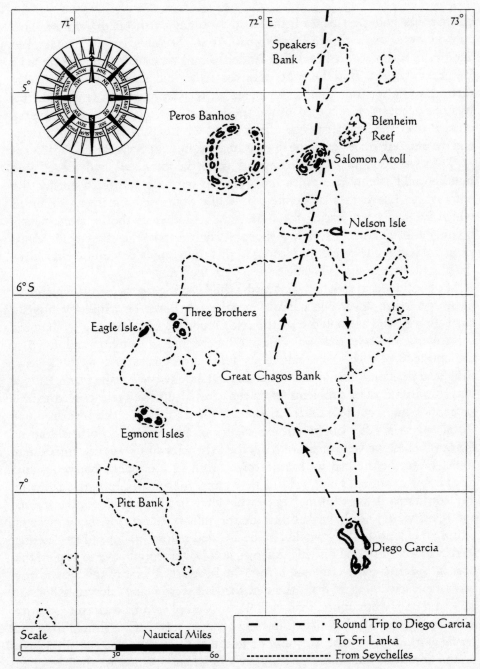

Map 6: Chagos Archipelago

all that was going on beneath the boat. I caught a fish on the trolling line, nabbed by a shark before I could haul it in. Seconds later I had hooked another, but this was tailless when landed. Third time lucky, and we landed a fair sized bonito. But the echo sounder never did show less than twelve metres, and after four minutes it increased to twenty metres (eighty metres was the deepest we recorded inside the lagoon). At ten minutes to nine we crossed over the southern edge of the bank, with depths of fourteen metres, and we entered, once again, the deep waters of the Indian Ocean.

Twenty-two hours after setting off from Salomon, we had logged one hundred and twenty-five miles and were tacking back and forth outside the entrance to Diego in a moderate sea. While doing so, something occurred which we had been fearing for some time. Another of the temporary stays holding the tabernacle together snapped. Fortunately the mast held. Once again we had come so close to losing it, this time only a few miles away from the place to which we had come to deal with the problem.

We continued to tack back and forth while waiting for the escort which had been detailed to cover our arrival. We were overflown by a military surveillance aircraft and we could hear the pilot reporting our presence to the port controller as 'a vessel that looks like a Chinese junk cruising up and down at the entrance passage'. This caused us some amusement and we took great delight in prancing around on deck making 'Chinese eyes' at the plane. After a few communications problems had been cleared up, we were guided to the quarantine buoy where we were moored. We were then boarded by a group of Royal Marines. After our recent experience of authorities and officialdom in the Seychelles, we were anxious to say the least. How different this turned out to be! Never before had we been received with such efficient, courteous and pleasurable treatment on arrival in a new place. All formalities were dealt with in record time. It was explained to us what plans had been made for the repairs and that I would be allowed ashore (under military escort) for the purpose of visiting the dentist. Tony would also be allowed ashore (under military escort) so that he could phone his wife, Sharon, and David would have to stay on the boat in order to receive the men from the boatyard. None of this was in any way unexpected – apart from the fact that we were being allowed ashore at all – and we were more than willing to comply with whatever security measures they wished to take. Our only concern was that we should have the repair work done so that we could continue our voyaging without the worry of the foremast tabernacle giving way completely. Once we had reached agreement with the Marines, they indicated they would leave us to get a few hours sleep and that they would return to escort *Tin Hau* to the dockyard in the afternoon.

As soon as we had tied up in the inner basin, we had a swarm of boatyard personnel on board to examine the damage with their critical professional eyes. There were so many of them we despaired of ever sorting them out into individuals. Not helped by the fact that at least three of the gentlemen involved were known as Bill. Inevitably the boatyard came to be known by ourselves as 'Bills' Boat Basin'.

The Bills made several proposals as to how the job could be tackled, and each proposal was accompanied by an estimate of time and cost. As soon as one of the plans had been approved and the relevant paperwork and the transfer of funds completed, preparations for work began. Within two days of arrival, everything that could be moved from the chain lockers and the deck was lifted ashore. The sail, foremast and windlass were taken off. *Tin Hau* had to be turned in her berth to allow easier access for heavy lifting equipment. The new orientation meant that dust from grinding work would blow into the sea. Then the real work commenced.

From seven in the morning till seven in the evening we heard again all the noises associated with steel boat building. While all this was going on we had numerous visits from the British customs officers (Royal Marines doing double duty) and naval staff who, because of the restrictions imposed on us, came to entertain and help us in any and every way they could. We had an exceptional opportunity to meet and get to know a few of those wonderful people who, in peacetime particularly, we all take so much for granted. I believe I speak for all three of us when I say that it was a rare privilege to have met the men and women serving in the Royal Marines and the Royal Navy on Diego Garcia at that time.

While we were in Diego Garcia, *Tin Hau* celebrated her first birthday. Although we were unable to go ashore, people ensured that we celebrated the event in style. In fact, we did so three times over. The first party, the night before the actual date of the launch, was more of an impromptu party – the Filipino labourers brought a crate or two of beers to share with us and I ended up inviting them all to eat with the crew. The Bill contingent arrived with loads of bottles the following night. The Brits devised the celebrations for the following day and baked a huge cake in the galley ashore (half eaten by the dog); and with a gigantic tray of artistically presented Sushimi and loads of bubbles to wash it all down, they really did *Tin Hau* proud.

Many things happened to us during our two week stay at Diego Garcia. We were on their local TV station news. We had a request played on the radio station for Peter and Barry back at Boddam (we knew Peter would be listening). We lent the authorities various magazine articles we carried on board, full of information about the Illois people who used to live on the islands. These were photocopied avidly and passed around. We helped with the repair work, although just about all of this was efficiently and effectively done by the professionals.

I asked the Navy medic what could be done about a verruca David had on his foot which was causing him a degree of pain. 'Cut it out with your scalpel,' I was told. David, there at the time, asked whether or not there would be an anaesthetic. 'Of course not,' said the medic. Turning to me again he continued: 'Use the scalpel like a corkscrew and you will know you have got it when he starts to yell and bleeds like a stuck pig.'

This operation was duly carried out with David desperately trying to prove he was as tough as any Royal Marine. The operation was performed on the wheelhouse settee with Tony standing guard on the wheelhouse roof to warn off any potential onlookers. The best thing that can be said about the entire episode is that we must have got it all out as David had no further problems with it and there is no scar.

Perhaps I have already said more than I should have done about Bills' Boat Basin. We did honour their request that we say nothing about Diego Garcia whilst we were in Sri Lanka – understandably they did not want a flood of boats seeking repairs. But years later I feel our time there can safely be mentioned. The authorities were so incredibly good to us. We owe them so much, there is little we can do to express our thanks. It wasn't actually the last we saw of the Marines. They called on us at Salomon Atoll a short while after our departure from Diego Garcia. We were able to reciprocate on some of their hospitality, throwing a party on *Tin Hau*. They brought plenty of crushed ice so the beers were cold. Barry didn't disappoint us either – a couple of taps on the bread board and he showed up, keen to meet our new friends.

We set sail late in the afternoon of 14th March, back to Boddam where we planned to spend another three weeks until the winds changed. Predictably, the wind was adverse, but it was not particularly strong. With some use of the engine we had reached the entrance of Salomon Atoll by twenty-five minutes to midday on the 16th. Once again the Chagos Bank was interesting and exciting. We sighted whales, sharks and dolphins, as well as numerous sea birds.

The return to our atoll was like returning home after a long journey. Peter was still there at Boddam, and Barry took up station below us as soon as we had anchored. The only difference was that there were two other boats, one anchored off Ile de Passe and one off Ile Takamaka. Later, one of them vanished overnight, presumably to Peros Banhos. The other eventually moved over to our anchorage. On board were Frank and Elise – a Canadian couple who had been cruising for some years. We stayed on long enough to be able to help Elise celebrate her birthday. Our gift to her was a jar of Boddam-made lemon curd (and a recipe to enable her to make more). The lack of shopping facilities certainly made for unusual gifts and bartering arrangements. We had already traded beers (ours) for potatoes (Peter's). Frank and Elise asked us to post mail for them when we reached our next port of call. In exchange I was given a lovely pair of silver and sea-urchin-spine earrings made aboard *Ouais Ouais* (their boat).

We are often asked how we occupied our time when not fishing or foraging for food or tackling the never ending list of boat jobs. One of our more enjoyable activities was beachcombing. There were all sorts of interesting items washed up on the seaward facing beaches. Sadly, however, some of the these beaches were also strewn with the most appalling man-made litter – rubbish that had obviously originated from Indonesia or from the Malay peninsula, well over a thousand miles to the east.

Peter decided it would be worth his while bringing one of the large and very well seasoned teak logs from this area across the reef and into the lagoon. This teak log had presumably broken free of a log raft up some river in Burma and had been brought by the currents to the atoll. Some one to one and a half metres in diameter and between three and four metres long, it was an exercise in ingenuity to drag it round the islet. Tony was a willing helper in this venture. Once the log was dragged on to the beach in the lagoon, the two of them proceeded to drive wedges into the end grain in order to split it into crude planks. These were eventually put aboard *Shahla*, taken to Mauritius and machined into proper teak strips. We later heard (the yottie grapevine is infallible) that Peter had decked *Shahla* with these. It was an enterprise that kept two people happily occupied for ages and improved the value and appearance of Peter's boat no end.

At some point, on one of his logging jaunts, Peter had left a tog bag open on the beach. A while later he realised he had carried a mouse back to *Shahla* in the bag. The mouse caused untold havoc aboard, eating its way through the bases of innumerable pots of long-life yoghurt, chewing through the rubber seal of the liferaft canister, and breaking into and urinating over all of Peter's tea bags. Hours of planning went into each attempt to catch the miscreant but when Peter finally came face to face with it, he was unable to kill it. In his words, it was 'too pretty'. I cannot recall how he eventually captured it, but he did and was able to return it to the island alive.

Our own pest problem was a plague of cockroaches. We had unknowingly moved a colony aboard, in the form of eggs, from the Seychelles. We discovered them on our voyage when they were still few in number and small in size. By the time we reached the atoll, we had what could be termed a fairly severe infestation and they were breeding at a fantastic rate. One of the things we requested of the Brits during our first contact with them was some form of pest control to combat the plague. On overhearing our radio plea, Peter announced that he had an Australian silo fumigator which might do the trick. He kindly gave us his only smoke bomb, which we used with great effect. The morning after we fumigated, I picked up three hundred and sixty (yes, I counted) dead cockroaches. That bomb was so effective that we had no further problems.

As you can see, a great deal of time was spent dealing with things like this. The rest of the hours in the day were given over to our personal interests – in my case, the collecting of shells, mainly beachings. I cleaned, labelled and classified hundreds of collected specimens, as well as making pen and ink drawings of the islands and some of the flora and fauna that helped to support our existence there.

David enjoyed his sailboard for quite a while. He would have continued to do so had he not become aware on one occasion that he was being shadowed by a shark at least the length of his board. How he ever made it back to *Tin Hau* with his knees knocking as they were (and without falling into the jaws of the shark below) we shall never know. After that he was reluctant to risk too much boardsailing.

Looking back on it all, even the hard work was fun in that environment. Had we been on our own, and had *Tin Hau* been more prepared for it (for example, we could have done without the necessity of the weekly hull scrub), David and I might well be castaways on our semi-desert island to this day.

The decision Tony made to help us out of our difficulties had been at considerable cost to himself and his family. Initially we had hoped to be able to give him the holiday of a lifetime in return for all that he had done to see our dream become a reality. His reward for his labours and loyalty was instead to be virtually marooned on an uninhabited island. It must have been a severe shock to his system. We had, after all, chosen and prepared for the life that cruising entailed. Tony had had no such preparation, and had just come along for the ride, as it were. It is to his credit that he managed to cope so well. In spite of our widely divergent interests and temperaments we got on very well together. It couldn't have been much fun being the spare wheel at times. Whenever we got too much for him or he felt he needed space, he took himself off to spend a few hours with Peter. When we hear some of the stories owners tell of their horrific experiences with crew it makes us realise how incredibly lucky we were with Tony. The only time irritation was openly expressed was when Tony remarked to David that had I been a man he would have hit me! I don't think he was used to dealing with bossy females.

Before we departed from Salomon for ever, we spent a few days at anchor in the passage between Takamaka and Fouquet islands. This was purely for pleasure – to enjoy a change of scenery and rest ourselves before setting out on the next leg of our journey. As usual, David had chosen the date for our departure to coincide with the full moon, thus giving us the benefit of natural night illumination for the start of the eight hundred and fifty mile haul to Sri Lanka. We set off at twenty minutes past nine in the morning on 9th April.

6. Onwards to Sri Lanka

During our first few days out of Salomon Atoll we had enough wind to carry us in the direction we wished to go. We covered the ground very slowly, with wind strengths varying from force one to force three. We ghosted along under sail in quite calm seas. Every now and then we chose to improve progress by using the engine.

On the fourth day we picked up the breeze we had been waiting for – a force three to four south-westerly. It lasted only twenty-four hours before dying again. At this point we could have put in to the Maldives to wait for the south-westerlies to strengthen. The nearest island, Gan, was only thirty miles to the west. Officially, however, the sole port of entry was on the island of Malé, two hundred and fifty miles away. We decided to give the Maldive islands a miss. They would have been very like Chagos, with one difference – people. The Maldives had a reputation which reminded us of the Seychelles – the officials were known to be most unwelcoming towards visiting yachts. Tempting as Gan was, we did not want to run the risk of being arrested as spies.

On 13th April at sunset we celebrated a great event – we crossed the equator. At the same time as we entered the northern hemisphere, we enjoyed the sight of a huge rainbow archway. By night we could still see the Southern Cross and the other stars of the southern skies that had grown so familiar, but we were also beginning to pick up some of the well known northern constellations such as the Plough. A few days later we sighted the Pole Star itself.

We spent Easter Day (19th April) hove-to, completely stationary. What little wind there had been had died out. We watched a school of dolphins race by. Ten minutes earlier we had been staring in amazement at a school of smaller fish just below *Tin Hau* swimming round and round in a tight anti-clockwise circle. Why were they doing that? Another mystery for us to solve.

By the thirteenth day (21st April), we were heartily sick of drifting in mid-ocean. Where were the prevailing westerlies? Tony, in particular, wanted to get to our destination. So on went the engine, and we started to eat up the miles. Galle was only two hundred miles away.

Our approach to Sri Lanka was hectic. At 10 p.m. on 23rd April, Dondra Head and Barberyn lighthouses were sighted and positively identified. Galle was fifty miles dead ahead. The weather started to deteriorate as we entered one of the busiest shipping lanes in the world. There were ships and trawlers heading in and out of the Sri Lankan ports, together with ships bound to and from the Persian Gulf, Suez, India and Singapore. Visibility conditions worsened rapidly. The rain bucketed down.

By dawn the rain had stopped and we could see the land clearly with all its various features. We were five miles away from the coast, and the view of Sri Lanka in the early morning light was magnificent. All the mountains and hills in varying shades of blue and purple with streaks of mist swirling around and over everything. Once again, as in Mauritius, it took a while to get our bearings. Eventually it was decided we had overshot the entrance to Galle and we had to backtrack southwards a few miles. We were close enough to the shore to be surrounded by fishing canoes. These were dugouts with outriggers powered by four or five men wielding oars. It surprised us to find such frail looking craft so far offshore – the swell and the waves that distance out were quite big. All the boats were very brightly painted in primary colours. The crews greeted us with beaming, friendly smiles.

7.   Back to the Bustling World

We had no success in contacting the authorities on the VHF, so we made our way into the harbour and picked up a mooring. As soon as we had everything shipshape we sat down to await the arrival of the officials. We waited. And we waited. Realising that we were not going to be visited, David and Tony went ashore to report our presence at the customs office and went

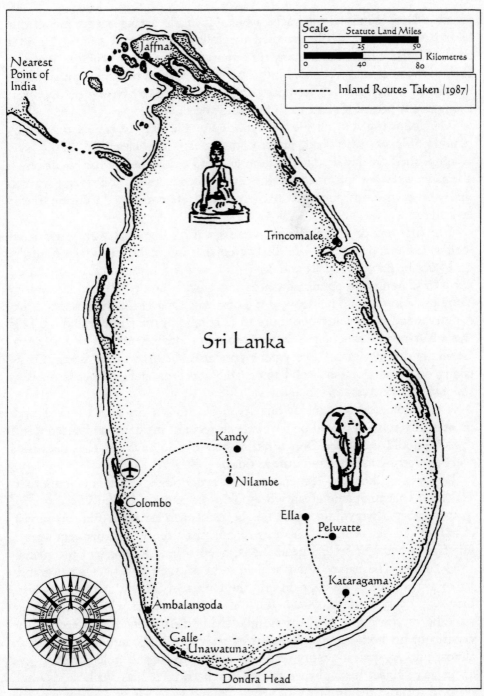

Map 7: Sri Lanka

to meet Don Windsor, the yacht agent. He made arrangements for all our clearance procedures to be handled the following day and handed David a stack of mail he had been keeping for our arrival. The chaps brought all of this back to the boat, and we settled into a two hour session of catching up with all our family and friends – interrupted only by the need to have a meal. Don had thoughtfully provided some fresh fruit and vegetables.

The following morning David reported at the jetty to collect the shore-bound officials who had arrived to effect our clearance. This was accomplished quickly despite the thousand and one forms we had to process – a legacy, we were informed, of the British occupation. The doctor arrived under his own steam, and once his formalities were completed we were free to go ashore.

Our first few days in Sri Lanka were spent having a hasty and superficial look at Galle and the fort. We discovered that international money transfers could not be handled locally and, as Tony was anxious to be off, we organised a trip to Colombo to arrange finances and a ticket home. We said farewell to Tony in Colombo and he flew out the next day. One of Don's sons, Moditha, had driven us the seventy-two miles to Colombo in the family minibus. This was a hair-raising experience I refused to repeat during our stay in Sri Lanka. Generally driving was of a very poor standard, but his was the worst. Over-taking on blind rises and solid lines, and travelling at high speeds on wet, slippery surfaces was too much for me.

A chronological account of our seven months in Sri Lanka would be a pointless exercise. It would be far better to recount incidents and anecdotes. I think I should introduce Don Windsor before I do anything else, because I will be referring to him from time to time.

Don was a Sinhalese businessman with every finger in one pie or another. He was a charming gentleman who took great pride in his unofficial title of 'yotties friend'. Everything he did for the yachtsman carried a (hidden) service charge of ten per cent, and this earned him the subtitle 'ten per cent agent'. His family had, for several generations, been ardent admirers of the British royal family. The name 'Windsor' had been adopted by Don's great-grand-father at the time of his baptism into the Christian faith. When we met him, Don was a very active sixty-two year-old with a wide knowledge and under-standing of world affairs. A throne-like chair was strategically placed on the veranda of his home and surrounded by chairs for his 'courtiers'. He had an almost photographic memory, and was willing to sit and hold forth on just about any subject his audience saw fit to choose. He was available day and night to sort out the problems of people far and wide. He was a Justice of the

Peace, and was regularly called upon in that capacity too. His family handled all manner of yacht related activities and provided all sorts of services including meals, laundry, sail repairs, carpentry, mechanical work and so on. No job was too small to handle, Don had the biggest ego of any human being we've ever met and took great pride in everything that had ever been written about him, whether good, bad or indifferent. He kept a scrapbook full of cuttings relating to himself and his activities. Articles had been sent to him from the four corners of the earth. I know he sounds larger than life, but he had to be seen to be believed.

Our first few weeks following Tony's departure saw us busy tackling the usual endless list of boat jobs. They always mount up on a long voyage and our experiences thus far in the Indian Ocean had taught us that the sooner they were done after arrival in a new port, the more we could relax in the knowledge that we were ready to put to sea at a moment's notice, if necessary. We had been assured we could stay as long as we liked – just as long as we paid our harbour dues (US $66 per month) and agent's fees (US $25 per month). There was also an initial fee of US $31.

Sri Lanka considered itself to be a developing nation. Having lived in a real developing country for some years, I would prefer to describe what I saw and experienced of Sri Lanka as a re-developing nation. The country has a history which goes back to around 500 BC. It has seen colonial rule three times, first under the Portuguese, then the Dutch, and finally the British. Each of these left a mark. The fort at Galle had architectural samples from each period in a good state of preservation. The fort itself was added to and modified during each phase of colonial rule. When we saw it, the fort area was used mainly as a business and office district and had a quiet dignity quite unlike the bustle that assaulted one elsewhere. In the new town area there was a confused mixture of noises, sights and smells that left one fighting for breath. Apart from the very modern post office building with its electronic equivalent of Big Ben all the buildings were of indefinite date and parentage. Some attempted to be modern. Others were dilapidated centenarians. Everywhere were crowded shops with goods spilling out on to the pavements in wild profusion. At closing time, one took pity on the assistant whose duty it was to cram everything back inside. When visiting these shops, it was almost impossible to weave one's way between the sacks of rice, lentils and other grains and spices which cluttered the floor. Once having negotiated that obstacle course, we had further difficulty seeing the contents of the shelves along the walls.

There were one or two yachts already in the harbour, and we quickly got acquainted with their crews. Yotties are always helpful when new yachts arrive, particularly in directing new arrivals towards the best bargains and places to have work done. One of these was an Irish girl who had been some time in Sri Lanka learning about acupuncture and homeopathy. She and I became friendly and I was glad to have her as a guide for the few days she had left before sailing to Thailand. It was she who took me down the coast to Unawatoona and introduced me to the owner of the vegetarian restaurant and also to a British ex-architect turned Buddhist monk who was running a mission station there. On the same day we went further down the coast to the home and workshops of Dr and Mrs Da Silva of Habaraduwa. These introductions all played an important part in our life in Sri Lanka. Mary had met these friends through her studies in Colombo. Both she and Ozren (her Yugoslav sailing companion) were qualified doctors who had a serious interest in alternative medicine. They had been studying at a world renowned clinic of acupuncture where Western medical practitioners went if they wished to learn more about Eastern medical practices. During our visit to Chagos I had strained my back and pulled an old injury, and had been suffering some pain. Ozren offered to manipulate me on board *Tin Hau* and added some acupuncture for good measure. The manipulation was brilliant and got my back into shape in no time. Ozren taught me how to self-manipulate in the event of a recurrence. Apart from providing an amusing subject for David's camera, I don't think the acupuncture was of much value.

On one of our visits to Unawatoona, I introduced David to Asvajit – the Buddhist monk. During the course of conversation that afternoon, we learnt that there was going to be a meditation retreat up in the hills at Nilambe, near Kandy. It seemed to us that we had nothing to lose by joining the retreat. Neither of us knew the first thing about Buddhism, and we saw it as a rare opportunity to find out. It was also a chance to have a few nights away from *Tin Hau* (we had only had one night off the boat in sixteen months). I had practised a form of meditation as a means of relaxation for many years, but had never taken it beyond the physical plane. We'd no idea what we were getting ourselves into.

We set off on a Friday morning and walked the two miles into Galle where we met the other participants at a pre-arranged rendezvous. We boarded the minibus which would take us all to Nilambe, stopping in Colombo to pick up the rest of the party. After Colombo it was all new territory for us, and very interesting too. The journey took twelve hours, with frequent stops at watering holes along the way. Lunch was provided at the home of a friend of one of the party. The route wandered through paddy fields and tea plantations as it wound ever higher into the hills. The air became crisper and cooler.

We arrived at our destination at half past five in the afternoon. David and I were sent off in different directions to our sleeping quarters. The latter consisted of concrete blockhouses subdivided into tiny cells. Each cell had two concrete benches along the walls, which served as bunks. The only other furnishing was a grass mat for each person to sleep on, and an enamelled candle-holder. There was no electricity, and no wardrobe to hang clothes – just a hook on the wall above each bed. I shared with an American girl for the duration. The ablution facilities were nearby in another concrete blockhouse. They comprised one shower (cold only – no hardship, as it was all we had on the boat anyway), one Eastern style loo (footpads with a squat-hole, tap and bucket for flushing), and one Western style loo (missing its cistern and ball valve). David told me afterwards that his loo wasn't as good as this and he had suffered the additional problem of having to remove large leeches from his legs whenever he went there in the dark. It took a few minutes to unpack my belongings and head off to the kitchen, from where we were guided into a long hall with concrete benches along the four walls. The floor of this room was covered with thick rush matting and there were loads of scattered cushions on the benches. There were a number of Buddhist converts and several Western tourists, who had enrolled for courses at the centre, already meditating at one end of the room. These people had been at the centre for a week or so and seemed quite at home in their lotus positions.

After our first session of instruction – where, quite frankly, we hadn't a clue what was going on – we returned to the communal kitchen. We were served a meal of dhal (lentils), bread and sweet milky tea by the light of the woodfires and a number of candles. Another session of meditation followed before we retired to do battle with our grass mat covered concrete bunks. An uncomfortable night ended at a quarter to five in the morning, with a quick visit to the blockhouse at the bottom of the compound and a stumbling climb up to the meditation hall. I grabbed the nearest thick cushion, slithered into a sleeping bag and nodded through the entire session of meditation which lasted just forty minutes.

The next stage was 'walking meditation' accompanied by mantra, the chants used to calm the mind and provide the right atmosphere for successful meditation. A further fifty minutes of silent meditation followed – silence punctuated by growls from tummies protesting at the long wait till breakfast. The morning meal was a thin porridge bulked out with soya flakes and bananas and the inevitable sweet milky tea. Community work followed. Nobody was assigned a task, but all were expected to do something useful in the way of cleaning, gardening or preparing food. We endured four days of a routine like this with only the occasional lapses (or bouts of rebellion). David was rooming with a Sri Lankan freelance journalist who was fascinated with our lifestyle, so much so that he tried several times to conduct whispered interviews during the meditation sessions. David was reprimanded like a naughty schoolboy for this misdemeanour. The meditation finally came to an end and during our final session in the hall an initiation ceremony was held for two Sinhalese men who were officially entering into the Western Buddhist order.

We rose early on the day of our departure, meditated for a short spell, then ate breakfast before we sank thankfully into the comfortable seats of the minibus that was to take us home to the boat. The route of our return was even more beautiful than that of the outward journey and on the way we visited several of the ancient temple sites near Kandy. The most interesting was the Rockhill Hermitage at Wegirikanda. We climbed up a steep hillside in order to visit the hermits. There were dozens of small caves hewn out of the rock. Each cave was the home of a solitary monk. One of these men spoke a little English and was kind enough to tell us how he had become a monk in later life, on retirement from the merchant service of Sri Lanka and was now living as a hermit in a cave with a skeleton for company. His abiding fear was of his eventual death. The skeleton was providing a focus for meditation which, he hoped, would help him overcome this fear. Our interesting chat with this very worldly monk ended when we were called to the alms house in the valley for lunch. Altogether, it was a most enlightening weekend. Though we did not feel drawn to Buddhism, we like to feel that our experience gave us a deeper understanding of the people and their beliefs.

The local bus services in Sri Lanka are an experience not to be missed. Most of the vehicles are twenty-seaters, excluding the driver and conductor. The bus stops are a matter of local knowledge rather than officially signposted points. One would wait at the stopping place till a bus came along and prayed, while waiting, that the vehicle would not be full. It was not a case of missing the bus if it was, but the fear of being the fiftieth passenger crammed into an already bulging bodywork, or being held in the wide open doorway by the conductor who was likely to stand outside with his arms and legs spreadeagled around the luckless passenger's body to keep it aboard! A bus conductor would never admit to his vehicle being full – no matter how many bodies were clinging to the open doorways or roof racks by their fingernails. Travel within this crazy system was very reasonably priced. A few pennies would transport one quite some distance. The buses were not scheduled, but ran very frequently so were pretty good for getting about, particularly between towns.

David and I would more often than not forego the pleasure of such a ride when going the two miles into Galle town – preferring to trust our own two (or four?) feet. If loaded down with shopping or such then we would either go to the bus station for the 'big bus', a vehicle with forty seats and no over-crowding, or take the Bajaj for the return journey. The Bajaj was no more than a three-wheeled scooter with a saddle seat for the driver and short bench seat for two passengers. A perambulator like canopy structure was pulled over to protect riders from the sudden onset of a tropical downpour. It provided a colourful though comparatively costly way of getting about.

Shortly after our return from Nilambe, I took David down to Habaraduwa to meet Mrs Da Silva and her family and see the batik factory. We arrived about midday and were pressed into staying for an impromptu meal which consisted of all sorts of locally grown goodies and the most wonderful succulent prawns caught in the sea just in front of her home. The afternoon was spent browsing through all the work being done in her batik factory.

Mrs Da Silva was Indian by birth, and a trained nursing tutor who had worked for many years in Delhi. It was there that she had met and married her husband Dr Da Silva. They returned to his country after their marriage and settled in Habaraduwa. For many years they had battled to start a family without success. Mrs Da Silva was known for her gentle caring ways and was looked to for help in dealing with the problem of abandonment of teenage girls by their families. To solve two problems she started up the batik factory which was manned by and run on behalf of these girls. They did all the work and they reaped the benefits. Over the years their home had grown to encompass a huge dormitory where the 'orphans' lived, and the factory premises where the most amazing designs were brought to life on fabric. Two of her girls had shown enough promise for her to have extended their training to a course in Indonesia. Six years prior to our arrival in Sri Lanka, the Da Silva couple's prayers were answered when a foundling baby arrived on their doorstep and was eventually legally adopted by them. They made a vow – the day Sulani became theirs officially – that they would make a pilgrimage every year, on her birthday, to the temples at Kataragama to give thanks for their child.

David and I were very honoured indeed to be included in the group making the pilgrimage in 1987. The annual procession began from the Da Silva home, where close friends and family assembled the day before. By this time David and I were being treated as members of the family and no special concessions were made to our Western way of doing things; for example there was no cutlery at meal times other than a spoon for soup or liquid dessert. We were expected to behave as they did and we really appreciated this. A forty-seater bus was hired and had been packed with food and drink for the journey. The Sinhalese have a wonderful way of travelling about their country. They take their own provisions wherever they go, but never stop to prepare or eat food by the wayside. Everyone in the country, it seems, has a friend or relative living in each town or village. It was customary to drop in at the homes of whichever friend happened to live along the route being followed. There one was welcome to use the facilities of the home for washing and refreshing before joining the resident family who shared the travellers' meal. We met and enjoyed the hospitality of many families when travelling with the Da Silvas on some of their frequent forays into the countryside. Our trip to Kataragama was such a one as this and we found it fascinating. Mrs Da Silva went out of her way to ensure that we saw all the sights, with side-trips to tiny cave shrines and scenic viewpoints en route. The most notable of these took us to the rock temples of Mulkirigala. Here, the vihara (temple) is actually a series of caves reached by climbing successive flights of steps cut into the hillside-rock. The nature of the caves dictated that each shrine had a reclining Buddha as opposed to the more usual sitting or standing ones. The higher one climbed, the larger and grander the shrines became. Each shelter was decorated with the most elaborate hand painted patterns – not unlike bright modern floral wallpapers. At the summit, perched on a huge rock, stood a small whitewashed dagoba (a reliquary), from which there was a superb view of the surrounding countryside. Dagobas, incidentally, appear dotted about all over the country. Generally they are domes with steeple like structures perched on top and, more often than not, painted white. There is almost certain to be one at every temple, but there are many wayside shrines which consist of nothing else. The largest we saw was on the main road half way between Galle and Colombo, and there were few Sinhalese motorists who did not stop to say their prayers when passing.

Kataragama itself is the religious Mecca of Sri Lanka. Set in an enormous, fenced off parkland we found Buddhist temples, Moslem mosques and Hindu temples side by side. Before entering, many of the pilgrims bathe in the river near the park gates and shed their travel-stained clothing for fresh, snowy white garments, ready to enter their chosen places of worship refreshed in body and spirit. Those with less time simply wash hands and feet at the pumps situated near the shrines. Just before we went in, many of our party bought garlands, oil and incense to offer up inside. These offerings were taken first into an outer temple for blessing. On bare feet we made our way along a beautifully kept shale road to the main Dagoba, where the offerings were left for the Gods. David and I each left a beautiful lotus blossom as a mark of respect and token of thanks for being privileged to witness such an important event in the lives of our friends. Although we did not understand much of the ritual, it was, nevertheless, a moving experience.

We had arranged to leave the party after the visit to the temples, because we had met and made friends with a couple who lived and worked on the sugar estates up at Pelwatte. Nick and Julie White had invited us to spend some time with them at their home on the border of the Yala national park. Mrs Da Silva dropped us off at the Traveller's Rest in the village of Kataragama, where we were to await the arrival of the Whites later in the day. Nick and Julie's home turned out to be a very comfortable colonial-style bungalow, with a lovely view of the highland foothills and a pretty irrigation lake in the foreground. It did not take us long to settle into their guest suite and make ourselves at home. We had a delightful week of being waited on hand and foot, and driven around to see the nearby towns of Buttala, Wellawaya, Ella and Bandarawela. What struck us forcibly was the marked difference in the cleanliness of the countryside in this region compared to the steamy coast. There was also a distinct lack of tourists, beggars and touts. We visited one of these small towns on market day and were intrigued by some of the gambling games being run in the streets, especially a form of roulette with a home made wheel which must have been biased!

We returned to Galle a week later, refreshed and ready to begin the long task of getting more complicated jobs done on board *Tin Hau*. The journey home was undertaken in a Ceylon Transport Board bus. It was a vintage Leyland – no doubt held together with chewing gum and hair grips – bursting at the seams as usual and being driven like the proverbial bat out of hell. We disembarked at Matara at lunch time and had a wander round before continuing to Galle on a more modern version of the same vehicle. One thing we had never seen before even though we had driven through the area was the stilt fishing at Welligama. The shallows are a veritable forest of forked stakes set in the seabed. Fishermen wade out at low tide and perch themselves in the crook of the fork. There they remain throughout the high tide, catching fish by handline. Anything they catch is dropped into a keepnet or basket floating in the surf at the base of their stilts and is collected at the next low tide when the fishermen climb down from their perches and wade ashore.

Back on board *Tin Hau*, we proceeded to tackle the aforementioned list of jobs. The timber frames round our portholes were rotting and had to be replaced. Sri Lanka is a good place to obtain brass and bronze articles, and there are lots of small foundries hidden away just waiting to be asked to carry out any work. It took David a while to find one he considered competent enough, with pricing suited to our budget. Eventually, with the help of Don's son, Indra, he succeeded. We were asked to supply a good wooden template. This was not difficult as we had a spare frame for each size of porthole on board. The order was placed in May and delivery was promised by mid- to late June. Meanwhile, the hatches, made of the same wood as the original porthole frames, were also in dire need of replacement. For these we ordered local timber on which we worked ourselves. To prevent future saturation of the wood, we decided to coat the whole with fibreglass – a very messy job, especially in the humid atmosphere.

David spent a lot of time continuing what he started in the Seychelles – the hunt for manufacturers of powered automatic steering systems. Having sailed *Tin Hau* seven thousand miles, he felt we knew her well enough to be able to install an autopilot. Letters flew back and forth between ourselves and companies in various parts of the world who made such goods. Unfortunately, the more we learned, the more confused we became. David was also in correspondence with the manufacturers of our radar, which had not performed as it should from the day it was installed. Though well beyond its guarantee, the manufacturers, Mars Electronics, had agreed to check – and if necessary replace – whichever of the parts they suspected were at fault. We received detailed directions for the removal of the relevant bits and planned to send them back to England. The echo sounder was still in England after having been sent back from the Seychelles, so we had to arrange for its collection too. Routine maintenance of all steelwork on the boat was carried out in parallel with these other jobs.

As in Africa, time meant little to the local inhabitants and we were very frustrated with the delays that held up our work. David had a few component parts made up for the installation of a new exhaust system for the generator – to make it possible to use the genny in a big sea. After the inevitable delays and various modifications, Don's mechanically minded son, Moditha, came aboard to fit the new system. A few trials showed that this was going to be a great improvement and we would no longer have to worry about possible flooding of the generator motor.

By this stage we began to realise that getting everything we wanted in the way of new equipment from abroad was going to involve a lot of tedious dealings with bureaucracy. Our attempts to return our faulty radar bits and bobs had required very patient hours with the authorities. We had been considering a possible holiday flight home in October, but decided in July to return earlier than that and combine it with the opportunity of sorting out our purchases and returning with them to Sri Lanka ourselves. We set a tentative date for flying back to the UK in early August.

On the local scene, things had been hotting up politically, and violence – until then mainly confined to the north – was breaking out all over the country. Suspected terrorists from Jaffna were being shipped by naval vessels down to Galle, where the wharf warehouses had been hastily bricked in to form a makeshift detention centre. We watched hundreds of prisoners arriving daily, each man chained to the next by the ankle. They were marched off the ships in shuffling lines to be incarcerated in the old warehouses, no more than a couple of hundred metres from our boat. From *Tin Hau* and the other boats in port we had a grandstand view of the activities. Don, as Godfather of the local Mafioso, was heavily involved in the comings and goings of the military and civilian officials concerned with interrogation and welfare matters. His veranda became the local gossip shop, where rumours – if not actually invented there – were told and re-told with much embellishment. The yachts were virtually put on red alert at one point. Most of us were rather shocked at the way the prisoners were being handled and lodged complaints, on humanitarian grounds, with Don. Thereafter all prisoners were unchained before being moved off the transport ships.

At about this time Mrs Da Silva wrote a note asking us to join her on a cultural expedition to Colombo, and also to a tea and rubber plantation. We wanted to go to Colombo anyway, in order to finalise our travel arrangements for August. The opportunity to join another of her progressions through the countryside slotted in very neatly with our own plans. David went up to Colombo under his own steam a couple of days early and arranged to meet up with us there. I remained behind to close up the boat for the few days we would be away. I had to be up two hours before cock-crow to meet the bus at the customs post at the harbour entrance. Our first stop was at an old and very important temple where David was waiting to join us. He had with him a young Englishman whom he had met in the hostel at Dehiwala, who was interested in the possibility of joining us for the onward voyage. By then we had decided to forget about the very tempting alternative of proceeding eastwards to Thailand. There were just too many maintenance jobs to be carried out on *Tin Hau*. The more we heard about Larnaca Marina in Cyprus, the more we were coming to realise that this was the place to go to for such work. So we made the decision to continue with our original plan of heading for the Mediterranean via the Red Sea. Cyprus would be the destination, and our departure from Sri Lanka would be in December when the winds changed.

Our next stop was the Colombo Museum. Most of the halls were of no interest to me, although there were several exciting special exhibits. One of these was a magnificent and very large collection of musical instruments of Asia. The other, which was positively outstanding, was the children's puppet museum. If I had only known of these two exhibits at the outset I would not have bothered trailing round the rest of the museum.

After the usual traveller's lunch we headed for Colombo Zoo which, while of a fairly high standard as such places go, was really rather sordid. I really don't appreciate seeing animals cooped up behind fences and bars. The main attraction was the trained working elephants that gave demonstrations of their skills for visitors. We never did see them, however, because rumours started circulating that a curfew was being imposed in and around Colombo as a result of the imminent arrival of the Indian Premier, Rajiv Gandhi. He was due to sign a peace accord to end violence in Sri Lanka. Mrs Da Silva made some enquiries to try and verify the rumours. Finally, we decided to cut our stay in Colombo short and head for the tea plantation, where she had arranged for us to spend the night.

The bus crawled through the southern suburbs of the city. Roads were very congested because everyone wanted to be somewhere else on hearing the threat of curfew. Eventually we made it out into the open roads and were on our way heading south-east for Horuna, a so-called 'low' tea area. We arrived on the estate which had been our destination around sunset, to be greeted by the wide open arms of our host and hostess Tudor and Jo Jayawardene, an utterly charming couple.

Tudor was the director of twelve governmental tea and rubber estate projects in the area, and lived high on a hill in a huge bungalow overlooking one of the tea plantations. We were ushered into a cool room with a high ceiling, furnished with two double beds and with its own en suite bathroom. We felt like two very small peas in an overly large pod as we rattled around in the sumptuous quarters we had been allocated. After a bath and change we joined the others on the front lawn for pre-dinner drinks. Dinner was a very lavish Sinhalese affair with a waiter for every diner. The company was stimulating, though we'd have liked to have had more time to have enjoyed it. Everyone goes to bed so early in hot climates!

We awoke, after a refreshing sleep, to the news that there was an island wide curfew. Only vehicles with special permits would be allowed on the road.

Tudor was a man of influence. He disappeared after breakfast in order to try and sort out some means by which we could continue our journey. It was becoming clear that the best thing would probably be to abandon our sight-seeing and head for home if we could obtain a travel permit. Tudor accomplished this and we set off along country lanes, now deserted because of the curfew, to rejoin the main coast road at Bentota – as close as possible to 'home'. A few miles south of this point we reached Ambalangoda. We were stopped by a police blockade at this point and told we would not be allowed to proceed further in spite of our travel permits. Rioting was still in progress and it would not be safe to go on. Our driver turned the bus about and attempted to find a route round the back of the town, but found our way barred there too. There was no option but to return to Ambalangoda which, being on the main road, was likely to re-open first. The town was quite sizeable, but was a ribbon development strung out along the coast. It had a number of hotels but all of these were at the southern end, and there was no way we could get through to them. The police were unable to say how long we were going to be held up, but said it could be quite a while.

We obviously had to try and find some form of accommodation. Mrs Da Silva made for the Buddhist temple not far from where we had pulled over and was offered refuge in the temple grounds. The bus was moved from the blockade and driven under the palm trees at the temple to be hidden. Buses were a favourite target of the rioters! The thirty-five occupants, including ourselves, became refugees under the protection of the high priest. This worthy gentleman opened up the 'Pilgrim's Rest' for the children of the party, provided us all with sleeping mats, and even found a couple of pillows for David and myself.

Mrs Da Silva organised the group into foraging parties, sent off on foot to try and buy or scrounge foodstuffs to supplement what was carried on the bus. What she had was quite considerable anyway, but she obviously foresaw a siege of some duration. David and I climbed up to the inevitable Dagoba and were invited to join two very young monks for afternoon tea in their cell. They were desperate to practise their limited English and were determined to make the most of the opportunity afforded them by our stay. By the time we returned to the camp a substantial meal of rice and dhal had been prepared. It was gratefully scoffed by all. We paid a moonlit visit to the temple well to bathe before bed. David spent the night being violently sick. We weren't sure if it was the food or a tummy bug.

There was no change in the situation that day or the next. By this time we were fretting a bit as we had only four days left before we were due back in Colombo to fly to England. We begged and pleaded with the police to allow us to walk the twenty or so miles to Galle along the beach. They refused to have anything to do with our idea. However, they did agree that if the situation had not changed by the following day they would escort us through themselves in an armoured vehicle. We had to be satisfied with that and we went off to while away another day in the company of some locals who had befriended us. They took us round the neighbourhood, visiting homes of their relatives and friends where we had the chance to meet the local medicine man, a cinnamon farmer, and a group of tea packers. We were served tea in exquisite cups of the finest china with a watermark depicting a regal figure which they believed to be Queen Victoria.

By the third day quite a few more refugees had arrived, some on foot from Colombo – from where they claimed to have escaped with their lives from burning buildings. Others were the survivors of buses which had been set upon by rioters. There were also a few stranded tourists who had been making their way up from the south, stopping for tea or a simple meal with us before moving northwards. It did seem odd that people were managing to get through from the other direction. We went to see the police again. They were still saying it was not safe to go through on our own but that they would help us the following day. In the event, at six o'clock on the Friday morning, the curfew was lifted for a short while and we were allowed to get away as soon as the barricade was raised. The road was only partially opened up and our driver had to exercise extreme caution. Burnt out hulks of buses littered the route, as did burning piles of palm tree trunks and smouldering tyres. Telephone poles and lines had been brought down and pylons turned over. Along with railway lines and sleepers, these had been dragged on to the road. Bulldozers had been used to shift great boulders off the beaches and on to the tarmac too. All of this meant that it took us almost two hours to reach Galle. Shortly after we arrived the curfew was reimposed. We felt vastly relieved to be back, though we still had the problem of how to get ourselves to Colombo for the outward flight if the situation remained unchanged.

Don Windsor was not particularly alarmed at our absence, but the other yachtsmen had been planning all sorts of wild moves to save *Tin Hau* in our absence. They had experienced petrol bombs flying across the harbour and had been quite worried.

Our trip to the UK started with our cadging a lift to Colombo with an American study group staying at the nearby Closenburg Hotel. We did this to ensure permit-documented transport. We were uncertain whether or not the troubles would allow passage between Galle and Colombo. We left with a day in hand but the situation had quietened considerably. Although the entire seventy-two miles was littered with riot debris, there was no active rioting and we made it through to the city. The Americans dropped us off on the southern outskirts of town and we hired a Bajaj to take ourselves and our luggage to the bus station in the city centre.

At the station we were able to get a minibus which gave us a hair raising ride out to the town of Negombo which is the nearest settlement to the airport. Negombo is a pretty town built on the banks of lagoons and canals and we managed to find a clean and homely guest house for the overnight stay. David's body chose that inopportune moment to rebel, staging a recurrence of the tummy problem. By the following morning I realised he was in no state to travel and would not be unless I got him to a doctor or medic immediately. I managed to find a doctor who was very helpful and supplied what I required, which included rehydration material.

David was well enough to go about an hour before we were due to take off. We made it to the plane – an Aeroflot Ilyushin bound for Karachi. It was very comfortable, apart from a tendency to shower the unlucky aisle seat passengers on takeoff and landing. The humidifier system wasn't functioning too well and caused a deluge of water to be released through vents either side of the aisle. The plane was pleasantly underbooked and, as there was no formal allocation of seats, we made sure we were not in the 'shower zone'. We did not see much of Karachi as it was a night stop, but the shops in the transit concourse were full of fascinating goods. 'Make order, Make order,' we were told by a weedy looking army officer backed up by burly uniformed soldiers, as he whipped us into a single file on the walk across the runway back to the plane. Several Russian engineers joined us, on their way home after being seconded on aid to Pakistan. They were not very communicative in spite of glasnost and all that. We amused ourselves by trying to spot the KGB agent, for we felt sure that there must have been one around to make the men clam up. The victim on take-off from Karachi was a gentleman with a haircut like a hedgehog sitting in the aisle seat a row in front of us – he had everyone in hysterics when he was caught in the downpour. The man who sat next to me was obviously familiar with this habit of Russian planes because as soon as we had taxied out to the end of the runway he had folded his magazine over his head.

Our first stop in Russia was Tashkent. It was still dark, so we saw nothing beyond the incredibly scruffy airport. We arrived in Moscow at four o'clock in the morning and were transferred to the Moscow Hilton – actually the Scheremetyvo Hotel, alongside the airport of the same name (one of Moscow's seven airports). We were allocated rooms; all doubles, so single travellers had to pair off. We were issued with vouchers to cover all the meals we would be entitled to during our brief stay. We had been advised by our travel agent in Colombo to ask for the free tour of the city when we got to Moscow. Incredibly, we were the only passengers who had been told this was a possibility, so we really started something when we asked to be allowed to do the tour. In the end they organised two coaches to accommodate eighty requests.

The tour was scheduled for ten o'clock. We had time to have a nap, shower and then go down for a meal. When we got to our room we discovered that the hot water was not functioning. It was a cold shower or nothing and the cold water was icy. The bedroom was quite well appointed and the bed comfortable, so we had a good rest. To us the whole thing was positive luxury after some of the places we had been and some of the things we had seen. However, in retrospect, I realise that the hotel we stayed at in Moscow was actually rather rundown. The curtains were hung with paper clips and safety pins. The plumbing was very poorly installed. The food was incredibly basic for a so-called international hotel, and the service was like nothing I'd ever experienced before.

At ten, as arranged, we piled into the coach and drove into Moscow centre to pick up an Intourist guide. We had a really fascinating tour of the city and were allowed to photograph anything that took our fancy. Red Square was paved with red stones; the Kremlin was far more beautiful in reality than I had been prepared for from pictures seen on television. We drove to the University of Moscow with its imposing architecture set in lovely park-like surroundings. We were allowed (unofficially) to get out of the coach for a short stop at one vantage point on a bridge overlooking the whole of Moscow, with the Olympics site in the foreground. By the time we had been up and down all those streets I had read about in spy novels, and passed familiar sounding landmarks like the GUM department store with long queues of shoppers waiting to gain admittance, seen Dzerzinski Square – home of the KGB and its associated departments – and seen the Bolshoi and Tchaikovsky theatres, our heads were ringing. After the tour, we lunched in the hotel dining room and then napped till it was time to go back to the airport. There we boarded the biggest plane in the Aeroflot fleet on its inaugural flight to Heathrow.

Derek and Frances Chidell were at Heathrow to meet us and take us to their home for our first few days back in civilisation. I cannot describe how wonderful it was to be back in merrie Englande, or describe the culture shock we experienced after so long in what seemed like alien lands. The efficiency, cleanliness and organisation of the most basic things was what struck us most forcibly. Fruit shops had bright and sparkling stock, attractively presented to the buyer. Supermarkets displayed goods we hadn't seen for years because they were unobtainable abroad. Packaging was so appealing we just wanted to buy the product to enjoy undoing the wrappers! The joy of being able to pick up a phone and place an order for a complicated mechanical part that had to be made to our design and to have it delivered to our home the following day was immense. Being able to hand in our defective radar parts at the factory and know they would be sent by courier in time for us to take them back on our return was most satisfying, as was the politeness and helpfulness of those working in service industries – they could have taught the Sinhalese a thing or three.

We left Derek and Frances in order to get to Chichester for Margaret's birthday. In fact the cat was let out of the bag because she just happened to phone Derek the night we arrived, so our arrival was not a surprise. Mark cut short his cycling tour of France in order to come home and spend some time with us. We hadn't seen any of the family since Mauritius. Mark, David and I went up to London to meet Tandy, and that morning managed to sort out all the problems we had been wrestling with for months in Sri Lanka. With everything bought or ordered in one morning, we had three weeks we could devote entirely to catching up with friends and family. Lazy days playing croquet on the back lawn, having pub lunches, visiting the theatre and watching the latest movies and TV (latest being anything made in the previous four years!) – in other words, indulging in all the landlubberly activities which were a novelty and treat for us.

We went to Southampton and saw *T'ai Shan* (sister ship to *Tin Hau*) after locating Tony Richardson. It was a very eerie feeling stepping aboard a boat we knew so well, yet not at all. *T'ai Shan* is a great credit to Tony. We tried many times to make arrangements to get the two junks together. It was not until years later that we finally managed it.

Far too soon we were thrust back into the heat and filth of Sri Lanka to get on with the business of readying the boat for the long voyage into the Mediterranean.

We were disappointed on our return to find that the porthole frames were still not ready for installation. You may remember that they were to have been completed by mid-May. Three and a half months later there was no sign of them. It took no time at all installing the newly acquired solar panel and David was able to get much of the Autohelm 6000 installation done without recourse to the yottie co-operative. Most of the work involved the fashioning of supporting brackets, a task made more difficult because the local steel workers could not read drawings. This meant hours over at the slipway workshops, with David interpreting his own drawings for the fabricators. Added to that was the 'ninety per cent syndrome' – a phenomenon which was peculiarly Sri Lankan. Nothing was ever a one hundred per cent job. The final ten per cent which would produce a perfect piece of work always seemed to elude the Sinhalese.

A typical example of a ninety per cent job was the new exhaust fitted to the generator early on during our period in Galle. Just before returning to the UK in August, I turned on the generator. I had to turn it off again quickly because it was making a dreadful noise and there were large sparks issuing from the fan vents. What had happened was that Moditha or his assistant had somehow managed to drop a stainless steel nut, which had worked its way down and finally entered the fan casing. There it proceeded to shatter fan blades one by one, ultimately jamming the starter motor. With Wilf's help we had partially stripped it and had managed to fish out a number of the broken blade bits with a flexible strip magnet. This freed the starter motor enough to fire it up. We got the thing going but there were still sparks, coughs and wheezes.

At this point we called in the local 'expert' mechanic. He, poor man, was only on board five minutes before he felt so sea sick he had to be ferried ashore (he had politely asked David's permission to vomit). Rather than do any further damage we decided to shelve the whole thing and wait till some-one with a little more knowledge happened along. The alterations to the pilothouse seating had been made and I was anxious to cannibalise the existing cushion covers and make new ones for the new seats. In order to use my sewing machine I needed electricity. We decided to temporarily 'import' my machine into Sri Lanka and rent a room with electricity from Don for a day. It was a devil having to organise to pay bond on the machine. A lot of paperwork was involved. Once we got the machine to Don's we discovered we hadn't the right type of plug. We went out and bought one, fitted it, plugged in and... Wham! David got a nasty shock and the electronics and motor of my machine blew up. 'Oh,' said Don, 'so sorry – I forgot to tell you the earth could be live!' Where else in the world would one find a live earth?

During the first six months of our sojourn in Sri Lanka we had the company of crews from quite a few transient yachts hailing from Sweden, Switzerland, USA, Germany and Australia. There were vessels of all shapes and sizes with a wide variety of rigs. These had arrived from far flung parts and most were heading east to Thailand or beyond. Their stays in Galle varied from a week to a month. We had boats of between twenty-five and seventy-five feet in length and almost all were manned by couples on their own. We were the first boat in Galle that year waiting to go west. Eventually we were joined by a whole fleet of boats going the same way. There were one or two other 'long stay' boats, notably a very spaced-out Swiss couple who owned an Indian dhow, *Aum Gaia*. They had spent many years in India, and the final three of those cruising up and down the west coast learning to handle their boat. The man, Fidibus, had gone native in habits and mannerisms. They left to sail to Thailand at the tail end of the south-west monsoon season with very patched-up sails, a borrowed VHF radio and charts, and no engine. The day they left blew up very nasty with forty-five knot winds lashing us in harbour. We dread to think what it was like for them. They were relatively inexperienced and their boat's windward ability was even worse than ours. Those remaining at Galle really worried about them, and were relieved months later to hear that they had made it. However, long after we reached Cyprus, a rumour reached us that they were back in Sri Lanka again – by accident! They had attended a yottie wedding on an island off Phuket. Unable to get back to the Thai coast, their day trip had turned into an unexpected 1,200 mile downwind passage to Sri Lanka, with very little food and no water by the time they got in.

There was a German single-hander in port for some months. He had the misfortune to be tied to the buoy closest to the big ship berth. While he was in Colombo on business one day, we watched in horror as a berthing cargo vessel was caught in a cross wind and went out of control, picking up *Birgitt* and the buoy on its rudder. We stood by helplessly but David had the presence of mind to take a series of photographs of the incident in the hope that it would help Löthar get some compensation for the damage. Claims were submitted and the pilot who had been in charge at the time had the nerve – even when confronted with the photographic evidence – to deny the incident had ever happened. Eventually Löthar had to leave in order to use the monsoon, and he never did get his damage paid for.

My birthday was celebrated in Don's home, with all those yotties in port at the time. Maggie, an ex-actress on board *Tanda*, a large British schooner, attended as if dressed for the Queen's garden party. She was wearing a large and flowery picture hat, worn with a lovely white broderie anglaise cotton dress. She arrived by bicycle! Her husband Wilf attended in his usual scruffy boat clothes, which consisted of ripped shorts barely covering his bottom, paint-bespattered tee-shirt which rode up at the front and gave a hint of furry pot-belly, and to complete it all a towel round his neck and a farmer's hat on top. Kenny and Richenda from the yacht *Sarah* went to town with painted faces, which totally bewildered the customs officers and utterly confirmed their belief that yotties are crazy (most of us are). Various others attended, including Nick and Julie White, who had come down from Pelwatte for the weekend. We were kicked out of Don's at midnight and continued aboard *Tin Hau* until half past two in the morning. Everyone was distinctly under the weather the next day – especially ourselves, as the Whites were staying aboard *Tin Hau* and we had taken up where we had left off the night before.

The tail end of the yachts heading east brought those boats sailing down to Australia to wave the British and Polish flags at the Australian bicentennial celebrations early in 1988. The tall ships of the world were congregating in Freemantle, then sailing from Hobart to Sydney. The British contingent consisted of two Nicholson 55's (*Sabre* and *Adventure*), with their support vessel, a trade wind motor-sailer of some seventy tons gross (*Aztec Lady*), and three crews totalling thirty-four persons.

The Polish entry was the thirty-one year old steel ketch *Joseph Conrad*, with a crew of ten. Suddenly Galle was livening up socially and, with a number of nasty squalls and the British not having sorted out their anchoring techniques, there was lots of fun in the harbour with dragging anchors. Hot bunking meant the Brits were playing a kind of musical berths. We made our spare berths available to the female crew members of *Sabre* and *Adventure* to ease that problem a little. The Poles turned out to be a particularly friendly and lively bunch of young people, with a fair command of our language and a highly developed taste for folk music and sea shanties. There were several talented guitarists among them, and we enjoyed many evenings singing folk songs with our own words (English and Polish) accompanied by tunes common to both nationalities. David's accordion was a popular addition to the band. Their final night was open house on the *Joseph Conrad*, and a heavy night it was – Polish vodka just about blew the tops of our heads off.

We seldom experienced less than five yachts in harbour, but the numbers had not got above ten until November, when the 'Red Sea fleet' began to arrive. Then yarn swapping started in earnest. The grapevine – where vital bits of information and gossip are exchanged – is a very important part of the small boat sailor's way of life. We always found the co-operative efforts between vessels to be outstanding, and we wish there was more of this open, giving attitude in evidence on land.

Once the Red Sea fleet started to arrive, we suddenly had a wealth of expertise on which to draw. The generator was totally stripped down by Geoff from *Arnak* and Glen from *St Combs*, the fan was rebuilt locally, the starter motor eventually had to be repaired, and the yottie engineering team got it all back together again. Our repayment was guiding the new arrivals through all their teething troubles in Galle, boat-sitting for them when they wished to travel inland, and introducing them to the best suppliers.

The porthole frames finally arrived towards the end of September. Fitting twenty-seven portholes at various places on the cabin sides could only be done in stages manageable between downpours. Each old frame had to be removed and the new frame offered up to the space it was to cover. This was to ensure that the boltholes were correctly positioned. In order to drill the holes accurately, David had arranged to use a drill press facility ashore. The procedure was, therefore, to mark out about six portholes, row them ashore, take them through customs, drill the holes, bring them back through customs, row them back to the boat, insert rubber gaskets to isolate the bronze from the steel, and bolt them in position. Bang in the middle of this exercise the customs six monthly rotation happened and we got a new chief. David was on his final trip when he was stopped by this new manager who proceeded to create problems where before none had existed. After much argument, David was allowed to pass through to get his drilling done and returned through customs with neither sight nor sign of an officer.

The following day we were busy applying the final coat of sealant to the installation when the customs boat pulled alongside. On board, looking like a fat red turkey, hopping up and down with fury, was the new chief. Very rudely, he ordered David to report to his office immediately. David, equally angry and shaking with it, hurriedly dressed in shore clothes and rowed off to get Don before the chief returned to base. David made his appeal to Don (the friendly ten per cent yacht agent) outlining the entire farce to him. Don said that there was nothing he could do and that David would have to sort it out for himself. (What were we paying him his fee for I wonder?) David had to go and face the angry turkey and argue the toss with him as to whether or not we should have to pay 1,000 Rupees 'cess' tax (whatever that was). We were pretty certain that there was no export tax on brass or bronze ware, which was freely available to tourists and not listed as a dutiable item at the airport. Anyway, this mad official strutted around yelling at David that 'rich' yotties could afford to pay 1,000 Rupees (about £20) easily, and why shouldn't the customs get revenue from yachts? He ended up telling David that he would not issue our clearance papers without our paying the tax in question. David laughed that threat off with the news that we weren't leaving till December and he agreed to pay the so-called 'cess' tax if the chief could produce the customs tariff code book and show the category under which we were liable. Nothing further happened for several weeks. Then, out of the blue, the officer visited *Tin Hau* with about thirty friends and relations. We gave them a free guided tour and some suitable refreshment. Miraculously, the whole business of 'cess' tax was forgotten. Another battle with officialdom was over. Although worn down, this time we felt we had won.

The longer we stayed in Sri Lanka, the more we realised the depths of corrupt practices that were not immediately apparent. During the British forces visit we discovered that Don had presented a bill to the captain of each boat for food and drink. We all knew that the individual crew members had paid for their own drinks. The final insult was delivered when the British High Commissioner was also presented with a bill for the same food and drink.

I had got myself into some hot water during that visit. Two of the girls who had used our bunking facilities had asked me to take them to Mrs Da Silva's batik factory. This I had willingly done, and we had a lovely morning with her and her girls. We were, as usual, pressed to stay for lunch; this was really appreciated by the two young ladies, as they had seen nothing of Sri Lanka during their brief stay. They had also enjoyed the novelty of the CTB bus rides there and back. Don got to hear of this visit and of how much they spent down at Habaraduwa. He was furious with me because I had done him out of a twenty to twenty-five per cent backhander which he would have had for sending them to his 'pet' batik shop.

It appeared that we were already in his bad books for having chosen to shop where we did and not at one of his suppliers. Our suppliers, Bandula and Mike, were new to the yacht provisioning business. David and I were their first non-Sinhalese customers. We requested items they did not stock, and even though they were a small family business, they were willing to take the chance of buying in things that we required. This forward-looking attitude, the service they were prepared to offer, and their efforts to please paid off for them in the end. We recommended them to all the yachtsmen. This turned them into stiff competition for Don's suppliers. They had, quite rightly, refused to give Don any commission.

Bandula and Mike became much more than just the local village store. They became good friends, too, with whom we are still in touch. We understand that they are now quoted in the pilots and guides used by yotties and seamen in that part of the world. Their good fortune is well deserved.

It may appear, from what I have written about him, that Don Windsor was a bit of a crook. This was not the case. One must remember that we were dealing with a system different to our own. What we call corruption others see as good business practice. Unfortunately, some of the yotties were not prepared to see the difference and were convinced they were being ripped off by all and sundry, but especially by Don. The ringleader of this group of yotties was Wilf of *Tanda*. By virtue of the fact that we had been there longest, and probably knew him best, we felt it was our duty to defend Don, many an hour was spent trying to convince Wilf (known as 'the Filth') that Don was running a business according to the customs of his country, not waging a vendetta against foreigners. Our words fell on deaf (or heavily inebriated) ears, and eventually there was a showdown between the two. Don solved the whole thing by banning Wilf the Filth from his home and grounds.

One of the features of Sri Lanka which I have not yet mentioned are the cool spots. A cool spot is a small wayside stall providing refreshment for the traveller. They mainly sell tea and soft drinks and snacks called *appa* (more commonly known as 'hoppas'), a sort of pancake with a fried egg in the middle. There was a cool spot right outside the customs post at Galle harbour, which we used regularly. Cooking could be a pig of a job in the heat and humidity. We had a regular booking for a Sunday evening meal with the family who ran the cool spot. They opened up specially for this group of yotties and provided us with a super meal for 25p each. The meal consisted of a pile of rice with four vegetable curries and a little omelette or dried fish, a glass of tea, a small soft drink, and a tiny wrapped sweetmeat to finish. The cool spot was in a small block-built garage-like structure, with a door at the back leading to the garden of the owner's home. There was nothing other than a glass counter and four tables and chairs in the 'shop'. There was no front door. When we arrived – usually in torrential rain – we had to call out and the grandfather would come round through the garden in to the shop and pull out three long planks from a hole in the front wall to let us in. Power cuts were frequent, so there were always plenty of candles ready stuck on saucers and bottle necks for our use. There was no menu – the food would just be what we were given. Our only choice was the type of soft drink we could start with. Simple though it was, it was a place we always felt welcome and at home and had many happy hours both with other yotties and the delightful family who ran it.

By the beginning of December, we had finished all our re-fitting jobs and were only awaiting some work we had put in the hands of a local carpenter. We decided we'd like to get away from Sri Lanka by mid-December and have Christmas at sea once again. David had arranged to take on the young man we had met earlier in the year as crew, together with another chosen for us in England by Derek Chidell, the main reason for crew being that we had not tested our Autohelm and didn't know if or how well it would work. David felt that the extra hands and eyes could be vital in the Red Sea. I must confess that

I was reluctant to have anyone else on board and was feeling very anti-crew, principally because I disliked the loss of privacy and freedom, and having crew doubled my own workload. In addition to standing all my usual watches and so on, I had double the provisioning to work out, and double the planning and cooking. Skipper's decision overruled my reservations and word was sent to Darren (who was in India at the time) and to Martyn in England that they should report aboard by 15th December, ready for departure a few days after that.

David got on with planning the route, allowing for various possible stops to take on water, fuel and provisions. This was an important preparation for the voyage ahead, as there were so many politically sensitive areas and places it would be advisable to avoid. Time had to be allowed for the fact that there would be long stops in the northern part of the Red Sea waiting for the right weather. Because the prevailing winds in that sector are from the north to north-west, it was unlikely that *Tin Hau* would be able to do much under sail. Calms or near calms would be necessary for economic progress under power. Our pilots and routeing charts showed that these happened only rarely.

At the time there were rumours galore that Aden (South Yemen) had an epidemic of meningitis. The Australians were being advised by their embassy to head for Djibouti on the African mainland instead. David wrote to the British authorities in Aden, who replied that the incidence of meningitis was no worse there than anywhere else in the region – that food, water and fuel were freely available, and that they would love us to visit. What a change to find an embassy that welcomed cruising yachtsmen.

Whatever the outcome of David's planning deliberations, there was no doubt that the next leg of the voyage of *Tin Hau* was going to be challenging. The route is known to be one of the more difficult passages for ocean cruisers to make. We would be relieved to have it behind us.

PART FOUR

The Arabian and Red Seas

David Chidell

198

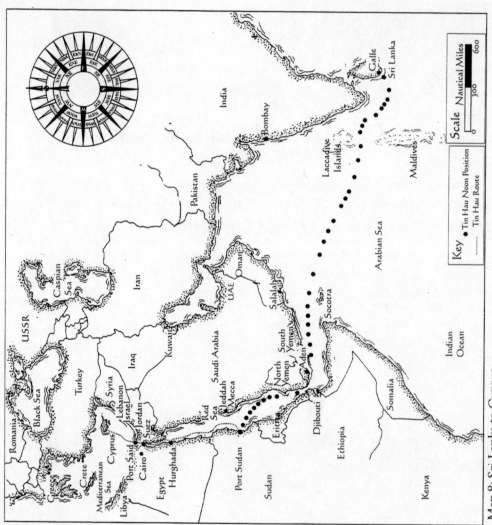

Map 8: Sri Lanka to Cyprus

1. Decisions

At long last the time had come for *Tin Hau* to be on the move once again. We had arrived in Galle in April in the knowledge that we could be there for perhaps as long as eight months, but there were no immediate pressures on us to decide where to go to next. As we had seen it, there were two main options and we could wait until July or so before making a decision as to which one to follow.

Plan 'A' was to turn right and go east. This would mean departure from Galle any time before November to pick up the wet south-west monsoon for an 1,100 mile ten to fifteen day crossing of the Bay of Bengal to Phuket in Thailand. We would then remain in that area and commence life as a charter boat.

Plan 'B' was to turn left and go west. This would mean departure from Galle in December to pick up the dry north-east monsoon for a 2,200 mile twenty to thirty day crossing of the Arabian Sea to Aden at the southern end of the Red Sea. There would follow a further six hundred or so miles of generally following winds to Port Sudan, half way up the Red Sea. Then seven hundred miles of strong headwinds and steep seas to Suez – no problem for vessels with powerful enough engines or with good windward sailing ability, but an altogether different matter for a beamy Chinese junk with a relatively small engine. Then ninety miles of the Suez Canal itself, fine as long as the political troubles of the 1970s did not flare up again (the canal had been closed from 1967 to 1975 due to the Israeli-Arab war which had resulted in the 'entombment' of some ships within the Bitter Lakes for seven long years). Finally the Mediterranean and a short two hundred and fifty mile hop to Larnaca Marina in Cyprus. Perhaps the whole voyage would take three to four months and be extremely enjoyable. Or just possibly we would not make it at all.

These were the two options, an easy passage to a fascinating country with a good climate just opening up to tourism and the charter market; or a difficult passage back to a Western country well used to tourists and yachts.

It would seem obvious. Go east. The opportunity was there. Change our original plans of becoming a charter boat in Greece or Turkey. Phuket and Thailand were so close. The potential seemed endless. And the cost of living was low. But...

The 'but' was *Tin Hau*. She needed attention. After the experience of living aboard her for well over a year in all sorts of conditions and climates, the list of improvements that we wanted to make filled eight pages of our 'defects book': improvements to the running rigging and other specialised 'junk matters'; improvements to the interior; removal of certain rust traps such as the deck boxes; changes to features such as the sea-cocks, which were causing considerable anxiety; finally, we badly needed to have her hauled out of the water so that we could repaint the hull in local spots and apply antifoul paint over the whole area below the water-line.

On the latter point I was becoming disenchanted with the weekly 'hold your breath and scrub the hull' routine. I had always been a bit worried by the knowledge that just behind my kicking flippers there were probably sharks lurking, who might want a nibble, if hungry. At least in the clear waters of Chagos we could see them when they were in the lagoon. Galle harbour, however, was murky and polluted. The discharge point of the sewer serving the town was clearly visible on the beach one hundred metres away and there was abundant food for fish and other creatures of the deep. I would often have to flush wriggling creatures out of my ears and bathing trunks after a hull cleaning session, but the job had to be done. My three attempts to pay a local to take on the work all ended in failure. It seemed that no one wanted the job more than once, whatever the pay.

There was a slipway in the harbour which made a haul-out and repaint possible, at least in theory. Having heard about some of the disasters which had happened – boats falling off their cradles and so on – I did not want to risk losing *Tin Hau* in this way. All our enquiries about Thai or Malaysian boat-yards did not yield anything more promising than Galle. Whereas Larnaca Marina with its large travel lift seemed to present no problems. We could haul *Tin Hau* out of the water in safety and at an affordable price. We could spend months working on her with no worries about where to obtain certain materials; and there would be no anxiety that the immigration or custom authorities might force us to leave the country before completion of the work.

By about June we had made our decision. We would go west. We would aim for Larnaca Marina. A tentative booking was made for 1st April. *Tin Hau* would be given all the care and attention she deserved. Our infatuation with 'our lady' came first – anyone who has ever owned and loved a boat will understand this. We would stick to our original plans and still try to become a charter boat in Greece or Turkey, even though there were one or two difficulties to overcome first before getting there.

So, by October or so, we were planning for our next voyage – Sri Lanka to Cyprus.

Arrangements were made with Darren (Pain), a twenty-five year-old carpenter and yoga teacher from East Sussex and Martyn (Kalina), a twenty-one year old decorator and Operation Raleigh veteran from near London, to join us. Darren only had to make a short journey from southern India. But Martyn had to fly from London (a flight which was to include a rip-off during a fuelling stop in India, when all transit passengers were persuaded to part with about £20 for an unnecessary visa). Both Martyn and Darren agreed to pay us £5 per day to cover food and certain boat costs; and to take full responsibility for the costs of transport in joining us and the costs of flying home from Cyprus or wherever. Having heard many horror stories from other yotties of crew arrangements that had gone wrong, particularly when items such as money and return flights were not discussed at the outset, we were always most careful in our choice of crew. For me at least, one of the highlights of our life afloat was the pleasure of getting to know those individuals who joined us on our longer passages. Darren and Martyn were no exception, although no one could beat Jeff, Jax, Barry and Jean-Marc on that very special maiden voyage.

2.   The Fleet

By 21st November, 1987, most of the current year's Red Sea Fleet was present in Galle Harbour. With the help of a German friend we had made in Galle, Volker Otto, I recorded the historic moment on video camera. Of the twenty-eight boats moored in the harbour only Nick White's *Alepha* was to remain; and he had already done his fair share of cruising from Madagascar to Sri Lanka via Kenya. Nick had built *Alepha* himself and had received some divine help when the launching problem was resolved by a convenient flood!

The most dramatic vessel was the one hundred year-old eighty-five foot wooden Norwegian brigantine, *Svanhilde*, a comfortable home for four families. Even the youngest children had a part to play in the running of this beautiful ship, of which we were to see more in the Red Sea.

Probably the next most interesting boat (besides *Tin Hau*, but we were biased!) was a wooden schooner named *Passat*, formerly a Portuguese trawler and about sixty feet in length. She had been brought in to Galle about two years earlier by a German crew, only to suffer a mysterious fire whilst on the slipway. The fire had been put out, but rumours were rife that it had been started deliberately with an insurance claim in mind. The new owner was an

American called Mike, who lived in England. He had plans to sail her up the Red Sea with the rest of us. 'How do you aim to do it, Mike?' I asked. 'Easy,' he said, 'just motor up the middle.'

We were to see more of *Passat*, but not until much later in Larnaca, where she created quite a stir not just by the story of her voyage but also by a strange event that happened there in front of many witnesses.

Of the other twenty-five yachts in Galle Harbour on 21st November, ten originated from Australia. Many of these were built by their owners, often of steel – yachts such as *Dalliance* (owned by Charles); *Top Knot* (Ted and Barb); *Lady Catrin* (Robert and Liz); *Yemanja II* (Rick and Julie); *Roama* (Doug and Yvonne); *Sundancer III* (Noel); and *Endurance II* (Steve, Warren and Michelle). There was also *Koonawarra* (a wooden yacht owned by David and Gail), *Quiet Achiever* (a thirty-three foot plywood catamaran owned by Graham and Gillian); and finally *Aquilla* (also a plywood catamaran, owned by Bob and Judy, who had with them their four children, Clare, Bruce, Lucy and Emily. One of the children later helped save *Tin Hau* from a serious accident while we were absent.)

There were three yachts from the United States – *Verity* (a fibreglass sloop owned by Karl and Patty); *Sauvage* (a fast aluminium schooner owned by a Pan-Am pilot; so fast that we never got to know him and about the first yacht of the year through the Suez Canal); and *St Combs* (probably the most luxurious of all the yachts in Galle that year – a fifty-foot fibreglass sloop with all mod cons including two Perkins 4.236 engines to our one and a desalination plant. *St Combs* was a beautiful yacht, owned by Alan and Gwen Buchan of Washington state).

Three yachts came from Sweden – *Miss My* (a fibreglass sloop), another fibreglass sloop whose name we never learnt, and *Lady Rosi* (a fibreglass sloop owned by Roger and Siv, who had with them their three year-old daughter, Rosita. This was to be the only yacht we ever encountered well out to sea in the Indian Ocean.)

Two yachts came from Holland – *Narai* (a catamaran – we never met the owners) and *Klepel* (owned by Nico and Hennie, whom we were to meet again on several occasions).

Two yachts were Swiss – *Fam* (a steel sloop owned by Ramon and Erica), and a ketch whose name we never learnt.

Arnak was the only yacht from New Zealand, a forty foot fibreglass Spray replica built by Geoff and Linda Gentil, immaculately maintained. Geoff was one of those people with a positive outlook on life, the ability to fix just about anything, and the generosity to help anyone in need (us included) at a moment's notice.

Boreas was – surprisingly – the only French yacht, a small aluminium sloop owned by Gilles and Christine. Possibly, most French cruising circumnavigators take the alternative South African route around the world as opposed to the Red Sea route – we certainly saw a number of French yachts in Mauritius, often constructed in aluminium.

Tara of Meath was the only Canadian registered yacht, a small steel sloop. The owner, Mike Kelly, was English, having originated from Porkellis in Cornwall. His family were known, he says, as the 'Poor Kellys'. We never ceased to marvel at the courage shown by Mike in overcoming a horrific accident in Canada which had left him in a coma for months. In spite of this – and still suffering from his injuries – he had managed to sail *Tara* most of the way around the world, often on his own. His ambition on reaching England was to continue life afloat, but in less strenuous circumstances in a canal narrow boat with his wife, Liyun. All of this he achieved.

Finally – besides *Tin Hau* – the only boat in harbour not yet mentioned was a small fibreglass sloop (a Nicholson 31) named *Baraka A*. Although flying a British flag (of convenience), this yacht was special in that it was crewed by the first Saudi Arabian man, Jameel, and the first Egyptian woman, Sherry, attempting to sail around the world. I later witnessed the official welcoming in Suez when their circumnavigation was nearly complete. Some years after this we purchased their book – *The Voyage of Baraka A* – and learnt that they did complete their circumnavigation, on reaching Casablanca in September 1988. They had many adventures. As is so often the case, it was their guts, determination and perseverance that got them around the world, not their initial sailing experience, which was almost nil.

Two yachts had left Galle already – the first being the twenty-four foot engineless sloop *Tola*, the baby of the fleet. Mike and Karen, the American owners, wanted to spend some time exploring the western coast of India before setting off for Aden from the former Portuguese colony of Goa. When we next saw them we learnt that Karen was pregnant, as there had been problems – discovered too late – with their Indian condoms. It seems that in India it is quite normal for ants to make small holes in condoms. Beware!

The other yacht was the Freedom-rigged *Bonaventure II*, the first of the Australian yachts to arrive in Galle and crewed by the owners, Bob and Dawn Buick. Again, we were to see a lot more of this boat, which always seemed to be at the centre of the action. Bob, like many of the Aussies shortly to arrive in Sri Lanka, was a keen radio ham.

Four other yachts did arrive in Galle after 21st November and before our departure – the American sloop *Windsong* (owned by Dick and Bonnie Bhyre); the New Zealand yacht *Freedom Hunter*; the Hong Kong yacht *Dreamtime* (owned by John Watson); and, on the day before we left, the British yacht *Didicoy*, with a mast temporarily held together with G-clamps and crewed by a retired couple, Bill and Betty, from England.

We did come across a further dozen or so yachts in the Red Sea proceeding northwards with the fleet. However we were still nearly alone in being British. Why were we seeing so few genuine British cruising yachts?

It was also surprising that in spite of so many people dreaming about cruising and sailing around (or part-way around) the world – people with the time, money and skills to do it – the number of boats actually passing through the Indian Ocean in 1987–1988 (with stopovers) was so few. I would estimate there were one hundred and fifty at the most.

3.   Preparations for the Voyage

By December we were starting to prepare in earnest for the voyage. Our immediate destination would be Salalah, in Oman. This was six hundred miles east-north-east of Aden along the coast of the Arabian peninsular, and not far off our route. Reports from yachts which had visited Salalah the previous year were very favourable. It would be interesting to have a quick glimpse of yet another country, although whether we actually stopped or not would depend on the strength and the slant of the north-east monsoon. If it turned out to be under-strength, or too much from the north, we would be forced to head straight for Aden.

It was disappointing that we would have to miss India but all recent accounts of the behaviour of the customs officials in the nearest major port, Cochin, were discouraging. Apparently, it was normal for the captain of a visiting foreign vessel to be asked, on arrival, to list every movable item to be found on his boat or ship. On departure, any items spotted by the eagle-eyed customs officials as 'not on the list' were immediately confiscated. For this reason the skipper of just about every yacht in Galle harbour decided with regret to give India a miss. I wonder if anyone in India noticed?

Even more on route, five hundred miles out of Galle, was the small island of Suheli Par, one of the Laccadive Islands administered by India. It seemed that we would have to miss this too. Again, the problem was the unpredictable behaviour of officials. Apparently, the previous year, two yachts had been detained there for three weeks for no good reason. We definitely could not afford a delay of this length.

So, bearing in mind that our provisioning would have to last for nearly four months (with some additional fresh food provisioning in Aden, Port Sudan and Suez), we made a final shopping visit to Mike and Bandula at 'Somebody Stores' to top up what was already held in *Tin Hau's* larders. Together we worked out a large order. In all we spent 9,804 rupees (£204) on non-perishable items such as beer, arrack, cigarettes (necessary 'currency' in the Red Sea), tinned and bottled goods, brown sugar (about eighty kilograms of the best), tea (again, of the highest quality), coffee, milk powder, flour, rice, liquid laundry soap, toilet paper and so on; and we spent a further 3,672 rupees (£76) on perishable items such as potatoes, tomatoes, a large branch of a banana tree complete with unripe bananas, eggs, cheese, bread, margarine, chocolate and meat. We also took on a good supply of Sri Lankan 'specials', such as locally produced strawberry jam labelled 'GUARANTEED NO STRAWBERRIES'; marmalade labelled 'Orange Marmalade Jam'; and the excellent locally made curd, packaged in terracotta bowls which were useful afterwards as ash trays.

We sadly said our farewells to the two brothers in their family room at the rear of the shop, where they entertained us royally and made a formal presentation of two traditionally carved and painted Sinhalese face masks. We learnt from Bandula two pieces of news: the good news that he was about to get married and the bad news that he would first have to work for two years or more in Saudi Arabia to save up the money needed to pay for the wedding. This is in fact exactly what he did.

A train journey was made to Colombo to collect US dollar traveller's cheques and cash (in small denominations) for the onward voyage. Dollars were considered the best currency to use in the Red Sea. I noted that we had spent about 210,000 rupees (£4,400) during our eight months in Sri Lanka, 115,000 rupees (£2,400) on *Tin Hau*; 60,000 rupees (£1,250) on our personal food and other living costs; and 35,000 rupees (£750) on our trip to England.

Darren moved aboard *Tin Hau* on 7th December and started helping on tasks such as hull cleaning. We paid particular attention to the propeller, knowing that in Galle harbour (with its polluted waters and sea temperature of thirty degrees centigrade) it only took six weeks or so for even a well-anti-fouled propeller to be rendered totally useless by the barnacles and other growth.

Similarly, we started on the long task of cleaning the two bow anchor chains and the two stern mooring lines. These had expanded to a diameter of about six inches with material that would have fascinated a marine biologist. Armed with a knife and chisel, it took us about six hours to clean each line.

Martyn arrived on 14th December, bringing with him a video camera (a gift from my mother) and some vaccine for meningitis which Lynda duly administered by injection. We were now ready for anything that Aden might throw at us – or so we hoped.

Christmas newsletters were hastily written, copied and posted. Last minute visits and preparations were made. Gas, diesel, petrol and water supplies were topped right up. The sun awnings were taken down. *Bizzy* was deflated and stowed. Clearance papers were completed. *Knot Often* was secured in the davits.

On 17th December, as planned, we were ready to go. The two anchors were successfully pulled out of the oozy seabed and cleaned. We motored slowly out of the harbour past the other yachts. By midday we were clear of the breakwater and all three sails were hoisted fully.

We were free once again.

4. Galle to Aden

For the first four hours we motor-sailed in a slight sea up the coast of Sri Lanka towards Colombo. It was good to view, from the seaward side, so many of the little settlements that we had come to know. But by four o'clock, the true wind had revealed itself. It was from the north-north-west – right on the nose. The sea state had increased to moderate, and we could no longer motor into the steep six foot waves. There was no alternative but to turn well to port, go onto the starboard tack, set Number Seven and head west out to sea under sail alone.

As night fell we settled in to the watch-keeping routine, Martyn being partnered with Lynda, Darren with myself. We adopted the watches we had grown to like for a crew of two or four on *Tin Hau*, which worked well for Lynda's meal preparations and my sextant sights at dawn, mid-morning, noon and dusk:

2200–0200 Lynda and Martyn
0200–0600 David and Darren
0600–1200 Lynda and Martyn
1200–1800 David and Darren
1800–2000 Lynda and Martyn
2000–2200 David and Darren

0630	Breakfast
1230	Lunch
1830	Supper

Darren washed up the dishes arising from the cold meals of breakfast and lunch; Martyn washed up the dishes from the hot evening meal. An efficient ship (with clearly defined routines and responsibilities) is a happy ship – so they say. We would certainly agree with this philosophy.

On this particular voyage, most of my sights were of the sun, which was usually visible when I needed it. Lynda would often jot down the readings for me, using the normal shorthand of a circle sitting on a horizontal line to show that the sight was of the lower limb of the sun. She went a degree further than normal by drawing a face or other feature on the circle to illustrate the mood – happy, sad, exhausted, terrified, angry, puzzled or whatever.

As well as 'shooting' the sun, I also took sights of the moon (usable for the first time on Day Twenty); the planets Venus (clearly visible at an altitude of about twenty-six degrees in the evening) and Jupiter (also visible high in the sky in the evening); and the stars Arcturus (a bright star at the convenient altitude of about fifty to sixty degrees, by far the most useful star on the voyage), Spica, Rigil Kent, Regulus, Dubhe, Procyon, Alphard, Alkaid, Capella, Rigel and finally – for fun – Polaris! (a sight with the very low altitude of thirteen degrees was taken for the first time on Day Twenty-Three). This made a total of one hundred and twenty sights over twenty-eight days, which never left me in any doubt as to where we were. Most of the other yachts had the luxury, ease and accuracy of Satnav (Satellite Navigator), but we learnt later that about one set in five had broken down, and in certain localised areas off the coast of Oman just about every set stopped working for a while due to some sort of interference.

On the second day we continued to sail due west away from Galle in uncomfortable moderate to rough seas, crossing the busy shipping lanes during the night and the early hours of the morning. Remarkably we did some shopping in the afternoon, even though we were ninety miles from land! We traded a packet of cigarettes for a fish from a Galle fishing boat.

Darren worried us a bit, as some untreated cuts he had picked up on his leg from the sharp barnacles on *Tin Hau's* hull were going septic. He continued to decline Lynda's offer of medical assistance, preferring instead a 'natural approach' of applying onion compresses.

On the third day the wind and sea moderated. By half past one I considered it worthwhile turning the engine on and going about on to the port tack. At long last we could head northwards again, although it was a pity that we had to consume fuel. With Number Seven no longer steering the boat we could test our new Autohelm 6000 autopilot (which we had named 'ERNI' – Electronic Rudder Nudging Instrument). It worked brilliantly! Figure 10 of *Tin Hau's* steering system, shows how the autopilot motor was installed in the lazaret, together with an additional slaveshaft. From that moment on watches became much, much easier. In fact *Tin Hau* became what we had always wanted – a boat that could be easily handled by just the two of us. Erni steered a better course than any human being could. All we had to do was to keep a lookout, tend the sails and watch the ammeter to see that Erni was not having to work too hard. Often the needle would sit for long periods at zero amps, showing that Erni was simply holding the wheel, not turning it. Once every thirty seconds perhaps – depending on the conditions – Erni would apply a small correction and the needle would show that, say, two to five amps of power was being consumed. It was all so simple to operate.

Later that afternoon we were visited once more by a Sri Lankan fishing boat, in fact two of them. This time, nothing was offered to us. Instead the fishermen begged desperately for food, water, cigarettes, diesel or anything else we cared to give them. We shouted at them to wait and made signs that we would throw them some bananas. They weren't interested in bananas and started preparing to come alongside. By this time we didn't believe for one minute that they were in any plight. We did our best to look aggressive. Sure enough, as soon as it was clear that we were not an easy prey for whatever they might want, they both revved up their engines and disappeared at great speed.

A couple of hours later we turned off our engine – our diesel supply had to last for a month at least – and we sailed gently towards the north-north-east and some distant lightning. Darren's leg had become much worse and had produced a large swelling in his groin. Lynda and I discussed the feasibility of returning to Sri Lanka. She was most disturbed by what seemed to indicate a serious case of blood poisoning, and insisted that Darren took some anti-biotics. Thankfully he agreed. We decided we would just have to wait and see what happened next.

By seven the next morning it was raining heavily. I decided to turn the engine on again and get away from the funny weather so characteristic of the ITCZ (Inter-Tropical Convergence Zone). Also by this time we were back in the main Singapore to Suez shipping lane. There were ships everywhere. We tracked them on the radar and took avoiding action for one or two. The weather became stranger and stranger. We motored through a plague of small flies, then moths (two hundred miles from land). Then the sea seemed to boil with jumping fish.

By the next morning my sextant fix showed that the ocean current, which the previous day had been setting two knots towards the west, was now setting one knot towards the east – back towards Sri Lanka! I had been half expecting this, having with us a book entitled *The World is All Islands*, written in 1957 by a Danish circumnavigator called Carl Nielsen. He had been in these same waters thirty years before us and had written about getting 'into a gigantic eddy'. Twice, in spite of using his meagre petrol reserves in an attempt to motor out of the eddy, he had failed. On the third attempt he had broken free, but only with the help of gale force winds which destroyed his headsail. He had then put in to a port in nearby India to carry out repairs and observed that a distance which normally would have been covered by his boat *Nordkaperen* in two days had in fact taken seventeen!

Not wishing to repeat *Nordkaperen's* experiences, I decided to use our engine to get out of the ITCZ and into the favourable prevailing north-easterlies which could not have been too far to the north of us. Luckily Darren's sores were beginning to look healthier and the swelling in his groin was not quite so bad. It looked as though we were going to be able to get away from Sri Lanka after all.

The funny weather, however, had one more surprise in store for us, which sent me scurrying down below to consult that wonderful book *The Times Atlas of the Oceans* which we were lucky enough to have in *Tin Hau's* large library. I looked in the index under 'waterspouts' to learn how common they were and what to do about them if encountered at sea. We could see four! The highest appeared to be well over a thousand feet in height. And it was close!

I told Lynda to steer any course she liked to dodge these massive spiralling pools of water. Martyn and Darren did what they could to improve an already well-stowed deck. All hatches were battened down and the forward companionway door was bolted securely. We were ready to dart inside the pilothouse doors, if necessary, and bolt them from the inside. There was nothing we could do to save the three sails if a waterspout 'hit' us. They would probably be sucked high into the sky.

All I could do was to continue to read what was said about waterspouts in the *Atlas*. Firstly, it appeared that the three most common areas in the world for waterspouts were The Gulf of Mexico, the mid- to south Atlantic, and the area where we were currently situated.

Secondly, even in these high risk areas, the chances of sighting a waterspout were extremely rare – only twenty to thirty sightings had been reported per 10,000 ships making weather reports over the last fifty years.

The next section I did not read out to Lynda and the others – it appeared that waterspouts travelled faster than a boat of *Tin Hau's* size could motor and 'even the most seaworthy of ships may be damaged if a spout passes directly overhead'.

For thirty minutes or so Lynda did her best – and we prayed!

Then, to our great relief, the danger was past – as quickly as it had appeared in the first place.

We motored onwards for just one hour when at long last (at a position of about seven degrees north and seventy-seven degrees east) the wind we had been waiting for appeared. A light easterly breeze set in. The engine could be turned off and we started sailing again, slowly but steadily. The gentle sound of the bow wave as we ghosted forward in the right direction (north-west) was music to our ears!

So we continued for days and days; in fact, for just over three weeks all the way to Aden (it became apparent on about Day Eighteen that we would not be stopping in Salalah). On Days Six, Seven, Eight and Nine (the latter being Christmas Day), we chose to motor for a short spell as the wind was decidedly fluky. But from Day Ten to Day Twenty-Eight, when we arrived in Aden, we hardly used the engine. The winds, although often on the light side (force one to three), were sufficient and always from the right direction for sailing. Day Twenty produced a strong breeze (force six), which whipped up a rough sea. But, apart from that, the winds were normally perfect – force four to five. Erni did much of the steering whilst we enjoyed the sun and clean air. Only when the wind was near to dead aft and of a strength to be worrisome did we steer manually.

Christmas Day was a real highlight (our position was about nine degrees north and seventy-five degrees east) – our second Christmas afloat on the high seas, and every bit as good as the first one the year before. The entry in the log was: 'Perfect sea and wind for Christmas dinner'. Lynda managed to cook a meal that was as good as anything we could have had ashore. We had our Christmas tree and decorations, carols on deck by lamplight and simple presents. Other than a sighting of two ships at four o'clock in the morning, we saw no signs of the human race all day, even though the visibility was exceptionally good (thirty miles or so).

We passed through the Nine Degree Channel of the Laccadive Islands on Boxing Day; and at half past eight the following morning we spotted the low lying atoll of Suheli Par about ten miles distant on the port bow. We drew closer rapidly, enjoying the benefit of what I estimated to be a 1.8 knot current. At twenty minutes past ten, just as we were toying with the idea of altering course for the island so that we could perhaps drop anchor for a few hours, or possibly overnight – we saw a small boat close inshore off the southern end of the northern island. It looked like a fishing trawler. The land was only one and a half miles away by this time, just forward of abeam. Through our binoculars we examined a long sand spit joining the two islands. These were clad with swaying palm trees reaching down to the golden beaches. We were so tempted to stop.

Then at twenty to eleven we spied a second boat, this time much closer and on our side of the northern island. This boat had obviously just seen *Tin Hau*. There was a flurry of activity on deck followed by a decisive alteration of course towards us. That was enough for me to make up my mind. We could not afford the risk of being detained by officialdom. I altered course twenty degrees to starboard and we raced past the island. The pursuing boat was not quite able to catch us – she turned round to head back for the island. It was with great regret that we watched Suheli Par disappear in our wake, which incidentally contained several eight-foot long brown coloured sharks, swimming in pairs. They too left us after a while as we left behind the Laccadives and entered the Arabian Sea proper.

A few days later it was New Year's Eve – time for another celebration. Once again the weather was kind to us. The evening started with a beautiful sunset which had prompted Martyn to get out his camera for a photograph. The rest of us sat around on deck enjoying the usual 'sun-downer'. At quarter past six a ship we had not seen before suddenly appeared – in silhouette – on the horizon right in front of the setting sun. We watched the sun sink lower and lower until it had just disappeared, when to our amazement we realised that the ship had also gone. I told the crew that this had something to do with refraction, the bending of the sun's rays. But to this day I still do not exactly understand why that ship, which was heading in the same direction as us, vanished in the way it did, long before darkness set in.

Darren and I went for some sleep at nine o'clock, with the request that we be wakened just before midnight so that we could all see the new year in together, at which point Lynda and Martyn would turn in for an early night. Just before midnight we were awakened, but not in the way we had expected. Instead of the usual gentle shake and the 'Dozey, it's your watch', I woke up to the sound of gunfire and explosions. Darren also woke up abruptly; and we both ran up on to the deck in great haste only to find Lynda and Martyn killing themselves with laughter. They had set off firecrackers just beside our open hatches.

The only other memorable thing about that New Year's Eve was the fact that midnight – and 1988 – came three times! First came midnight in the current time zone (+0500). Then we moved our clocks back an hour for the new time zone (+0400). Sixty minutes later came the second midnight and a second rendition of Auld Lang Syne. Finally we put our watches back a further second in order to comply with an announcement we had heard on BBC World Service that this had to be done worldwide so as to make a necessary correction to world time. One second later came the third midnight!

As mentioned earlier, the long haul across the Arabian Sea proceeded without too much incident – just lots of easy, pleasant sailing. We often had dolphins for company and never ceased to wonder at these incredible creatures. They would swim in schools beside us for hours at a time, squeaking gleefully and occasionally jumping out of the water and landing with a splash, as though they were saying to us and to *Tin Hau*: 'look how happy we are to be alive in this beautiful sea – are you happy as well?'

On Day Twenty-One we logged our best day's run of the voyage – 142 miles, although twenty miles of this could be attributed to the favourable current. Salalah was now one hundred and sixty miles to the north of us; and the large island of Socotra off the 'Horn of Africa' was one hundred miles to the south.

The following day (8th January, 1988) was an exciting one. At quarter to seven in the morning we spotted a yacht coming up behind us with a multi-coloured spinnaker set. By quarter past twelve she was dead abeam and only fifty metres away, as close as she would get – she was the Swedish sloop, *Lady Rosi*, from Galle. We exchanged news with Roger and Siv and took photographs of each other, both crews saying how beautiful the other boat looked! I confirmed by VHF their Satnav position at quarter past one – thirteen degrees fifty-eight minutes north, fifty-two degrees forty-seven minutes east. Later that day we picked up Aden and Masirah RDF (radio direction-finder) beacons. Aden was only four hundred and fifty miles ahead of us, and Masirah was about five hundred miles to the north-east well up the Omani coast.

On Day Twenty-Five the sea became quite rough, and the deep blue colour changed to green. The first land flies appeared. There was a spicy smell in the air. We were getting close.

During the night the wind increased in strength slightly and the sea became rougher (it always seems to do this as land is approached!) *Tin Hau* was speeding along at six and a half knots at one point; and we were also being helped by a favourable current of perhaps two knots. We started seeing many ships the next day – a warship, a luxury passenger liner and many coasters and fishing boats.

We were treated to a wonderful display by the dolphins the following night, as they jumped and played around us in the phosphorescence, while baby dolphins surfed at the bow. At times it seemed like an underwater fireworks display. Star sights taken at eight o'clock in the morning showed that Aden was now only fifty miles distant.

At 4.25 a.m. on Day Twenty-Eight (13th January, 1988), we picked up the seabed on the echo-sounder; and at five o'clock lights were just visible off the starboard bow. We gybed to the port tack at half past five from a course of 270° to the more southerly one of 240°. By half past six the Aden peninsular was clearly visible.

It is always most exciting to see land again after a long spell at sea, particularly if the terrain of the new country is completely different to that of the country left behind. In this case we were staring for the first time at brown, barren land – *Tin Hau's* first desert. What surprised us was how rocky and mountainous it was.

We started rounding Aden's headland at half past eleven under power, having taken in the log. The wind had all but disappeared. Port Control called us on the VHF as we approached the harbour. There followed a most pleasant conversation during which I was asked questions about *Tin Hau* and her crew. The port controller took down all the relevant details, officially welcomed us to Aden, and advised us where to anchor in the harbour. We proceeded to weave our way past a large number of moored ships, many of them Russian.

At quarter to one we dropped anchor amongst a handful of other yachts, as directed. As soon as we had finished – but not before – a launch came up to us and tied alongside. Customs, health and immigration formalities were very speedily and effectively dealt with. Fifteen minutes later we were free to do as we pleased. Seldom before had we come across such efficient and courteous officials; it was an easy end to a relatively easy voyage.

5.   Aden

There are always so many interesting things to look at in a new anchorage. Aden, the main town of the People's Democratic Republic of Yemen, with a population of about 300,000, was no exception. Near to us were anchored other yachts from our fleet. Just three of them – *Lady Rosi*, *Yemanja II* and *Aquilla*. We compared notes on the passage from Galle. All around us was the bustle of a busy bunkering and refinery port, with a noticeable military presence. Towering above the town were steep, bare mountains. We couldn't wait to go ashore.

Eventually we launched *Knot Often* and rowed over to Customs Wharf, the designated landing point for dinghies from foreign yachts. We were allowed to proceed into the town, but two important rules were first explained to us. Firstly, no cameras could be taken past the customs check point; and definitely no video cameras. Secondly, we were to be subject to a curfew. We had to stay on our boats between the hours of sunset and sunrise every night.

We had no difficulty in understanding the reasons for these rules, given the political instability still very much present in Aden. Only two years earlier there had been a bloody coup and some fierce fighting in the streets, together with gunfire across the harbour. A moored British yacht, appropriately named *Innocent Bystander*, had been sunk. Four other yachts had been damaged, one beyond repair; all crew members safely evacuated, leaving their yachts behind. We learnt later at the British Embassy that all the embassy staff – and other foreign nationals – had had to evacuate the country, many of them being taken off by the royal yacht *Britannia*, which had happened to be nearby at the time.

We were quite happy to return to *Tin Hau* each night during our nine day stay there – we never did like leaving *Tin Hau* for too long anyway. The skipper of another yacht, which arrived after us, felt rather differently. He liked to sample the night life ashore in ports; and Aden wasn't going to be any different. He solved the curfew problem his own way – by the risky method of sinking his dinghy in deep water at Customs Wharf whenever he intended to stay overnight, thus rendering it invisible to the patrolling soldiers. Luckily for him, he was never caught.

On our second day ashore we cashed some traveller's cheques at the Bank of Yemen (the currency being the Dinar, worth about three US dollars, and divided into one thousand fils or twenty shillings), Darren and Martyn returned to the boat, while Lynda and I took a bus to the British Embassy further round the bay at Khormaksar. We did not quite know what to expect – normally we avoided embassies unless there was a real problem. However, having had such a warm letter from this particular embassy when we had written from Galle, we felt we had to pay a visit. We were immediately welcomed. The embassy staff, particularly Andy Goodwin, could not do enough for us.

I was asked if I played golf. 'Not very well,' I replied, 'and I have not played for five years – but, as it happens, I do have a set of clubs on the boat.' This was one of many items totally unrelated to life at sea that we were still carrying after our days in Swaziland. A game of golf was arranged for the following Saturday.

We were asked if we wanted to run with the Hash House Harriers. I had never heard of this sport before. But once the rules had been roughly explained – it seemed like a cross between a treasure hunt and cross-country running – we said yes. That was arranged for the Sunday.

Having read the latest international papers at the embassy and generally caught up on any news we might have missed during the past month (not much), we were driven back to the harbour by Andy.

But where was *Tin Hau*? Just for a moment our hearts stopped – she wasn't where we had left her! Then we saw her – lying happily at anchor with the other yachts. But hadn't she moved a bit?

We rowed out to her quickly, only to find Darren and Martyn looking quite unconcerned and relaxed. However, they had a story to tell. Apparently, a couple of hours earlier, the anchor had failed to hold during a strong gust of wind. *Tin Hau* had become entangled with *Yemanja II*, denting her pulpit. At this point young Bruce (aged twelve) on *Aquilla* had noticed the commotion and had immediately shot over in *Aquilla's* dinghy to help.

None of the three of them had ever started *Tin Hau's* engine before. Darren and Martyn had only once witnessed the process of winching in *Tin Hau's* anchor by hand. But – all credit to them – they managed to do all of this without inflicting any damage to *Tin Hau* or any further damage to *Yemanja II*. Having broken free, they had gone for a jaunt around Aden harbour, inspecting the Russian ships and so on – which Martyn in particular had thoroughly enjoyed – before returning to drop anchor in a slightly different location.

We were obviously most grateful to our crew – and also to Bruce – for saving *Tin Hau* in this way. That act alone more than justified our choice in having crew, although I suppose if it had been just the two of us, Lynda would have stayed on the boat and I would have gone to the embassy on my own.

Later on I worked out where I had gone wrong. This was the first – but not the last – time *Tin Hau's* anchor had ever dragged. The problem was that prior to Galle we had always used a system of painted marks on the chain to know how much of it we had let out (we had not at this stage changed to the better system of ribbons). But in Galle harbour, with all the marine growth, these marks had disappeared, and it had been impossible to re-apply them while still at anchor. As a temporary measure I had worked out that each turn of the windlass handle was equivalent to about half a metre of chain. So sixty turns of the handle was the equivalent of about thirty metres of chain – which we had needed in this case. In my haste, I had forgotten the 3:1 gearing built in to the windlass and my calculations had been out by a factor of three! I should have counted one hundred and eighty turns on the windlass handle, not sixty! No wonder we had had a problem, even though I had still added a generous length of anti-snub line to what had felt like a well dug in anchor. Unfortunately, it had been impossible to view the anchor and chain underwater, as the water had been so murky.

Later that day we saw Rick and Julie (French and English respectively) of *Yemanja II* to apologise for the accident and to see what we could do to make amends for *Yemanja II's* dented pulpit and scratched paintwork. Rick insisted the pulpit needed replacing anyway. There was nothing we could do to make them accept any money or gift in lieu. Such a reaction was absolutely typical of those people we met in the Indian Ocean on long distance cruising boats. It was wonderful to feel part of this group of sailing folk, who believed in helping each other, whatever the cost. Nationality did not matter. Assistance from the outside world was not needed. It was only when we reached western Europe that attitudes changed and phrases like 'you must pay for this', 'I will sue you' and 'this has to be an insurance claim' were used.

The following day we took the bus into Crater, the nearest 'town' to the harbour. The area around the harbour had included several buildings built in colonial style in the days prior to 1967 when Aden had been a British colony. Crater, however, was much more of a traditional Moslem town with a large open-air market, minarets and narrow alleyways. We had a meal at a street cafe, drawn in more by the smell than by the looks of the place. What a good meal it was – it proved to be about the best tasting fish we have ever experienced.

My game of golf took place as planned. It seemed very strange playing on a course without grass. I had to carry a small mat of artificial grass (or Astroturf) for use on fairways (which I kept forgetting to pick up); and putting took place on 'browns', not greens. In reality these were black and as fast as a table top. They consisted of desert sand, held together with oil, and were well rolled.

On returning from the golf, Andy visited the boat for a drink before taking all of us out for a meal in Crater at the Red Sea Restaurant. We were surprised to see nearby hundreds of iron bedsteads lined up in rows, open to the sky and facing a large black and white television set, apparently an 'outdoor' hotel. It hardly ever rains in Aden – so I suppose a low-cost hotel such as this made sense.

The Hash House Harriers run was an equally new and enjoyable experience. It was also good exercise for the calf muscles, the only muscles that are not well exercised on long ocean voyages in small boats.

Soon it was time to start preparing for the onward passage. This involved more hull scrubbing and an extensive shopping session at the western-style supermarket where many bargains were to be had, including excellent Russian vodka. We also topped up our supplies of gas, water and diesel. The latter was cheap – it cost us fifty US dollars (or £30) to fill up our tanks with eighty-four gallons (three hundred and eighty litres) of fuel. We had managed to reach Aden with half of our diesel supplies intact.

On Thursday, 21st January, we were ready to leave. Clearance formalities took a mere fifteen minutes. We slipped out of the harbour at noon, with the expected ideal forecast of a ten to fifteen knot easterly breeze, good visibility, a maximum temperature of twenty-three degrees centigrade and – of course – no rain.

6.   Aden to Port Sudan

It took us just twenty hours to sail the one hundred miles to the island of Perim, the Yemeni (formerly British) island at the southern entrance to the Red Sea. We kept close to the coast all the way, in depths varying from twenty metres to fifty metres; and so had wonderful views of the rugged mountainous terrain to starboard. To port there were many ships bound to and from the Straits of Bab-el-Mandeb.

The main shipping lane lay between Perim Island and the coast of Africa (Djibouti), ten miles to the south-west. For years I had remembered a phrase from my diary, written twenty-nine years earlier (aged six) while on passage from Hong Kong to England with my parents and brothers on the liner, the *Hamburg*. The phrase went something like: 'I fort Djibouti would be horridle, but it was even more horridle than I fort.'

I think that this childhood memory had tipped the scales in deciding me to stop in Aden instead.

Years later, however, I saw this diary again and read it with renewed interest as *Tin Hau* and the *Hamburg* had sailed in so many of the same waters. I was amazed to see that the *Hamburg's* time from Colombo to Suez (3,400 miles) had been a mere eight days, including the stop in Djibouti (at that time the capital of French Somaliland), compared to one hundred days on *Tin Hau*). I discovered also that my uneasiness about Djibouti had been ill-founded – I hadn't actually felt it was too horrible. My words had actually been: 'We came to Djibouti. I went ashore. I fort it was horridle but it was nicer than I fort. They are funny trains there.'

So much for the accuracy of childhood memories!

Returning to *Tin Hau* and the Straits of Bab-el-Mandeb, we chose to take the less used Small Strait – the narrow channel between Perim and mainland Yemen. This was a definite short cut when turning the corner into the Red Sea, and it was out of the shipping lane.

We approached the strait at five o'clock in the morning under full sail with the easterly wind dead aft, sailing goosewinged. Erni steered. The closer we got, the more the wind increased and the steeper the waves became. I think we had quite a strong current with us, as the land on both sides appeared to shoot by at tremendous speed. It was exciting to pick out more and more detail, first with binoculars and later with the naked eye. The lighthouse, which we had spotted during the night at ten minutes to four, was by eight a.m. only a few hundred metres away. The echo sounder showed the depth was decreasing fast.

Suddenly we were through. The sea became much calmer and the depth started to increase. We began to turn to starboard, expecting to gybe the main. But, as so often happens at headlands, the wind followed us round, gradually veering from east to south-east to south – and increasing in strength to force five. In the relatively calm seas *Tin Hau* shot along at six to seven knots. Soon, however, it became time to reef. Sailing overcanvassed and goosewinged in these conditions, although exhilarating, was hardly safe. A violent gybe could happen from either direction. Also, we could expect the sea to become rougher, with every mile covered, as the fetch increased. We gradually reefed the sails from six-six-six to six-five-four to five-five-four. In the middle of all this activity, Lynda noticed a tug on the fishing line (which we nearly always trailed) and hauled in a one metre long wahoo.

By ten minutes past one we had sighted the buoy marking the entrance to Mokkha (a town of North Yemen, visited – we heard later – by Rick and Julie on *Yemanja II*, who had also made an interesting trip inland). The water depths remained steady at about twenty-two metres; and the sea state was moderate to rough, the steep eight-foot waves still chasing us from behind. I wanted to reduce sail further and alter course. First, before I could decide which sails to gybe, I had to work out exactly where we were. Unfortunately the radar – still the original one at that time – did not help at all. I did not want to stray too close to the North Yemen shore on our starboard side, as the authorities had a reputation – similar to that of the Ethiopians twenty miles to the south-west of us – of being unfriendly to foreign yachtsmen. We were all spy ships or gunrunners, they thought. Nor did I want to become entangled with the busy shipping lane a mile or so to port.

The crew were becoming increasingly agitated as they awaited my decision.

At twenty minutes past one I had nearly finished my furious plottings at the chart table, when... Bang! Crash! Something had come adrift in a nasty unplanned gybe. It did not take long for us to realise that the mizzen yard had broken in two – just aft of the eye where the halyard was attached.

We gathered in the sail bundle as quickly as possible – scrambling around on the pilothouse roof – and lashed it to the gallows. Then we gybed the foresail and reefed both foresail and main to only three panels of each, thus sailing three-three-zero. We should have done this twenty minutes earlier, but I had been too engrossed in other things.

Although everything seemed much safer under the reduced sail, our speed was still 4.2 knots (plus current). I wanted to anchor somewhere to recover from the shock and assess the damage, but the only possibility – the twenty-five mile long Hanish group of islands thirty miles ahead – would be passed during the hours of darkness. I considered various ways of slowing down still further, but with such little room to manoeuvre between the Yemeni shore and the shipping lane – and with unknown currents – I decided against this idea. It was a pity, as there were some attractive anchorages and beaches on these nearly uninhabited islands.

Instead, I decided that we would stop at the Zubair Islands, seventy miles beyond Hanish, and reachable, I calculated, before darkness the following day.

The wind continued to increase during the night and the sea became rougher, but under such reduced sail we had no real difficulty in tacking downwind, gybing every three hours or so. Several reefs had to be identified and avoided; we made certain that we never, quite, joined the shipping lane.

By the next morning, Lynda and Martyn felt refreshed enough to spend several hours on the pilothouse roof fitting a new yard. First they released from the sail the two broken pieces of the original mahogany yard. These they secured to the main cabin top in place of two of the spare bamboos that we had been carrying around for so long and which had never been needed until that moment. Painstakingly, in the continued rough seas, they lashed these two bamboos together to form a new yard, which they tied once again to the sail and halyard. Their repair work was so good that we did not have to make any more changes until Cyprus, where the original yard was fixed.

At ten minutes past two, the Zubair Islands were sighted dead ahead. I decided that we would still try to stop there. We all needed the rest.

Leaving the main island close to starboard, we made our approach. We spotted four or five dhows at anchor within a small bay on the leeward side of the island. Towering over this anchorage was a steep extinct volcano, the most barren piece of earth we had ever seen.

At half past five, just before dusk, we dropped anchor amongst the dhows in water ten metres deep. The wind howled in the rigging and the wind generator worked overtime in gusts of thirty-five knots. But, with seventy metres of chain and nylon warp let out, we were more than safe. We could relax over a sun-downer, enjoy a good meal and sleep.

We ended up staying nearly three days at Zubair. Darren and Martyn went ashore and climbed the volcano. I tried to video the two small dots as they worked their way up the steep incline, but it was difficult to hold the camera still with *Tin Hau* rolling so much in the open anchorage. Lynda – by now the expert video camera operator after hours of dolphin filming between Galle and Aden – left me to it. She was feeling very sick, as she had been in Aden. There was definitely something amiss with her health. Hopefully things would just get better on their own.

I made the most of the opportunity to give the hull a really good clean, appreciating the first clear water for this job since Chagos ten months earlier. The sea temperature was still nearly twenty-six degrees centigrade, quite warm enough for all sorts of weed, molluscs and other marine creatures to flourish.

I also carried out a thorough service of the engine, checked the batteries and generally gave *Tin Hau* the TLC (Tender Loving Care) that she deserved. We gazed across in admiration at the beautiful dhows. These were lovely brightly painted vessels with large crews. There were no covered cabins on deck – the men slept out in the open. One of them came by to give us a large fish, a gift much appreciated by all of us.

On the morning of Tuesday, 26th January, the dhows started to leave the anchorage, which was a sure sign that we could go as well. We set off at ten o'clock, bound for Port Sudan four hundred miles distant.

For the first forty-eight or so hours, in winds of less than five knots and waves no higher than two feet, we drifted gently in the right direction, and no more. I resisted all temptation to turn on the engine, as I knew that, if we waited long enough, a wind of favourable direction and strength would arrive. Besides, it was pleasant just to drift. Martyn passed much of his time sprawled out in the hammock reading more books from *Tin Hau's* library (he confessed to never having read a book for pleasure before joining us – in Galle we had started him off with *The Secret Life of Adrian Mole Aged 13¾*). Darren squatted on the foredeck wrapped in his lungi (a sarong-like garment), contemplating the horizon and looking like a native of southern India. Lynda always seemed to be busy with something below decks, yet she invariably spotted the ship on the horizon long before her watchful crew – or skipper – had seen anything. I kept myself occupied at the chart table – immersed in charts, pilots, atlases and any other books that would tell me more about the fascinating Red Sea.

On the third day we made some reasonable progress in the afternoon breeze, enough to leave North Yemen behind. The land to starboard of us was now Saudi Arabia.

After another comfortable but windless night spent hove-to, I decided to motor for a while. Our immediate reward was landing a small barracuda; and by midday we were again enjoying a pleasant sailing wind which allowed us to make good progress.

At six o'clock in the evening we entered a strange area with extensive weed where the two opposing swells of the Red Sea met. It was time to motor onwards to Port Sudan before any adverse northerly wind sprang up.

So, much of the final three and a half days of the voyage was spent under power. This included the crossing of the shipping lane to get over to the African side of the Red Sea. We took avoiding action for two ships – the *Bunka Tiga* and the Danish *Sally Maersk*. Port Sudan's lighthouse was sighted at ten minutes to ten on 1st February, and we reached it at twenty minutes past four. As there was no wind and the sea was flat calm, we decided to turn off the engine and simply rest in silence under the full moon until dawn.

At quarter to six we spoke to one of the Port Sudan pilots on the VHF radio and were given permission to enter the harbour. Half an hour later we were ghosting in towards a town that had not yet woken up. I decided to anchor as quietly as possible amongst a dozen or so foreign flagged yachts in the western corner of the harbour. *Aquilla* was the only one we recognised.

7.   Port Sudan

Once again we found ourselves in an intriguing new world, totally different to anything we had seen before.

Sudan is a huge country, Africa's largest and twenty times the size of England. Much of it is desert, although along its lifeline – the River Nile – the terrain is often lush, and tasty fruits and vegetables are grown. The capital, Khartoum, is located at the important junction between the Blue Nile, which starts its life in Ethiopia, and the White Nile, whose source – about one thousand miles to the south – is Lake Victoria.

I had been to Sudan twelve years earlier as part of my Africa Overland journey, having entered it in the south-west from the Republic of Central Africa, driven through the only large town in the south – Juba – and left via an unmanned border post into Kenya. My main impression then was, as in Nigeria, that I was in a country split very broadly into two parts – the Arab Moslem north and the African Christian south. I had been horrified to learn about some of the massacres that had happened over the years, particularly in the south. I remember seeing little crosses stuck in the ground, at fifty yard intervals, for mile after mile beside the road (if one could call it that) near to the RCA border.

For centuries Sudan had been part of a collection of warring states and empires extending from the Red Sea westwards as far as the Atlantic Ocean. In the late nineteenth century, the fearsome Mahdi controlled much of the present Arab part of Sudan. He captured Khartoum from the British under General Gordon in 1885. Thirteen years later, however, it was re-captured by an Anglo-Egyptian force led by General Kitchener; and Sudan remained under British control until independence in 1956.

Port Sudan, a town of about 150,000 people, is modern Sudan's only port of significance; it is connected by road and railway to Khartoum, four hundred miles inland. Thanks to this, the large open-air market was stocked with some wonderful fresh produce – particularly the Nile valley grapefruits, which we had heard about long before reaching Sudan. These lived up to our greatest expectations and were certainly the biggest, juiciest and least expensive grapefruits we had ever come across. They lasted for six weeks – nearly all the way to Suez; and really meant a lot to us! In a country like Sudan – as in so much of the third world – you learn to appreciate the few things that are available, rather than complain about what is unavailable, as is done in the west.

The other supplies for which Port Sudan was known amongst yotties were also very good. The water was excellent – we filled up all our tanks and loose containers. How could a town with hardly any rain, hundreds of miles from the nearest river, have such a good supply? Diesel was reasonably inexpensive – we bought a forty-four gallon drum of diesel for seventy US dollars. Our appointed agent, Ali, took care of all of this, together with an order from the market worth two hundred and fifty Sudanese pounds (eight Sudanese pounds were equivalent to about two US dollars at the bank, or one US dollar on the black market, a facility that was recommended to me by a policeman at the main police station, although I wasn't sure whether or not he was seeking a reason to arrest me!) On our second day in Port Sudan, the morning after we had placed the order, Ali arrived in his car with the entire contents of the order. There was no fuss. No extra money was demanded. We were pleasantly surprised by his efficiency, and felt instantly guilty that we had ever doubted his honesty or abilities.

The town itself gave the appearance of anything but cleanliness and organisation. I think it was the large number of free-grazing camels that struck us first. These seemed to be everywhere – along with goats, Toyota pick-up trucks, large lorries heavily laden in readiness for lengthy journeys across the desert, tall dignified looking men in long white robes, old men squatting on the top of sacks of interesting smelling spices, and children playing in the dusty streets. There were some fine old buildings in the centre of the town, built to give plenty of cool shade. Once away from the centre, homes tended to be built of old sheets of corrugated iron, scrap pieces of timber or anything else that happened to be at hand.

We were free to wander around at will; and, although we were stared at with great curiosity and perhaps sometimes regarded as dollar notes on legs, the looks were open and friendly. On balance, I liked Port Sudan very much.

Everything that happened from our second day onwards at Port Sudan was, however, clouded by a serious downturn of fortune.

Lynda started the day being violently sick. I went backwards and forwards to the heads with countless buckets until I thought she could not possibly have anything left inside her. But still she went on, until she was just about losing consciousness.

I really did not know what to do. Port Sudan was new to us. *Aquilla* had already left. *Dreamtime* had just arrived, but we knew more about Port Sudan than they did. Ali, our main Sudanese contact, was busy delivering the provisions and might be able to help us. First I rowed over to the Australian yacht *Copper Lady*, whose owner, Brian, had been most helpful the previous day in telling us this and that about Port Sudan and – in particular – in recommending Ali. He was in fact based in the area, undertaking some casual charter work.

'There are some English nurses in that boat over there,' Brian said. 'Let's see if they are in.'

We rowed over and knocked on the hull; sure enough, they were on board. I told them about Lynda and they were immediately most concerned. They had no hesitation in recommending one particular private hospital in town – Al Ahly Hospital.

I rowed back to *Tin Hau* and asked Darren to take charge of her – I didn't know when we would be back. We gently helped Lynda into *Knot Often*.

By now Ali understood exactly what was going on. He was there on the shore waiting for us. We got Lynda into the back seat of his car (she remembers none of this) and drove across town at high speed. Ali refused any payment as he dropped the two of us off at the hospital entrance.

What to do next? There was no reception in the hospital, just hundreds of people. The corridors were full. There were patients on stretchers, apparently abandoned. The few notices on the otherwise bare, unpainted walls were in Arabic, which I couldn't read. I had to get Lynda to a doctor soon.

I started opening doors and wandering around different parts of the building, supporting Lynda as I went, just saying one word, 'Doctor'. Eventually I was told to sit in the corner of a room and wait.

The next few minutes were unbearable – I had to find someone who could help us. I had never seen Lynda in this state before. Usually, nothing would knock her down. Again I started making a nuisance of myself, pestering anyone who didn't appear to be a patient.

At long last, a door opened and a man of obvious authority, dressed in crisp white suit, came in. This was the doctor.

He had one look at Lynda, said he would examine her immediately and they both disappeared.

I sat and waited. Nearly all day. No one spoke to me and I had no idea what was happening. All I could do was pray.

Eventually the doctor appeared again. 'Your wife is all right now,' he said, 'but she must stay here.' He tried to explain exactly what was wrong – something to do with the gall bladder. I wasn't hearing the details. I was just so relieved that Lynda was okay.

I wondered what to do with myself for the night. Lynda was in a hospital bed with all sorts of tubes coming out of her in various directions. There was an empty bed next to her. I decided to lie on it and keep watch.

This continued throughout the next day (Thursday, 4th February). At one point in the afternoon I was dozing on my bed, when suddenly I became aware that Lynda had woken up and was agitated about something. She was calling for the nurse (who, like so many of the nurses, was a male refugee from Ethiopia). She was pointing to her drip where a large bubble of air was working its way towards her bloodstream. Luckily the nurse moved quickly when he saw his error and serious trouble was averted. Amazingly, even when heavily drugged, Lynda proved herself to be more vigilant than either myself or a trained nurse!

The following day, being a Friday, was the Moslem day of rest. I was astonished to see a beautiful bunch of flowers arrive at Lynda's bedside. These had been picked by the doctor in his own garden during the only few spare hours he had every week. By this time, I had grown to admire him enormously and wonder at our luck in finding probably the best-qualified person in the whole of Sudan's Red Sea Province to deal with Lynda's particular problem. Dr Abu Sin had worked previously at a hospital in Aberdeen in Scotland, but, being Sudanese, I suppose it had always been his intention to return to his native country. Lynda's sickness had in fact started in Aden, and her trouble in Zubair had been more of the same thing. Somehow she had not allowed her body to rebel totally until her part in seeing us safely to Port Sudan was over.

Later that morning Lynda was told that she could eat for the first time in nearly three days. However, there was a slight problem. In an African hospital such as this, it was up to the family to provide food. For once, I was not there. I had returned to the boat and joined the others and some of those off *Dreamtime* for a quick visit to the famous old town of Suakin just south of Port Sudan. It was known for being the last slave trading port in the world, still used for this purpose until the Second World War. The old town was an archaeologist's paradise – so many ancient buildings remained. My mind was more on what was happening at the hospital; when I returned there I found a very hungry – but much better – Lynda.

On Saturday the Doctor was prepared to discharge Lynda from the hospital. When I told him what the next six weeks or so might hold in store for us and that we would be totally out of touch with the outside world, he was horrified. 'She must not be over-stressed. She must eat the right food. Her symptoms could well reappear.'

It seemed that there was just no way Lynda could join us on this part of the voyage. We could hardly wait indefinitely in Port Sudan, or abandon *Tin Hau* there. So the decision was made that Lynda would fly back to England to stay with my mother and seek further medical care there. Hopefully she would be able to rejoin *Tin Hau* before too long. Martyn, Darren and I would have to take the boat northwards to Suez and possibly all the way to Cyprus – without the mate. This was a very sad state of affairs for all concerned.

We were presented with a bill for hospital care. It was a mere 365 Sudanese pounds (£27), inclusive of the hospital bed, drugs, nursing staff and the attention of the best doctor in Port Sudan. 'Your wife is a colleague,' he said (he had learnt that she was a paramedic), 'I cannot charge any more.'

Back at the harbour we discussed our predicament with John Watson and the crew of *Dreamtime*. We knew that two crew members, Richard Henry and his son, were flying out of Port Sudan on the following Monday. We asked if Lynda could go with them. 'Of course,' Richard said. 'No problem at all.'

So it was agreed that Lynda would fly with them, first to Cairo on a local plane, then on to London. That left me the following morning to arrange the flight details and sort out all the paperwork with the authorities. I decided that I would clear *Tin Hau* out of Sudan at the same time so that we could also leave town.

The next morning the first place I had to visit was the Sudanese airline office. I learnt that the cost of the one-way flight was a horrific US $950 (about £550). This had to be paid in foreign currency. Richard very kindly allowed us to use his American Express card for most of this amount, as we did not have enough traveller's cheques with us (Lynda repaid him in England).

Before I could buy the ticket, I had to go through the process of signing Lynda off *Tin Hau's* crew list and getting her a temporary visa to enter Sudan for one day. This took me until eleven o'clock, which left only three hours to take care of the rest of the paperwork, as everything closed at two in the afternoon.

I consider the next three hours to have been my most intense battle with bureaucracy ever – and by this time I was pretty experienced at filling in forms in triplicate, quadruplicate or whatever. It was also my biggest triumph. The clock was against me all the way. I only had to visit about six places, but some of these had to be returned to more than once, and they were all a long way apart – some in West Town near to the dinghy jetty, some across the creek in East Town.

At first I walked, but after a while I saw that I would never finish on time in this way. So I started running between the port office, the police station, the customs office, the immigration office and so on. I hitched a lift at one point with a donkey and cart. I crossed the creek once by ferry before realising that it was much quicker to run up one bank of the creek across the bridge and back down the other bank. If I did not finish everything I would have to start all over again from scratch the next morning.

Finish I did, thanks to a phone call being made to the final office, which stayed open two minutes past the closing time on my account.

I returned to *Tin Hau*, hot and thirsty, but feeling really good about the morning's marathon.

During the afternoon there was a chance to visit one or two of the yachts in harbour, some bearing familiar faces from Galle. *Lady Rosi* had just arrived after delays due to engine problems near Djibouti. Also there was *Endurance II* with Steve, Warren and Michelle. We heard on *Dreamtime's* radio that *Klepel's* Satnav had still not been fixed in Djibouti and that she was being navigated via *Top Knot's* radar. We learnt that many of 'the Fleet' had stopped in Hanish or were still there.

There were several other yachts anchored in the harbour, new to us since Galle. *Boo*, from St Vincent, had arrived with a broken engine, a broken Satnav, and no steering. The skipper was an ex-Hong Kong policeman. The crew, soldiers based with the British forces in Cyprus, were keen to get back.

There was *U-Matalu*, a sleek French aluminium sloop with one incredibly tall mast. We were to see more of this boat later. *Bug Off*, *Nalu IV* and *Cheval de la Mer* were all from the United States. *Aurora*, a large seventy-five foot schooner, was one of the Italian charter yachts operating in the Port Sudan area. *La Sacrée Thérèse* and *Sinbad* were two French yachts, each about thirty-eight feet in length, sailing from Suez to southern Sudan and back.

Then there was *Ann Judith*, a forty foot steel ketch from Australia, crewed by father and son, also going north; *Couchen*, a thirty-five foot Swiss sloop with a yellow hull; and *Guinevere*, sailed single-handedly by Bill Belford, a Kiwi vet whom we were to get to know better at Larnaca.

Finally there was a black hulled wooden ketch – whose name we never did learn – skippered by a pirate-like figure, Alistair, from Scotland. He seemed very much at home in the Red Sea and had a large family on board, complete with monkey. He had many exciting stories to tell, including one about hitting a reef in Saudi Arabia, abandoning ship, and subsequently being rescued – at no charge – by the Saudi navy.

We took Lynda to *Dreamtime* early on Monday morning, so that we could get clear of Port Sudan before the usual headwinds and seas had had a chance to build up. It was a very sad moment, waving goodbye to her as she stood in the cockpit of another boat. She disappeared from sight as we rounded the harbour's breakwater and turned to the north. It was quarter past five in the morning.

For thirty minutes we motor-sailed into waves which were already increasing to a critical height. At quarter to six I decided we were wasting our time. We would only get a quarter of the way to Suez at that rate. Reluctantly I turned round; but at least there was the consolation that I would see Lynda again.

We entered Port Sudan once more and I looked across towards *Dreamtime*. But Lynda had already left.

We returned to our old anchorage, notified port control that we would leave as soon as the weather allowed; and prepared ourselves for a long wait on board *Tin Hau*.

8. Port Sudan to Hurghada

On the following day, Tuesday, 9th February, we had to move *Tin Hau* three times to allow ships clear access to the coal jetty – all good practice for Martyn and Darren. Shortly after this the wind seemed to drop slightly and I decided to set off up the coast, bound hopefully for Marsa Darur, fifteen miles to the north. Anything to get away from Port Sudan. By ten o'clock in the morning we had rounded the breakwater and were once again in clear water.

As I had expected, motoring straight into the choppy waves was just not worth it. But I found that motor-sailing, with plenty of power from the engine and with full main and mizzen, was feasible. We could tack through ninety degrees, which was not bad for *Tin Hau*. The price was high fuel consumption.

I discovered also that navigation in the narrow channel between the inshore reef and the offshore reef was not easy. Land was too far away and featureless to be of use for compass bearings. The echo sounder did not help either – the change from the deep water of the channel to the reef just below the surface was far too rapid. All we could do – besides dead reckoning – was to use our eyes, tacking just before each reef.

So it continued all day. The tension of 'reef spotting' even got to the crew, underlined when coffee was made at one point with salt water instead of fresh. The wrong galley tap had been used!

By quarter past five, just before dark, we had still not spied the entrance through the inshore reef to Marsa Darur. Standing on the pilothouse roof, I used the binoculars to scan the long reef to the north and to the south. The problem, with which we were to become familiar, was that we would often find ourselves in the difficult position of having to look directly towards the sun when trying to spot a reef. In the evenings the way in to a marsa or khor (the Arabic words for 'anchorage' and 'inlet' respectively) would be towards the west – and the setting sun. In the mornings the way out of the marsa or khor would be towards the east – and the rising sun. Either way we would be breaking the golden rule of navigation in reef country: never eyeball up to a reef against the sun.

Underwater features are clearly visible when the sun is behind you, but almost impossible to spot – until really close – when the sun is ahead. In this respect, the eastern side of the Red Sea would have been much easier for coastal hopping between reef anchorages, but the east coast would have meant Saudi Arabia; and unfortunately Saudi Arabia was a no go zone for foreign yachts, at least in 1988.

On this particular day darkness was approaching and we had still not found a break in the inshore reef. Panic was beginning to set in – I really did not know what we would do if we could not drop anchor. A whole night spent sailing backwards and forwards in the two to three mile wide zone between the two reefs – without being able to see either of them – was too nightmarish to contemplate.

At the last minute, however, we saw a small fishing boat at anchor on the landward side of the inshore reef. We motored at top speed towards it; and, sure enough, there was a small gap in the reef through which we could squeeze. Gratefully, we dropped anchor in calm sheltered water five metres deep. The fishing boat departed five minutes later, leaving us all alone in the strangest of anchorages, a long way from the shoreline.

Due to the strong adverse winds, we stayed in this anchorage for three days, during which time I used the sextant – and anything else I could think of – to try to work out where we were. Were we just to the north of Marsa Darur or just to the south of it? I never did find out!

I also had time to work out – with the crew – some new routines on a *Tin Hau* without Lynda. We decided that the usual high standard of three meals a day was difficult to maintain, and changed this to two meals a day – brunch in mid-morning prepared and washed up by Martyn (grapefruit, muesli and delicious homebaked bread) and a hot supper in the evening (with pink blancmange for dessert) prepared and washed up by Darren. We had to be very careful with our water consumption, but found that this was no problem provided that we used salt water for most washing purposes. We managed to keep to a very steady fifteen litres (about three gallons) of fresh water per day (twenty strokes on the header tank pump).

Day Five (12th February) brought a change in the weather and for a while we were actually able to turn the engine off and sail! We passed the first possible anchorage – Marsa Arus – at quarter to nine and the next one – Marsa Arakiya, with its army lookout post – at eleven o'clock. We decided to head for Marsa Salak, fourteen miles further on. The next anchorage beyond this would have been too far to reach before nightfall.

By two o'clock we were starting to look for the beacon which was meant to be situated at the entrance to Marsa Salak, but we could not see it anywhere. Three fishermen in an open boat realised that we were having problems and they approached us at great speed, making signs that we should turn round and go southwards, back towards Port Sudan! They seemed to know what they were doing. So – reluctantly – I decided to follow them.

One mile later they turned to starboard through a tiny gap in the reef. We followed cautiously, entering a deep channel thirty metres wide and fifty metres long. How could we anchor in this? The fishing boat had reached the western end of the channel and was turning ninety degrees to port. Still we followed, down an even narrower channel. Were we being trapped? One more ninety degree bend to starboard, however, and the channel shallowed and opened up into small pool. We could just make ourselves secure by using two anchors, one at the bow and one at the stern. Again, it felt really strange to be at anchor so far from the mainland in such an unusual setting, but it was snug and safe. We asked the fishermen on board for tea, and later helped them fix their outboard engine.

The next day, we were off again at the crack of dawn and managed to win another fourteen useful miles to the north. This time there was a wide open anchorage available in the lee of the low lying Taila Islands. As there was plenty of swinging room and no coral on the seabed, we could let out a good length of chain and feel totally secure. The anchorage commanded a wide view of the southern entrance to an interesting inland sea, about twenty-five miles long, south of Ras Abu Shagara ('ras' means headland). We watched in envy as *Lady Rosi* tacked up from the south under sail alone, and disappeared from sight to the north.

The whole of the next day – Valentine's Day – was spent at anchor in fifteen to twenty-five knot winds from the north-west (veering as was normal in the afternoons to the north-east). The wind generator kept up a steady tune from treble to base; and the rigging shrieked. I remained in the pilothouse, with my charts and pilots, staring out of the windows at the views beyond. To the west of us, there was not a soul to be seen on the barren land. In the distance – about fifteen to twenty miles inland – there was a never ending line of mountainous peaks. Behind them, I knew, there stretched for 3,600 miles the biggest desert in the world – the Sahara. A mere 125 miles to the east-north-east of us, however, on the other side of the Red Sea, was the Saudi Arabian port of Jiddah – in whose design I had played a tiny part in 1974, when working for Sir William Halcrow and Partners in London. So frustratingly close – one day's sail – but, as mentioned earlier, foreign yachts were believed not to be welcome.

Only forty miles inland from Jiddah was Mecca, the holy city that Moslem people worldwide seek to visit at least once in their lifetime. Again – a really special place, so close but so far.

By the following morning the wind was light and from the north-east. We were able to motor-sail for another ten miles northwards up the coast to the beautiful safe haven of Khor Inkeifal. While we were there, two rugged looking overland vehicles from Austria came over to investigate us. What really surprised us was that they had Satnav. I think they were even more surprised to learn that we had no Satnav. They disappeared as unexpectedly as they had arrived.

We got up at twenty minutes past five in the morning for a quiet motor up the next section of the 'inland sea' between the mainland and the island of Mukawwar, following clear marker beacons all the way. By half past seven we were past the shallowest part of the channel (about seven metres in depth) and approaching the open sea. One look, however, at the white caps in the middle distance and the rougher looking water beyond, was enough. The next anchorage to the north was twenty-two miles away – we would have to turn round. I decided to sail back for two miles or so to the lovely anchorage we had noticed earlier in the lee of the tiny island of Mesharifa, merely a sand spit with a little grass on it.

We had not been there long when we noticed a sail approaching us from the north. It was *Lady Rosi* again. What were they doing heading south? Before long, Roger, Siv and Rosita were on board *Tin Hau* and telling us how impossible it had been to make any headway against the nasty, steep waves (the usual story for the Red Sea).

We ended up spending five days at Mesharifa island, pottering around on the shore and doing various jobs on the boat. I was able to help the crew of *Lady Rosi* with a problem they had endured for five long months – no toilet! They had the same type of toilet as we did – the Lavac, which has a separate Henderson Mark V hand pump. We carried spares for just about every part which could go wrong; and one such part was exactly what they needed – the pump diaphragm and seal. Roger fitted it on *Lady Rosi* – and they were back in business, to their great relief.

The crew of *Lady Rosi* in turn did us a great favour in trying to get a relayed ham radio message through to Lynda to say where we were and that we were okay; and the news came back to us that Lynda was safely in Chichester with my mother. We also learnt on the radio the sad news that *Bonaventure II* had had major engine problems whilst approaching Port Sudan and that she might not be able to continue with the trip. *Aquilla* and *Tola* were apparently over two hundred miles ahead of us at Ras Banas, which was good to hear.

On Sunday, 21st February, we were able to set off once more. The wind was not ideal in that it was from the north to north-west again. At least it was not too strong and the waves were less than four feet in height. We rounded Ras Abu Shagara successfully and spent an eventful day identifying reefs and wrecks as we motor-sailed amongst them, tacking to and fro on our way northwards. I decided to go as far as Khor Shinab, forty miles from Mesharifa island.

By three o'clock in the afternoon we had reached the entrance to this narrow inlet. Martyn and Darren were stowing the sails and I was using Erni to bring *Tin Hau* slowly in towards the land. As was usual, I had perched myself half way up the starboard pilothouse ladder so that I was as high as possible to see the water colour ahead, but near enough to Erni and the engine controls if I wanted to alter course. The sun was exactly wrong – dead ahead of us. I was not unduly worried, as I could see the reef closing in on us on both sides of the channel.

Suddenly, to my horror, we came to an abrupt standstill. I looked over the side of the boat and saw to my surprise that we were hard and fast on top of an uncharted 'bommie'. I engaged reverse gear immediately but *Tin Hau* would not move – even at maximum throttle. We had a quick look round underwater and saw that the bommie was about fifteen metres in length and five metres in width, with very deep water all around. The main reef to leeward of us – the south-eastern side of the channel – was only thirty metres away; the windward reef was about the same distance to the north-west.

Immediately, we launched *Knot Often*, picked up the bow anchor, and dropped it just clear of the bommie. Then we winched in the chain so that the anchor was hooked under the edge of the coral. This was to protect us, if the wind broke us free, from drifting on to the main reef to leeward. If that had happened, I do not think we would ever have been able to get *Tin Hau* off again. There would certainly have been no external help and I imagine *Tin Hau* would eventually have been a wreck. Not a pleasant thought!

A brief look at the tide tables revealed that we would get no help from that quarter. In fact the tides – such as they were – could not have been worse. We would have to re-float *Tin Hau* as quickly as possible.

I instructed Darren to get his mask and flippers on and report on what things looked like from underwater. This he duly did. Spluttering from below us, he described the bommie in detail. It appeared that the weakest looking piece of coral was that nearest to the bow an the starboard side. Darren said that, if I was to make a series of moves under power, it might be possible to break it.

Following his instructions, I first manoeuvred *Tin Hau* gently astern (taking care not to damage the rudder); we were able to move slightly. Then, with full throttle and wheel hard to starboard, we battered the reef as hard as possible! Gently in reverse again, wheel to port. Full throttle forward. Kill that reef! So we continued again and again. Darren popped up every so often to make encouraging noises. The coral was suffering.

Suddenly we were clear – thank goodness!

Having pulled up the dangling anchor, Martyn joined Darren in *Knot Often* and the two of then rowed ahead of *Tin Hau*, scanning the seabed for more offending bommies. It was a relief to reach the calmer waters within the inlet.

Once we had anchored, I dived down to inspect the hull. The only damage was some superficial scratching of the paintwork on the keel, which was about what I had expected. Still it was gratifying to have had an experience at long last that really justified our choice of steel as the construction material. Most fibreglass or wooden boats would not have stood up to that sort of treatment; but then I suppose most skippers do not place their boats on a reef!

It took a triple vodka and orange each before the delayed shock wore off and we felt better!

The next day we started early again at half past five (I would usually be up at four o'clock in all our Red Sea anchorages to sniff the wind and decide whether or not an early start was desirable). On this occasion, the wind behaved fairly typically. We were able to make good progress under power in smooth seas until nine o'clock when it started blowing at a strength of about force three from the north-north-west. For another hour or so it was still feasible to head straight into the wind and make progress under power alone. After that we had to hoist the main and mizzen, keep the engine on, and bear away to motor-sail on a new course forty-five degrees off the one we wanted. At this point I decided to head for a sheltered but deep anchorage called Marsa Wasi, which we reached at eleven o'clock, just as the wind was blowing up in earnest.

We ended up staying two further days at Marsa Wasi, during which time the wind gusted force seven to eight in the afternoons. Our wind generator generated more power than I could dissipate in the freezer. At least we had plenty of ice to put in the sun-downers.

On 25th February (the day of the week was no longer considered important), we managed eleven miles to reach the interesting anchorage of Marsa Gwilaib, another of those narrow creeks not visible until we were actually opposite the entrance. This one had a sand spit almost all of the way across the channel and various reefs and bommies to watch out for. Once inside, the remoteness and wildness was as beautiful as ever. Darren and Martyn continued to enjoy the exciting underwater world of the Red Sea, spending much time swimming and snorkelling amongst the coral reefs.

A further ten miles were achieved the following day. We anchored in a bay with reef protection only, just south of Marsa Umbeila. At ten minutes past eleven the sleek French yacht *U-Matalu* motored by, slicing through the waves with no pitching whatsoever. We spoke to each other on the VHF. I learnt that *U-Matalu* had left Port Sudan sixteen days earlier, just after us, and had seen no other yachts. At three minutes past seven – from an anchorage just to the north – *U-Matalu* relayed the Jiddah forecast to us, which was for seventeen to twenty-one knot north-west winds with five to seven foot waves – in other words, a fairly typical Red Sea day.

We saw *U-Matalu* in her anchorage at seven o'clock the following morning as we motored past, a mile or so out to sea. By now, although I had not yet met him, I knew the name of the skipper – Hippolyte. We had an exciting radio conversation with him on VHF channel six. He was able to speak on his long range amateur radio set to Dick and Bonnie of *Windsong*, who were well to the north of us at Ras Banas (in fact we could speak to them directly via *U-Matalu's* two radio sets). *Windsong* had received a message from *Freedom Hunter*, anchored to the south of us, who in turn had received the message from a UK amateur radio operator named Bill, that Lynda's medical tests were negative and that so far no operation was being proposed. Amazing how news travels, if it really has to, via the yottie grapevine!

The rest of that day went reasonably well in that we were able to travel twenty-nine miles, round the exposed headland of Ras Hadarba, and onwards to the large sandy bottomed lagoon of Marsa Halaib, the best anchorage we had yet encountered in the Red Sea, which – amazingly – we had almost to ourselves. We anchored near to the entrance in the northern part of the lagoon, where there was shelter from the northerlies in the lee of the reef and island known as Gezirat Halaib. At the southern end of the lagoon, about two miles away, was a small settlement and army post with a high look-out tower. My twenty-two year-old Michelin map of north-east Africa showed that politically Halaib was in Egypt (although for administration purposes it was shown to be in the Sudan). All my other more recent books, charts and guides (including our Bible – *The Red Sea and Indian Ocean Cruising Guide*, written by Alan Lucas) showed that we were still in Sudan, and therefore there illegally, as we had officially left the country nearly three weeks earlier in Port Sudan, the only place where clearance formalities were possible.

I say all this, because it was my intention to visit the army post the next day to see if I could purchase any diesel – and perhaps some fresh fruit or vegetables. I had been monitoring the diesel position day by day since Port Sudan and doing everything I could to conserve supplies. The current situation was that we had 588 of our original 770 litres of fuel remaining, of which perhaps 550 litres were usable (allowing for the outlet pipe positions, heeling of the boat and so on). Yet Hurghada, the nearest certain place where diesel could be bought, was still 340 miles away. Given that there were so few anchorages ahead of us where we could take shelter and wait during inclement weather, I felt that the fuel we still carried was not sufficient. The one hundred mile open sea crossing of Foul Bay lay immediately ahead.

On the other hand, looking at it optimistically, it might be possible to use as little as three hundred litres of diesel, if the sea was mirror calm all the way to Hurghada; but how likely was this, on past performance? We would need a miracle!

After weighing it all up, I decided to motor over to the army post the next morning to see whether they could help us. We anchored right opposite the settlement, launched *Knot Often*, and rowed ashore.

The welcome was hostile in the extreme. Why had we been anchored at the northern end of the lagoon the previous night? Why had we not called at the army post straightaway? What were we doing in Sudan? Who were we? Our passports and ship's papers were scrutinised.

I was unable to get a word in edgeways for at least ten minutes, but things calmed down after a while. I explained how I had deliberately come to this army post because I needed help. Could I purchase any diesel? Could they please help us?

Their attitude changed. They would help if they could, but unfortunately they had no food or diesel to spare. I could, however, go to Port Sudan by lorry (about two hundred miles) and pick up a forty-four gallon drum there. 'Fine,' I said. 'When is the next lorry?'

'Not today,' said one officer.

'Not tomorrow,' said another.

'Possibly Wednesday.'

So we prepared ourselves for a long wait, anchoring *Tin Hau* securely with several anchors. I spent the following day sitting on a stool outside the main building, chatting to Omer, chief of the army post and chief customs officer. Omer's English was excellent and he welcomed the chance to practise using it.

I learnt that one of the buildings near to us was the new customs control centre, which had been opened only the previous month. Things were changing in Halaib.

On the next day, Sunday, 29th February– the 'leap day' that occurred only once every four years – the miracle started to take place. The wind blew gently from the south-west and then backed to the east. We had never seen this happen before. At half past eight in the morning I decided that we would abandon our plans of acquiring more diesel by road. We would instead gamble on the weather and set off across Foul Bay. I went ashore to tell Omer about our change of plans.

By ten minutes past nine we were outside the entrance to Marsa Halaib. There was no wind, but quite a big swell. We set off northwards under power alone.

For the whole morning the sea stayed smooth and we made good progress. There was a time in the afternoon when a breeze threatened to pick up. But by sunset it had died again. The sea became calmer and calmer. We rejoiced as we crossed more and more of the dreaded Foul Bay with no problems at all. We enjoyed a beautiful clear moonlit night – the temperature was a warm twenty-two degrees centigrade.

At twenty minutes to four in the morning, the tiny island of Zabargad was spotted in the moonlight just off the starboard bow. By dawn, as we crossed the Tropic of Cancer, the island was abeam – I took a photograph of the sun rising right behind it. Our next excitement was to sight land on the port bow: this was mainland Egypt at last! We left the thirty-four metre high island of Mikauwa a few miles to port at quarter to ten. Ras Banas was only four miles distant when, for the first time in twenty-four hours, a head wind threatened. Just a puff, but was this a forerunner of stronger stuff to come?

I decided to anchor in the lee of Ras Banas for a breather while we assessed what the wind would do next. Whatever it chose to do, we felt triumphant. The most difficult part of the Red Sea must surely be over.

At two o'clock the breeze started to drop and we decided to carry on. Could there be still more of this miracle calm?

As though they sensed our mood, a school of dolphins joined us, leaping and dancing all over the place. After nightfall, with Erni still steering, the wind changed to a very slight following breeze; for three and a half hours the engine was off and we sailed.

Strangely, it had suddenly become very humid (one hundred per cent relative humidity). From this point onwards until Suez I maintained a graph showing (two or three times a day) barometric and hygrometric (humidity) readings, together with a score out of a hundred representing how easy or difficult it was to make progress to the north (see Figure 14). Zero meant that it was totally impossible to go anywhere; one hundred meant that it was possible to proceed reasonably quickly in the right direction under sail. Later, I used the graph, together with the current humidity reading (this seemed to be of greater significance than the barometric reading), to help me decide whether or not to leave an anchorage in an attempt to go northwards. There was precious little else to go on – I was receiving no weather reports or forecasts.

We considered anchoring at the island of Wadi Gimal (latitude 24°39' north) at eight o'clock the next morning, but, after nosing around it for an hour or so, we decided to continue. The calm was too good to waste.

On we went, with mainland Egypt about six miles to port (for once our radar was working – I think it liked the calm sea!) Mile after mile went by with little incident, although there was plenty of navigation to be done.

At midnight the wind changed to its usual direction of north-north-west – dead on the nose. Only lightly at first, but the waves threatened to increase to a size we could not motor against. As there was a possible anchorage nearby – Marsa Wizr (latitude 25°47' north), open only to the east, I decided to stop. First we had to wait for dawn, maintaining position by tacking to and fro under sail alone. I managed to get a number of star fixes in the moonlight so as to pinpoint our position as well as possible. As soon as it was light we sailed closer to the land. We found, however, that the anchorage was not quite where I had hoped and we still had to motor for a couple of miles up the coast. At half past eight we eventually found Marsa Wizr, which was bleak and feature-less, and we anchored with relief – I was very tired.

The wind did increase in strength from the north-west during the morning, but at dusk it changed to the east. With hindsight, we should have gone then, as the wind remained easterly for much of the night – which was most uncomfortable for us at anchor, and a waste of a favourable wind direction for making progress to the north. How was I to have known in advance how long it was going to remain favourable?

As it was, we left at ten minutes past eleven the next morning, under power as usual and in moderating seas. We passed the Egyptian port of Quseir at twenty-five past four, glad not to be stopping there as it had a bad reputation amongst yotties. Port Safâga, forty-two miles further on, also had an appalling reputation – hopefully, we would get beyond it. However, at five minutes to eight that evening, still twenty-five miles short of our target, a vicious twenty-five knot blast of wind hit us from ahead. We had two choices – turn back

Direction	Knots	Points	Direction	Knots	Points
SW (225°)	0-5	85	NE (045°)	0-5	80
	5-10	90		5-10	75
	10-15	95		10-15	70
	15-20	92		15-20	50
	20-25	85		20-25	25
	25+	75		25+	0
W (270°)	0-5	80	E (090°)	0-5	85
	5-10 ✱	75		5-10	95
	10-15 ✱	70		10-15	98
	15-20 ✱	50		15-20	95
	20-25 ✱	25		20-25	85
	25+	0		25+	75
NW (315°)	0-5	60	SE (135°)	0-5	90
	5-10 ✱	40		5-10	95
	10-15 ✱	10		10-15	100
	15-20 ✱	5		15-20	98
	20-25 ✱	0		20-25	92
	25+	0		25+	80
N (000°)	0-5	60	S (180°)	0-5	90
	5-10 ✱	40		5-10	95
	10-15 ✱	10		10-15	100
	15-20 ✱	5		15-20	98
	20-25 ✱	0		20-25	92
	25+	0		25+	80

✱ The most commonly occurring winds.

This system of "Wind Points", based on wind direction and strength, was devised in the northern part of the Red Sea to assist in *Tin Hau's* passage north-north-west towards Suez. The score, 100, represents optimum sailing conditions and 0 represents impossible sailing conditions.

Figure 15: Wind Points - Red Sea & Gulf of Suez
sheet 1 of 2 - Definition of "points"

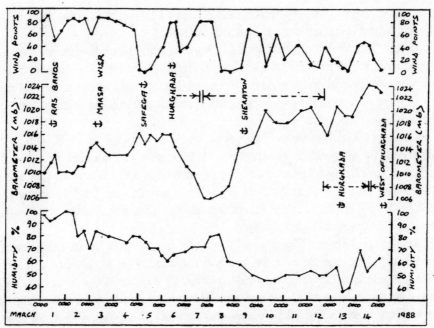

These graphs were plotted in an attempt to correlate air pressure, humidity and favourable sailing conditions. Efforts to make headway were not generally made in wind points of less than 50.

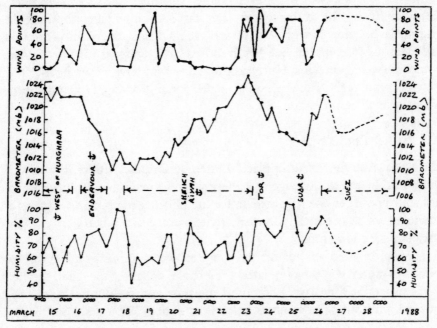

Figure 15: Wind Points - Red Sea & Gulf of Suez – March 1988

towards Quseir or try to make Port Safâga. I decided on the latter – I have always found it difficult to go back on my tracks.

There followed one of those nights I would rather forget, as we motor-sailed against steeper and steeper seas, Darren was horribly seasick, but he kept up with all the sail changes and only retired when no further help was needed from him. We got there in the end, gratefully dropping anchor just inside Safâga Bay at 8.43 a.m.

I had on board some useful 'yottie notes', compiled in 1985, which had a worrying little anecdote about a yacht, anchored just where we were, being arrested for failing to proceed to the commercial port. We were just too tired to go anywhere that afternoon. However, as no one had disturbed us, I resolved to leave for Hurghada (thirty-three miles away) as early as possible the next day, weather permitting.

Luck was with us. There was little wind in the early hours of the morning of Sunday, 6th March; and the sea had subsided. We were away at quarter to five and made good progress under power all day. At about seven o'clock we were surprised to spot at anchor *Svanhilde* with two yachts rafted up alongside her. These turned out to be *Klepel* and another *Windsong*, a German one this time, not the American *Windsong* belonging to Dick and Bonnie. The three boats got going an hour later and followed in our wake.

At ten o'clock we were even more surprised to spot *Top Knot* and *Sundancer III* in the distance off the starboard bow, also homing in on Hurghada. So, after having seen so few yachts during the twenty-eight days it had taken us to complete the five hundred or so miles from Port Sudan, we found ourselves entering Hurghada together with five other boats. It was a truly beautiful sight. Between us we represented Norway, Holland, Germany, Australia and Great Britain.

9.   Hurghada to Suez

Hurghada. Another exciting place. Different sounds. Different smells. I felt stimulated by the knowledge that there were so many new things to explore. Just the opposite to the hemmed-in feeling of being trapped in a rut and going nowhere, which occurs all too easily (with me at least) when living on land in one place for a long time.

Having dropped anchor off the town at twenty minutes to one in twelve metres of water, we contemplated the change of landscape ashore. This was Egypt proper at long last. I savoured the moment, feeling both relieved and satisfied with our achievements since Port Sudan. What a shame that Lynda couldn't have been with us to share the occasion, especially after all the work she had done to prepare *Tin Hau* for one of our most challenging voyages.

Knot Often was launched and I rowed ashore, armed with the ship's papers, ready to face officialdom once more. This time it was going to be slightly less lonesome. With me were the captains of *Svanhilde*, *Klepel*, *Windsong*, *Top Knot* and *Sundancer III*. It was more a case of poor officials. They would be outnumbered for once.

All went well at first. Customs clearance was effected quickly, immediately followed by the harbour office. But there it stuck. The remainder was going to have to wait until the next morning. Being a Sunday was not the problem; Friday is the day of rest in the Moslem world. The trouble was that we were trying to enter Egypt during an afternoon. This was obviously not the normal thing to do.

So back we went to our respective boats for the evening and night. I rowed over to speak to Ted and Barbara on *Top Knot* and then on to the beautiful *Svanhilde*. There I was in for a surprise. It was possible to use the ship's radio equipment for a 'patched' telephone call (via Oslo) to Lynda. It was amazing to hear the phone ringing in Chichester, followed by Lynda's voice. I learnt, however, that, even though there was no talk of an operation, there was still no way that she could yet return to *Tin Hau*. How I missed her, as did *Tin Hau* and her crew. Sadly, it seemed that we might have to manage without the mate all the way to Cyprus.

The next morning (Monday, 8th March, 1988), the international yottie onslaught on Egyptian bureaucracy commenced at an early hour. A shared taxi was taken into the middle of town, where we went to government offices and met an Egyptian colonel. After protracted interviews we were all granted Egyptian visas at a cost of US $8 per person (although we had been unable to get Egyptian visas in Port Sudan, we had learnt that the cost of a visa granted there would have been US $30). At the bank we obtained our first Egyptian pounds (their pound is subdivided into 100 piastres), the rate being US $1 to Egyptian £2.23. Thus armed, we were able to revisit the customs office to hand over E £18 for the entry fee and we could pay E £10 to the doctor for his part in the clearance formalities. We learnt that a special permit was needed to anchor off the Sheraton Hotel, which was located at the end of a small headland a couple of miles from the harbour. Mooring there would cost E £10 per day, but reasonably priced diesel could apparently be arranged and it was a shallower, safer anchorage than the harbour, as well as a pleasant place to be. We all decided to acquire the necessary permits and enjoy a few days of rest beside the Sheraton.

The final job to carry out in the town was that of food shopping. In this respect we were very pleasantly surprised. The market was full of the most delicious looking fruit and vegetables, grown in the fertile Nile basin one hundred miles inland. E £1 (about 30p) bought us a cauliflower, half a dozen tomatoes, two dozen bananas, five oranges and a whole lot of onions! We were overwhelmed to have such wonderful fresh provisions again and generally felt a bit culture shocked to be seeing tarred roads, bustling traffic and dignified old buildings. Tourists coming to Egypt by plane may have viewed Hurghada as a sleepy, dusty old Egyptian backwater. To us it was a modern twentieth century metropolis!

At quarter to four we pulled up the anchor and sailed round to the Sheraton, anchoring in five metres of clear water beside *Fam* and *Lady Rosi* (the latter having been towed in to Hurghada by *Freedom Hunter* after engine problems). We marvelled at the sight of the ultra-modern hotel, all lit up in turquoise blue with the floodlit desert hills immediately behind. As the distant mountains merged with the darkening sky, we sipped our sun-downers and relaxed in this most beautiful of anchorages. We slept deeply right through the night without any disturbance.

The next morning I went ashore to the hotel and started making arrangements for diesel (one hundred and forty litres remained of the seven hundred and seventy litres with which we had left Port Sudan). One meeting followed another, until eventually I was the only skipper still pursuing the trail. My patience paid off in the end and I found myself a somewhat bemused passenger on the hotel motor launch, bouncing out at great speed towards *Tin Hau*. We were in the middle of using the spare halyard to lift the first of two forty-four gallon (two hundred litre) drums full of diesel on to *Tin Hau's* deck, when Ted of *Top Knot*, anchored nearby, started making frantic signs that I must turn on my radio. 'Channel seventy-three,' he shouted.

I duly turned on the VHF. 'How did you get the diesel?' he spluttered. 'How much are you paying?' I was aware that he was not the only one awaiting my reply, but I told him to wait. I was content to proceed in the Egyptian way, where tea comes first and time moves at a civilised pace. Price negotiations could be concluded later.

In the meantime I was getting to know Mustafa from the hotel – and his two assistants. I was impressed by their dignity and willingness to help. They insisted on personally organising the siphoning of the diesel into the main tanks. I was happy to use three-quarter inch hose, but they considered this too slow, preferring instead to use some spare one and a half inch toilet hose, even though this meant that they swallowed copious quantities of the foul tasting fuel. Although I knew that the price of diesel in oil-producing Egypt was low, I was still pleasantly surprised by the sum demanded – E £40 (equivalent to 3p per litre). I was happy to pay this without any bargaining. Also I gave a tip of E £10 to each of the helpers – all to Ted's great annoyance when he found out later. He felt I was paying too much.

The following few days saw the return of the strong north-westerlies. We lay safely to two anchors, whilst three of the other yachts dragged. *Roama* arrived in the anchorage, as did *Bonaventure II* (following her engine problems, she had been towed by *St Combs* for four hundred miles). We learnt through *Top Knot's* ham radio that *St Combs's* arrival was imminent. News of the whereabouts of the rest of the fleet trickled through by the same route.

As we were relatively close to the ancient tombs at Luxor, ten of us decided to leave our boats, hire a van and speed one hundred and seventy-five miles across the desert to see the world famous historical site. The opportunity was just too good to waste. What a disappointment it proved to be! There were thousands and thousands of tourists of every conceivable nationality. One guided tour after another was rushed through the Valley of the Kings, the Tombs of the Queens and into the well known burial chambers. Prices were astronomically inflated. We encountered aggressive, noisy behaviour such as we had not seen for years. It was beyond our comprehension that the tourists we watched regarded this as a holiday. The only proper way to have experienced Luxor would have been in solitude and in silence. We had obviously picked the wrong time. I, for one, was very happy to be returning to the boat, where the pace of life was slow and there was time to contemplate one's surroundings in peace.

On Saturday, 12th March, we pulled up the anchors and motored round to Hurghada town, in order to follow the official instructions of reporting to the authorities (again) for clearance to proceed northwards towards Suez (one hundred and eighty miles). With hindsight it was probably a mistake to have been so law abiding. Nothing much was achieved on the first day. On the second day, I thought that I had completed all the formalities, having paid the customs officer E £24 (which included E £20 for 'overtime'). I had been given clearance papers and told that we were free to go. I had just finished stowing *Knot Often* in the davits when there was a loud shout from the shore.

'Tinooo, Tinooo, Poleez, Poleez.' I was needed ashore again. Urgently.

I launched *Knot Often* and rowed to the quay. Awaiting me was an absolutely seething police officer, who was really angry that I had not been to see him earlier. He wanted E £51 payment for harbour dues – to cover the period whilst we had been dealing with the customs officer. If I chose to pay the following morning during normal office hours, this could be reduced to E £15 (US $7). I decided that the latter course was preferable, even though it meant more delay.

Early the next morning (the third day of our official clearance from Hurghada town) we waved to four of the 'Sheraton fleet' sailing by on their way towards Suez. Knowing what had happened to us, they had chosen to forget about a second visit to the Hurghada authorities. We, unfortunately, were committed. I duly reported to the harbour office, as soon as it was open, and handed over E £15. We were free to go. However, by this time, five hours after dawn, the wind had got up and any progress in the right direction was clearly (in my eyes) impossible. I asked if I could wait until the sea was calmer, perhaps leaving at half past four the following morning. Although the harbour master was happy with this, the customs officer was not. We would have to enter Hurghada officially again and then go through the clearance process a second time. It was a catch-22 situation. Heads they win. Tails I lose. It could go on for ever (unless I resorted to bribing my way out of the difficulty, which I always refused to do on principle). I therefore decided against my better judgement to leave straightaway and anchor in the lee of a tiny island one and a half miles from the town. I had a large scale chart of this island and anchoring appeared possible although uncomfortable.

Once again, I was forced into a dangerous position by marine officials who appeared not to understand the sea, let alone the limitations of a Chinese junk or its crew. Of the eight countries we had been to so far – South Africa, Mauritius, Seychelles, Chagos, Sri Lanka, South Yemen (Aden), Sudan and Egypt – only in Chagos and South Yemen had there been no problems. So few officials seem to understand the harm they do by not allowing small boat owners the freedom to pick their own times for departure from a port or country. Skippers and crews need time for physical and psychological rest before setting off on voyages of twelve hours or more. Boats need to be properly prepared and maintained. Financial – or indeed any other – pressure should not be brought to bear to force a yacht's early departure.

Anyway, depart we did. At first sight the chosen anchorage seemed satisfactory. We were sheltered from the rough sea the other side of the reef. I laid out a second anchor for safety. However, as the day turned to night, the wind was strengthening, rather than abating, as happened normally. A heavy swell started to turn the corner into our bay. Still no problem, if it wasn't for one factor – coral heads. There were many more of these than shown on my chart. Slowly but surely our anchor chains started to foul on some of them, which meant that our effective chain lengths reduced from forty metres to thirty metres to twenty metres. At two o'clock in the morning one of the anti-snub ropes broke while Darren was carrying out an inspection. A length of rope whistled past his head, just missing it. By now, the violent jerks on the anchor windlass and the one remaining anti-snub rope were frightening. In the dark, there was nothing we could do. We just had to wait for dawn.

In the daylight we could see the waves at last – they were about four to five feet in height. I considered returning to Hurghada town. However, this would have necessitated buoying and temporarily abandoning our main anchors; also it was now difficult to see the coral heads on the way out of the anchorage. So I decided to stay put. We did at least manage to shackle on a new anti-snub rope, which took the pressure off the windlass. To our dismay, we saw that the damage had already been done. One end of the main shaft had been bent, thus rendering the starboard side of the windlass unusable. This meant that all raising and lowering of the number two anchor would have to be done by hand until a repair could be effected in Cyprus. Not an easy task. Once again we cursed the Hurghada customs officer.

On the following day, the wind had moderated to force four and was no longer blowing straight from the direction towards which we wanted to go. With a sigh of relief we weighed anchor and left Hurghada, bound for the island of Shaker and beyond.

By lunchtime we had covered twenty-five miles and reached our intended destination, Endeavour Anchorage, a huge, nearly totally enclosed, anchorage – one of the best in the entire Red Sea – part of the small uninhabited island of Tawila (27°34' north, 33°47' east). Our only neighbour was a forty-five foot ferrocement French sloop named *Nomad*. As is the norm in the yottie world, it was not long before we were making friends with the owners of the yacht, René and Chantal, and swapping stories. These two were amongst the most experienced sailors I had ever come across. They had lived for many years on *Nomad*. Sadly, although they were about to complete a circumnavigation, they explained they would not be stopping in their home country, France. The reason was that they could not afford to comply with France's strict rules on expensive safety equipment such as annually serviced liferafts. France's loss, not theirs. It was ironic that one of the safest yachts in existence should be deemed 'unsafe' by the French authorities.

We were still enjoying the sun, sea and tranquillity at our anchorage the following afternoon when the wind dropped and started blowing very gently from the unusual easterly direction. This was most favourable for passage making northwards into the Gulf of Suez. As if on cue, *St Combs* and *PF Flyer* chose this moment to ghost past the entrance under full sail. I spoke to them on the VHF and, as a result, decided that the conditions were too advantageous to be ignored. Even though we were committing ourselves to a night passage, which would mean no turning back, the calm period (or better still the easterly breeze) only had to last to two in the morning for the next shelter to be reached safely. So, off we set once again, praying for a lucky spell.

For the first two hours we made good progress under power as we entered the southern end of the Gulf of Suez. There were ships and oil rigs all over the place, some of the rigs with huge blazing gas flares. I had never seen anything like it.

So far so good, but then the worst happened, just as darkness fell. The wind changed to north-north-west. At first a light breeze, then by nine o'clock it had reached force four. A moderate steep sea developed, against which we could no longer motor without help from the sails. We hoisted the main and mizzen, bore away forty-five degrees to starboard and started motor-sailing. Our semi-operational radar chose this moment to be really useful for the first time since Agalega! Not only was I able to pick out the nearby land, but I could also plot the movements of shipping and navigate by the position of the oil rigs. Some of the latter had Racon beacons, which were new to me. There were also a few abandoned and unlit oil rigs, which, without radar, we might have been in danger of hitting.

The situation went from bad to worse. The wind strength increased to force six and the very steep seas had reached ten feet in height. What a place to be in the pitch dark in a Chinese junk! Would we be swept out of the Gulf of Suez back through the Straits of Gubal into the Red Sea again? Or could we make way to windward?

At midnight the log reading was: 'Struggling! Oil rigs, ships, headwind and big seas.' At eight minutes past one: 'Tack badly – snarl up. Broken main sheetlets. Reef to 3 panels. Sail setting horribly.'

Some hours later, I think we were all feeling seasick; I was so cold my teeth were chattering violently; the engine was at full revs; and the sails were reefed as far as they would go. However, we were winning. We *were* making progress – at a rate of about one mile directly against the wind, and perhaps current, every hour. *Tin Hau* was pulling through her first real test of this nature. It appeared that an anchorage on the far (eastern) side of the Gulf of Suez on the Sinai peninsular *was* attainable.

At half past seven in the morning we reached the shelter of Sheikh Riyah and dropped anchor. We just had time to register that there was another yacht there – the sleek French sloop *U-Matalu* with her enormous single mast – before collapsing on to our berths and falling asleep.

Two hours later there was a loud sound of knocking on the hull. I staggered up on deck to find that we were being invited to tea. A crew member from *U-Matalu* had come over to deliver the invitation. He immediately understood that we needed sleep and changed the invitation to drinks that evening. He even offered to collect us to save us the bother of launching *Knot Often*. I thanked him and went down below again.

All our energy had returned after our sleep and we were looking forward to a good evening out. The speed boat from *U-Matalu* arrived right on time. We raced over to the French yacht at a tremendous rate. The first surprise revealed itself as we approached. *U-Matalu's* transom opened up, James Bond style, to reveal what they termed 'le garage'. The speed boat was winched within and the stern closed silently.

Inside, we took stock of our surroundings, which were luxurious in the extreme! *Tin Hau* seemed positively shabby in comparison. Hippolyte, the skipper, welcomed us on board and offered us a choice of drinks from the bar. After I'd had a few, I learnt that there was a 'telephone' on board. 'Could I make a call to England?' I asked.

'Of course,' said Hippolyte, picking up the headset. Within seconds I heard the dialling tone, and Lynda answered. Unbelievable – to us simple folk, that is! This time we had been patched through Paris.

The next morning we were surprised to see *U-Matalu's* anchor being lifted. Hippolyte had obviously decided to proceed towards Suez in spite of the continued headwind and rough seas. We watched as she rounded the headland and reached the white capped water beyond. Surprisingly no sails were raised. She continued onwards as though there was not a wave in existence. A very slight pitching motion commenced. Amazing! *Tin Hau* would really have been struggling.

About five minutes later, however, we were equally surprised to see *U–Matalu* turn round. She was returning to Sheikh Riyah! Why? Hippolyte had the answer as he motored past. 'The girls were having difficulty with the cooking,' he said.

We remained at the same anchorage for six days – after one false start in an effort to leave on the second day. There was plenty of time to talk, read and think.

On 23rd March, the wind had moderated enough for us to be able to win another five miles up the coast to the town of Tor. In fact we went four miles beyond Tor before turning back, owing to a sudden change in the wind direction. Tor harbour was entered in the darkness of night.

We reported to the authorities the following morning. They were utterly charming and couldn't do enough for us. Many things were 'not permitted' – at least officially. But the army officer took the view that as long as he accompanied us everywhere there would be no problem. We were shown around the whole town and entertained royally.

Unfortunately we couldn't stay for long, as the wind changed again, this time favourably. We pulled up the anchor at quarter past six and were motoring north-westwards once more by half past six into a slight sea with very good visibility. Navigation was very easy owing to the radar set and the abundance of well lit oil rigs. It was like something from another world.

All through the night – and throughout the next day – we motored at a good economical engine speed. Martyn produced his usual excellent brunch. Erni steered and life was easy.

The only problem was that at this rate we would reach Suez in the middle of the night. So at three o'clock, as we approached the headland of Ras Sudr, we decided to drop anchor. We would thus enter Suez the next morning in daylight, refreshed and ready for anything that might be thrown our way.

The night, however, was by no means the restful one we had been expecting, given the calm weather of the preceding twenty-four hours. Strong northerlies blew from sunset until midnight, creating four to five foot waves, even where we were anchored. We took turns keeping an anchor watch, glad not to have been out at sea trying to make progress.

At 5.23 a.m. we started hauling in our full length of chain (seventy metres). The sea had calmed down as quickly as it had been whipped up. We set off for Suez, about twenty miles distant.

By half past nine we were passing the first of a long line of anchored ships, awaiting their turn to pass through the canal. We listened on the VHF to a Chinese skipper being bawled out by an Egyptian pilot in broken English that even we could hardly understand. I wondered whether to call up the authorities on channel sixteen, but decided to continue as far as I could towards the canal before creating any disturbance.

At ten minutes to ten the Prince of the Red Sea's 'brother' came alongside us in a launch as we entered Suez Bay. He confirmed that we could proceed to Suez Yacht Club just inside the canal entrance. This was a convenient encounter, as we had already decided three months earlier in Sri Lanka that the self-proclaimed 'Prince of the Red Sea' would be our 'agent' to assist with the canal transit. The papers required for the two day, ninety nautical mile, transit are quite complex, and an agent – specifically this one – had been strongly recommended.

The Prince's brother left us and we continued under power, drawing closer and closer to the canal entrance. The variety of anchored shipping was fascinating – ocean liners, smart cruise ships, plenty of rusty old traders, oil and gas tankers of all shapes and sizes, car transporters, and numerous smaller local craft. There was activity all over the place. It felt good to be part of it all.

Our happy daydreaming was brought to an abrupt standstill as two largish launches, each about the size of *Tin Hau*, broke away from the clutter of small craft and headed straight for us. Each one had about a dozen jabbering Egyptians on deck, all making signs that we should alter course to port and enter Port Ibrahim, the large commercial harbour at the entrance to the canal. They drew up each side of us and started turning to port themselves. A few of the deck hands started trying to board *Tin Hau*. No fenders had been put out. It looked as though we were about to lose some paint – and perhaps more.

'Get hold of the boat-hooks,' I shouted to Darren and Martyn. 'Darren, take the port side. Martyn, take the starboard. Wallop any knuckles that come anywhere near to us.'

Even though the helmsmen of the launches were shouting that they were Suez Canal officials, I was not going to allow our beautiful boat to be squeezed and damaged in this way. I increased our speed to over six knots and grabbed hold of the VHF transmitter.

I called out on channel sixteen: 'Prince of the Red Sea. Prince of the Red Sea. This is *Tin Hau*. Over.'

No answer. I tried a second time. Darren and Martyn were doing what I had asked them to do – with great enthusiasm. Knowing what the normal procedure was for yachts transiting the canal, I was not going to be diverted into a commercial harbour, which would almost certainly have meant delays and extra costs.

'*Tin Hau*. *Tin Hau*. This is the Prince of the Red Sea. Channel seventy-three,' an American voice answered.

I duly switched channels and found myself speaking to Alan of *St Combs*. He just happened to be in the Prince of the Red Sea's office in Suez at the time! He advised me to proceed to the Yacht Club without delay and ignore any other instructions.

I waved the microphone at the two launch skippers and tried to look menacing! It must have worked, for they peeled off and left us on our own.

We reached the canal entrance, and fifteen minutes later dropped anchor opposite Suez Yacht Club near to four yachts from the Sri Lanka 'fleet' – *St Combs*, *PF Flyer*, *Endurance II*, and *Roama*. Glen from *St Combs* helped us secure a stern line to a buoy. A small boat drew up alongside. It was another of the Prince's 'brothers', arriving to welcome us to Suez. He gave us some forms to fill in, explained the procedure for the canal transit, told us that we could use the showers and laundry facilities ashore for as long as we chose to stay – the daily mooring and yacht club charge was E £6 – and then to cap it all he had a present for all of us – a delicious assortment of Egyptian cakes.

'Welcome, welcome,' he called as he drew away. We certainly felt welcome; and we were most impressed with the Prince's efficiency (we never actually met the shadowy Prince himself). A fitting end to our forty-eight day, seven hundred mile passage from Port Sudan.

10. Suez to Larnaca

We stayed for nearly a week in Suez, a large and strategic town of about 370,000 people; and very enjoyable it was too. After the initial excitement of collecting our post and meeting up again with friends on the other yachts, we spent quite a bit of time wandering around the town looking for this and that. I remember the satisfaction of locating a genuine tin of WD40, after a two hour hunt which took me through a maze of back streets. This felt much more like the 'real Egypt' than Luxor, for example, where I had ended up viewing most local people with suspicion. Everywhere I went in Suez it was 'Welcome, Welcome'.

Diesel was arranged and taken on board. Knowing that we would shortly be leaving the land of cheap fuel, I bought numerous plastic jerrycans and filled these as well, storing them on deck.

We learnt that about fifty to one hundred ships proceeded up and down the canal each day in distinct 'convoys' under the care of Egyptian pilots. A north-bound convoy would pass a south-bound convoy at one of the three lakes part way along the canal – Lake Timsah, Great Bitter Lake and Little Bitter Lake. The canal, which has no locks, was supervised by Ferdinand de Lessops and opened in 1869. After the 1967 Israeli-Arab war and the subsequent closure of the canal, it was cleared, widened and deepened to handle larger ships including tankers (unladen with oil) of up to 200,000 tons in size.

A yacht intent on travelling northwards through the canal was required to set off in the dark well before the first convoy. It was compulsory to carry a pilot. The cost was a reasonable (or so I thought) US $140, plus tips.

I arranged our departure date for Saturday, 2nd April. I was told that the pilot would board at twenty minutes to three in the morning and that I was to re-moor fore and aft between two designated buoys. This would enable a 'quick getaway'. Only one other yacht would be sailing with us (or rather motoring with us, as it was forbidden to use sails) – the Swedish yacht *Amat Berani II*. We met the owner – Stephan (Bo Erik), and learnt that he had worked for many years as a marine engineer in Singapore. He had bought *Amat Berani* there and was taking her back to Sweden. She was a lovely fifty footer, constructed of Indonesian ironwood, with a centre cockpit, two masts and a brightly painted red hull. Interestingly, Stephan – probably the most experienced person in small marine diesel engines that I had ever met – admitted to being very nervous about how he would cope if his engine failed. It was a case of 'the more you know, the more you fear'. I felt slightly less bad about my own fears of engine failure and maintenance.

We were all ready to go at the appointed hour. It had taken a long time the previous day to clean the filthy harbour mud off our anchor and chain. Our first pilot – Ali – arrived at 2.35 a.m. and the canal transit began with *Tin Hau* leading the way and *Amat Berani* immediately astern.

As bad luck would have it, there was a headwind, which increased in strength as the day went on. There was also an adverse current of two and a half knots to contend with at one stage. Ali kept pushing the throttle forward as far as it would go – he was not happy with our slow progress. We hugged the port bank, keeping in shallow water to port of the beacons marking the edge of the channel. Dawn came at twenty minutes past five and Ali started becoming fidgety – like a cat looking for somewhere to go. He walked all around the boat. We wondered what the problem was. Finally he climbed on to the aft cabin top and produced a small mat from his bag. As he laid this out on the deck, we realised what was coming next. It was time for morning prayers. We should have known that Ali – as a devout Moslem – would need somewhere with a bit of space where he could bow down to face Mecca. We were glad that there was enough room for him on *Tin Hau*.

We reached Little Bitter Lake just in time. The first convoy of ships was coming up behind. It felt very strange to see so many huge ships at such close quarters, apparently steaming through a sea of sand.

At Great Bitter Lake more ships passed us. We also watched, with interest, some beautiful Egyptian feluccas sailing with great efficiency. Three further packets of cigarettes were handed over at the canal station at the northern end of the lake. The stock of Sri Lankan cigarettes left behind by Lynda was proving valuable, especially as there was something about these cigarettes that never seemed to produce greedy demands for more.

It was as late as twenty minutes to four by the time we reached our destination for the first day – a collection of mooring buoys at the northern end of Lake Timsah near to the large town of Ismailia. We rafted up alongside

Amat Berani for the night. I think Ali was glad to leave us to return to Suez and his normal job as a crane driver. It had been a long day – we had only covered forty-five miles but, owing to the strong headwind and adverse currents, this had taken thirteen hours.

Our pilot the next morning was called Salah Mohammed. He boarded at ten past eight, nearly four hours later than we had been expecting, owing to problems that had arisen concerning two southbound supertankers. Unfortunately, the wind was still strong and from the north. I had officially cleared out of Egypt in Suez, the plan being that we would not stop in Port Said, but would proceed directly into the Mediterranean. However, this was beginning to look impossible due to the adverse wind direction. When the northbound convoy started passing us from half past one onwards, I made contact over the radio with the captain of one of the ships (the Panamanian registered *Pointe de Carsen*) and obtained a forecast for Area Delta, which was: Wind north-east force five, locally six, moderating to four. I decided that this was not good enough and we would have to stop.

It was dark by the time we reached Port Said. Salah Mohammed left us and a new pilot named Shaban joined us to guide *Tin Hau* to Port Said Yacht Club. We were the only foreign yacht there. At eight o'clock an immigration launch came alongside and the formalities were dealt with by a very courteous and efficient police major. I decided not to apply for official entry to Egypt again, and told the major that we simply wanted to wait for suitable weather before leaving. He understood totally. We could stay where we were and use the yacht club facilities as we pleased (the charges were E £6 per day). On departure we would just have to notify the policeman on duty at the yacht club gates, who would retrieve our passports.

The highlight of what turned out to be a three day stay at the yacht club was meeting Commodore Hassan Luxor and his son, Ashraf. Commodore Luxor was a retired Egyptian naval officer, obviously of some note in Egyptian yachting circles. Like so many Egyptians, he was very courteous and helpful. Unfortunately, we were meeting him at the wrong time – just as we were leaving Egypt, rather than on our arrival. He very kindly gave us an autographed copy of his excellent booklet published the previous year, entitled *Egypt for Yachtsmen*.

On Wednesday, 6th April, the forecast was slightly better – east-north-east, eighteen knots. I decided to go. Passports were retrieved, bills paid and we were free to enter the Mediterranean.

We started off just after midday by sailing beside a long dredged murky channel leading north-westwards away from the canal entrance. It was good to be making way at long last without the use of the engine. The huge Nile Delta lay ahead of us just off the port bow, but, as the hours went by, we appeared to be clearing it. At quarter to ten the main part of the delta was about eight miles abeam and we crossed the twenty metre contour to enter the deeper waters of the shipping lane once more. By midnight the echo sounder was reading fifty-five metres. We ghosted along silently in the night with Number Seven steering and Darren on watch, the wind north-north-east, force three to four.

I was semi-awake for the rest of the night, even though my watch started officially at eight in the morning. We were receiving rather an interesting and enjoyable radio station broadcast in English – 'The Voice of Peace'. We never did find out exactly where it was based, but we think it was on a ship anchored near to the Israeli coast about one hundred and twenty miles away. Useful weather forecasts were given at regular intervals.

It was such a joy to look all around us and see neither land nor ships. The sea below was a deep blue colour such as we had not experienced for a long time. I spent as much time as possible at the bow, listening to the gentle splashing of the bow wave, relieved at leaving another busy port behind. It was magic; and it went on for three whole days as we drifted ever closer to Cyprus in lighter and lighter winds.

In the end we were forced to start the engine, as in the light airs we were being pushed further and further to the west – towards the wrong end of Cyprus. Larnaca was our ultimate destination, but without the engine we might not even make Paphos – also on Cyprus's south coast, but about seventy-five nautical miles to the west of Larnaca. During the course of the day (9th April) we alternated between heading for Larnaca and heading for Paphos, as the wind and swell varied.

We started to pick up all the signs of land. First we saw a floating container, with only one corner visible above the surface – highly dangerous to shipping. Then we came across some tame land birds, followed by a swarm of dopey flies. When the flies started to die all over the deck, yet more birds arrived, drawn by the free feast.

The coast of Cyprus was sighted at dusk. I finally made the decision to head for Paphos, rather than motoring for an additional eighteen hours to Larnaca. I preferred to wait for the prevailing westerly wind for an enjoyable sail along the south coast of Cyprus from Paphos to Larnaca.

As we approached Paphos in the dark, a most amazing fireworks display commenced on the shore, such as we had never seen before. It was as though it had been laid on for our benefit.

We entered the small harbour at quarter past ten. All was quiet – not a soul was around. I spotted a gap at the end of the pier where we could moor stern-to. This was to be our first experience of the 'Mediterranean moor', not quite so easy in the pitch dark, but at least no one would be watching. I picked a spot to drop anchor and reversed gently towards the pier, allowing for the light crosswind. Martyn was poised on *Knot Often*, slung in her davits right across the stern of *Tin Hau*. At the critical moment, he jumped down on to the quay (from quite a height), clutching the end of a mooring line, which he then made fast to a bollard. I engaged forward gear quickly in order to stop *Tin Hau's* large rudder hitting the pier. Darren took in the slack on the anchor chain and checked that the anchor was holding.

In this instance, all went very smoothly, but I knew that *Knot Often* would have to go. She would have to be replaced by a smaller dinghy, so that Lynda and I could carry out this manoeuvre on our own. There would have to be room to use the gates each side of the pilothouse; and we would need a gangplank.

A few minutes after we had settled down, an official in a smart uniform ambled over to greet us.

'Captain,' he said, 'You must be tired. I come back tomorrow. Late, because tomorrow Easter. You rest. Welcome to Cyprus.'

With that, the initial formalities were over. After so many difficult encounters with officialdom, I was overjoyed. This was wonderful – we were going to like Cyprus.

But what was that about tomorrow being Easter? The official had been quite sure; yet, according to our reckoning, Easter Sunday had already happened – six days ago, while we had been in Egypt. What was going on? Had we lost a week somewhere? It was some time before we worked out that the Greek Orthodox Church's Easter usually takes place on a different day to 'our' Easter. By chance, we had chosen to arrive in Cyprus on the evening before the most important and celebrated day of the year. Hence the fire-works; and hence the reason for the official's unwillingness to visit us at an early hour the next morning.

My plan the following day was to get to Larnaca as soon as possible – by bus or taxi – to find out Lynda's news. Maybe she would even be there?

But all my efforts to reach Larnaca failed. On Easter Sunday in Cyprus, it seemed, *everything* stopped. I had to be content with booking a 'shared taxi' to leave Paphos at the crack of dawn on the Monday. We listened anxiously to the headlines on the radio, which were all about the closure of Larnaca airport due to a hijacked aeroplane.

The shared taxi journey went as planned, very comfortable and low priced. I have often wondered since why the shared taxi concept – a door to door service between key towns at fixed prices and semi-fixed times – is not widely used in England and elsewhere. My companions in the taxi included a couple of policemen about to take up their day shift at Larnaca Marina. So, on arrival there at about eight o'clock, I had no problems about not being allowed through the main security gates!

The whole Marina appeared to be still asleep, with the exception of young Bruce from *Aquilla*, whom I encountered near to the shower block. It was Bruce who had helped to save *Tin Hau* in Aden. 'Have you seen Lynda?' he asked me. 'She is on *Windsong* half way along North Quay. That way!' he exclaimed, pointing.

I couldn't get there quickly enough. Again, there was not a sign of life on the long line of boats, moored stern to the quay. Except on one boat, where someone was sleepily emerging from the cockpit. My heart skipped several beats. It was Lynda!

We ran to hug each other – it was like something out of a film. But this was for real. It was a truly wonderful moment. She looked so much better than when I had last seen her just out of hospital in Port Sudan. We both felt overwhelmed by emotion.

Lynda soon asked the practical question: Where's *Tin Hau*? I was glad to be able to give her the news that we had made it to Cyprus in one piece and without any damage, the only slight problem being that we were in Paphos, not Larnaca. We made plans to return to Paphos that day.

'When did you arrive?' I asked.

'Yesterday,' she replied. She had seen the hijacked plane, but her flight had not been affected. She had been welcomed by several friends from the 'Sri Lanka fleet'. *Aquilla* had arrived safely on 26th March; Dick and Bonnie of *Windsong* (who had immediately offered to have Lynda to stay) had arrived at the end of March, followed by Mike and Karen of *Tola* (who had received a tow through the Suez Canal), Ted and Barbara of *Top Knot* on 2nd April, and Noel of *Sundancer III* on 5th April. There was also news of many of the boats equipped with ham radio.

I went to the marina office and met Glafkos, the Marina Director, who had been nothing but encouraging and helpful in all the correspondence I had had with him. More detailed arrangements were made about *Tin Hau's* stay at the marina, including the haul-out by travel-lift. We anticipated spending much of the summer 'out of the water', attending to the long list of things that needed doing.

Mike and Karen decided to join us in the shared taxi back to Paphos. It was their first wedding anniversary and they fancied a break away from *Tola*. We invited them to stay on *Tin Hau*, possibly sailing back with us to Larnaca.

Darren and Martyn had looked after *Tin Hau* well in my brief absence. They had started making plans for their departure, having booked berths on the ferry, the *Europa*, due to leave Limassol at about midday on the 14th. As it was the 11th already and the weather was still not suitable for a passage to Larnaca, it was agreed that they would leave us from Paphos.

On the morning of the 14th, the time had come for Darren and Martyn to step off *Tin Hau* for the last time. We said our farewells. 'Blancmange will never taste the same,' were Darren's last words. They had achieved everything they had set out to, and had played an important part in getting us all back to the Mediterranean safely. We were sorry to see them go and grateful to them for all their help.

Mike and Karen had left the previous day and so Lynda and I were alone once again. Since the wind was now favourable, we decided to pull up the anchor and get sailing immediately.

Four hours later, we were under full sail and sailing happily towards Larnaca when a large ship appeared on the horizon coming towards us. I turned on the VHF just in case it should be needed. A few minutes later, to our surprise, the radio crackled to life: '*Tin Hau*, *Tin Hau*. This is *Europa*. Over.'

The Cockney voice sounded strangely familiar. '*Europa*. This is *Tin Hau*. Channel eight. Over,' I replied.

It was Martyn! He and Darren had managed to get on to the bridge of the *Europa*. When Martyn had finished telling us what it was like to steer a big ship and what *Tin Hau* looked like from on high, we were close enough to wave to each other. It must have seemed very strange from their point of view, seeing their home of four months sailing past.

Lynda and I carried on at a good speed into the afternoon and night. By half past two we were approaching Larnaca and we started making our preparations for arrival. As it was still dark, we decided to anchor outside the marina until there were some signs of life ashore.

At nine o'clock we turned the engine on. We had been noticed by the marina staff and given instructions on what to do. Our life at Larnaca Marina was set to begin. *Tin Hau* was about to receive the tender loving care she deserved.

After that, Greece, Turkey and the lovely islands of the Aegean were now well within our reach. Our dream boat had been built. We had taken her to the Mediterranean. Soon we would be in the position to realise the third and final part of our original dream: to make a living by giving others a holiday afloat they would always treasure.

Christmas morning at sea-Darren and Martyn

Sunset along the Sudanese coast

An overtaking ship in the Suez Canal

Larnaca Marina haul-out-work in progress

Dotting the eye on the oculus

Re-launching by travel lift (28th August, 1998)
Photograph: John & Barbara Fletcher of S.Y. Anglesea

Turkish anchorage-Çineviz Liman

Kastellorizon, Greece's easternmost island

Cleopatra

On the gangplank at Larnca Marina
Photograph:Rhoda of *Sunchaser*

'Admiral' Vangelis
Photographer Helmut Gabriel

Vangelis' cottage at Panormos Bay, Skopelos

Land-bird taking a rest on the Walker Log
between Sicily and Sardina

Don Durham on galley duty in southern Spain

Mark's 20th birthday-Villamoura, Portugal

The two Marks on the beach at Baleeira, Portugal

Cape St Vincent, Portugal
Photograph Nigel Boulton of *Avalon*

Crossing the shipping lanes in the English Channel

Alongside town quay, Truro
An unknown Cornish Photographer

PART FIVE
The Eastern Mediterranean

Lynda Chidell

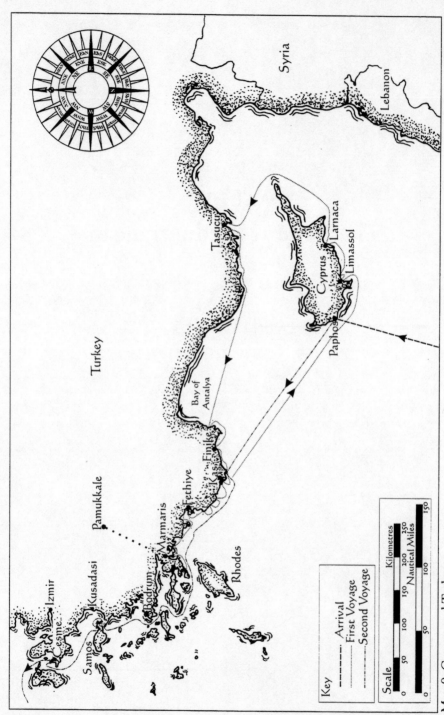

Map 9: Cyprus and Turkey

1.   A Summer on Land

Larnaca Marina probably has one of the biggest floating communities in the Mediterranean. Apart from boats belonging to local sailors, and boats laid up for the winter, there are so many permanent live aboard cruisers that the marina actually becomes a village for the winter.

Because of an incident some years prior to our arrival, the marina was protected by a security system which only allowed access to permit holders and their guests, who had to be signed in. The marina was administered from an office block which also housed a convenience store and small bar/restaurant.

There was a single building devoted to other facilities such as laundry and ablutions. The centre of this unit housed an enormous circular counter around which was arrayed a huge bank of lockers. These functioned as mail boxes and storage for toiletries and the like. The counter came into use at weekends, when the yachtsmen held a book swap. During the rest of the week, it acted as a discard table where one could leave anything for which one no longer had a use, but considered too good for chucking. There is no saying so true as that which declares 'one man's junk is another man's treasure'. Seldom was anything left on the counter which did not quickly find a new home. One had to remember to warn visitors not to leave valuables there – it was very embarrassing on one occasion for a yottie to have to advertise for the return of his visitor's coat and handbag!

The winter village did not generally start to disperse till the end of April. The marina was bursting on our arrival and the only berth available was right at the end of the north quay – the most exposed position in the marina. Although it was lumpy, we realised we were not going to have to endure it for long as we were scheduled for haul-out just as soon as a suitably large hard-standing became available.

Meanwhile, we had the time to get to know our new location and get bearings on such diverse places as the best timber merchant, chandler, paint supplier, restaurants, sailmaker, supermarkets and so on. Given the size of the town and the distance between some of these, it became obvious that we would need some form of land transport. Initially we hired a moped, but eventually invested in a pair of folding bicycles, which grew to be invaluable for every land-based activity.

In the event we had only a week to wait before *Tin Hau* was raised and transported by the marina travel-lift to her new place on the tarmac hard-standing. The most anxious moment was when the keel appeared out of the water; we were dying to see what – if any – damage she had sustained during her hours of reef bashing down in the Red Sea. All that came to light were a few slight scratches in the paintwork, which hardly reached bare metal! This was the first time we had seen her out of the water since her launch way back in March 1986. David had been scrubbing her bottom religiously at every opportunity, and we were pleased that she did not look totally neglected.

It was our intention, apart from the obvious scrubdown, repaint and re-antifoul, to make a number of changes to things with which we had never been satisfied, or to rebuild things we had got wrong. For four and a half exceedingly hot months (forty-three degrees centigrade in the shade) we laboured to carry out extensive interior renovation work in the cabin area. We made major changes to the plumbing system to make it safer, replacing virtually all the through-hull fittings with standpipes, to which valves were attached above the waterline. We had had nightmares about the dissimilar metals used in stopcocks, valves, inlets and outlets. Large scale metalwork improvements were made to the exhaust system and dinghy davits. Deckboxes were removed and replaced with stainless steel framework, and deck seating was added.

We had lived so long in fear of flooding the engine through forgetting to close the exhaust valve, or blowing the whole thing by forgetting to open it before turning on. The solution was simple, but needed the facilities of the marina to carry out the work. A stainless steel tubular loop was built to carry the fumes up and out through the deck, then back down again to rejoin the original exhaust port. The deck seating was built over the loop, so it was not even visible. Most of the new steelwork was done to replace excessive corrosion areas with stainless steel, or to change the design so that no corrosion was likely.

We had the sails off the masts for the first time since launch, and they were taken to a part-time sailmaker called Louis, who patched them where necessary. More importantly, he added pockets at both ends of each batten position. One of the enduring problems had been the snagging of running rigging in the batten projections at sail edges. We decided to try out PVC waterpipe in graded sizes instead of bamboo battens. The larger diameters were reserved for the higher battens, the smaller for the lower. Each batten was sleeved in a length of larger diameter pipe at the point where it came into contact with the mast. We also took the opportunity to add chafe battens to the opposite side of the sail (see Figure 5).

Louis made us a new centre deck awning, to our own design, which shaded the new seating area. This wonderful man became a valued friend, with whom we enjoyed a sociable evening every Friday we were in Larnaca. We would cycle to his shop, where he would mount his bike and ride with us to a roadside shack. The best souvlaki, pitta, sheftalia and iced beer on the island were to be found here. As luck would have it, Panikos, the greatest confectioner in town, had his establishment right across the road. We almost always rounded off our meal with a visit to him for some home made ice-cream or cakes and Greek coffee.

All in all we managed to remove a lot of potential disasters and a number of minor irritations from our worry list during that time. *Tin Hau* was relaunched on 28th August. This left us sufficient time to make a short cruise to Turkey before winter.

A number of our Red Sea fleet spent all or part of the summer out on the hard with us. Some locked up their boats and returned home for a longer spell. Bob and Dawn Buick of *Bonaventure II* returned to Australia for well over a year leaving their boat in the marina. Those of us who remained were thoroughly entertained by the arrival, eviction and subsequent re-entry of *Passat* during the months we were beavering away on our boats. Mike, the owner, had left his boat in the hands of a paid crew to deliver the boat to Larnaca. While in Djibouti, they had been boarded by a stowaway. We don't know the exact details of his discovery, but *Passat* was denied entry to Cyprus as a result. We heard later that she had made for Israel where the stowaway jumped ship and caused the crew untold problems. These having been sorted out, they returned to Cyprus where they finally effected entry. The crew were very disgruntled because they had not been paid and the marina staff were looking to them for payment of marina charges. The upshot of this unpleasant saga was that the crew abandoned ship, having first locked the boat and dropped the key in the sea! The next episode in the drama came when *Passat* was seen to be aground on the shallows in the outer basin of the marina. No one had any idea how she had got there. Tugs were called in to drag her off and it took two whole days to do so. There were all sorts of rumours flying around, but we never got to the bottom of the story. It did appear, though, that *Passat* was continuing to be an unlucky boat.

2. A Quick Whirl in the Land of the Dervishes

We were joined in Larnaca, two days after relaunch, by our son Mark, who had just finished his A levels and had been planning to take a year out. He arrived with the announcement that he would not, after all, be spending the year with us, but only a six week holiday. This meant that we would be taking him to Turkey and leaving him to find his way back to the UK from there. This news did not significantly alter our plans – though we were disappointed that we were not to have his company for very long.

We were a while longer in Larnaca – tidying up a few loose ends and waiting for suitable weather to set sail for Turkey. On 9th September, there was a gentle westerly wind and as we had no insurance restrictions we were able to take the decision to do the 'eastabout' route into Turkey. Many boats had to take the 'westabout' route to comply with their insurer's exemption clauses. The wind held all day and we were able to sail right through till sunset, when the breeze dropped to the point where we had to turn on the engine. This was our first real engine run since relaunch, so David was carrying out a series of important checks on various parts of the system at regular intervals. It is just as well he did because at nine o'clock he discovered the stern gland was leaking heavily. He managed to tighten the plate and reduce the rate of flow, but could not stop it. By midnight we had taken on another two and a half inches of water in the aft bilge. This was a situation which required careful monitoring. In the end, adjustments and occasional pumping sessions kept the water to acceptable levels. By eleven o'clock the next morning we had sighted the coast of Turkey and we had enough breeze to motor-sail. Lunchtime saw us broad reaching at six knots, enjoying the force three to four west-south-westerly breeze and slight sea.

We tied up in Taşucu harbour at three o'clock that afternoon, and awaited the arrival of the authorities to carry out the cumbersome entry procedures. These couldn't be completed because the only medical officer qualified to deal with such matters was attending a birth in a village some fourteen miles distant. Everything else had been done in spite of the fact that none of the officials spoke English. Although we had been through all the rigmarole and had not stepped out of line, we realised that something about *Tin Hau* was causing upset among the officials. The problem was finding out what. Eventually we found a local petrol pump attendant who had a smattering of French. He and David managed an exchange in which we learned that they were not happy with our home-made version of the Turkish flag. Apparently I had unwittingly used the Ottoman alignment of the star in the cusp moon.

They preferred that we flew a correct four inch by three inch tourist pennant than the incorrectly marked courtesy flag. It took us all weekend to gain entry to Turkey, but the people were so friendly and we were on holiday, so it did not really matter to us. David's abiding memory of that brush with officialdom will be the arm-wrestling sessions between himself and the doctor.

Yachts seldom enter Turkey as far south and east as Taşucu, partly because of insurance restrictions owing to the proximity of Syria, and partly because this part of the coast is relatively straight with few harbours and anchorages. Although we had made arrangements to meet family further up the coast, we had allowed enough time to amble along and enjoy the peace of this lesser known part of Turkey. As soon as we had permission to proceed, we made a beeline for Agalimani, a small bay on the other side of the Gulf of Taşucu. Here we experienced our first anchoring in heavy weed conditions. Our route then took us on pleasant day sails, sometimes motoring, but mainly either sailing or motor-sailing to places with very foreign sounding names like Ovaçik Adasi, Aydinçik Liman, and Söğüksu. Our next hop was overnight, across the large bay of Antalya to reach the Lycian coast. During my early morning watch I was called on the VHF by a ship closing fast astern, to find out why I was signalling! It transpired that our stern pilothouse window, tilted open, reflected the rising sun as we bobbed up and down on the slight swell. This caused an effect like a flashing light. Having established that we were, in fact, okay, the captain of the ship MV *Beograd* passed us half a mile to port.

The scenery was very dramatic, with mountains coming right down to the sea. So lovely was our first anchorage at Çineviz Liman that we idled away a couple of days before continuing along the coast to Finike. Here we chose to do some shopping, and take on diesel and water. We were tied stern-to a beautifully clean quay wall alongside two of the smartest yachts we had ever seen. They were obviously either privately owned by very wealthy families or very high class charter boats. The crew were all smartly uniformed, in keeping with the clean, shiny brightwork and dazzlingly polished brassware. Thank goodness *Tin Hau* had her bright new paintwork to keep up standards at our end of the quay.

Filled to the gunwales with wonderful sweet melons and other fruit, we set off up the coast to the Kekova Roads, a truly enchanting area with so much to see and experience. At the entrance to the bay of Uçagiz stood the village of Kale Köy, with a castle towering above. The surrounding waters contained relics of ages past, including semi-submerged sarcophagi which probably dated back to the crusades. The bay of Uçagiz was virtually surrounded by land and there was a lovely village which was relatively unspoilt as it was difficult to reach by land. The villagers were incredibly kind and very keen that David and Mark should join them to watch a football match. We had visions of them being driven over rough roads to a big town to watch a game. Instead, they were taken to the village square where rows of seats had been arranged round a large television set fixed to an overhead gantry. As guests of honour, the visitors were given the best seats and treated like royalty.

Many of the offshore islands had ruins about which little or nothing had been written. We visited one island in the area where we were able to walk through ruins and explore tunnels, the origin of which we could only guess. Remains of beautiful mosaic work still covered sections of the floors. The style of building and the decorations were decidedly Middle Eastern in appearance, but the remains of frescos suggested at least some Christian influence. On one small island we were delighted to find an open sarcophagus-type tomb that had been completely decorated with frescos inside. The ceiling was painted a midnight blue with all the elements of the night sky visible. Around the walls were headless figures, but there was sufficient costume detail remaining to see hose, pointed shoes, and well draped mid-calf and full length tunics. This kind of costume suggested the frescos were painted around the early part of the twelfth century. What I would dearly love to know is why someone had gone to such trouble removing the heads of all the figures. I don't suppose I shall ever know.

We stopped very briefly in Kaş where we managed, at last, to buy a proper courtesy flag for *Tin Hau* to replace the car aerial pennant we had been flying. Kaş was a pretty town, with less than usual concrete-block building work going on. Five days of short hops, with long stops between, took us to our next big town, Fethiye, which nestles attractively at the foot of some very steep hills. To me it was memorable for its wonderful market. The knitting yarns on sale there were absolutely beautiful. The displays of herbs and spices were unequalled anywhere we'd been before, and the variety of Turkish delight was unsurpassed. Happily we passed Fethiye on several occasions and were every bit as delighted with the market each time. In all our years of travel abroad I have only two shopping regrets. The first is that we did not fill the boat with rugs from the village where we bought the few we acquired. The second is that we did not buy out the wool stalls in the market in Fethiye. This particular part of the Lycian coast was still in the early stages of tourist development when we first went there. Judging by travel guides and reports of holidaying friends, it has been opened up and developed considerably since. David took the opportunity in Fethiye to make enquiries about chartering. It was our intention to try and start chartering the following year. Initially we fancied being tied into a tour company. That way we would have administrative backup and practical support. David managed to find an interested company and got all the information we needed to make our official applications for licences and so on. We only made one further stop between Fethiye and Marmaris, as Mark's six weeks were rapidly coming to an end and the date for meeting my parents (whom we had not seen since we left South Africa) was fast approaching. We berthed in the unfinished Marmaris new marina.

Mark managed to overlap with my parents by a few hours – they flew in at three o'clock in the morning and he ferried out at eleven. We knew roughly where they would be staying, so Mark cycled over to the hotel to be there when they arrived and spent some time with them. We, meanwhile, prepared the boat for an onward passage we planned to take with Mum and Dad. After seeing Mark off on the ferry, we sailed the boat along the Marmaris waterfront and anchored her right in front of the Koçer Hotel, where Mum and Dad had been installed by their package tour guide. I believe they were somewhat relieved to know that we were taking them sailing along the Carian coast for a large part of their holiday, as their hotel was situated between two further hotels-under-construction, with jackhammers and other noisy implements running all through the daylight hours.

Before we did this, however, we joined them on a round trip inland to see the mineral springs and the beautiful 'cotton castle' of Pamukkale. It made a delightful change for us to do something out of the ordinary. That is if you can call a bus trip (albeit four hundred miles worth) extraordinary.

We had six days of glorious weather, lovely sailing and lots of chances to play our newly invented game called out-guletting the gulets. A gulet is a wooden sailing ship peculiar to Turkey, and now mainly used for ferrying parties of tourists up and down the coast on short overnight charters. Every bay or inlet has its prime anchorage position, and we quickly learned that if we headed for it, then in all probability we would pay heavily for the privilege. Gulets would anchor dangerously close (so you couldn't rest easy at night). They would have noisy parties on board (so you couldn't hear yourself think). Sometimes their guests would prove to be very intrusive and nosy about privately owned boats if they were within swimming distance. The game, then, consisted of working out where the gulets were most likely to plant their hooks, and then finding a spot where we could be secure but as far away from them as possible. This sometimes led us into funny or difficult situations, but generally worked to our advantage.

Nearing a chosen anchorage late one evening, David decided to attempt a shortcut which presented itself. It seldom pays to change your planned route, as we found out when we became aware of breaking water on a submerged reef spanning the passage between the mainland and a small island. We were about to turn round and pass outside the island, as originally planned, when a local boat overtook us and motioned us to follow. Though, again, not generally considered to be good practice, we decided to chance it rather than negotiate the passage back in the dark. In the event, we were safely guided over the reef at its lowest point and shown the way into the bay we wished to visit. The kindness was repaid with a small bottle of Russian vodka (after establishing that the gentleman who helped did not feel bound by the Muslim anti-alcohol laws). We dined, that night, in the tavern owned by our rescuer. I was particularly interested in the activities of his daughter. She was weaving wool into broad bands or belts using a mobile loom system. I managed to show enough interest to be invited to a full demonstration of her work and methods the following day.

We reached Bozuk Bükü before turning around for the journey back to Marmaris. The winds were very much in our favour on that part of our travels and we had some wonderful sailing for a change.

We based *Tin Hau* in the marina at Marmaris and used our bikes for the last few days with Mum and Dad. This enabled us to fuel, water and provision again, prior to the arrival of David's cousins, Heather and Nigel, who were to join us for a short holiday. Our aim was to work our way back down the coast to Fethiye visiting some of those places we had missed with Mark. These included Ekinçik and Baba Adasi, from which anchorage we took a side trip to Dalyan through the reed beds to see the rock tombs built high in the hills. We then visited various anchorages in the area of Kapi Creek, before sailing, once again, into Fethiye.

By this time David was feeling decidedly under the weather with what we took to be flu. After Heather and Nigel had left us to fly back to England, he took to his bed with a raging temperature, and the most appalling headache and stiff neck. This lasted two days and coincided with the onset of very cold weather. There was snow on the mountains close to the sea, and we experienced severe electrical storm conditions with heavy hail. While David was incapacitated, I ferried jerrycans of fuel back and forth from quay to boat, in order to top up the tanks for the return journey. We planned to clear out of Turkey in Kaş, pop over to Greece at the nearest point (three miles distance), and from there set sail for Cyprus. As soon as David felt well enough to be up, we left in near calm conditions to motor down to Kaş. We completed our formalities early the following morning, and sailed in a lovely force three to four on the beam to Kastellorizon.

We spent three nights in Kastellorizon waiting out a series of nasty squalls and frightening ourselves silly by climbing the mountain behind the town to look at the atrocious weather! We met up with several yachts of our acquaintance in the harbour, which helped to pass the time. We also introduced the local taverna owner to Trivial Pursuit, and in exchange for including him in our games were fed the most delicious lobster meals on the house.

We had the easiest possible conditions for the return journey, with mostly south-westerly winds of between forces zero and one. In other words, we motored all the way back to Cyprus. This was not the first time we'd experienced a long passage under motor, but time was not on our side. It was now nearing the middle of November and the conditions were not likely to change in our favour. Cyprus was in sight by morning twilight and it was then I caught our first Mediterranean fish. I had to play the line for one and a half hours and eventually landed a small swordfish. In fact that turned out to be the only catch we ever made in the Mediterranean.

We bypassed Paphos in order to make use of the still light airs, and finally were headed somewhat short of Limassol. In spite of strengthening wind, we managed to make our way into the commercial port and dropped anchor in seven metres of water out of the way of shipping at twenty minutes past one in the morning. By twenty past six, there appeared to be a northerly force two blowing, so we decided to make a dash for it. Within an hour and a half the wind had veered to east-north-east and increased beyond the point where we could make progress. We were not far off the Sheraton marina a few miles east of Limassol, so we radioed for permission to enter. The entrance is very tricky, especially for a big and difficult to manoeuvre vessel like *Tin Hau*. We negotiated the tight turns and found ourselves in a snug berth for the next twenty-four hours. We were not the only boat doing this. To our surprise there were several awaiting a change of wind direction.

The desired south-westerly arrived the next morning and we high-tailed it out of the Sheraton, soon cutting the engine and sailing in some style into Larnaca seven hours later. It took that long because we had to make a large detour to avoid naval exercises along the coast. We spent the first night in the outer basin while the staff worked out where they were going to put us for the winter. Our allotted place was between *Cusar* – an American flagged Taiwanese-built ketch of roughly the same length as ourselves, and the somewhat smaller, but nonetheless elegant, *White Friar II*, a Taiwanese-built motor cruiser flying the red ensign. The poor owners of these two boats looked on helplessly as we cautiously backed our way into the rather tiny-looking space available. *Tin Hau*, when viewed from the stern, is rather a daunting sight. She towers above other vessels and appears to be about to batter them with her ram-like deck structure. I might add that, although we stopped their collective hearts for several seconds, we managed to get *Tin Hau* neatly tied up without causing a scratch to either neighbour.

We had had a wonderful cruise to Turkey and we were now ready to settle into a spell of marina life for the first time. Our previous experience had been almost totally on the hard, working our guts out to get the boat shipshape again. This time we were going to savour the advantages of being part of a floating village and living close to like-minded people.

3.   Winter in a Floating Village

Even though we had had a full summer of work with the boat out on the hard, there were still several changes we felt we would like to make. A whole winter based in a place with good facilities was too good an opportunity to miss. First, though, we wanted to get to know our new neighbours and enjoy our first Christmas in the company of other yachts. There was only one job which needed urgent attention, and that was getting a specialist to have a look at the still-leaking stern gland. We had visions of an enforced second haul-out. In the event, this was not necessary as the engineer was able to squeeze into the aft bilge and re-stuff the stern gland housing with the boat in the water.

David was glad to be back in Cyprus and to know that we had no commitments (other than social ones) for a number of months. He was not feeling at all well, the stiff neck and headache persisting and now affecting his back too. In fact, he was so unwell that we visited a doctor and got a referral to an orthopaedic surgeon. Inconclusive X-rays were taken; anti-inflammatory drugs were given, along with analgesics. Eventually David was sent for physiotherapy to a young Cypriot called Athos, who had trained in England. Nothing seemed to help, and instead of getting better, he appeared to be suffering more and more. Normal static positions such as sitting, lying down and standing were difficult to maintain without pain. All through the winter, this problem overshadowed our every activity.

Quite a few of the yotties we had met while on the hard had returned for the winter, and there were still a few of our own Red Sea fleet in Larnaca. Of our immediate neighbours, we knew *White Friar II's* crew slightly, but *Cusar's* not at all.

I had stayed aboard *Windsong* on my arrival back in April and they had been moored close to *White Friar II*. I clearly remembered Peter, her skipper, declaring at a quayside party, while scoffing strawberries and cream and drinking champagne, that he really had no time for Germans. I recalled thinking this was a bit 'off' – especially in a multi-national society such as that in which we found ourselves. He had been introduced to me simply by his first name, as is the yottie way. He spoke with a highly cultured accent and, to all intents and purposes, appeared English to the core. One day, shortly after our return, I emerged from *Tin Hau* to see Peter on the quay sporting a brilliant sweatshirt with 'SUPERKRAUT' emblazoned across the chest. I could not resist referring to his comment of the previous spring, and discovered he was in fact a German national. From then on, he was known to us as Superkraut. His lovely ladyfriend, Angela, we referred to as 'Petal'. Living so close to them, we could not but be aware of him using this term of endearment whenever he wanted anything. The rest of the time we believe he did use her given name.

Cusar is a Turkish word meaning pirate or corsair, but is also an acronym for 'Colonel US Army (Retired)', which is what Rick was. He was married to a bundle of energy called Sheila – a physical therapist (to use her own terminology) turned sailor. Sheila kindly gave David a number of massages to try and help his back, and she also 'vetted' Athos before he submitted David to a series of epidural and other injections.

We had arranged for a friend of ours, Mark Sylvester, who was based in Italy, to come over and join us for Christmas along with Margaret, David's mum. Prior to their arrival, we also offered to have Cleopatra to stay for a few weeks. Cleo was an English bulldog belonging to Danish friends Torben and Helle Jorgensen. Torben was abroad working as a plastic surgeon somewhere in the Caribbean. Helle, meanwhile, was anxious to help a desperately ill mother in Denmark but was unable to go there because she could not take Cleo for quarantine reasons. She could not believe her luck when we volunteered to have her stay on *Tin Hau*. Cleo turned out to be one of our most endearing visitors and we had loads of fun with her. The Jorgensen's own boat had been on the hard for months and Cleo had had to be winched on and off *Nicoline Magrethe* in a specially designed harness. By comparison, life back on board a floating boat was a doddle. The wheelhouse and deck became her domain. As long as she had her green tartan blanket to sleep under, a couple of salty crackers to eat before bed, a couple of reasonable walks, a daily game of ball and the odd chopped cucumber treat to eat, she was happy.

Rick and Sheila were keen bridge players and we discovered that there were quite a few others in the marina. One of the American skippers, Don of *Sunchaser*, was running a class for beginners. We decided it would be fun to introduce them all to duplicate bridge. Starting with some of the better players, we got a group going once weekly in a restaurant near the marina gates. As soon as they were all familiar with the differences between rubber and duplicate bridge, David set up a handicap system. At this point the beginners who had been learning from Don joined the group. The better players had the satisfaction of pre-handicap point wins, and the less able were in with a fair chance of taking home the prizes. During the winter we held various competitions. Teams comprising single nationalities played against one another. We formed a Larnaca Marina team which challenged teams of expatriates and locals in Paphos. This was just one of the activities which united the floating community. We understand that the Larnaca club was still running some years after we left, and that another had been started in Kuşadasi Marina.

Sinbad Severn was moored several boats along the quay. She had recently changed hands, though her new owners were unable to move aboard at that stage. They had pressed a non-sailor friend called Billy to boat-sit her for the winter. Billy was a brilliant musician, who, together with David and myself, had volunteered to be the 'band' for the yottie carol evening. We had a number of rehearsals on *Sinbad*, David on his accordion, Billy and myself on guitars. Billy managed to persuade a Cypriot music shop owner to lend us a sound system for the actual night, and David used an electronic keyboard instead of his accordion. Don of *Abask* was MC and choir master, and he cobbled together a group of singers from the liveaboards. Volunteers wrote out the words for the carols on the back of reject rolls of wallpaper, different verses in different languages. Non-singers from the European boats organised glühwein and mince pies for the evening. Cypriot customs made an old unused warehouse available to us. We were joined there by a large number of ex-pats from town and had an enjoyable singsong by candlelight.

The marina staff organised a 'silly party' on Boxing Day, which consisted of a number of games and races with silly or back-to-front rules and instructions. For instance, there was the slow bike race. The idea was to ride your bike as slowly as possible between two points without actually stopping or falling off. Dinghy and swimming races in the ice cold marina water were also included.

New Year was celebrated with a tramp's ball and pig roast. The American boats handled all the catering for this, taking one hour tricks at turning the spit. They started at some unearthly time in the morning to have all ready for eating at midnight. The same customs warehouse was borrowed and decorated, with the flags of all the nations represented together with the courtesy flags of many nations visited.

Apart from these seasonal and winter activities, we passed quiet evenings aboard *Tin Hau*, or enjoyed the company of other sailors on board their boats. Sundays were designated barbecue days. A huge fire was lit every week and we were free to join in or not. Everyone provided their own meat and drinks as well as a communal salad or sweet.

During the earlier part of the winter, some of the American ladies, headed by Sheila, buzzed about the marina taking pictures of yotties going about their daily business – carrying out routine winter maintenance and daily chores which, on a boat, are somewhat more primitive than their land counterparts. We discovered that these pictures were to be used to illustrate a talk the ladies were giving to an international club in town. We were intrigued that live-aboard life was to be the subject of such a talk and begged the opportunity to see the show ourselves. They had managed to capture so many aspects of our lives which we never really considered particularly unusual. The show took the form of slides with an extremely humorous commentary delivered by Sheila. I do so wish that I had thought to video record her performance, as it was vastly entertaining and would have made a wonderful keepsake for us all.

Over the months spent in this unique village, we got to know a number of people from different countries, cultures and walks of life. There really is no better way of promoting international understanding. As in any small community, we rejoiced at the arrival of several babies, and we experienced the shock and sadness of death when one of our number fell overboard, was trapped between two boats and drowned on the night before Christmas Eve. The members of the community stood by and helped one another through such crises in a way which is no longer so common on shore.

After the Christmas and New Year celebrations were over and our visitors had all returned whence they came, David and I proceeded to rip out and rebuild the galley/saloon area. Our seating arrangements had always been a bit of a nuisance because there was only one way into these areas, and, once in, the first person was trapped. The fridge and freezer were not being used much because the former was too small and the latter too large. This desperately needed sorting out. Generally, the galley was no longer suited to my needs and we had much better ideas we wanted to try out now that we had lived aboard for some time.

For a period of about two months we had no food preparation facilities. Nor had we any dining area. There are many small tavernas in the town of

Larnaca, and most of them produced good meals almost as cheaply as I could on the boat. David and I had our favourites and it was to these that we now made our way on a strictly rotational basis for our daily dinner. We visited 'Chips and Chips' along the esplanade on one night of the week (nicknamed thus because their limited English and our limited Greek had once caused a misunderstanding that resulted in David being served two plates of chips as his meal). We went to 'Two Pound' on another – again a nickname we had devised, as everything we ever ordered totalled two pounds on the bill at the end of the evening. On Fridays we continued to visit our wayside souvlaki hut and cake shop in the company of Louis. Funnily enough I never tired of the Greek taverna food. Very simple, most of it, but wholesome and very tasty. I doubt I could have lasted so long on English café grub.

Meanwhile, we had to start rebuilding our galley and saloon. Absolutely everything had been removed. We ditched the main section of the stainless steel freezer tank, the old gas cooker, and the remaining microwave. Our new layout made provision for the installation of a full-size domestic cooker to be placed fore and aft, with a guard rail to hold it in place. We had the latter fabricated, along with other stainless steel projects, by Manolis and Melitas of the engineering workshop in the marina.

The new freezer/fridge arrangement was to be made of timber, lined with Formica. The design was for a moderate sized box in which we installed the eutectic plates. This would be the main freezer compartment. This was divided from the next compartment by an insulated divider with a spill-under gap. We constructed several of these compartments, each getting progressively further away from and therefore warmer than the freezer. Any of them could be expanded by the removal of a divider panel. This system worked very well and was far more efficient in terms of power requirements.

The new saloon settee arrangement made use of all the stripped-out black-wood set up on a different framework. This time we went for two settees facing one another across a table. The table was fixed at one end and at the other end was supported on a specially fabricated stainless steel pedestal. The new galley and saloon ran athwartships, galley at the engine room end and saloon aft.

We now had an island in the centre of the saloon/galley area. Most of this was devoted to counter space, but the rest housed the sink and the stainless lids from the old freezer. These acted as a place for draining pots and so on, as well as providing a good safe stowage area for thermos flasks and the like when making passage.

I managed to obtain virtually enough teak parquet tiles to resurface the cabin sole. Nick, from the timber workshop, was able to supply me with offcut strips of teak, which I used as borders along all the edges. This eked out the tiles to completely cover the area. The finished effect was very good indeed.

Finally, I cribbed an idea for our new tabletop from *White Friar II*, constructing it from laminated layers of ply with an inlaid teak and cherry wood top.

While I was busy with the detailing down below, David worked up designs for, and supervised the fabrication of, new boom gallows and various other deck fixings. Our neighbours were very tolerant of all the mess and noise these involved.

One of the saddest tasks we had to perform that winter was the sale of *Knot Often*. She had been in storage on the hard while we had been in Turkey, but the time had come to sell her if we could. We found a buyer, a local gentleman, but this created a real bureaucratic tangle because the dinghy had, first, to be imported. David is endlessly patient in these sort of dealings and managed to find a route through to completing the sale, but not without some annoying financial loss in the form of customs duty payments. We had already found and been using our replacement dinghy, a second-hand aluminium 'tubby' dinghy from one of the Australian boats. She was christened *Tin Tack* and proved to be a perfect substitute for *Knot Often*. We now had access through our stern gates over our gangplank or passarelle. We had constructed this from a long aluminium ladder, some substantial threaded bar, nuts, bolts and washers, and a pair of nylon wheels. White painted plywood was attached to the ladder and coated with non-slip material. This was a standard method of making simple boarding equipment in Cyprus. The top of the ladder had hooks fitted, which slotted over some specially placed bars at the stern gates, enabling us, with a system of ropes and pulleys, to raise and lower the drawbridge.

Mid-March was our deadline for completion of these alterations and improvements. We wanted time to refresh ourselves and get ready for the push into the Mediterranean. David's back was not getting any better in spite of the variety of treatments he had undergone. By this time we were convinced that the best thing was for him to return to England to try and find out what was wrong and get whatever treatment he could.

First, though, we had to find somewhere for me to stay with the boat. We could not remain in Cyprus without incurring customs charges. My criteria were to find somewhere interesting, where I would feel safe on my own, and where the boat would be okay. My inclination was to find a Greek island port. Talking to all the experienced Greek hands, one town seemed to come up quite frequently: Mitilini on Lesbos. We made the decision to leave in the middle of April.

One final task remained before departure. We had to take the boat out of the marina and swing our main compass. We had bought some new magnets for this purpose. I had given David an Autohelm digital compass for Christmas, which was incredibly accurate and could be used to help us with this task. Rick and Sheila went out with us for the day. The idea was to do the work while the weather was calm, then have a sail later in the day when the wind got up. The compass swinging went well, and, as soon as we had taken a light lunch, a breeze sprang up sufficient for us to raise sail. It impressed our higher-tech neighbours enormously how easy it was to get such a big boat going in airs as light as force one. The breeze gradually increased to a respectable force three to four and we had a fun afternoon's sailing.

We were very glad that we had taken the trouble to do this run prior to departure. When David carried out his post-excursion engine room check, he found the aft sole nearly awash with salt water. The siphon-breaker water trap had corroded right through at its base. A replacement had to be specially made. We had to wait a few days before Manolis was free to construct an entirely new water trap from stainless steel, with a much heavier, thicker base than previously. Once that had been installed, we were virtually ready to leave Larnaca.

Memories of shortages experienced on previous trips to Greek islands prompted us to do an enormous purchase of certain food items. We cycled to the largest supermarket in town, some two miles distant, on bikes fitted with crates and baskets at front and rear ends. We also carried large rucksacks on our backs. We returned laden with goodies for the store cupboards to see us through the weeks that lay ahead.

4.   In Quest of a Quiet Anchorage

Despite having left our berth a week previously, we still found our anchor chain was under that belonging to another yacht, *Wizardry*. It took some time and work with boat hooks for us to free ourselves and for them to relay their anchor. Friends waited patiently while the untangling process took place – praying, no doubt, that their own boats had not also become snarled with others. Some of them, we knew, we would see on our travels. Others we would possibly never meet again. This is one of the sad facts of life for the itinerant.

This time we were following the more usual westabout route out of Cyprus, aiming directly for Rhodes. We did not get very far, however, before being headed. So, within sight of Larnaca Marina, we anchored in shallow water at the end of the runway of the main airport. By evening the wind had changed and we were able to make progress at the rate of three to four knots. The following morning, around breakfast time, we were treated to a wonderful display by the Red Arrows, who were flying, we believe, from the Royal Air Force base at Akrotiri. To be drifting along on a relatively calm sea in one of the world's slowest forms of transport and to be 'buzzed' by a flight of some of the world's fastest planes must be a unique experience.

About this time, we discovered that the freezer pump was not functioning properly and decided to put into Paphos to rectify it while we still had the benefit of Cypriot facilities. This was not nearly the hardship it might have been, in that our bridge playing had made us a number of friends in the town. As the repair took a while to effect, we had the bonus of five days in their company. On our second day in Paphos, which is rather exposed in certain directions, we found ourselves with a dragging bow anchor and a stern repeatedly hitting the quay wall. We had to use the engine for forty-five minutes, to hold ourselves off the quay while our second anchor was laid for us by a Lebanese fisherman. Once this was holding, our first anchor was relaid, so we had the security of two anchors out. Confident that our holding was finally good enough, we left the boat for a night to join Jerry and Pat Seavers at their home in the hills. Jerry had been a senior officer in the RAF and had retired to Cyprus. One of his many interests was sports cars, and he had built himself a Bugatti as his runabout. He had also been involved in the building of a light aircraft. I did not see this, but David was very impressed.

Five days later, we set off from Paphos with an east-north-easterly forecast of ten to fifteen knots. Sadly those light airs never appeared and we ended up motoring or motor-sailing for forty-two hours before deciding to head into Kaş, on the Turkish coast, once again. We were greeted like long-lost friends by the harbour master – indeed our invitation to take tea aboard was accepted with alacrity. Being the first boat of the season to arrive in an area has its advantages. This time the clearances were effected very quickly. We were issued with our cruising documents, which meant that we were now committed to cruising up the Turkish coast rather than Greek island hopping, as had been our intention.

278

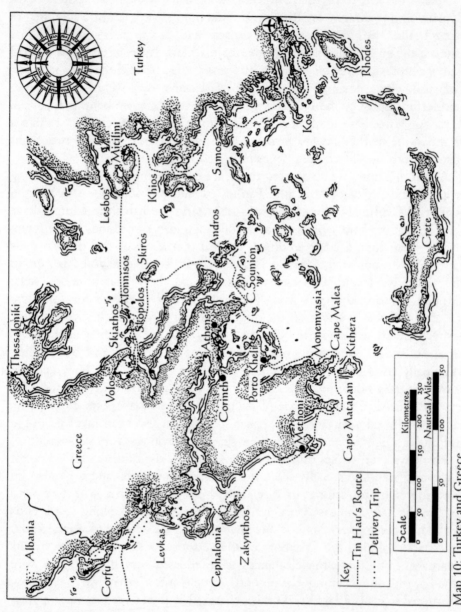

Map 10: Turkey and Greece

We tried to take in as many new ports, bays and anchorages as possible. These included Karacaören, Baba Adasi, Serçe, Kargi, Knidos, Gümüşlük, and Talianaki. Where possible, we tried to sail rather than use the engine.

Our next leg involved passing through the strait between the island of Samos and the Turkish mainland. We had been sailing with a steady force three to four on the approach, but by the time we were lined up at the entrance, the wind had increased to force six, dead astern, and the water was quite choppy. At one point our log showed we were touching nine knots. The nearest port along the coast was Kuşadasi, but David did not fancy the entry there with the following wind. We decided, therefore, to take shelter in the lee of Samos, at Mourita Bay. Technically this was not legal, as we had no clearance for being in Greek waters. However, we were not going ashore, merely sheltering from adverse winds.

We visited several more anchorages in Turkey before clearing out at the port of Çeşme. The procedure would have been relatively simple but for the fact that the harbour officials tried to fleece David for more than they were due. The customs officers discovered a discrepancy in the figures on the paperwork; this meant that David had to cover double the usual amount of ground visiting every official department twice, taking three and a half hours to do so. The actual harbour dues were L2,500 and the harbour master had tried to take L14,000!

Our port of entry in Greece was Mandraki on Khios. There we were joined by the Danish boat *Jo*. This lovely ex-trawler had been painstakingly restored by a group of young Danes. They took it in turns to sail *Jo* for several months at a time with other young friends. When we first met her she was being skippered by a nineteen year-old girl. Most of her crew were students taking time out to do something adventurous.

We didn't remain long in Khios, but headed for the island of Ouinoussa. The large bay there was used mainly as a merchant naval training centre. The island was owned, we understood, by the well-known shipping families of Greece, and used by them in the summer months as a retreat. It was very quiet. We planned this to be our last cruising call for the year as our next stop was Lesbos, from where we hoped David would fly home for a miracle cure.

We were met, on arrival in Mitilini, by the port police and instructed where and how to anchor *Tin Hau*. Even though it was now mid-May, there were relatively few boats in the port. Among them were two British flagged vessels, *Sagittaire*, sailed by Bill and Janet, and *Thalassa*, sailed by James. We came to know James very well over the following months.

In a matter of days it became obvious that, though Mitilini was ideal in many respects, the harbour staff were not content to have a boat tied up in one place for long. If David were to leave me here, I was in danger of having to shift *Tin Hau* myself or with the help of people who did not know her handling characteristics as we did. We were not happy with this possibility, so we decided to look around the island for a more suitable berth.

Our first anchorage was in Skala Loutra in the Gulf of Yeras, in the company of *Thalassa* and *Ping*, the latter being Freedom-rigged. James was making for the western islands of the Sporades group, and managed to persuade us that they were worth visiting. As we had not yet found anywhere which suited our needs, we agreed that we would sail more or less in company to Sigri, and spend a night or two there prior to making the crossing to Skopelos. James peeled off at Plomarion to make a telephone call to the UK. We carried on, in worsening weather conditions, before finally deciding to take refuge in the Gulf of Kalloni. We actually spent four full days anchored off the island of Erimonisi with strong winds buffeting the boat and listening to a screaming wind generator. Though we only recorded winds varying between force seven and eight, we were receiving severe gale warnings and reports of very high seas. We finally pulled out on the fifth day and made our way to Sigri, where we found a shattered James. He had continued on to Sigri in the worst of the weather, and had been knocked down. He thought his last hour had come when he discovered water pouring in through an open porthole in the heads. We allowed a couple of days for the sea to go down, and for James to lick his wounds, before attempting the passage to the island of Peristera.

From then on we decided we would just hope to meet up with *Thalassa* rather than be worrying about James or he about us when planned meetings did not happen. We left Sigri together and headed out into a still high and lumpy sea but with a reasonable forecast of a force four to five north-easterly in the north-east Aegean and force three to four north-westerly in the north-west Aegean. Although the Greek Waters pilot we used suggested we might hear forecasts in English, we seldom came across one. I learned to take the forecast from the Greek. We logged seventy-four miles as we entered the Northern Sporades. Twenty-two hours after leaving Sigri, we were snugly anchored with three charter yachts in Vasiliko Bay on Peristera.

James had headed off to Skiros, hoping to catch up with us in Skopelos a few days later. We, meanwhile, were content to potter about for a day or two, visiting little bays on Peristera and Alonnisos. On 31st May we dropped our hook in Agnonda Bay on Skopelos. The following day we moved on to

Panormou Bay, where we hoped to meet up with James again. The pictur-
esque anchorage was full of boats, mainly flotilla charterers, and we had to
place ourselves in a decidedly uncomfortable spot. Within minutes of setting
our anchors, we were visited by a small wooden craft bearing what appeared to
be a local fisherman. In fact this gentleman turned out to be Vangelis, a quite
well-known and somewhat sought-after individual, who was the central
character in *The Gates of the Wind*, a book set in Skopelos.

Our anchor didn't hold all that well. Being tied to the shore as well meant
that we were badly affected by beam winds. We were not happy with the
anchorage in Panormou and planned to leave as soon as we had breakfasted.
Vangelis came down early that morning and was horrified that we were
contemplating leaving his domain so soon. He begged us to postpone our
departure, saying that he would set us up in the prime anchorage in the bay.
He kept his word on this and we were soon snuggled into a very secure
holding.

We learned that we had found an absolute gem in Vangelis. It was his usual
policy to ignore boats coming into his anchorage (yes, he owned all the land
surrounding it and more besides), but *Tin Hau* had really caught his eye. He
owned a lovely wooden sailing boat of his own, and was fascinated by things
nautical. When he heard where we had been and what we had done with *Tin
Hau*, he was even more disposed to be friendly.

David was woken many a morning to help Vangelis bring in his nets. I was
taught (both in his cottage and aboard *Tin Hau*) how to prepare and cook
'proper' Greek food. It was not unusual to be hailed by a shrill whistle and
virtually ordered to 'come for squids'; a meal of calamari and skordalia would
follow. Or stuffed tomatoes would be brought to the boat ready cooked, for us
to share a meal with him. Occasionally the makings of a meal would be left for
me to deal with – as on the day I found an octopus crawling over the deck. I
had to be shown how to prepare it for dinner. We met Helmut and Heidi
Gabriel, Austrian guests renting Vangelis's waterside cottage, and found
ourselves in yet more congenial company.

A message reached us that James would be staying a while in Skiros as he
had, while climbing aboard *Thalassa* in the dark one night, tripped and fallen,
breaking several ribs in the process. Our few days on Skopelos turned into two
weeks and we were enjoying ourselves so thoroughly that we really did not
wish to leave. However, we were running short of gas, and were still no nearer
finding the ideal place for me to be left with the boat. Tandy and her friend
Kay were due to visit us soon and we needed to be able to let them know
where we were going to be. It seemed sensible to plan a return to Skopelos

after a period of further exploration and provisioning. We had dined, one evening, aboard a boat belonging to friends of Vangelis based in Volos. They gave us an open invitation to visit them should we ever be in their home port. To Volos, then, we decided to go.

We were happy to be saying 'so long' rather than 'goodbye' to Vangelis, as we sailed out of his beautiful bay. Heidi and Helmut sailed the eight miles to Skiathos with us and returned to Loutraki on the 'Flying Dolphin' later that day. We heard from them later that it was the highlight of their holiday that year.

We stopped briefly in a number of places including Koukounaria, Pegadi and Vathoudi on our journey into the Gulf of Volos. We delayed our arrival in port by a day, to allow the Greeks to recover from election mania. Tied up at the outer breakwater just astern of us was a wooden sailing boat called *Hekla*, owned by Klaus, who was resident in a nearby town. Klaus was very hospitable. Beside taking us to his home, he treated us to a rare trip inland, up Mount Pelion in the Thessalian mountains. Described in a Greek travel manual as 'a real hanging garden between the blue of heaven and the emerald of the sea', it was, indeed, a magical place.

Volos itself proved to be quite a large city. The harbour was commercially important and generally full of cargo boats. We had discussions with the harbour master on the suitability of Volos for a long-term stay, and he was encouraging to the point of offering to arrange a job for me as an English teacher! We were, by then, well into the summer and enjoying the cruising so much that we decided to carry on a while longer before making decisions about where to stop for David to return home. He had short-listed Porto Kheli in the Saronic as a likely stopping point. (We had anchored there years earlier and remembered it well.) On 24th June, in a flat calm, we motored out of the Gulf of Volos and back to Koukounaria on Skiathos. The following day we sailed back to our special berth in Panormou.

Vangelis greeted us with the news that James had been in and then pushed on to Skiathos. Tandy and Kay arrived for their brief visit, and spent most of their time snorkelling, lazing on a nearby beach, trying to hitch rides into discos in Skopelos, and generally disapproving of the wonderful peace and tranquillity of our lovely anchorage.

At sunset on the first day of July, we were delighted to see *Cusar* sail into the bay. They came right over and moored alongside – quite like old times. They had arrived with a mission – to try to get to meet Vangelis! Friends of theirs had been sailing in and out of Panormou for years trying to do just that, but had never been successful. Imagine their surprise when they discovered that we could introduce them. Vangelis was more than pleased to have yet another galley to cook in, and more galley slaves wanting to learn the art of Greek cuisine. James returned in time for the Fourth of July celebrations. Rick and Sheila took his references to British Thanksgiving in good part, and a good party was enjoyed by all.

That party was also a farewell to Skopelos, because we had decided to take Tandy and Kay over to Skiathos to try to satisfy their craving for a busier nightlife. We could not persuade them to carry on with us for a longer cruise. They preferred, instead, to leave us in Skiathos and continue their travels through Europe by train. After their departure, there was little to keep us from heading south.

Rick and Sheila sailed across to Skiathos and we had a final meal with them before starting out for Skiros. We stopped in Skantzoura through lack of wind, then moved on to Linaria Cove on Skiros. The anchorage there was particularly evil – both anchors dragged. It was only in the shallows that we could get clear of weed. We went by bus into Skiros town from Linaria.

The fifty-mile sail from Skiros to Gavrion on Andros was great. There was a gentle breeze astern for the first three and a half hours, followed by a moderate following wind for the remaining eight. The autopilot was able to cope with the sailing and sea conditions, so we had little to do other than watch the world go by. We experienced gale force gusts on the approach to Gavrion and were happy to anchor off the beach near *Lady Catrin*. Liz and Robert had been 'sheltering' in this anchorage for days, with *Lady Catrin* tied to a telegraph pole on shore for extra security. The wind howled as it tore down from the surrounding hills and raced across the bay. Robert did not believe that there were pleasant sailing conditions outside. We spent a further day there, and were joined by six more cruising boats. Finally convinced that it was okay outside, *Lady Catrin* crept out of the anchorage at the same time as we left. From that day onward, we termed such anchorages 'Robert Holes'.

Destination Sounion. The bay itself turned out to be so crowded with yachts that there was no room for us. We anchored off Arki instead, but the holding was so poor that we dragged twice and had to keep an anchor watch all night long.

Our first Saronic island was Dhokos. The anchorage at Skindos Bay was awful. To quote the log: 'Checked anchor by diving. Sitting badly. Pull with engine to reset. Drags. Re-anchor with Danforth. Drags. Re-anchor with Northill. Drags. Decide to give up east side of bay and motor one mile to cove in NW of bay. Drop in 10 m, with 40 m of chain. Also tie to rocks. Seems okay now.' We only dared to stay one night before moving round to Porto

Kheli. What changes had taken place there! The fondly-remembered small village, comprising a few houses served by a taverna, bakery and butcher's shop had turned into a massive development which sprawled right around the enclosed bay. Approximately one quarter of the water surface was laid out with buoys for yachts to tie to. The rest was designated for other water activities such as paragliding, water and jet skiing and so on. This was not the place for me to stay in either. We would just have to continue our passage round the Greek islands till we found what we sought. There was nowhere else in the Saronic area that we considered suitable. The decision, then, was whether to transit the Corinth Canal (expensive and we had done it before), or to round the 'dreaded capes' of the Peloponnese peninsula.

The latter option was chosen. *Tin Hau* duly sailed southward for about thirty-five miles before turning into an incredibly scenic lagoon at Ieraka. The views from the steep hill above the village were quite stunning. Even the patchwork of walled fields on the hilltop itself was worth seeing. Returning, at sunset, to a meal at the excellent taverna on the beach, locals told us that the lively summer population dwindled to a mere fourteen souls in winter (all men). Much as we'd have liked to have stayed, we left the next day, bypassed Monemvasia, rounded Cape Malea with a good following breeze, and sailed to an anchorage at Elaphonisos.

With the weather still in our favour, we crossed the Gulf of Lakonika to Porto Kaio, and anchored overnight before rounding Cape Matapan and heading north to an anchorage at Limeni in the Gulf of Messinia. A mixed forecast suggested the weather might not hold much longer, so we didn't dally at Limeni, but crossed the gulf, sailed by Cape Akritas, and made our way to Longos. There we found buoys, floating platforms and fencing all over the area we believed to be available for boats to anchor. A motor boat later appeared and tied up to this strange structure. David hopped in the dinghy and went over to find out what it was all about. It turned out to be a government-sponsored fish farm. The owner, a retired naval commander, lived in Methoni; he invited us to visit his home the following day. We duly anchored off Methoni and met up with the commander at the appointed time and place. He drove us out to his almond farm, where we sat on his terrace and watched the sun set over a distant *Tin Hau* while eating garlic toast and drinking ouzo in the company of his family.

As the following day, 25th July, was my birthday, we were delighted to receive our new-found friend aboard *Tin Hau* accompanied by his tax inspector. I doubt the latter gentleman had been warned of this visit, as he was dressed in a very smart suit and shiny leather shoes. *Yemanja II* was anchored close by, so Rick and Julie were also able to come over and swell the numbers for an afternoon tea party. It was a couple of days before the winds were suitable for the journey northwards into the Ionian.

We made our way from Methoni, via Proti, to the isle of Zakinthos (Zante). Apart from the shock of meeting with western Mediterranean prices – such as astronomical charges for laundry and stainless steel welding – we had nine happy days pottering about the coast. We met interesting people such as Johnny and Vanessa, who were starting up a dinghy sailing club offering activity holidays. Friends of theirs, Claire and Ian Ferguson, were staying with them while on a sort of working holiday. Claire was collecting recipes for a new cookery book, while Ian was preparing himself for the start of another business venture. They joined us for some afternoon sails while we were in the area, and there was a very real possibility of Ian joining us for a longer sail at a later date.

Departure from Zakinthos was taken when we had a good forecast of force four north-westerly. Three hours of motoring positioned us three miles east of Cephalonia, at which point we cut the motor and decided to drift a while. The drift lasted a full six hours, until the promised wind finally arrived and we sailed to the mainland, north of the Gulf of Patras. Our anchorage that first night, between Petalas and the mainland, was wild, remote and beautiful. We coast-hopped, stopping frequently in lovely little villages and islands along the mainland west coast, finally crossing to Nidri on the island of Levkas. Here we met up with Paul and Soraya on *PF Flyer*, last seen in the Larnaca Marina bridge club the previous winter. We took leave of them three days later to transit the Levkas canal and travel on to Vonitsa Bay in the Gulf of Amvrakia.

The Gulf of Amvrakia is a small inland sea. Unusually calm weather conditions allowed us to move *Tin Hau* across Vonitsa Bay to moor off the beach at the north-east side. Close to sunset we were visited by a swimmer. He had come to invite us to join himself and his friends on shore for whisky. We gladly rowed to the beach, and followed his instructions to land in the area cleared of mines, which was marked with lines and floats. The gentleman who had swum out to us was General Kalamaki (retired), lately of Greek National Security and Intelligence, and we had been summoned to join his friends – including General Kosta Theoghitis and his wife Helen – all of whom were the guests of Peter, Kiki and Eddie Papapetros, on whose land we were now being feted. The Papapetros family were tobacco farmers. These charming people entertained us lavishly over the next few days, and were able to tell us much about modern Greek history. The two Generals had been in the army at the same time as the Colonels – on the opposite side – and had some hair-raising tales to tell. We were able to help General Kalamaki to recover his drowned spectacles, wristwatch and other items when his sailing dinghy was capsized by strong winds. We became aware of his predicament when I heard him crying 'catastrophe, catastrophe' from the shore one afternoon. The word 'catastrophe' will never have the same ring to it as it did that day. (The 'mines' we had been warned about turned out to be sea urchins.)

We reluctantly raised anchor once again and moved to Amphiloca for a night. We then moved to a remote anchorage in reedbeds near River Arakhthos, another at Korakonisa, and finally to Preveza at the entrance to the gulf. We were escorted for much of this journey by several schools of dolphins. At one stage we felt they were seriously trying to warn us of shallow ground ahead of the starboard bow.

We dined aboard *Alpine Rose* with Anne and Tom Devine – another opportunity for a few hands of bridge. They were making their way back to Larnaca for yet another winter in the marina. We went on to Paxos; stopping in Mongonisi, where David was forced to spend ages tying stern lines to rocks either side of a totally naked golden sylph. Those knots were infernally difficult to get right, and had to be inspected regularly throughout the afternoon.

We made a very brief stop in Porto Gaios to see the town, before going on to anchor for the night at Lakka. We were joined by two of the staff of the sailing club for our next hop to Sand Bar Bay near Mourtos. There was only one other boat in the anchorage. We seemed to be anchored rather close, so David apologised and offered to move. Instead he was invited aboard *Marpekie* to meet her owners. Nadine and George were a highly entertaining pair. When asked about his occupation during his working life, George replied that he was a 'condomologist'. In fact he had been a designer and manufacturer of machines which were used by condom manufacturers for testing their products. His business card graphically illustrated his line.

Our final port of call was Igoumenitsa, a harbour on the mainland just south of Albania. We spent one night there before crossing to the island of Corfu and, more specifically, the marina at Gouvia. It was, by then, early September. David had put up with his aching back all summer long. He did not wish to have to undergo yet another pain-wracked winter. Provided we found the marina secure, David planned to leave me on Corfu and fly back to England. The few days till his departure were filled with all the usual end-of-season activity, as well as organising his travel. The marina provided buoys for securing the bow, but to make sure *Tin Hau* could withstand just about anything, we laid out a heavy bow anchor as well.

The day of parting arrived. We said our farewells at the bus stop in Kondokali and I watched as the rackety old bus trundled off towards the town of Corfu. When it was lost to sight, I walked back to the boat, unsure when I would next see David.

5.   Another Winter, Another Marina

September was really quite early to be settling for the winter. The advantage for us lay in the fact that as there were few boats around, we had the pick of the berths. Our spot was well protected from both wind and swell.

C-shaped Gouvia Bay lay some five miles north-west of Corfu town. The marina occupied approximately one-sixth of the entire bay, and was situated in the south-west corner adjacent to the village of Kondokali. Like Larnaca, it was in a fenced compound. There was a single motor vehicle access point at one end of the village and a narrow path through to Takis Taverna in the village centre. Unlike Larnaca, the facilities within the compound were minimal. The marina office and a small, expensive, chandlers shop were the main buildings. There were two uninviting ablution units, which resembled nothing so much as circular blockhouses complete with embrasures all around. These 'arrow slits' were left unglazed, thus providing excellent ventilation and a grandstand view for passers-by. Only one of the units was in use because the keys to the other had been lost at the time of the official opening.

Every berth had a pod for electricity and water, but the main supplies to these were run through an open channel alongside the pavement that skirted the quays. Unwary and inebriated yachtsmen were constantly at risk of stumbling or cycling into these 'ditches'. There was at least one broken limb during my time there.

Takis Taverna was the closest thing to a yacht club serving the marina. The restaurant side was run by a Brit and the food was, therefore, mainly English. This was very common on Corfu. I have never understood why, wherever they go, the English have to have their own kind of meals served in restaurants. Thankfully most of the rest of Greece has managed to resist this appalling tendency to pander to its tourists.

The village had a small, well-stocked supermarket; a pharmacy; half a dozen bars and discos catering to the requirements of tourists, and one or two local tavernas patronised by inhabitants who merely tolerated visitors. There was also an interesting knitwear factory. The tourist hotels were some distance from the village centre.

Most of the activity in the marina during September was charter based. Several small flotillas operated out of Gouvia, as well as a few large crewed boats. These came and went on a regular fortnightly schedule. One or two privately owned yachts were occupied and it was to these I turned for companionship in David's absence. Keith and Diane on *Snuller*, Bill and Carole Kerley of *Kerley Tops* and Norman and Pauline Sheriff on *Summersong*, all included me in their social activities. I also got to know a few of the people staffing and crewing the charter operations, as well as a few locals.

There was a bus service into Corfu town. Though cheap, it was decidedly irregular, so one could wait ages to get into town. The trip by bike was relatively flat, quite suitable for our non-geared cycles.

At the beginning of October, my parents booked a package holiday to Corfu for a fortnight. Their hotel was not far from the marina, so I cycled back and forth daily. We set out by bus to find new places to explore. Mum and Dad are tireless walkers, so once we reached our destination, our adventures continued on foot. At the end of each day we returned to their hotel, where I luxuriated in the endless supply of hot water. There I had my first bath since my visit to England, and my first proper hot shower since Larnaca. We were forced to take a break in this routine when, for three days, the heavens opened and created the heaviest deluge I have ever known. The streets were awash under twelve inches of thin mud. Walking, only possible if wearing sea-boots, was infinitely preferable to cycling. I spent one of those days mooching round the hotel with my parents, but they (and I) were happier killing time on *Tin Hau*. The games cupboard on board had more to offer rain-weary souls than did the hotel.

After Mum and Dad had gone, a party was got up to sail down the coast to Petreti. I was invited to sail aboard *Snuller*, and the rest of the group on *Salambo*. Sailing a boat with a western rig was an almost-forgotten experience. Keith was very generous in allowing me hours of helming time. We had several nights in the quaint fishing village of Petreti. The taverna owner and his family knew Keith and Diane well. They prepared delicious seafood meals for us. As it was the weekend, the villagers were in the mood to let their hair down. Both evenings were given over to strenuous dancing once the feasting was over. The owner/skipper of *Salambo*, Ivor Henderson, offered me the opportunity to sail back aboard his boat. We were blessed with a terrific sailing breeze for the sixteen-mile return journey. Later, I was able to sail to Ayios Stephanos and Kassiopi aboard *Salambo*, and had great fun doing so.

Norman and Pauline organised an enormous bonfire on 5th November. There were few fireworks to be had, but that didn't really matter. The main thing was that it gave an excuse for a yottie 'knees-up'. The few children in the marina were content with a large guy made from bits and bobs scrounged off the liveaboards. Embers from the fire were raked into a pit, then used for cooking meat and potatoes. I remember it as being a very cold night with a brilliant starry sky.

As the month wore on it became clear that few yachts were likely to be occupied throughout the winter. Gouvia was a place to park your boat and fly home. Planes stop flying into Corfu on a regular basis from mid-November, so most yotties who were going home did so then. Diane flew out with them, hoping to be back for Christmas, returning by road. She and Keith had a car and belongings in England that they wished to move over to Greece.

The final sailing of the season took place in November, after the last charterers had returned home but before the charter boats were 'put to bed'. The charter companies organised a fun regatta for their staff and crews and all occupied boats in the marina. Unable to de-winterise *Tin Hau* for the event, I was invited to join Keith, with a few ex-pat friends, aboard *Snuller* for the race. Nobody took the regatta too seriously – a good thing, as there was virtually no wind once we reached the turn-around buoy! Getting back by any means other than engine or auxiliary became the challenge. Boats were towed by swimmers or crew paddling on sailboards; or they were propelled by dinghy oars. The flotilla crews bombed anyone in range with water filled balloons. Generally, it was an opportunity for everyone to let off steam and we did just that.

Looking after *Tin Hau* was fairly straightforward. I drew up a chart listing all the regular chores usually carried out by David. I attended to these on a certain day each week, and noted every check made and any changes or worries to keep an eye on. I had one slight concern over the leakage of current into the hull, but was able to straighten that out with the help of Bill Kerley before he and Carole returned to the UK.

We had several gales in the middle of November. Our berth was uncomfortable, especially in a northerly blow, but it was secure. My only real worry in that sort of weather was the boat along our starboard side. Its mooring was in a parlous state, to say the least.

Correspondence and phone calls from England indicated that David was getting very frustrated with the lack of diagnosis. He had been through some horrendous investigative procedures which had revealed nothing of significance. He was issued with TENS equipment to help him manage the pain, and virtually told that that was all that could be done for the present. TENS is an acronym for transcutaneous electrical nerve stimulation. The

TENS equipment comprises a small battery pack with controls to adjust the level of electrical pulse delivered, and electrodes to connect to the body. The patient administers his own treatment by delivering the electrical pulses, via the electrodes, to the area in which he is experiencing pain. This treatment is supposed to relieve the pain.

Diane contacted David while she was in England and asked if he would be ready to return for Christmas and if so, would he help her to drive out? In view of the lack of progress and a desire to get back to *Tin Hau* and myself, he agreed to this plan.

Keith and I were delighted to see our partners return late in the second week of December. They had a journey fraught with difficulties, which started with a cancelled, rescheduled and re-cancelled ferry sailing from England. As a result, the rest of the trip was rushed and David was relieved to reach Ancona in time for the ferry crossing to Greece.

I believe David was surprised at how little camaraderie there was in the marina; so few boats occupied, and many of those having little or no common language. Most of our social life was turned towards the young ex-pats in Kondokali. Jerome aboard *Crusader*, whom we secretly believed to be an MI6 agent, became a fourth at bridge along with Brian Hodges. Games were generally played in the rather noisy and smoky atmosphere of Takis Taverna, with a pool game going on in the background. Two east-bound yachts, *Raddy* and *Pennylee*, turned up a week or so before Christmas. We were delighted to see them as both crews were English and both were willing to enter members in the marina quiz team. A local pub/restaurant was drumming up business by running a winter quiz competition.

All the drama usual among ex-pat communities was, meanwhile, unfolding in Kondokali; various fallings-out leading to certain cliques not talking to each other, and several partnerships splitting up and re-forming differently. David and I got caught in the middle of one such triangle as all parties were good friends of ours. (The two of us probably knowing more about the situation than any of the three personalities involved.)

Pete and Ellen of *Raddy* managed to get their engine troubles sorted out by New Year and were anxious to be off. Pete had taken a year's leave of absence from work and was intent on getting through Suez and back. He and Ellen were keen scuba divers, determined to explore some of the wonderful reefs of the Red Sea. We sailed with them to Porto Gaios (Paxos) when they left Gouvia. We enjoyed every minute of their company and were sad that our time together was so short.

Our friend Brian was temporarily short of cash and very anxious to return to England for a holiday. We bought his motorcycle for the price of an airfare and used it to explore the island. Numerous things went wrong with it. The first month we owned it, I spent more time fitting new clutch and brake cables than riding the thing. Eventually we had it running well. The only snag was that it really didn't like carrying both of us up hills. This meant that one of us had to hop off and hoof it up to the top. However, it was great fun and gave us a lot more freedom than the bus and push-bikes ever had.

When we arrived in Corfu, we came across a small junk rigged boat called *Hui Mar*. During the winter she was bought by Geoff Leigh-Ford and Gill Brooks, who had also recently acquired a small flotilla. Their plan was to base themselves on board *Hui Mar*, while supervising their five-strong fleet and some windsurfers. The boats were fitted out during the late winter. During David's absence I had been asked to help deliver one of these boats to Cephalonia in the new year. The time to do this was fast approaching, and Gill came over to confirm that our help was still needed. In fact, they were short of a skipper or two so I recklessly agreed that we would take a boat each!

I had sailed *Tin Hau* many times without David present in the wheelhouse. I had even sailed her when he was not on board. On each occasion, though, there had been someone else around to help if I got into difficulties. This was the first time I had ever had sole charge of, or single-handedly sailed, a boat of any size larger than an Optimist. I had not had that much experience of roller reefing genoas either. The boat I was to deliver was twenty-seven feet LOA – just over half the length of our own, but a fraction of the tonnage. Even though she had a modern roller reefed jib, she proved to be quite a handful – the sails were far more difficult to deal with than those on *Tin Hau*. I also had a few problems with the engine controls, which kept slipping into neutral. This made the daily business of mooring a bit problematic and affected the canal transit at Levkas. We had a mixture of conditions which meant I had sail handling as well as helming to cope with. The final leg was a brilliant sail from Levkas to Cephalonia with the boats racing each other. I did not win, but was very proud of my effort. I did better than several experienced skippers! More importantly, I'd proved to myself and David that I was more than capable of handling a boat on my own.

One of several boats along the quay was the yacht *Nabob*. Alan and Cilla Hull were her owners. Throughout the winter, this couple struggled to come to a decision about which way they should go when they left Gouvia. They kept a tally in which each recorded a daily vote of either east or west according to their inclination at the time. By the end of the winter they were no nearer reaching a decision. The votes were inconclusive. Eventually they opted to tag along with us and sail in company. We had decided that we should head for the western Mediterranean and, eventually, England. David was not coping with the back problem. As a result, chartering was looking less likely. We thought it might be best to give the British medical system a longer try. Two weeks or so prior to departure, the Hulls discovered that they had no insurance certificate for cruising in Italy. They went back to casting votes.

As was our custom, we took *Tin Hau* out of mothballs before departure date in order to check that everything was still as it should be. Crews of other boats were returning and getting themselves ready for the summer. On 18th April we took a number of these people out for a shakedown sail to Corfu Town, round the island of Vidha, and back again. For many of them it was their first experience of junk rig sailing. To make it more memorable, David gave each a line to operate. Junks are notorious for having miles of rope associated with their sails, so there was no shortage of lines for fourteen crew. Each person was given his or her task to carry out at a prearranged whistle command.

Everything went very well. So well that we had one skipper offer (half-seriously) to trade his boat and three landlubbers wanting to join us for part of our journey westwards. Two of these, David and Janey, were wanting to try an out-of-sight-of-land sail. The third, Terry, was a friend of Gill and Geoff of *Hui Mar*. After some discussion with them, we agreed that we would take all three as far as Sicily. We were essentially ready to go as soon as we had favourable conditions. All three crew moved aboard in anticipation that night.

On the night of the 20th we all went to a restaurant in town as the guests of Christophe on *Topqot*. After a very merry evening, we returned (three sheets in the wind) to *Tin Hau*. At quarter past one, with calm seas and a force five forecast, we decided that we should head off to Paxos. Without any more ado, we weighed anchor and made our way out of the bay. Once into the open sea, we raised sail and set course for the headland at Corfu. We had just about reached that point when the wind arrived and headed us. Unfortunately it arrived with a dreadful squall, which included quite large hailstones. One of the visitors was at the wheel at the time and lost control of the steering. The rest of the crew were out on deck trying desperately to reef the sails. I got the engine on again and took over the helm. The scene outside was incredibly dramatic, with lightning illuminating the island and surrounding rocks. Deafening thunder rumbled all around and wind buffeted *Tin Hau*. It was a scene of which any horror movie director would have been proud. We turned around and went back to Gouvia, tails very much between our legs. No-one on shore was even aware that we had been out.

PART SIX
Beyond Corfu

Lynda Chidell

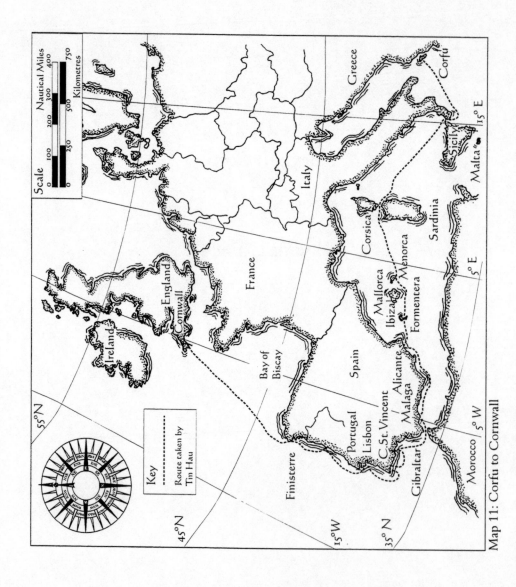

Map 11: Corfu to Cornwall

1. Following the Sun

Four days after our aborted night departure, the right conditions were forecast. Messages were sent to the crew, who had been allowed home on shore leave. All hands reported for duty at 9 a.m. and, by twenty past ten on 24th April, we were once again passing between the buoys marking the entrance to Gouvia. There was little wind to sail by, so we pulled into Lakka on the island of Paxos, called it a day and anchored till better breezes blew.

A light north-easterly arrived at breakfast the following morning. Hoping for the best, we left as soon as it appeared. It fluttered off and on for the first twenty-four hours, so all progress was made with the help of the engine. We had a moderate breeze the following day, which increased to the point where we had to heave-to for a few hours. The crew were not surprised to learn that we were quite close to the Gulf of Squillace – otherwise known as the Gulf of Squalls.

The mini-gale didn't last long. Once round Cape Spartivento, the wind had backed and dropped considerably. This state of affairs did not continue. The fickle wind veered again and headed us. With engine on, we crawled along the Italian coastline, logging four knots but actually only gaining two miles of ground. We were watching our progress on the radar. When the tidal current was at its strongest, we could see *Tin Hau* actually moving backward in relation to the coastline. This phenomenon didn't last too long, thank goodness. We eventually passed through the narrows at the Straits of Messina in the early morning. We did not see any whirlpools, but the water was quite choppy.

We altered course to port once we had passed the north-eastern tip of Sicily. The light airs were very variable so we were motoring once again. Janey expressed a wish to be hoisted to the top of a mast. We sent her up in a bosun's chair and left her there for a couple of hours. The rest of us were busy dipping buckets into the sea to collect floating jelly. This turned out to be some sort of fish roe. The tiny eggs contained even smaller fry. The babies appeared to be all eyes and not much else.

We tied up at the quay in Milazzo harbour in time for lunch. There were no entry formalities, and no harbour dues. The harbour master moved us, within hours of arrival, to a different part of the quay. What he actually wanted was to get rid of us altogether, but we stubbornly refused to go. The annual festival of the sea and boat-blessing ceremony was due to take place that weekend, and they wanted to be able to get all the boats and ferries into the harbour. No matter that there was nowhere else we could reasonably move to.

Terry had a good working knowledge of Italian (having spent many years in the 'rag trade' in Italy). The local Sicilians were not impressed by that or anything else we could offer. It was our impression that they didn't want anything to do with us at all. How Terry had the nerve to submit to a cut-throat razor when having a shave at the barber shop, I shall never know. Obtaining money was incredibly difficult. Finding a bank that was open was the first problem. The second was that it also had to be amenable to exchanging foreign currency. The security at the entrances to these establishments was tighter than that protecting the Crown Jewels. Spending money was almost as difficult, in that shopkeepers didn't seem keen to serve us.

Our three guests wanted to take us out for dinner the night we arrived. It was their final night, as they were leaving the following day to return to Corfu. We wanted an early night and were feeling tired anyway, so asked them to try and find a takeaway meal to eat on board. They returned with the biggest pizza either of us had ever seen. It arrived on a special tray, in a rope cradle, suspended from Dave's fully extended arm. It overhung the width of the saloon table by about six inches. Surprisingly, we managed to eat the whole thing at one sitting. It was absolutely, lip-smackingly, gorgeous.

David and I remained in Milazzo on the Sunday – St Francesco's Day – and watched the festivities ashore from the grandstand of our wheelhouse roof. We could not leave till Monday anyway – the bunkering jetty was closed till then.

First thing in the morning we tried to get ourselves lined up for fuel. We found the berth impossible to get into. Finally we tied up to the main quay alongside the fuelling jetty, in very shallow water. We filled up, at three times what it cost in Greece. David went off to pay what we owed. There was much gesturing on both sides in the process of paying the bill. As he was leaving, David realised the surly attendant understood English very well and was just being stroppy. On showing that he had rumbled the Sicilian, he was treated to a mouthful of very English obscenities.

There was no such thing as a weather forecast, so we left without one. Once out of the bay, David set course for Sardinia. The most dramatic of the Aeolian islands, Stromboli, was out of our way. However, our route took us close to the islands of Vulcano, Lipari and Salina. We did not stop at any of these, however, because we were just beginning to enjoy a good sailing breeze. We contented ourselves with seeing steam rising from Lipari and smelling the sulphur from a distance. Some of the rock formations to the north-west were like giant sculptures rising from the sea. Light airs of around force two to three accompanied us all the way to Sardinia. One hundred and ninety miles from Sicily, we recorded having twelve land birds hitching a ride. We had experienced this before, but never a large number at once. Thirty miles further on we noted: 'birds all over the boat'!

Land showed up on the radar at ten minutes to eight in the evening on 2nd May. Silhouette land formations were visible as the sun set, but there was nothing for the eye to see after it had gone down. A heavy mist descended with the dark. We had to use the radar to make our landfall as there was no sign of the lighthouses which should have been guiding us in.

We dropped anchor in Coda Cavallo at half past one in the morning on 3rd May. We awoke to find ourselves in a beautiful emerald anchorage. There was little sign of habitation. Later that morning we were visited by three policemen acting as coastguards. They gave our passports a cursory inspection and went on their way. We raised anchor shortly after and moved on to Golfo Aranci to provision.

The next four days were spent bay-hopping along the east and north coast of Sardinia. We visited Cala di Volpe and Porto Cervo before passing through the southern channel of the Bonifacio Strait. This took us between mainland Sardinia and La Maddelena archipelago. The architecture on shore was very different to anything we had seen before in the Mediterranean. Our anchorages on the north coast included Porto Pollo, Isola Rossi and Cala Yacca. At that point, we tried to get a forecast for the onward passage. The best we got was from the supermarket owner, who predicted fine weather. We carried on to the Fornelli passage, where we anchored near Piana island for the night. This was to be our 'jumping-off' point for the crossing to the Balearics.

2. Islas Baleares

Wind. Not nearly enough, or a full blown gale. That is the lot of yotties sailing outside the trades. We had no immediate deadline to meet in Menorca, but the sooner we arrived there, the longer we would have to enjoy the island. Like most early mornings since Messina, 8th May was bright and breathless. As soon as breakfast had been cleared away, we completed the Fornelli passage between two tiny islands; Piana, and Asinara. The beacon system marking the route over the shallows was very good and we recorded a minimum depth of three metres. There was an adverse current of one to two knots.

The breeze that day got up to a force two – we were going so slowly we were actually overtaken by a bumblebee. The evening log shows we were still taking birds aboard, with at least four swallows and one other visitor seeking perches for the night. At midnight, five swallows were roosting in the rigging and a little brown job was snuggled into the port docking line. Rarely did any of our avian passengers live to see land again. By mid-afternoon on the 9th, we had lost all the swallows. The LBJ took off from the stern rail and was swooped upon by a gull.

We were within range of the lighthouses on Menorca by eight in the evening. We entered Puerto de Mahon in the moonlight at half past midnight. There was enough gentle breeze for us to ghost along the entire length of the fjord-like natural harbour under full sail. Passing the naval base on Isla Pinto near the far end of the inlet, we dropped sail and turned on the motor. There were not many spaces along the quay, especially one big enough for *Tin Hau*. We eventually found one and managed to tuck ourselves into it neatly and without fuss. We didn't plan to stay long, just needing sufficient time to effect clearance, visit Poste Restante, fill water tanks, and buy fresh food.

Mahon was a huge harbour with many different parts, each like a small harbour in its own right. The main quay is an extension of the promenade. The yacht club and marina were based at the entrance to Cala Figuera. We wanted to move away from the hustle and bustle of town and anchor at Cala Teulera, between La Mola and Isla del Lazareto.

As we got ready to move, a stiff breeze sprang up, blowing us onto the quay. *Tin Hau's* tonnage and windage made hard work of leaving such a berth. The direction of the wind in this instance dictated that we should spring out the stern. I had released the stern mooring lines in preparation and slipped a short spring line onto a bollard at the bow. David did his stuff at the wheel and got the stern out nicely. I slipped the bow line and signalled David to take her out. To my horror, instead of gliding out backwards, we dived forwards and hit a submerged obstruction! I looped a spring line over the bollard again, tied off and went forward to assess damage. I gulped and swallowed hard on seeing a multitude of bubbles rising from the stem area. I thought we must have been holed. Closer inspection revealed we had hit a concrete ramp several feet under. A chunk of concrete had broken off and this was where the bubbles were coming from. Poor David was dumbstruck. He had somehow confused ahead and astern on the engine controls. Relieved that we had sustained no obvious damage, we repeated the exercise correctly and pulled smoothly away from the quay.

The stiff breeze hampered our next job too. We motored down to Cala Figuera to take on fuel. We had no option but to berth alongside, though there was little room to manoeuvre. We got in without any hitches, but held up a number of trawlers when we left as we hadn't the room to spring out. We had to tie two mooring lines together, fastening one end to the bitt on the foredeck. David then walked the other end several hundred metres along the shore to a bollard. Our own muscle power was used to pull *Tin Hau* round. Quite hard work.

Cala Teulera was glorious. Five days in such a well sheltered anchorage was bliss. Sometimes we had the place to ourselves, at others there were one or two yachts for company. The local gin factory ran cruises around the harbour, and these occasionally intruded on our peaceful existence. One afternoon, while dozing in one of the hammocks, I awoke to hear 'Jack-eye, the Captain's Parrot' pointing us out to her charterers. As the days went by, we acquired the most marvellous fictional history; pure invention on the part of the courier, Jacqui. It gave us, and those who knew us, a real giggle.

On Friday, 18th May, we raised anchor and sailed out of Mahon and up the east coast to Cala Mesquida. We had promised to be anchored off the village of Es Grau when David's mum arrived to stay in her nearby villa. We had met up with *St Combs* on one of our dinghy forays into Mahon. The crew arranged to follow us to Cala Mesquida. It was pleasing to be able to raft up and spend some time with Alan and Gwen, whom we hadn't seen since Larnaca. Alan kindly offered to take our sailing generator on ahead to Gibraltar for us. It had stopped working between Sardinia and Menorca. This would save us a bit of time later.

Margaret hailed us from the shore when she drove in. David rowed over to fetch her. We had prepared a seafood meal, on board, which she shared with us before we all went to spend the night in the villa. On our return in the morning, we discovered that our dinghy had been stolen. It turned out, in fact, to have been borrowed; used by some children to get from one side of the bay to the other. We were glad to have it back, though rather annoyed at this cavalier attitude towards other people's property, which we were meeting for the first time. Margaret joined us aboard to return *Tin Hau* to Mahon. The mosquitoes of Mesquida were too much for comfort. The sail back was great, with a beam reach virtually all the way.

We had a week left in Menorca before we were due to meet Don Durham. He was flying in from South Africa to join us for the sail to Gibraltar via the Balearics. David used this time trying to locate a highly recommended Swiss doctor in yet another effort to do something about his back. José Jorge was finally run to earth in Villa Carlos. He turned out not to be a doctor at all, but a Swiss physiotherapist specialising in sports injuries. He did his level best to help David, giving him massage and exercises to relieve pain. When he heard what we were doing, he would take no payment for his work, but accepted an invitation to spend an afternoon aboard *Tin Hau* with his French wife Françoise. It was the first time we had ever come across land people who saw, without being told, the difficulties inherent in our lifestyle. They noticed we hadn't a washing machine and offered to do our laundry for us. They saw the problem of provisioning without a motor vehicle and offered to take us to the out-of-town supermarket. They cottoned onto the fact that we had no hot water or bath and insisted that David, at least, should have a good hot soak at their home prior to a thorough massage.

Don and his wife arrived on 27th May. Audrey was not a sailor. After a couple of nights aboard she was going on to England by plane. José and Françoise had arranged a farewell fondue party for us on the night of the 28th. We had an unforgettable evening with these incredibly warm, hospitable people. They did not stop at that, either. José had, supposedly, been helping David to find a pair of pearl earrings to match my necklace. This was to have been a birthday present from David. When it came down to it, David was not allowed to buy them. The Jorges did that and presented them to me as an early birthday-cum-parting gift. Their generosity was overwhelming. It was with heavy hearts that we waved farewell to them from the deck of *Tin Hau* as we sailed by Punta de St Carlos. We sailed south, then altered course to the south-west to pass between the main island and Illa de L'Aire. Our first stop on the south coast was at Binibeca.

We had given ourselves a month to make the passage from Mahon to Gibraltar. This would not allow extensive exploring, but would give a taste of each of the Balearic islands and a little of the Spanish mainland coast. We were sailing south about Menorca. A gentle north-easterly enabled us to cruise close to the shore. We made a number of stops, visiting most of the tiny coves en route to Cala Turqueta. The eastern part of this coast was quite steep-to and each of the coves was surrounded by high ground. Cala Covas, with its prehistoric caves occupied by modern cave dwellers, was very beautiful. Don was fascinated by these hippy-like people. Other coves also had occupied caves, but not on the scale that existed here.

After a night anchored in Cala Turqueta, we made a leisurely start from Menorca with a light following wind. Nine and a quarter hours later, we were anchored at Cala de San Geroni on Mallorca. We had little sleep that night in the increasingly rolly anchorage. There was nowhere more suitable to go, so we stayed put till dawn. The place we were aiming for was Porto Colom, about eighteen miles south-south-west. We didn't call at any of the places in between, most of them offering no more shelter than San Geroni. A lot of the visible development along that coast was quite hideous to our eyes. Mostly multi-storey buildings with little to recommend them that we could see. Porto Colom was quite built-up, but still retained a native charm.

On 2nd June we left Porto Colom and sailed to Cabrera island just off the southern tip of Mallorca. We were having such a good sail that we prolonged it by circumnavigating the island before dropping the hook in the main harbour. There were more boats at anchor than we had seen for a while. We had to move when a traditional Spanish boat, under charter, anchored too close and threatened to cause problems in the night.

Don was now familiar with most of the routines followed on *Tin Hau*, so we opted to make a night passage from Cabrera to Ibiza. We left at half past eight with a very light beam wind. David set a course to take us into the bay at the north-eastern end of the island, passing a kilometre north of Tagomago island. I took my usual night watch (from ten to two), then handed over to David and Don and bunked down in our cabin. Erni was steering the boat and, apart from an unidentified lighthouse, everything was going according to plan. David instructed Don to keep a lookout for stray fishing floats while he took a few of the proverbial forty winks on the pilothouse settee. This brief nap turned into a deep sleep from which his sixth sense aroused him well after the end of his watch. I was called, and came up on deck to a scene of utter confusion. We were surrounded by land and heading for a shore a few hundred metres ahead. Don, blissfully unaware of anything untoward, was still hanging over the bow looking for fishing floats, as per orders. It never occurred to him that we were far too close to land – he assumed that it was all part of David's plan. In fact we had arrived at our way point far sooner than David had anticipated, having covered the sixty miles between the two lighthouses in record time. Yet our log only recorded fifty-two miles. We must have had quite a strong current in our favour. David was totally disorientated. We should have altered course to the south-west before the island of Tagomago which was now on our port side. There were numerous rocks around us which we had miraculously missed. It was vital that he established our position as quickly as possible. We hauled the log in and gave David time by motoring *Tin Hau* in a tight circle – more or less holding station. Once he had worked out where we were, we altered course to the south, passed between Tagomago and Mallorca, then south-west down the coast to Cala

Llonga, five miles from Ibiza City. This was a brief stop. As soon as we had all rested, we moved down to Ibiza.

In spite of the specific anxiety so recently experienced, we noticed, generally, that Don was visibly unwinding. He had arrived in Menorca still tensed up from the frustrations of his job. *Tin Hau* was working her magic on him, and he was relaxing into the laid-back ways of the seasoned sailor.

We anchored overnight alongside the mole outside the main harbour at Ibiza. We took the dinghy into town in order to explore the citadel. Several hours of pleasant wandering round the market and through little alleyways, trying on hats, buying and eating juicy oranges still warm from lying in the sun made for a memorable morning.

While sitting on deck, in the early evening, I spotted a large wooden object floating by. Never able to leave that sort of thing in the water, I heaved it onto my dinghy and then aboard *Tin Hau*. I had salvaged a solid teak door. Once it had dried out, we put it under the mattress in our cabin. Who knew when that sort of find might come in useful?

We were never overly fond of being in busy ports, and Ibiza was no exception. We longed for a tranquil anchorage. On the afternoon of 5th June, with a good forecast, we set sail for Puerto de Espalmador, a tiny island just north of Formentera. This was much more to our liking. There were comparatively few boats – a mere twelve besides ourselves. On arrival, David attended to a few maintenance jobs. The propeller needed a scrub, *Tin Tack* needed a new painter, and a fuse replacement was necessary on the radar. The pilot led us to believe that Espalmador was becoming overrun with day-trippers. There was little evidence that we could see. We walked all over the island, which I recall as being rather colourless, flat and a bit windswept.

Two days later, we motored three miles on to Puerto de Sabina on Formentera. We anchored outside the harbour, along with several other yachts, then used *Tin Tack* to get into town. We liked the little we saw of Sabina, though we only paid a fleeting visit before moving to Cabrito. The headland west of this bay provided shelter from the west-south-westerly wind. We climbed up to the top from where we had beautiful views of Ibiza, Espalmador and Formentera. All the following day the wind blew from the wrong quarter, but it finally dropped at four o'clock in the afternoon. We enjoyed the day at anchor, watching some interesting boats coming and going. We were especially intrigued by an enormous, modern, multi-masted French boat. When the wind returned, two hours later, it was from the opposite direction, ideal for our fifty-five mile crossing to mainland Spain.

We allowed six hours to make sure the wind was setting in. That also gave time for the swell to go down a bit. The sea was smooth. At five minutes into the new day, we motored round the headland and set off for Spain. The swell was still a bit high and caused uncomfortable pitching for the first four hours or so. A while later, we lost most of the swell and the wind strengthened to force three. We were making good progress. Several other yachts were heading westward with us. At twenty minutes to eleven we spotted land off the starboard bow. We closed the land rapidly, having logged fifty-three miles. We were going so well that we decided to gybe and make for Alicante, thirty miles to the south. Capital letters in the log note that we crossed the Greenwich meridian at twenty minutes to three. We whizzed by Benidorm, without regret, in the early evening. By then, the wind was dying gradually and we used the last of it to drift into Alicante bay at dusk. We had crossed the Mediterranean from east coast to west.

3. Dots on the Radar

Alicante bay proved to be an uncomfortable anchorage because the swell did not die down. There was also an increase in wind strength which didn't help matters. We laid out a second anchor to make sure we were secure because we did not wish to have to move into Port Alicante till the Monday morning.

The harbour was full of yachts, but the harbour master found us a place to tie our stern to the quay. We were surprised and delighted to find Hennie and Nico of *Klepel* in port, aboard *Klepel II*. We had not seen them since our first stopover in Cyprus. They had been home to Holland and had replaced their boat with a newer model. If my memory serves me correctly, I vaguely recall that this was in preparation for a second circumnavigation.

The 1990 World Cup soccer matches were in progress during this part of our voyage, so the men were pleased to be invited aboard to watch some of the football on *Klepel's* television.

Alicante was a pleasant town to visit. The quay on which we were berthed, which was also the marine parade, was planted with palm trees along the entire length. Centrally situated in the town, there was plenty of activity to watch, especially in the evenings when the inhabitants came down to the front to see and be seen. We stayed for two days; long enough to replenish our stores but without feeling overwhelmed by all the bustle of shore life.

Torrevieja was our next destination. The only remarkable thing about the six-hour sail along the coast was the dramatic and distinct colour change of the sea – from a dark azurine blue to a milky emerald green. There was a clear dividing line between the two where the River Sigura flows out to sea. The area close to the divide was covered in flotsam and jetsam. We did not attempt to go into either of the marinas, preferring, instead, to anchor near the salt loading quay. There was plenty of room for this.

We were interested in seeing the coast to come because Bill and Carole Kerley's friends had based their boat in Mar Menor, and they were wondering if they should do likewise. We were very disappointed, for them, at what we saw from *Tin Hau* during the sail past. First we were bothered by a huge plague of mosquitoes settling on board. Then the water around became absolutely filthy. Very tall buildings ashore did nothing at all for the landscape.

Not far beyond all this, at Cabo de Palos, was one of the loveliest light-houses we had ever seen. We bypassed Cartagena and Puerto Mazzaron and made for Ensenada de la Fuente, a remote anchorage tucked behind Cabo Cope. Considering that this was still very much part of the Costa Blanca, it was delightfully undeveloped.

Rounding Cape Gata and reaching the Costa del Sol was not without difficulties, mainly due to fitful winds and confused sea and swell. Most of the anchorages were good for wind shelter, but useless for comfort – rolly beyond imagination. Our first anchorage in the Gulf of Almeria was just outside the breakwater of the harbour at Roquettas del Mar. The waves were too high to negotiate the harbour entrance. The following day we made our way toward Adra. There was virtually no wind, yet a large swell and confused sea, occasionally breaking; very uncomfortable. We motored into it at higher revs than we had ever used before. Anchoring in Puerto de Adra was something of a relief.

We had not long left the shelter of the port when we entered a fog bank. We experienced minimal visibility for three hours, then came out into a clear patch for forty-five minutes before plunging once again into even thicker fog. This was why David had insisted on having a radar. He was tracking following and overtaking trawlers as well as keeping an eye on the not-too-distant coast. Don and I were on deck, keeping a lookout ahead and to either side. Visibility was down to three hundred metres. David, worried about an overtaking trawler four hundred metres to port, changed radar range to get a clearer picture. At the instant of doing so, the fishing vessel must have changed course, and within seconds came into our field of vision, heading straight for our midships section. Don saw it first and immediately alerted me. I yelled at him to blow, and keep blowing, on the fog horn. At the same time I ran back to the wheelhouse, put David in the picture and started to haul in the log line. David revved up the engine, the trawler held its course and at the last possible moment, the crew became aware of Don's long foghorn blast. The expressions of fear and horror on their faces were not at all surprising to us. They passed within inches of our stern. There was no one in their wheelhouse, though revolving scanners indicated that they had two radar units operating. The half dozen hands we saw appeared to be busy picking small fish out of nets. We were amazed they could be so casual in those conditions. All three of us were shaking from our incredibly close call. Don had more than made up for his earlier near-miss. Typically, the fog cleared five minutes after the incident.

Marina del Este was our destination, but when we got there we found it was really a marina for very small boats and we should have to anchor off the pontoons in a position exposed to the wind. It was altogether too open, so we carried on till we found a spot in Herradura Bay. That was barely suitable either – we were up half the night checking on our anchor. By five o'clock we had had enough and decided to move on to the west.

The pilot showed a marina in the vicinity, but to the west of Torre del Mar. There was no wind to start with but the sea was moderate to rough. We had two and a half hours of windless conditions, and then had to cope with a force four headwind as well. When we reached the point where the marina should have been, all we could see were a few scattered building blocks on a deserted beach. Disheartened, we turned about again. It looked like we would have to retrace our steps.

Then we saw a trawler making for the shore to the north-east of us. He had to be going into shelter, probably in Torre del Mar, though we had no information on a harbour there. We decided to risk following him. The trawler got closer and closer to the beach, virtually into the surf. We followed with some trepidation. Just when we were wondering if we had done the right thing, he made a ninety degree turn to starboard, heading for an entrance we still could not see. We executed the same manoeuvre in our turn and finally found ourselves in a crowded little fishing harbour with hardly room to swing a cat. We tied to the ice quay after several attempts, and remained there for half an hour while the officials decided what to do with us. Eventually we were told to anchor in the middle of the harbour. Later we added a stern anchor to prevent swinging. The wind increased, another yacht came in, more trawlers returned. Between four thirty and five thirty the following morning, all the fishing boats pulled out. They had obviously had word of a change. We waited till the wind arrived at ten o'clock. We watched it swing from south-west to east before setting off ourselves. Within an hour and a half it was heading us again. However, with a moderating sea, we were able to motor-sail.

We were welcomed into Malaga, on 21st June, by a large naval vessel which circled us, then called us on the VHF to tell us how beautiful we were! We hadn't the heart to ask him to keep his distance as he was blocking our wind. It was so nice to come across a naval officer with a spark of romance and appreciation for the more basic way of getting about on water.

Don's time was fast running out. The adverse winds of the week leading up to arrival in Malaga showed no sign of letting up. If they continued, we calculated, he would miss his plane out of Gibraltar. Forecasts were inconclusive, so he regretfully took the decision to leave us and head for Gibraltar by coach. This was sad, but sensible from his point of view.

While waiting for the windshift we got to know Nigel and Lynne of *Avalon*, the first boat we had met that was bound for England – more specifically, Cornwall. We had seen their boat earlier, but had not had the opportunity to meet them.

Don left the boat early on the 23rd. Not long after his departure came the news that a levanter (east-north-east) wind was on its way. By lunchtime we were motoring through a disgusting soup of scum, rubbish and empty bottles off Torremolinos. Shortly after clearing that we picked up a gentle breeze which allowed us to ghost gently past Fuengirola. Dozens of small boats came out from Benalmadena and we could have made a small fortune had we charged for all the pictures taken of *Tin Hau* that day. The wind strengthened and we reefed accordingly, but continued to sail goosewinged with a school of close to a hundred dolphins for company. At five o'clock we gybed to give room to a trailer-suction dredger working in the area. There were some seventy or so small fishing boats anchored nearby, making use of the waters churned up by the dredging. We had to weave a path through these, to avoid their trailing lines.

At 8 p.m. we had Gibraltar in sight, and had identified Sidi Musa in Morocco (forty-five miles distant) twenty minutes later. The Gibraltar lighthouse was visible at ten minutes to ten.

David called me to join him during his dawn watch as he was concerned about unidentified fast-moving objects appearing an the radar screen but which he could not see. We were only a few miles from Europa Point and entering busy shipping lanes. I was equally unable to work out what these dots on the radar were. We could only conclude that they had some military or naval connection.

At twenty past six, with an adverse three to four knot current running, we rounded Europa Point and left the Mediterranean behind us. The entry in the log shows a 'Mr Happy' type drawing of *Tin Hau's* skipper – delighted to have sailed his ship into British waters at last.

4.   In the Shadow of the Rock

Clearing customs was quick and easy, then we moved along to the bunkering quay. By the time we had finished refuelling, a strong breeze had blown up, putting us in the same position we had experienced in Menorca – unable to get off the jetty, with no room to work our way round. Tied alongside, we had a ski-boat with several really powerful outboard engines attached. We asked the owner for help in pulling out our stern. In spite of all his efforts (or should I say in spite of the power of all that machinery?) we were unable to get off. We ended up springing our stern out with less difficulty than we had imagined.

We were anchored beyond the runway, on the border between Gibraltar and Spain, by eleven o'clock. Soon after dropping the hook, we were joined by our powerboat friend for a mid-morning beer. We were intrigued by this chap, who solved the riddle of the 'dots on the radar'. His over-powered boat was one such dot – making regular runs between Gibraltar and a beach on the Spanish coast with contraband cigarettes. He was, in effect, a smuggler. Fed up with working as a carpenter in England, he had been persuaded by a friend to invest in a boat and suitable motors to run cargoes between Gibraltar and Spain. There were a number of young men involved in these escapades. Each operated his own boat, bought duty-free stock in Gibraltar, quite legally it seemed, then transported it round to a pre-arranged spot on a Spanish beach in the dead of night. All the cigarette boats ran without lights of any kind (which explains why we couldn't see them). The Spanish navy sent gunboats out after them, but they evaded these by running straight for fishing nets. As they reached the nets, they raised their motors, allowing them to cross the mesh safely. The gunboats, with their inboard engines, could not follow without getting their propellers fouled. The set-up was obviously more complex than this, but my description gives the general idea.

We had quite a bit to attend to in Gibraltar. We were being joined by our son Mark and his girlfriend Lynn, and our friend Mark Sylvester and a colleague of his, Anne, from The United World College in Trieste. They were hoping to sail with us back to England via the Azores. Crew were going to present the same problem we had from Corfu to Sicily – two men answering to the same name. Our Mark, being the younger, became Markie (as in 'little Mark') and our friend became Marko (because of the Italian connection).

The generator left by Alan of *St Combs* was ready and awaiting our arrival. Bless the Buchans, they had found a really good workshop, given explicit instructions for the repair and need for speed, and left us a receipt and directions for finding the workshop. So efficient.

A friend of ours from Hampshire had arranged to visit his mother in Gibraltar for a short holiday around the time we were there. This was great for us as it gave us an introduction ashore. Michael had long wanted to see *Tin Hau* and this was his first opportunity. He was not very pleased with us for sneaking in without warning, however. His mother's flat commanded a wonderful view of the approaches to Gibraltar's many harbours, and he had hoped to film our arrival from there. We gave ourselves time to see the sights and socialise a bit, which was good.

Once more, we found ourselves having difficulties with gas refills. Our cylinders, changed in Cyprus, then again in Greece, were being rejected by the fuelling station as non-standard. They could not (or would not) refill them for us. Neither could they supply us with new ones. We ended up having to cross the border into Spain and hunt through the shops in La Linea for some new cylinders of the right type.

David carried out a thorough servicing of the fuel lines and oil filtration system on our Perkins diesel. In the process he sheared the slotted top off a vital cylinder plug. Fortunately we were able to remove the stump and obtain a cannibalised part to replace it. I spent hours trying to sort out a problem with the outboard. It was essential with all the coming and going from the anchorage, and was not performing well at all. I ended up replacing the impeller which seemed to fix it, even though the old one did not seem particularly worn.

Anne accompanied me on a trip to the supermarket to buy provisions for the crossing to the Azores. It was the first time I had had anyone other than David with me on such an expedition and I found it very difficult having to enforce the sailing budget on someone who would obviously much rather have been buying what she fancied. As fast as she was filling the trolley with exotic foodstuffs I was (as surreptitiously as possible) emptying it again. We followed a well balanced and satisfying diet aboard *Tin Hau*, but it tended to be based on very economical ingredients. My health required a low fat diet, which imposed certain limitations; we also worked to a strict cost per person per day when travelling with other people. What we were charging realistically only covered what was on my shopping list. I could allow only a few of the less extravagant items chosen by my shopping companion.

We had asked all our crew to be ready for departure on 1st July. You have to set a date to get them all where you want them, when you want them. The forecast was not up to much for a day or two, so everyone was free to explore the town, laze about, or visit other yachts. *Avalon* was in port, so we had the chance to get some more information about Cornwall from Nigel. He and Lynne had half-persuaded us to try it, as we still had not settled on a suitable place to base *Tin Hau* on our return.

4th July brought an easterly forecast of force six in the straits. We completed all our formalities in the morning and were ready, by lunchtime, to start on our first voyage into the Atlantic. At five minutes to two we called Gibraltar Radio and Lloyds to let them know we were on our way. We made our figure of eight to cut the dragon's tail as we left the anchorage.

In the straits proper at quarter to four, we were in the tide rips with an advantageous current. The wind reached maximum strength (force five) three hours later propelling us through the remainder of the straits like a cork leaving a champagne bottle.

5. Atlantic Rollers

David set a course which would keep us in the northern inshore traffic zone for some distance beyond Tarifa Light. This was to ensure that we would clear the rocks and wrecks of Los Cabezos. Around sunset, we had a sighting of what appeared to be a boat being rowed by three men, some distance off the port bow. We were keeping a lookout to starboard for the rocks. After a while it became clear that the 'oarsmen' were, in fact, the rocks we were looking out for. The current was so strong it had set us well to the north-east of where we planned to be. Midnight saw us four miles to the south-west of Cape Trafalgar. The wind was dropping. So, with a one and a half knot current still pushing us towards the coast, we needed to get our engine on. All the while we were very conscious of the historical importance of the area we were sailing in.

The wind remained too light to work under sail alone and the swell was making hard work of helming. David found all the standing a real problem with his back. We were fast realising that a long ocean passage was going to be almost impossible for him to endure. A little light relief came when we passed the Russian sail training ship *Tovarich* heading for Gibraltar. She was probably returning after taking part in the Tall Ships race, which had just ended in northern Spain.

Eventually a good breeze did come up, but from the north-west, so it was quite useless. We changed our immediate plans and decided to head for Villamoura in Portugal. That would enable us to sit out the adverse winds and decide how to proceed.

At quarter to seven in the morning on 6th July, (Markie's twentieth birthday), we were mooring alongside the arrivals quay in Villamoura marina. We hadn't finished tying our lines when the mate from the boat ahead came asking for ice (if we had any). The lady in question looked very familiar and seemed to know my name. The need for ice was urgent, so I left off wondering who she was and dashed below to get what I could from the freezer. As soon as she had boarded her own boat, I flipped through our yottie record book to try and find a name to fit the face. It turned out to be Pat MacKay of *Lapwing*, whom we had last seen in Port Elizabeth when we were building *Tin Hau*. *Lapwing* was on the hard at the time. Pat and her husband, Gus, had been conducting pre-circumnavigation trials when they had hit a sleeping whale. *Lapwing* had been badly holed and they were lucky to have got her back into port. She was relaunched before our departure in 1986. It turned out that they had remained in South Africa till just three months before we met them in Portugal. They had taken part in the Vasco da Gama race from Cape Town to Lisbon; it had taken them that short space of time to reach the same place we had used four years to find.

We were allocated berth Q24 in the marina – the first time *Tin Hau* was tied to a floating pontoon. Supplied with abundant water and electricity, we got the washing machine going and did all our laundry. The abundant water also tempted Anne to have a prolonged shower on the deck. We tried to follow a policy of behaving modestly while in foreign ports so as not to offend local sensibilities. Though we were happy for crew to feel free to strip down at sea, we were not prepared to have them compromise our reputation in port by acting in a way which might upset our hosts. Anne did not take kindly to our views and we sensed this could lead to personality clashes.

David and I, meanwhile, were having endless discussions about how to proceed from Villamoura. He was inclined to believe that it was the end of the road. He was unable to envisage himself making the ocean passage towards the Azores and on to England. That being the case, I suggested that we try to make it home by coast hopping. In the light of his experience motoring against adverse winds in the Red Sea, David felt there was little to gain by motoring up the Portuguese coast. The prevailing winds were against us; the likelihood of our getting sufficient calm weather to make the northing, he believed, was very small indeed. Shelter along the way was virtually non-existent. I wasn't prepared to accept that there were never going to be any calm periods. My argument went along the lines that it would be at least as expensive to stay in Villamoura as to try and get home using the engine only. Given that it was going to cost money either way, would he not prefer to think that at least he was getting a passage home for his money even if it was a slow passage?

While the arguments swung this way and that, we made our way to Portimao. On 9th July it seemed we might be able to get round Cape St Vincent; the wind was very light and variable. Once we rounded Cape Sagres, we realised it was hopeless – wind from the north-west made the cape impassable.

We returned to Baleeira, where we anchored outside the tiny fishing harbour. We were eventually joined by *Avalon*. They had been anchored in Lagos. We got permission from the police to take on one hundred and fifty litres of diesel – this enabled us to top up our tanks and carry three jerrycans as well. David walked along the cliff tops to Cape St Vincent. It was probably a mistake to do so when he was already so wound up about the task facing him. Viewed from the lighthouse on the cliffs, the passage ahead looked like a pipe dream.

The BBC forecast for 14th July looked reasonable; a north-westerly becoming westerly. At 4.30 a.m. we turned on the engine and by five o'clock we were rounding Cape Sagres for the second time. Forty-five minutes later we passed Cape St Vincent, leaving it seven miles to starboard. We made our way northward despite the fact that our promised westerly wind never arrived. By midnight we were abreast Cape Espichel and just twenty-four hours after leaving Baleeira, we dropped our anchor in Cascais. We had cleared the first hurdle. David was still unhappy with the plan we seemed to be following. The coastline ahead offered little in the way of stopping places. The few ports along that stretch were not ideal for *Tin Hau*.

We had reached the point where our crew from Italy were getting a bit twitchy about our timing. Marko was concerned about possible problems with his visas which would not be valid for him to leave us in Spain. Carrying on with us to England might make them too late for the start of the new term. We were unable to commit ourselves to any ports of call in Portugal because everything was being dictated by the winds. Marko made a trip to his embassy in Lisbon to try and extend his Spanish visa, but this proved to be impossible. In the end, Marko and Anne decided to sign off in Cascais and make their way back to Italy from there. Markie and Lynn put no pressure on us at all. David was still talking about the possibility of calling a halt to the voyage. He was looking at the viability of stopping in Lisbon. I couldn't see any point in that other than taking immediate pressure off him. It would only have been a short-term solution because we would still have had to face the return to England the following year. The problem of how to get home was not going to go away.

We deposited Marko and Anne on the beach at Cascais on the evening of 19th July. The forecast for the 20th was such that we wanted to leave immediately and try to get ahead of the coming good winds. We set off as soon as we had secured the dinghy, left Cascais behind and approached Cape Raso. Initially the wind was westerly and light, but it soon veered to the north and strengthened to force four to five. It didn't seem likely that we would be able to continue, so we turned around. We backtracked two miles then decided we were being silly and had another go. We found ourselves back in Cascais by twenty minutes past nine. I didn't go to bed that night, preferring to stay up for the forecast after midnight. I woke the rest of the crew at half past three and said we should be off. The forecast was variable three with fog patches. Generally foggy conditions tend to be relatively windless, so I was banking on low visibility and minimal wind. The only other thing we needed was a drop in the swell height.

To start with we were recording swell as being one metre with either slight or smooth sea. The variable wind never reached stronger than force two. These conditions remained with us throughout the 137 miles to Leixões. We dropped anchor at lunchtime and rowed over to *Avalon* to catch up with Nigel and Lynne again. We spent the following day in port and left in similar conditions to those experienced on arrival. *Avalon* went around the same time. They were planning to stop in Viana do Castelo, then go on to Bayona. We were hoping that we would be able to make it all the way through to Spain.

We spent the night dodging fishing vessels using the radar. There were dozens of them milling around and it was quite a job working out what they were doing. When I handed over at the end of my night watch on the 23rd, we were still motoring along with a force one north-easterly. Two hours later it had backed to north-west and strengthened to force four. David recorded lightning to the west and the sky closing in. He decided to make for Viana do Castelo. It was the last place he really wanted to be taking *Tin Hau*, as it was a very narrow harbour with limited access. The attendant was, unexpectedly, available to open the bridge for us to go in at dawn. There was nowhere along the harbour wall to tie up, but Nigel had heard our engine, roused Lynne, and kindly moved *Avalon* so that we could tie up inside them. We invited them aboard for a bacon and egg breakfast to say thank you. Markie's Lynn slept through all the activity and awoke with the first crash of thunder and the lashing rain which then poured down.

We spent the day exploring the town and dined ashore with *Avalon's* crew. The swing bridge was opened for us at midnight and the two boats headed out together to find the southerly breeze that would carry us to Spain. Seven and a half hours later we were in Spanish waters once again and tied up south of the breakwater in Bayona. We took on four hundred litres of fuel at the yacht club quay.

Soon it was my birthday again. We set off with *Avalon* to Islas Cies. We had a lovely sail over there in absolutely ideal conditions. The youngsters had planned a barbecue on the beach. They had managed, somehow, to get a cake in Bayona and had smuggled it aboard without my knowing. We had a lovely evening together celebrating life beginning!

The next morning we set off in company to sail to Finisterre. We broad reached virtually all the way with a force three to four. The sea state was more or less what one would expect for the wind strength, but suddenly we were very aware of the Atlantic rollers. When we arrived in Finisterre, we were delighted to find *Scaffy* at anchor. We had last seen her owners, Tony and Kate, in Larnaca. They had been to England and had added to their crew while there. They were on their way back to the Mediterranean for a spell before crossing the Atlantic and returning to Australia. Their baby was just three months old.

It was sad that we hadn't the time to explore more of the Spanish Rias. The little we saw was exciting and unspoiled – just our sort of cruising ground.

On 27th Friday we cleared our anchor chain, which had fouled on a rock, and set sail for Camarinas. We planned to wait there for a south-westerly wind to blow us to England.

On 29th July we got the forecast we were hoping for – south-westerly, force four to five. As we left Camarinas Ria we passed some twenty or so boats packed to the gunwales with celebrating locals. There were friendly waves from them and fireworks ashore to send us on our way. We found our favourable wind as soon as we were out of the Ria. We turned off the engine at half past midday and sailed past the north-western tip of Spain. We lost the wind six hours later. The engine went on and stayed on all day, in spite of a slight following breeze which came up again later. The swell was the most memorable thing about that leg of the voyage. It reached a height of around five metres for a while just beyond the tip of Spain, then reduced to about three metres.

BODY OBSERVED : ☉ SUN	DATE : 30-7-90	SEXTANT ALT : 31° 45.6
LOG READING : 80	CHOSEN LAT. : 44° N	DIP $^{-2.8\ at\ 8'}_{-3.2\ at\ 11'}_{-3.6\ oe\ 16'}$: — 3.2
DR POSITION : 44° 30' N 8° 50' W		CORR. ALT : 31° 42.4
LOCAL TIME :		INDEX ERROR : + —1.2
WATCH ERROR (SLOW + / FAST —)	08 29 39 s 1 s	APPARENT ALT : 31° 41.2
CORR. LOCAL TIME :	08 29 38	CORR ᴀ. : + 14.5 (SEE BELOW)
ZONE : GMT +	—	TRUE ALT. : 31° 55.2
GMT :	08 h 29 m 38 s	

DAILY PAGES :	FROM NAUTICAL ALMANAC :	ALTITUDE CORRᴺˢ:
TAB GHA 298° 23.5	V (MOON, PLANETS)	SUN : 14.5
INCREMENT+ 7° 24.5	d (SUN, MOON, PLANETS) 0.6	STARS & PLANETS (EXCEPT VENUS, MARS) :
SHA (STARS)+ ° '	HP (MOON)	VENUS 1st CORRᴺ. :
V CORRᴺ. (MOON, PLANETS) ±	TAB DEC N 18° 32.8	MARS 2nd CORRᴺ. :
GHA 305° 48.0	d CORRᴺ. 0.3	TOTAL CORRᴺ. :
-360° IF REQ —	DEC 18° 32.5	MOON 1st CORRᴺ. :
GHA 305° 48.0		2nd CORRᴺ. :
CHOSEN LONG. W- 08 48.0 E+		TOTAL :
LHA 297	TAB DEC 18°	-30' IF UL :
-360° IF REQ —	SAME/CONTRARY	TOTAL CORRᴺ. :
TAB LHA 297	DEC INC 32.5	

FROM SIGHT REDUCTION TABLES NP401 :		
Hc : 31° 41.1	d ± : +39.3	1st ALT DIFF. :
TOTAL ALT DIFF : + 21.3	DSD (IF APPLIC) :	TENS : 16.3
COR. TAB ALT : 32° 02.4	Z : 93.8	UNITS : 5.0
TRUE ALT : 31° 55.2	TRUE : °	TOTAL 1st ALT DIFF + 21.3
INTERCEPT : 07.2	Zₙ : 93.8	2nd ALT DIFF (IF APPLIC.) +
TO/FROM	IF TRUE ALT > COR. TAB ALT , TO IF TRUE ALT < COR. TAB ALT, FROM	TOTAL ALT DIFF ± '

LATITUDE BY SOLAR MERIDIAN	LATITUDE BY POLARIS	SEXTANT/TIME ROUGH JOTTINGS
TRUE ALT AT MERIDIAN : ° '	TRUE ALT : ° '	08 - 29 - 39
SUBTRACT FROM 90° 00.0	SUBTRACT : 1°	taken in a trough
ZENITH DISTANCE : ° '	TOTAL : ° ' ADD a₀ :	- 4m swells.
DECLINATION AT MERIDIAN TIME ± ° '	ADD a₁ : ADD a₂ :	Horizon difficult
LATITUDE : ° '	LATITUDE : ° '	31° 45.6

Figure 16: Astral Navigation Sheet (sample page)(off north-west Spain)

We hardly saw the wind again, just a smooth sea and the swell. We motored alongside huge schools of dolphins, were followed by whales, and watched countless shooting stars falling to earth. Forty miles from Falmouth we picked up an easterly breeze. At quarter to ten on 2nd August, *Tin Hau* shuddered violently and our ears were assailed by the sound of a single loud explosion. I was convinced that we had been hit by something. There was no sign of any damage so we concluded that we might be approaching an area where naval exercises were under way. We had seen quite a few naval ships during the previous twenty-four hours. Customs officers in Falmouth solved the riddle of the explosion – Concorde.

By lunchtime we were picking up conversations between Cornish fishermen on VHF channels ten and seventy-three. It was very frustrating, we could not see land at all. We knew it was not far away because it showed up on the radar, but it was not until we were half a mile off the approach to Falmouth harbour that it became visible. What an emotional moment, when we first glimpsed the rolling hills and grazing cows. David and I got horribly soppy and sentimental. We put on a tape of patriotic music and opened a bottle of champagne. Tears flowed freely as *Tin Hau* slowly made her way into her first anchorage in England. Despite all difficulties placed in our way, we had brought our beloved *Tin Hau* home at last.

6. What Followed

Our arrival in England was not meant to be the end of our adventures with *Tin Hau*. Falmouth was ideal for us as a port of arrival and it also turned out to have a boatyard capable of taking *Tin Hau* out of the water almost immediately. While waiting for our date on the slipway, we explored the nearby anchorages, looking into various possibilities for a place to overwinter. The Helford, St Mawes, Penryn and Truro were all considered, but we had made no decision when our time came for the haul-out. Mark stayed on to help us.

We had three weeks of concentrated work on the boat – scraping, cleaning and re-antifouling. Several conversions had to be carried out to make *Tin Hau* suitable for living aboard through an English winter. We breached the water-tight bulkhead between the engine room and forward cabin areas. We reasoned that having to move fore and aft above decks in icy conditions was plain silly. Changes and sacrifices had to be made to accommodate the new arrangement. We installed a solid fuel stove in the new sitting area forward of the engine room.

While busy working on these changes, we had a visit from representatives of the harbour master at Truro offering us a berth for the winter. The rates and conditions were acceptable, and we agreed there and then to move to Truro at the end of October.

Our berth in Truro was quite unique. We were alongside Town Quay, floating and grounding twice daily, within sight of the beautiful cathedral. It was a three minutes walk to the city centre. When aground, *Tin Hau* sank into a nest she hollowed out for herself in soft mud. David was handily situated for getting all the medical attention he could possibly want. The best supermarket for miles was sited on the other side of the river, well within reach of our feet, bikes or dinghy.

We lived in Truro for ten months. David underwent further tests which did show some problems with his back, but nothing which really accounted for the severity of the pain he suffered. We realised that the chances of his finding treatment were very slim indeed and had to accept that our cruising life was not helping the situation.

I was emotionally devastated at the thought of losing *Tin Hau* and the life of the cruising yotties. However, David's health and well-being were far more important. We put *Tin Hau* on the market, bought a small cottage ashore and became landlubbers once more. I cannot describe how weird it was to be driving again; to have family and friends available at the other end of a telephone connected to where we were living; to have a permanent postal address. It was a while after moving ashore that David eventually went back to work. It was not an easy adjustment for either of us, having grown so used to being together all the time.

We had an enquiry from American junk rig enthusiasts living in Sweden. Arrangements were made for them to visit us and have a short stay aboard. Though they had obviously fallen in love with the boat they felt, under-standably perhaps, that she was rather too big for them. Twelve months went by before we had another serious bite. This time it came in the form of an offer from Spain – considerably less than we had been asking, and we were very loathe to let her go. The long, drawn-out business of selling her was wearing us down, so we decided to let the first viewers know that we were considering accepting an offer. Almost immediately they came back with a matching offer. The agony of the whole selling process, the feeling that *Tin Hau* was languishing in Truro when she should be out braving the elements, and various other factors persuaded us to accept the offer.

Tin Hau passed into the care of Andy and Marion Torchia eleven months after the sale was completed. I helped move her down to Port Falmouth boatyard for yet another haul-out. On the way down from Truro I explained to the new owners the Chinese ritual enacted to release evil spirits and demons from the boat. Given that *Tin Hau* had been tied in one place for so long, she was bound to have accumulated numerous goblins. Together we sailed a double figure-of-eight in the Carrick roads, thereby cutting the dragon's tail once more. After her relaunch, the Torchias berthed her in Port Pendennis for a month while they returned briefly to Sweden.

It was in August 1993 that we waved farewell as *Tin Hau* left to resume her cruising life. We had very mixed feelings about seeing her go. On the one hand we were glad she was going to continue sailing. There is, in our opinion, nothing more sad than to see an ocean-going boat permanently tied to the land and gradually losing her essential spirit. On the other hand we were very heartsore at losing a dear friend. *Tin Hau* had given us the experiences of a lifetime. We had lived close to nature in a very basic and meaningful way, an opportunity that is becoming more and more rare.

Andrew and Marion first took *Tin Hau* to Sweden. She was berthed in Stockholm while they cut their ties with shore life. A friend of ours, George Donaldson, joined them for the first leg of the return journey to the Mediterranean – a journey that was as filled with excitement and incident as any we encountered. However, that story properly belongs to Andrew and Marion. We are happy to know that they consider us an important part of *Tin Hau's* family and keep us informed as to their doings.

It never ceases to astonish us how the story of our life aboard *Tin Hau* captures the imagination of people we meet. Shortly after we arrived back in England, we were asked to give a talk to a local yacht club. For people who had become used to a fairly isolated existence, it was a daunting business addressing nearly one hundred people. Within months we had done several talks for local sailors and hosted the autumn rally tea party for the Junk Rig Association. Since David went back to full-time employment, the talks have become my responsibility. Very few of my audiences are sailors, but there is a magic about small sailing boats and the lives of cruising folk that seems to hold their attention, whatever their background.

We still dream about the possibility of rejoining the cruising fraternity. One day, if David's back is ever cured... In the meantime, David is designing our ideal little sister to *Tin Hau* – a junkentine.

David and I have well and truly swallowed the anchor. For the first time in our adult lives we have settled in one placed for a period longer than a couple of years. We moved from our cottage on a farm to a smallholding twelve miles away. We are privileged to be able to enjoy nature in quiet surroundings, though perhaps in not quite so elemental a manner as we did when at sea. Our daily life now revolves around our small animal family – a collie dog called Mungo and three goats – and caring for the woodlands we have taken over as part of our property.

Epilogue

The memory of *Tin Hau* lives on; we hope it always will. But this tale would be incomplete without mentioning what has become of some of the special people who played an important or particularly memorable part in our life with *Tin Hau*. The list would be almost endless if we mentioned all of those we would like to include. Close family have been excluded, even though certain members of our respective families gave us more physical and moral support than anyone else. The following, however, could not possibly be omitted:

Tom Colvin	The naval architect who designed *Tin Hau* and many sister ships. His own *Kung Fu Tse* was sailed to Scotland, to become the pride of another sailing family. Tom, we believe, is now land-based in Florida.
Ronnie Nel	Carried on working as a boat builder in South Africa. His son joined him in his new boatyard down at the harbour, which we visited in December 1993. We have since heard that Ronnie died after a long illness.
Tony Bryant	Became something of an entrepreneur on his return to South Africa. He remarried a few years after his *Tin Hau* adventure and, with his new family, now lives in a magnificent home in the Magaliesburg.

Jeff Perring	Is still living and working in Swaziland. He visits the UK regularly when we have the opportunity to rehash the maiden voyage yet again. One of our few regrets is that Jeff never had the chance of a holiday cruise in *Tin Hau*.
Jacqui Wilmot	Went on to qualify as a pharmacist and did so well that she represented her country at several international young pharmacists conventions. She was married in October 1997 to Lionel Nieburg. We hope he appreciates what a gem he has wed.
Barry Lamprecht	Is now the senior photographer for a leading Cape Town daily. Barry had the good luck to be in Mauritius with us when a big sailing news story broke. His 'scoop' was syndicated nationally and more than justified his trip. He took many of the photographs in this book.
Desmond and Terry Cohen	Sadly lost *Hummingbird* in a cyclone a year or two after we left. They bought a stunning riverside property in The Wilderness – an area of the Cape Province of South Africa, and changed direction to build up a unique crafts business. Natural disaster continues to rule their lives – a flood carried away their beautiful home in 1996.
Don Windsor	Continued to reign as king of the harbour for a few more years before his death. One of his sons now runs the agency and all the other enterprises set up by Don.

Mike and Bandula	Bandula set off for Saudi to earn the money needed to set up a home for his intended bride. We know he returned for the wedding but fancy he went back to Saudi for a further contract.
Darren Pain	Darren made his way back to East Sussex where, for a while, he continued to follow his new-found interest in sailing. He was involved with both cruising and racing, in the Solent and across the channel. Around 1994, about six years after his return from our adventure, he bought a rural property, in France, near to his work in Toulouse.
Martyn Kalina	Martyn returned to High Wycombe and to the career he had interrupted in order to join us. He married in 1996. When we last spoke to him, he told us of plans to take up sailing again by crewing for the local vicar who had just bought a dinghy.
Rick and Sheila Nelson	Carried on cruising in the eastern Mediterranean. They ran the bridge club the year after we left and handed over to Jim of *Gralyn* on their departure. Wintering in Kuşadasi ever since, they have run duplicate bridge and other activities for the live aboard community. During their summers they cruised the Black Sea extensively and produced the cruising pilot for that area, now published.

Superkraut and Petal	Progressed to the western Mediterranean and took up residence in Spain. There they settled to run an English style bar in the Benalmadena area.
Vangelis Hannas	Is still the sitting Admiral of all the Balkans. We have postcards from him from time to time and our Austrian friends, Helmut and Heidi, continue to holiday with him annually. They plan to build a home on Skopelos.
Don Durham	Refreshed himself sufficiently on his adventure to return to his work for a few more years before he retired a couple of years ago.
Mark Sylvester	Is back at the United World College in Trieste. He spends his holidays climbing and walking now, quite convinced that it is a more sensible way to enjoy the great outdoors than messing about in boats.
Andrew and Marion Torchia	The new *Tin Hau* family are very good at keeping us informed as to their whereabouts. They have based her, since returning to the Mediterranean, in Larnaca, from where they cruise to Turkey and the Greek isles.

Bibliography

The list of books we read prior to building and sailing *Tin Hau* are far too numerous to list here. There are several, however, which were of such enormous value to us as junk sailors and liveaboards that they really deserve a mention for the benefit they may bring to others.

Burke, Katy, *The Live Aboard Book*, Seven Seas Press, 1982
Colvin, Thomas E., *Cruising As A Way of Life*, Seven Seas Press, 1979
Colvin, Thomas E., *Cruising Wrinkles*, Seven Seas Press, 1972
Hasler, H.G., and McLeod, J.K., *Practical Junk Rig*, Adlard Coles, 1987
Heikell, Rod, *Greek Waters Pilot*, Imray Laurie Norie & Wilson
Heikell, Rod, *Turkish Waters Pilot*, Imray Laurie Norie & Wilson
Lucas, Alan, *Red Sea and Indian Ocean Cruising Guide*, Imray Laurie Norie & Wilson
Cruising Association Handbook, The Cruising Association, London
The Times Atlas of the Oceans, edited by Alastair Couper, Times Books, 1983
In addition, we found the Newsletters of the Junk Rig Association of tremendous interest and value. Back copies of these can be obtained from the Association's Honorary Secretary, Robin Blain, at 373 Hunts Pond Road, Titchfield Common, Fareham, Hampshire PO14 4PB.

List of Boats, Yachts and Ships

The index lists the names of boats, yachts and ships – together with the names of their crews – where known – mentioned within the pages of this story.

A

Abask	yacht	Don, Gail, Simon, J.P. and Rebecca
Adventure	yacht	HM Forces
Alepha	ketch	Nick White
Alex Bonnyman	supply vessel	(chartered to US Navy)
Alpine Rose	sloop	Tom and Anne Devine
Amat Berani II	ketch	Stephan Bo Erik and three others
Ann Judith	ketch	Arthur and Peter
Aquilla	catamaran	Bob, Judy, Clare, Bruce, Lucy and Emily
Arnak	ketch	Geoff and Linda Gentil
Asylum	yacht	Brock
Aum Gaia	Indian dhow	Fidibus and Bee
Aurora	schooner	(charter yacht)
Avalon	sloop	Nigel Boulton and Lynne
Aztec Lady	motor sailer	John and Joan

B

Baraka A	sloop	Jameel and Sherry
MV *Beograd*	coaster	
Birgitt	sloop	Löthar Lasson
Bizzy	dinghy	(tender to *Tin Hau*)
Blue Jay	tug	(Port Elizabeth Harbour Authority)

Bonaventure II	Freedom-rigged	Bob and Dawn Buick
Boo	yacht	
Boreas	sloop	Gilles and Christine
Brilliant Venture	tanker	Captain Anderson and crew
Brittania	Royal yacht	
Bubblehull	sloop	Jurg Weilenmann, Bruno, Max and Peat
Bug Off	yacht	
Bunka Tiga	cargo ship	

C

Cheval de la Mer	ketch	
Copper Lady	sloop	Brian
Couchen	sloop	
Crusader	yacht	Jerome Frier
Cusar	ketch	Rick and Sheila Nelson

D

Dalliance	sloop	Charles
Didicoy	sloop	Bill and Betty
Dreamtime	ketch	John Watson, Richard, Shaun and others
Drennec	trawler	

E

Elf Chine	Chinese junk	Niels Lutyens, and others
Endurance II	ketch	Steve, Warren Brooks and Michelle
Europa	ferry	Ferry crew, Darren and Martyn

F

Fam	sloop	Ramon and Erika
Formosa Glory	cargo ship	
Freedom Hunter	yacht	Sid and Mel

G

Gralyn	yacht	Jim and Jane
Guinevere	sloop	Bill Belford

H

Hamburg	liner	
Hekla	yacht	Klaus and Helma
HMS *Andromeda*	warship	Royal Navy
HMS *Nottingham*	warship	Royal Navy
Hui Mar	junk rigged	Geoff and Gill Leigh Ford
Hummingbird	sloop	Des and Terry Cohen

I

Innocent Bystander	yacht

J

Jo	ex-trawler	Anders, Anne, Mette and others
Joseph Conrad	ketch	University Sports Assoc. of Poland

K

Kerley Tops	yacht	Bill and Carole Kerley
Klepel	ketch	Nico and Hennie
Klepel II	yacht	Nico and Hennie
Knot Often	dinghy	(tender to *Tin Hau*)
Koonawarra	sloop	David and Gail
Kung Fu Tse	Colvin junk	Tom and Jean Colvin

L

La Sacrée Thérèse	sloop	
Lady Catrin	sloop	Robert and Liz Sauer
Lady Rosi	sloop	Roger, Siv and Rosita
Lapwing	yacht	Gus and Pat Mackay
Leisurely Leo	yacht	Maurice and Jennifer Day

M

Marpekie	sloop	George and Nadine
Miss My	sloop	

N

Nabob	sloop	Alan and Cilla Hull
Nalu IV	yacht	Jim and Jesse
Narai	catamaran	
Nicoline Magrethe	schooner	Torben and Helle Glarborg Jorgensen
Nomad	sloop	René and Chantal
Nordkaperen	yawl	Carl Nielsen and others

O

Okeanos	sloop	Jean-Claude
Ouais Ouais	ketch	Frank Cotton and Elise Gagnon

P

Passat	schooner	Mike, and others
Pennylee	sloop	
PF Flyer	sloop	Paul Finnell and Soraya Hughes
Ping	Freedom-rigged	
Pointe de Carsen	cargo ship	

Q

Quiet Achiever	catamaran	Graham and Gillian Pfister

R

Raddy	sloop	Pete and Ellen Saunders
Rajah Laut	Malaysian junk	Wolfgang
RFA *Orange Leaf*	supply vessel	Royal Fleet Auxiliary
Roama	sloop	Doug and Yvonne, Ben and Kathy.

S

Sabre	yacht	HM Forces
Sagan	sloop	Dusty and Mary
Sagittaire	sloop	Bill and Janet
Salambo	sloop	Ivor Henderson
Sally Maersk	cargo ship	Danish Maersk Company
Sarah	yacht	Ken and Richenda
Sarah La Noire	sloop	Pierre and Christine Zürcher

Sauvage	schooner	
Scaffy	yacht	Tony and Kate
Shahla	sloop	Peter Atwell Brown
Sinbad	ketch	
Sinbad Severn	yacht	Billy, Scott and Joan
Snuller	sloop	Keith Fenwick and Diane Dando
St Combs	sloop	Alan and Gwen Buchan
Summersong	sloop	Norman and Pauline Sheriff
Sunchaser	sloop	Don and Rhoda
Sundancer III	sloop	Noel
Svanhilde	brigantine	Four Norwegian families – skipper Oban

T

T'ai Shan	Colvin junk	Tony Richardson
Tanda	schooner	Wilf and Maggie Brophy
Tara of Meath	sloop	Mike and Liyun Kelly
Thalassa	sloop	James Grosvenor Alsop
Tin Hau	Colvin Junk	David and Lynda Chidell
Tin Tack	dinghy	(tender to *Tin Hau*)
Tola	sloop	Mike and Karen
Top Knot	ketch	Ted and Barb
Topqot	sloop	Christophe Weber and Konrad Franke
Tovarich	barque	Russian sail training ship

U

U-Matalu	sloop	Hippolyte and others

V

| *Verity* | sloop | Karl and Patty |

W

White Friar II	motor yacht	Peter (Superkraut) and Angela (Petal)
Windsong	sloop	Dick and Bonnie Bhyre
Wizardry	yacht	Mark, Jeanne and Eric

Y

| *Yamatama Maru* | cargo ship | |
| *Yemanja II* | sloop | Rick (Henri) Vessiere and Julie Addison |

General Index